# Guests of God

# Guests of God

*Pilgrimage and Politics in the Islamic World*

ROBERT R. BIANCHI

UNIVERSITY PRESS

2004

# OXFORD
UNIVERSITY PRESS

Oxford   New York
Auckland   Bangkok   Buenos Aires   Cape Town   Chennai
Dar es Salaam   Delhi   Hong Kong   Istanbul   Karachi   Kolkata
Kuala Lumpur   Madrid   Melbourne   Mexico City   Mumbai
Nairobi   São Paulo   Shanghai   Taipei   Tokyo   Toronto

Published by Oxford University Press, Inc.
198 Madison Avenue, New York, New York 10016

www.oup.com

Oxford is a registered trademark of Oxford University Press

Library of Congress Cataloging-in-Publication Data
Bianchi, Robert, 1945–
Guests of God: pilgrimage and politics in the Islamic world / Robert R. Bianchi.
p.   cm
Includes bibliographical references and index.
ISBN 978-0-19-534211-6
1. Muslim pilgrims and pilgrimages—Saudi Arabia—Mecca. 2. Islam and politics.
3. Islamic countries—Politics and government. I.   Title.
BP187.3.B53. 2004
297.3'52—dc22      2004041484

Printed in the United States of America
on acid-free paper

*Para Vicki,*
*quien me lee mejor que nadie*

# Preface

I've written books before, but this one got its hooks into me and I fell in love with it. The project grew far beyond my initial ambitions because the people who manage the hajj—or try to—kept giving me more data and insights than I expected, and the connections quickly multiplied in each country I visited. Shortly after I made the hajj myself, I started fieldwork in Pakistan and Turkey. The results were so encouraging that I decided to make additional trips to Malaysia and Indonesia, and eventually to Nigeria and Senegal. I never set out to tackle a work of this magnitude. One step led to another, and I just followed the trail.

Why did I get so wrapped up in the hajj, and why did so many strangers go out of their way to help me succeed? The simplest answer is that everything about the hajj is magical. In many ways, it represents the heart and soul of Islam, Islam at its best—at its most humanitarian and universal, its most pluralistic and egalitarian. These are the very ideals that give Muslims such pride in their traditions and that also cause them great distress when they are ignored or negated.

That raises the second reason for my fascination with the hajj. Although we know that these ideals are real, we also know they are elusive. For all its dignity and nobility, sometimes the hajj seems like just another commodity or business venture, just another status symbol and pool of patronage. The hajj's contradictions are an open secret in the Islamic world. I was constantly amazed at how candid people were in criticizing hajj organizations in their countries and around the globe. Wherever I went, even the directors responsible for shaping and implementing hajj policy expressed their misgivings. At times, it was like listening to friends describing dysfunctional families—once they started, there was no stopping them and no telling what would come next. I merely kept listening and learning to ask better questions.

To meet the needs of both general readers and specialists, I've summarized major trends in the text and created an appendix for those who want a more detailed view of the data. All of the items in the appendix are cited at relevant points in the text so that interested readers can delve deeper whenever they wish.

The original inspiration to write a book on the hajj came from Leonard Binder and the late Fazlur Rahman. Along the way, I had invaluable advice and encouragement from Iliya Harik, Marvin Weinbaum, and John Esposito. My research assistant, Jefferson Gray, did a phenomenal job in helping to collect the core data and make sense of it. I was fortunate to enjoy financial assistance from the U.S. Department of Education, the Division of the Social Sciences of the University of Chicago, and the Chicago Humanities Institute.

My greatest debt is to the dozens of hajj managers who opened their doors and files to me in country after country. Most of them were eager to help because they believed that people of all faiths would benefit from a better understanding of the hajj and its crucial role in Islam.

Several people were so generous with their time and attention that I would like to thank them personally. In Pakistan, I am particularly grateful to Omar Qureshi and his family, Samira Shah, Ijaz Gilani, and Hafiz Pasha. In Turkey, I enjoyed the kindness of Dilek Barlas, Bekir Demirkol, Levant Korkut, Carl Hershiser, Güneli Gün, and Metin Heper. Muhammad Zaini educated me about Malaysia, as did Qadri Azizi concerning Indonesia. My Nigerian experiences were especially enjoyable thanks to La Ray Denzer, Father Joseph Kenny, Father Iheanyi M. Enwerem, Shehu Galadanci, Sani Zahredeen, Kabiru Sani Hanga, Muhammad Sani Umar, Archbishop Peter Akinola, Msgr. D. E. Inyang, Dr. Efosa Oviasu, Michael Hanna, and Olu Makendi. And in Senegal, I received warm assistance from Souleymane Bachir Diagne, Hajj Rawane Mbaye, and Khadim Mbacké.

A number of legal scholars helped me think through the hajj's implications for international law, adding a special dimension beyond the advice I received from colleagues in the social sciences and humanities. In particular, I wish to thank Mark Janis, Abdullahi Ahmed An-Na'im, Alan Raphael, and Cherif Bassiouni. Vicki Mayfield and Theo Calderara guided me through multiple revisions of the manuscript, reading every word and critiquing every idea. Naturally, any remaining shortcomings in the work are solely my responsibility.

# Contents

# List of Tables

For a list of tables in the Appendix, see pp. 273–274.

# List of Figures

For a list of figures in the Appendix, see pp. 274–275.

And proclaim to humanity the Pilgrimage,
and they shall come unto thee on foot
and upon every lean beast. They shall come from every deep ravine
that they may witness things profitable to them.

Qur'an (xxii: 27–28)

All humankind is from Adam and Eve, an Arab has no superiority over a non-Arab
nor a non-Arab has any superiority over an Arab; also a white has no superiority over
a black nor a black has any superiority over a white except by piety and good action.
. . . This day have I perfected for you your religion and fulfilled My favor unto you.

Muhammad, 570–632 ("Farewell Sermon at Mount 'Arafat")

The longer the way, the more companions are necessary—the way to the Ka'ba is hard,
one needs a long caravan and a caravan-leader . . . and how much more difficult is it
to come closer to God through so many veils, steep mountains, and highway-robbers!

Mevlâna Celâleddin Rumi, 1207–1273 (Annemarie Schimmel,<br>
The Triumphal Sun, p. 293)

Behold the secret building before it is too late, and thou wilt see how it takes on life
through those who circle round it and walk round its stones, and how it looks out at
them from behind its veils and cloaks! And then I saw it take on life, as he had said.

Muhyiddin Ibn 'Arabi, 1165–1240 (Meccan Revelations, in<br>
Fritz Meier, "The Mystery of the Ka'ba," p. 161)

The darkest thing in the world is the Beloved's house without the Beloved. . . . When
the lover turns his eye away from created things, he will inevitably see the Creator
with his heart.

'Ali Bin 'Uthman al-Hujwiri, d. ca. 1072 (Kashf al-Mahjub,<br>
The Uncovering of the Veils, translated by R. A. Nicholson,<br>
pp. 327, 330)

I went to the Ka'ba, and from there I yearned for your street.
I beheld the Ka'ba, and remembered your face.
When I saw the black covering of the Ka'ba,
I stretched the hand of my desire towards the black dress of your hair.

When I seized the knocker of the *Ka'ba* with a hundred cravings,
    I made a prayer for your musk-scented curl.
The people in the sanctuary bowed their faces in humility to the *Ka'ba*,
    I turned, amidst all, the face of my heart to you.
In every stage I turned my footsteps to no other than you;
    The *tawaf* and the *sa'y* I performed in search of you.
The people stood praying at 'Arafat;
    I closed my lips for the prayer, and talked about you.
While the people in Mina were subject to their desire and their inclinations,
    I craved for you, empty as a cup.
                    Nur al-Din 'Abd al-Rahman Jami, 1414–1492 (Anna Livia F. A. Beelaert,
                                    "The Ka'ba as a Woman," pp. 118–119)

The King of the mice jumped back into his hole and rejoined his subjects.
    "How is the King of the cats after his Pilgrimage?" they asked. "Let's hope he
has changed for the better."
    "Never mind the Pilgrimage," said the King of the mice. "He may pray like a
Hajji, but he still pounces like a cat."
                    "The Cat Who Went to Mecca" (Syrian folktale in *Arab Folktales*,
                                    edited and translated by Inea Bushnaq, p. 216)

One day a pesky villager came to Sheikh Jaha's house. Jaha asked, "What are you
looking for?" and he answered, "I'm a Guest of God." Then Jaha said, "Come on, let's
go." The man followed him through the town until they arrived at the gate of the
Friday Mosque. Then the Sheikh said, "Since you're a Guest of God, you came to
me by mistake. This is God's house."
                    "A Guest of God Belongs in God's House" (Hausa folktale in
                                    *Hikayoyin Shehu Jaha* [Stories of Sheikh Jaha], edited by
                                    Tijjani M. Imam, p. 21)

Between us and the house of God there is a secret
Which even Gabriel the faithful does not know.
                    Sir Muhammad Iqbal, 1877–1938 (Annemarie Schimmel,
                                    *Gabriel's Wing*, p. 199)

He who does not realize the essence of the hajj only brings back from Mecca a suit-
case full of souvenirs and an empty mind. . . . These conventions are not assembled
by heads of states or their representatives, diplomats or political leaders, members of
parliament, cabinets, senators, university professors, scientists, intellectuals or spiritual leaders. No! No! Only Almighty God has the right to decide for the people because the people are His representatives on earth. This is the reason for the convention in Mina where God is the director of the people who have gathered by His
invitation.
                    'Ali Shari'ati, 1933–1977 (*Hajj*, pp. 83, 111–112)

You may be shocked by these words coming from me. But on this pilgrimage, what I
have seen, and experienced, has forced me to re-arrange much of my thought patterns previously held, and to toss aside some of my previous conclusions. . . . During
the past eleven days here in the Muslim world, I have eaten from the same plate,
drunk from the same glass, and slept in the same bed, (or on the same rug)—while
praying to the same God—with fellow Muslims, whose eyes were the bluest of blue,
whose hair was the blondest of blond, and whose skin was the whitest of white. . . .
We were truly all the same (brothers)—because their belief in one God had removed
the "white" from their minds, the "white" from their behavior, and the "white" from
their attitude.
                    Malcolm X, 1925–1965 ("Letter from Mecca" in
                                    *Autobiography*, p. 340)

# Guests of God

# Introduction

The hajj is the greatest gathering of humanity on earth. Each year, more than two million people from every corner of the globe come to the same place at the same time to visit "God's house"—the holy *Ka'ba* in Mecca—and participate in an emotional week of rituals that Muslims have been reenacting for fourteen centuries. Nowadays, much of the hajj is televised live so Muslims all over the world can accompany the pilgrims as they play out sacred dramas renewing their bonds with God, with ancient prophets from Adam to Muhammad, and with the entire community of believers.

For pilgrims, the hajj is the peak of spiritual life. Cleansed of all sin, they are as pure as the day they were born—assured of Paradise if they should die before returning home. For Muslims everywhere, the hajj is the most powerful expression of the unity and equality of all believers and their common destiny in this world and the next.

The hajj is a time of profound reflection, during which pilgrims critically examine their souls as well as the social and political conditions in their homelands, the global Islamic community, and the world as a whole. This explicit fusion of religion and politics makes the hajj both a pilgrimage and an annual congress of Islam—a massive spiritual assembly where international Muslim society reconstitutes itself and reconsiders its course in history.

## The Politics of the Modern Hajj

The hajj has always had far-reaching political ramifications, but today, after a half century of sponsorship and regulation by governments around the world, it is more politicized than ever. In one country after another, state pilgrimage agencies have taken over the lion's share of the booming market in religious tourism from private business. Politicians attempt to lure voters by outbidding one another with costly proposals for pilgrimage subsidies and services. Bankers and entrepreneurs scramble to attract investment capital from aspiring hajjis who prepay their expenses with installment savings plans. The media dispense a cascade of advice and exposés about every aspect of the hajj, beginning as pilgrims are preparing to travel and continuing for months after they return.

The hajj season is no longer confined to a few weeks between Islam's major holidays, the Feast of Fast Breaking at the end of Ramadan and the Feast of Sacrifice coinciding with the pilgrimage itself. Today's hajj is a yearlong cycle of planning, financing, teaching, outfitting, transporting, lodging, doctoring, celebrating, mourning, blaming, and correcting. In the biggest Muslim nations, pilgrimage demands as much mass enthusiasm and cooperation as any activity, including war.

Despite their great attention to organization, governments and politicians seldom envision the results of their own hajj policies at home or abroad. Pilgrims to Mecca are "Guests of God," not of Saudi Arabia or any other nation-state. Hajjis expect broad freedom to visit the holy places and to imagine their spiritual experiences individualistically. The principle of open access, combined with freedom of religious interpretation, preserves the autonomy of the hajj, no matter how many politicians try to manipulate it.

Freewheeling debates about the meanings of the rituals engage Muslims everywhere. Each state energetically publicizes its preferred interpretations, but their views are only a part of a global conversation that touches on every facet of Islam and politics. The more governments claim credit for promoting pilgrimage, the more they invite charges that they distort religion and exploit it for their gain. When it comes to managing the hajj, Muslim rulers learn that no good deed is above criticism.

As the world's greatest pilgrimage grows and becomes more politically charged, it demolishes deep-seated assumptions about religion in modern society, especially concerning the separation of the sacred and profane and the marginal role of ritual in daily life. It is impossible to imagine any set of entrenched powers controlling the hajj—turning it on and off according to their shifting interests or diverting its turbulent course to bolster the status quo while only appearing to question it.

Hajj managers regularly lose control over the institutions they create and the social forces they nurture. The prime example is Saudi Arabia itself. In the 1960s, King Faysal used the pilgrimage to lobby Muslim statesmen on behalf of his project to launch the Organization of the Islamic Conference (OIC). Although the OIC originated as an ad hoc coalition against Saudi Arabia's adversaries, it developed into the leading international organization of Muslim states—the so-called United Nations of the Islamic world.

Faysal's successors relied on the OIC to negotiate a new international regime for the hajj. The new hajj regime enforced an unprecedented and unpopular system of national quotas that checked a flood of revolutionary propaganda from Iranian pilgrims and attempted to curb mounting death tolls caused by disastrous overcrowding. By building an international consensus in the OIC, the Saudis pushed through controversial hajj reforms they would never have dared to adopt unilaterally. Yet their very success diminished Saudi influence over both the hajj and the OIC.

The large Sunni states that aided Saudi Arabia were more advanced than the desert principalities accustomed to dominating Islamic diplomacy. Saudis found they had to share power with important non-Arab countries where modern hajj management was well developed, especially Pakistan, Malaysia, Turkey, Indonesia, and Nigeria. Countries with professional hajj administrations were indispensable to enforcing the new quota system, and they enjoyed a host of advantages that strengthened their leverage in the Islamic world and beyond. Compared with Saudi Arabia, all these nations have economies that are diversified and internationally competitive, cultures that are pluralistic and cosmopolitan, and political systems that are responsive to popular demands for democracy and equality.

Leading Asian and African powers in the OIC helped Saudi Arabia fend off Iran's demand that Riyadh relinquish sovereignty over the hajj and holy cities in favor of an international administration run by all Muslim states. But they extracted a high price for their support. Saudis had to accept a compromise that preserved their sovereignty in the holy cities while internationalizing the pilgrimage. Non-Arab states agreed to a quota system restricting their participation in the hajj, but they insisted on a greater voice in the new pilgrimage regime and the OIC organs supervising it.

Although politicians in many countries are benefiting from Saudi Arabia's difficulties, their efforts to create national hajj monopolies are turning their own citizens against them. In country after country, governments have established centralized hajj agencies providing a full range of state-financed services at every step in the pilgrimage.

As hajj technocrats around the world imitate one another's innovations, modern pilgrimage management spreads with remarkable speed, offering subsidized package tours for all budgets and tastes. Today's high-end tours include online registration, computerized plane and hotel reservations, well-illustrated training materials and videotapes, mobile field hospitals, life insurance, and color-coded clothing and luggage.

But in nearly every case, hajj administration is tainted with favoritism and corruption. All the major pilgrimage programs are explicitly tailored to benefit voting blocks and businesses at home while cultivating prestige and influence abroad. Frequently, pilgrim management is so politicized it subverts the central values of the hajj. Instead of promoting unity and equality, it divides Muslims along every conceivable line—ethnicity, language, class, party, region, sect, gender, and age.

Pakistan's hajj rises and falls with the fortunes of the Bhutto family and the People's Party in their clashes with Punjabi elites who dominate the army and the Muslim League. In Malaysia, the ruling party turned the pilgrimage agency into a state bank that finances political cronies in the big cities and isolates Islamic opponents in the countryside. Turkey's pilgrimage is a revolving patronage pool for several right-wing parties. They compete for the same Muslim voters by trying to outdo one another in pouring hajj subsidies and contracts into pivotal electoral districts. When Suharto began losing support in the military, he tried to shore up his popularity by making the Indonesian hajj the largest in the world and dragging his whole family to Mecca to deflect outrage over their business scandals. Nigerian politicians threw so much money into the hajj that Christians became convinced they were creating an Islamic state. By the time Muslim army officers seized power, the specter of religious warfare drove them to sponsor a Christian pilgrimage to Jerusalem as well.

Discriminatory hajj policies are religiously self-contradictory and politically self-defeating. Manipulating sacred symbols of universality for partisan advantage is transparent hypocrisy unsustainable in even the most cynical environments. Gains in support are quickly outweighed by losses of legitimacy and credibility.

Aggressive sponsorship of the hajj generates at least as much anger as gratitude. Many Muslims, as well as non-Muslims, disapprove of government interference in religion. In their view, spending public funds on pilgrimage is just as offensive as spending them on mosques and religious schools.

Politically committed Muslims are unlikely to change their allegiances simply because a few thousand more people can go to Mecca for a few hundred dollars less. Especially in countries where Muslims are the majority, many believe all governments have an obligation to support the hajj, and they see no reason to reward politicians for simply doing their duty. Given such attitudes, it is no surprise when politicized hajj agencies prop up governments in the short run only to undermine them in the end.

# I

# What Is the Hajj and How Does Anyone Survive It?

The hajj is a time for centering and ordering, but it is also a time of tumult and chaos. Spiritually, the hajj is a steadying and stabilizing experience. Pilgrims reaffirm their ties to a single, worldwide community—creating it anew with each reunion and touching a common destiny that reaches far beyond their cramped lifetimes and imaginations. Physically, however, the hajj exposes everyone to pervasive uncertainty and danger. For at least a month, pilgrims are uprooted from everything familiar, disoriented at every turn, and thrown into countless perils—some unavoidable, others self-inflicted—shattering any illusion that they are solitary actors controlling their own fates.

The first casualty is a sense of time. Hajjis are constantly amazed at the tricks time plays on their minds and bodies. Everything is too slow or too fast. Speech, thought, and reflexes all go their separate ways. Someone says each day in the Holy Land feels like a month; another insists the days fly away in seconds. Neither uses the correct tenses, and neither remembers what day of the week it is.

The hajj is a grueling and perilous march. Sooner or later, it exposes the best and worst in everyone, as exhaustion dissolves into delirium, and serenity gives way to impatience, anger, and sheer panic. Even the most self-reliant pilgrims realize that being closer to God also brings them closer to death, and the ones most likely to survive are those who help one another. The constant struggle against heat, crowds, and confusion saps the stamina of all pilgrims, forcing them to build instant friendships with strangers from every corner of the world, knowing at several points that a split-second move by anyone can either save lives or end them.

The hajj works because of the good sense and mutual support of the pilgrims, not because of the staggering resources their governments marshal to assist and control them. All the money and technology, the planning and security, are impressive and growing every year, but it is never enough. The decisive factor is the pilgrims' self-control and mutual cooperation. When they pull together, they usually muddle through the thousands of breakdowns in order and services confronting them each day. When they fall apart, nothing else really matters, and no one can save them from disaster.

## Flexible Rites in Treacherous Places

Hajjis retrace the steps of Muhammad and Ibrahim, the founders of Islam and ancient monotheism. Even Muslims who never see the Holy Cities know the route and sequence of the rites.[1] Pilgrims flow in a mass procession and recession from the Grand Mosque in Mecca to the Plain of 'Arafat about twelve miles east and back again to the city. Overnight stops punctuate movement in each direction—in Mina on the way out, in Muzdalifa and Mina on the way home (Figure 1.1).

Much of the action dramatizes critical moments in the life of Ibrahim and his family. Circling the *Ka'ba* (the *tawaf*) pays homage to God by visiting his "house" on earth, the building Ibrahim and his son, Isma'il, constructed by following the instructions of the angel Gabriel (Figure 1.2). During the *tawaf*, pilgrims pray briefly at a spot just across from the door of the *Ka'ba* known as "Ibrahim's Place." Here, inside a tall glass showcase, is an ancient rock with an impression resembling a human foot. Many believe this to be Ibrahim's footprint, preserved in a stepping-stone he used while building the *Ka'ba*.

The *sa'y*—running back and forth between the hills of al-Safa and al-Marwa—commemorates the trials of Hagar, the concubine of Ibrahim and mother of Isma'il. When Ibrahim left mother and infant alone in the desert, Hagar frantically searched for water and discovered the sacred well of Zamzam. Pilgrims constantly drink the miraculous waters of Zamzam while in Mecca, and nearly everyone purchases several bottles as gifts for friends and relatives back home.

The highpoints of the hajj are not in Mecca but on the outskirts in 'Arafat and Mina. On the ninth day of the month of Dhu al-Hijjah (the last month in the Islamic calendar), all two million pilgrims assemble at the Plain of 'Arafat for the Day of Standing—a time of prayer and meditation from about noon until sunset. The congregation at 'Arafat replicates the gathering Muhammad addressed during his "Farewell Pilgrimage," when he revealed the final verses of the Qur'an just months before his death. Pilgrims crowd around the Mount

FIGURE I.I Major steps of the hajj

1    Put on the *ihram* garb and enter the sacred precinct on the outskirts of Mecca; chant the *talbiya* on the way to Mecca and perform the *tawaf* of arrival by circling the *Ka'ba* seven times (before the eighth day of Dhu al-Hijjah)

2    Spend the night in the pilgrims' camp at Mina (eighth day)

3    Gather at 'Arafat for the Day of Standing (ninth day)

4    Leave 'Arafat after sundown, spend the night in Muzdalifa, and gather pebbles for stoning the devil in Mina (evening of the ninth and morning of the tenth)

5    Arrive in Mina, stone the first pillar symbolizing the devil before noon, make an animal sacrifice, and remove the *ihram* (tenth day)

6    Return to Mecca, perform a second *tawaf* followed by the *sa'y*—running seven times between the hills of al-Safa and al-Marwa (tenth or eleventh day)

7–9  Shuttle between Mecca and Mina, stoning all three pillars and spending the nights in Mina (eleventh to thirteenth days)

10   Perform the *tawaf* of farewell and immediately depart Mecca (twelfth day or later)

of Mercy, where Muhammad delivered his sermon, and many believe their prayers reach God more readily from this point than anywhere else on earth.

At sundown, tens of thousands of buses, cars, and vans begin the painful return to Mecca. Throughout the night, they squeeze into the valley of Muzdalifa, where each pilgrim collects seventy small pebbles under a magnificent starlit sky. The pebbles are "ammunition" for the following day in Mina, when pilgrims begin stoning three pillars (*jamarat*) representing the devil. When God commanded Ibrahim to kill Isma'il, Satan appeared three times, telling the father to disobey. Each time, Ibrahim chased the devil away by throwing stones. In stoning likenesses of Satan, pilgrims reenact Ibrahim's struggle and remember it in their own battles with evil and temptation.

When pilgrims offer an animal sacrifice at Mina, they celebrate God's decision to spare Isma'il by allowing Ibrahim to slaughter a ram instead of the boy. Pilgrims make their sacrifices on the tenth of Dhu al-Hijjah—the same day Muslims all over the world observe Islam's greatest festival, Kurban Bayram or 'Id al-Adha, by slaughtering an animal and sharing its meat with neighbors and the needy.

The last three days of the hajj are the most hectic and frightening. From the eleventh until the thirteenth of Dhu al-Hijjah, pilgrims are constantly mov-

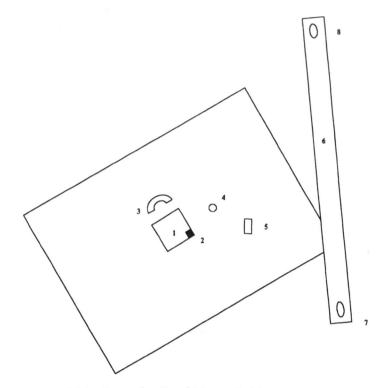

FIGURE I.2 Main sites at the Grand Mosque in Mecca

1 The *Ka'ba*
2 The Black Stone
3 The Hijr—burial place of Hagar and Isma'il
4 Ibrahim's Place
5 The Well of Zamzam
6 Al-Mas'a, the Place of Running
7 Al-Safa
8 Al-Marwa

ing back and forth between Mina and Mecca, rushing to complete ritual duties at both sites and preparing to return home or make a side-trip to Medina. This is when overcrowding and confusion reach their peak; it is also when the bulk of hajj-related accidents and fatalities occur. In the last three decades, about 2,700 pilgrims have perished in Mina alone, mostly because of fires in the campsite and crushing crowds on pedestrian bridges and in the tunnel leading to the stoning areas around the *jamarat*[2] (Table 1.1).

Saudi Arabian authorities have spent at least $25 billion to accommodate greater numbers of pilgrims and to ensure their safety. Yet death tolls rise year after year. Ironically, vast improvements in hajj infrastructure and services probably worsened the problem by attracting ever larger throngs to tiny areas

TABLE 1.1  Hajj-related disasters in recent years

| | |
|---|---|
| 2004 | 251 pilgrims die in Mina during stampedes at the *jamarat*. |
| 2001 | Crushing crowds at the *jamarat* kill 35 during the stoning of the devil. |
| 1998 | Overcrowding and trampling at the *jamarat* leave 118 dead. |
| 1997 | Fire sweeps through the pilgrims' camp at Mina, destroying 70,000 tents and caus- ing 343 fatalities and 1,500 injuries. |
| 1994 | Trampling kills 270 people near the *jamarat*. |
| 1990 | 1,426 pilgrims perish during a human stampede in the al-Mu'aisim pedestrian tun- nel through the mountains between Mecca and Mina. A power failure cuts the tunnel's air-conditioning and lighting, spreading panic among thousands who fear being trapped inside. |
| 1989 | Terrorists set off two bombs in Mecca, killing 1 and wounding 16. Sixteen Kuwaitis are arrested and executed. |
| 1987 | Police clash with pro-Iranian demonstrators in the Grand Mosque, leaving 402 dead. |
| 1975 | Fire kills at least 200 pilgrims in the camp at Mina. |

now more cramped and overburdened than ever[3] (Table 1.2). No matter how rapidly the Saudis demolish and rebuild, they can never keep up with the even stronger surge of pilgrims eager to come under any conditions.

Pilgrimage managers eased the pressure somewhat by adopting a quota system that freezes per capita hajj participation at 1990 levels. Nowadays, most countries can send no more than 1,000 pilgrims for every million people, holding the total number of overseas hajjis at about 1.3 million annually.[4] The international network of hajj agencies created to encourage pilgrimage is now a gatekeeper constricting the flow at its source.

Saudi officials also limit internal pilgrims—resident foreigners and Saudi citizens—who used to equal the number of hajjis from abroad. In 1998, the Saudi government required its own citizens to apply to local pilgrimage boards that grant permits only to those who have not made the hajj for at least five years. Pilgrims from within the kingdom have declined from 50 percent of all hajjis to less than 30 percent—and most of these are non-Saudis.[5]

Saudi authorities tried to lessen the sting of quotas by encouraging people to make fewer hajjis and more 'umras—briefer visits to Mecca that Muslims can undertake any time of year. In 2001, the Saudis liberalized the 'umra sys- tem, allowing foreigners to travel freely inside the kingdom. In granting 'umra visitors the equivalent of tourist visas, the Saudis hope to kill two birds with one stone—deflecting anger over new hajj restrictions while building a tourism industry that earns foreign exchange without admitting non-Muslims. Each year, Saudi Arabian tourists spend about $8 billion abroad, three times the amount hajjis spend in their country. A freer 'umra might offset these costs and lighten pressures in the hajj season.

Overcrowding and fatalities would be far worse were it not for the inherent flexibility of the rituals themselves. All pilgrims must perform essentially the

TABLE 1.2  Resources and services devoted to the hajj

| | |
|---|---|
| Mosque expansion in Mecca | A 5-fold increase in the area of the Grand Mosque after 1955 and another doubling of the area after 1988, permitting more than 1 million visitors at a time |
| Mosque expansion in Medina | Four expansions since 1951, creating capacity for 700,000 worshipers |
| Transportation | A separate terminal at King 'Abd al-'Aziz Airport in Jeddah, receiving 50,000 pilgrims daily (Indonesia alone accounts for more than 450 flights and Pakistan an additional 376 flights); port facilities in Jeddah admitting 70 ships carrying 80,000 pilgrims in less than 3 weeks |
| Security, health, and service workers | 15,000 police, 5,000 doctors and nurses, 35,000 traffic officers, cleaners, bakers, and rubbish collectors |
| Food | 95.2 million loaves of bread; 7.8 million ready-made meals on sale at 1,500 points in Mecca, 'Arafat, and Mina |
| Water | 50.5 million 1-liter plastic bags of water, 113 million bottles of mineral water, and 141 million liters of Zamzam water |
| Publications | 6 million books, 600,000 audiocassettes, 300,000 Qur'ans, and 117,000 videotapes in 5 languages |
| Health centers | 85 in Mecca, including 5 in the Grand Mosque; 133 in Medina, including 7 in the Prophet's Mosque |
| Fireproof tents | 40,000 fiberglass tents, 42,000 water pumps, and 27,000 toilets in Mina |
| Animals | 1.1 million sheep, 172,000 goats, 60,000 cattle, and 60,000 camels; the meat of more than 600,000 animals distributed to 27 countries |
| The Kiswa | 450 kilograms (992 pounds) of silk and gold embroidery woven by 200 people at a cost of $4.53 million |

same rites in the same places, but they enjoy some leeway in the timing and sequence of movements. Pilgrims can accomplish a valid hajj even if they fail to complete an obligatory act. A hajji's intention is always more important than her ritual exactness. If exigencies of health or safety disrupt her schedule, there are many ways to repair the breach: making an additional animal sacrifice, fasting a few extra days in the year ahead, or increasing her annual zakat contribution for the poor.

Hajj managers encourage pilgrims to stick to the basic rites and dispense with others that are only customary or that are potentially life threatening. Each year, they urge pilgrims making the tawaf to be content with beckoning to the Black Stone from a distance instead of pushing through the crowd to kiss or touch it. Nowadays, most people make their animal sacrifices by proxy rather than in person, knowing the excess meat is no longer incinerated or buried in the desert but frozen and airlifted to feed needy Muslims in about thirty countries.[6]

Two reforms are particularly vital to crowd control, though they are controversial for breaking revered custom. First, a longer timetable for stoning the jamarat in Mina allows pilgrims to pummel the devil throughout the daylight hours instead of piling on top of one another in the hottest part of the afternoon. Second, when the hajj ends, pilgrims must leave Mecca as soon as possible rather than staying on as students or permanent residents, as millions did for centuries.[7]

International management and ritual flexibility save countless lives each year, but neither can ensure a safe and successful hajj. In the end, it is the hajjis themselves who create a pilgrimage where disaster is the exception rather than the rule. The hajj works because two million hajjis of every race and nation are determined to make it work.

## Small Groups and Great Deeds: Making Friends on the Move

Even though the core of the hajj is a celebration of unity and equality, it takes time for pilgrims to learn the value of looking after each other instead of looking out for themselves. The group I joined in the United States was no exception. My fifty or so companions came from every part of the country, but most were Indian and Palestinian immigrants who quickly decided they did not like one another.

Their mutual antipathy expressed precisely the national and ethnic jealousy the hajj is supposed to transcend. In retrospect, though, they did us all a great favor. By setting such a bad example in the early days of our journey, they made the rest of us more determined to cement friendships that pulled the group together in the difficult weeks that followed.

### Taming Tribalism

The most embarrassing clash occurred in Jeddah, just after arriving in Saudi Arabia. We were getting ready for a pre-hajj visit to Medina, the city where Muhammad established what many regard as the ideal Islamic society. As we boarded, our laughter and chatter faded to awkward silence as we realized there were not enough seats to go around. Nearly everyone was in the throes of jet lag after two-day flights with long stopovers in New York, Frankfurt, and Amman, but somebody had to stand.

The last aboard were also the least capable of enduring more discomfort— elderly Indians, mainly women. No one moved and no one spoke. Then, all eyes turned toward four young men—all in their twenties and all Palestinian— seated together near the center of the bus. More annoyed than ashamed, one of the youths shouted, "The Indian men should stand so their women can sit down. It's their responsibility to take care of their own people."

At that, Dr. Hasan—a surgeon in his sixties and the sole male among those standing—jumped out of his skin. "What are you talking about?" he screamed. "Indian men, Palestinian men. There are no Indians and Palestinians here. There are only Muslims! In a few hours we will be at the tomb of the Prophet, and you are telling us some of these seats are for Indians and others are for Palestinians? What kind of hajj are you making?"

This was merely the first of many impromptu lectures Dr. Hasan gave us on social propriety and ritual correctness. He constantly worried we might "spoil" our pilgrimages by missing a required rite or destroying our state of purity with prohibited behavior. But now it was Dr. Hasan who was on the verge of invalidating his hajj even before it began. Not only did he let the cat out of the bag about how the Indians and Palestinians really felt about one another but also he unleashed a fiery temper that spelled trouble for everyone. We all knew the surest way to invalidate a pilgrimage was to get embroiled in a fight—even if someone else started it.

Within seconds of the doctor's outburst, half those seated jumped up, offering places to the latecomers. We all found some place to squeeze in, and no one cared if their new neighbors were young or old, male or female, Indian or Palestinian. The young men who set the doctor off stayed glued to their window seats, but they had sense enough to hold their tongues. They had gotten the message and, whatever their inner thoughts, were on their best behavior from then on.

Later, a brief crisis nudged the Palestinians a little further out of their cocoon. A Palestinian woman disappeared, and her companions were frantic. Police scoured missing pilgrims' camps all over Medina, hoping someone had found her and led her to safety. Finally, late in the afternoon, Muhammad, leader of our tour, came to me with good news—he was on his way to fetch her from a Turkish dormitory on the other side of town, and he wanted me to tag along.

In the next few hours, we realized the vanishing lady had triggered a spontaneous multinational effort that was repeated thousands of times every day of the hajj season. Muhammad and I—an Egyptian and an American—found a taxi driver from Yemen who knew enough of the city to unravel directions from several Saudi policemen. When we arrived at the Turkish center, the director introduced a withered Moroccan man smiling from ear to ear as he leaned on a wooden walking staff. It was he who had found the Palestinian woman. Then, he insisted on waiting at her side the entire day and personally handing her over to her friends.

When she described her dramatic "rescue," tensions in our group subsided considerably. The "every country for itself" approach was soundly discredited, and the young men who advocated it were doing nothing to watch over their compatriots. Most Palestinian pilgrims in our group were middle-aged and elderly women traveling without male escorts. The only young woman was a bright and dutiful daughter-in-law stuck with the impossible job of riding herd over a dozen bewildered grandmothers. Most of the time she managed to keep them in tow, but it was too much to expect of one person.

*The Doctor Learns to Relax*

As our companions created more friendships cutting across cultures, their initial squabbles and suspicions faded from memory. Everyone benefited from the comradeship, but it was Dr. Hasan who gained the most. He spurred others to abandon their "tribal feuding," but they, in turn, pressed him to give up his obsession for ritual perfection.

The turning point for the doctor came in the valley of Muzdalifa in the middle of the world's biggest traffic jam. At sundown on the Day of Standing, all two million pilgrims assembled at 'Arafat depart at exactly the same time. More than 100,000 buses, trucks, cars, and vans plunge into a couple of narrow mountain passes, producing complete gridlock. As darkness falls, the lucky ones crawl ahead at one mile per hour. Around midnight or later, they arrive at Muzdalifa, pausing until twilight before moving on to Mina.

Pilgrims do very little at Muzdalifa, and in the past that was exactly why many described it with such ecstasy. They pray and gather seventy pebbles to use later in stoning the devil, but mostly they camp out under the desert sky and gaze at endless stars dancing in the luminous canopy above. Before the hajj became gargantuan, Muzdalifa offered a few precious hours of peace and solitude to recover a bit of energy for the final days of ritual duties that keep pilgrims shuttling back and forth between Mina and Mecca.

Today, that respite is gone. The valley is a grisly parking lot—miles of jet-black asphalt under blinding light towers, where thousands of air-conditioned buses sit, their motors churning clouds of carbon monoxide thick enough to chew. There is room for a fraction of the early arrivals to pitch tents in the desert and pray at a tiny mosque in the foothills. They can bide their time until first light signals a renewal of the trek toward Mina. For everyone else, Muzdalifa is a bleak holding pen where those straying more than a few hundred feet from the bus will probably never find their way back.

For most, the "new Muzdalifa" is a disappointment, but for Dr. Hasan it was a calamity. The leaders suggested that, in view of the impossible conditions, we could legitimately leave the valley a few hours before dawn. This way, we might arrive in Mina early enough to complete the first ritual stoning of the devil before the heat and crowds became truly dangerous. But the doctor would not hear of it. For him, it was cheating, pure and simple. He insisted we stay through the night. "If the rest of you want to spoil your hajjs, I can't stop you," he said. "But let me get off of the bus right here."

Everyone understood the doctor would be exposing himself to great danger if he left the group and tried to catch up at Mina. It took us half an hour to persuade him to stay, marshaling every conceivable argument both personal and theological. We pointed out that sleeping at Muzdalifa was a custom, not a requirement. In recent years, it had become routine for guides to shorten the time there because of terrible overcrowding. None of this impressed Dr. Hasan. We were lazy and looking for any excuse to cut corners. Because the travel agents were motivated only by profit, they had no qualms about bending the rules, and they could always find scholars willing to spout any opinion for which they were paid.

Soon the debate widened as companions added reasons for the doctor to change his mind. Several reminded him that a sincere intention was far more important to a valid hajj than any ritual. Only God decides whose pilgrimage is acceptable and whose is irretrievably flawed. His decision depends on what is in a pilgrim's heart rather than on ritual precision, and no human knows the result for certain. These people said the doctor was the best judge of his own intention, and if he had more confidence in himself spiritually, he would be less distracted by legalisms and appearances.

Others pointed out that even if leaving Muzdalifa early was a technical breach, it was a minor fault that could be remedied by any number of compensatory acts. "Only God is perfect," said a woman near the front of the bus. "And he doesn't expect the visitors to his house to be perfect guests," said another toward the rear. "Especially if perfection means getting killed," added a man standing close to the doctor.

There was yet another argument that swayed Dr. Hasan, though it sprang more from desperation than from common sense or any religious authority we could recall. Several of us proclaimed we were willing to be held personally responsible for the decision to move on. If there was any infraction, the doctor would be absolved, and we alone would be accountable before God.

At last, Dr. Hasan relented. Stepping back from the front door, he nodded to the driver and took his seat. It was the most dubious and emotional argument of all that tipped the balance—a spontaneous declaration of shared responsibility by the very people he scolded in Medina for succumbing to tribalism. Now, everyone pooled their persuasive skills to cajole a proud and obstinate man who had painted himself into a corner and needed a graceful way out. After insisting he had to leave the group to save his hajj, the doctor seemed relieved to discover he could remain with us and enjoy even higher esteem.

## Our Composite Hajji

My companions could not have chosen a better time to pull themselves together, for the final days in Mina and Mecca were by far the most difficult. In previous weeks, I had become friends with a handful of men who were also traveling on their own, and before long our makeshift family blossomed into one of the most cohesive units in the group. I spent the bulk of my time with Muhammad, the Egyptian tour leader, who was a university student in Chicago, and Sultan, a towering African American postal worker from Oakland. Most days, we were joined by Ashraf, an Egyptian engineer from Milwaukee, and Hussain, a Pakistani who ran a tourist shop in New Orleans. There were also a couple of married men who enjoyed our company whenever their wives had to share sleeping quarters with the other women. We jokingly called them the "brothers from Ohio," but they were really brothers-in-law—Middle Western farm boys married to sisters from a family of Syrian immigrants.

Muhammad, Sultan, and I got acquainted in Medina. Muhammad arranged for Sultan and me to be roommates and visited us whenever he was free. Sultan spent a day and a half guiding us through the history of Islam among American blacks. He gave a masterly account of the rival factions—describing their social bases, their clashes and reconciliation with mainstream Islam, and their influence on the broader civil rights movement.

Afterward, Sultan asked Muhammad to translate a few verses from the Qur'an because he could not understand if their references to "infidels" and "unbelievers" included Christians and Jews. Muhammad claimed that all non-Muslims including "People of the Book" were unbelievers, so I noted that standard interpretations contradicted him. He readily acknowledged my point, arguing that differences of opinion were beneficial because they forced people to look to the Qur'an for evidence.

Reaching into his shirt pocket, he produced a small Qur'an he carried everywhere. He told us he and his wife had a pact to refer to the Qur'an and abide by its teachings whenever they disagreed about something at home. "If this is the way you read the Qur'an," I said, "your wife must win all the arguments." "That's almost true," he admitted smiling through his curly black beard, "but I win one too now and then."

In addition to the constant teasing and learning from one another, we also developed a keen sense of mutual protection. It began with small things like watching after each other in crowds and attending to constant signs of fatigue and dehydration. In time, it seemed we each lent parts of ourselves to an imaginary fourth hajji we had created to look after us all. Our composite guardian was everything we were and more. He pooled our size and stamina, our senses and instincts, our languages and social skills, our courage and prudence.

There were many occasions where mutual reliance saved us from physical harm, but two incidents stand out. The first was in Medina during a morning visit to the Prophet's Mosque. The focal point of the mosque is a small area toward the front where the Prophet's pulpit and tomb are located. A narrow passage between the pulpit and tomb is known as Rauda al-Nabawiya—the Prophet's Garden—because tradition says he was accustomed to praying there. No matter how many additions the Saudis construct to expand the space for prayer, everyone still wants to be as close as possible to this tiny corner.

Security guards in the mosque allow pilgrims to pray briefly in the Rauda and then to pass quickly by the Prophet's tomb. Pilgrims can greet the Prophet as they would any dear friend, but they are not permitted to pray in front of his tomb because it would seem they were worshiping another human instead of God, especially because their backs are facing the *Ka'ba*. The steady crush of emotion-filled visitors and their recurrent clashes with whip-wielding guards makes this a flash point under any circumstances. But since the Iranian Revolution, guards have become more willing to use force against stragglers, suspecting they might be Shi'ites protesting bans on visitations at Medina's other gravesites.

When we visited the Prophet's tomb, Sultan and I were astonished by the power of Muhammad's emotions. We had already made several trips to the mosque at different hours of the day and night, so we assumed this visit would be like the others—crowded but relaxed and convivial. Then, as we squeezed into the line passing in front of the tomb, we realized Muhammad was weeping uncontrollably.

Overcome by the surge of feeling he experienced in the Prophet's "presence," he froze, closed his eyes, and prayed in whispers, holding his open hands near his temples. Soon, others stood at his side, each in a similar posture. The flow of visitors slowed to a trickle and then stopped completely, putting unbearable pressure on the already weary crowd behind us.

As Sultan made his way to the exit, I pulled his arm. As soon as he saw Muhammad, Sultan's eyes told me he understood what I was just beginning to grasp—the security guards were ready to pounce, and the pilgrims were terrified. In a flash, we grabbed Muhammad, shook him to his senses, and pushed him toward the door. By the time the guards moved in, the lines had almost sorted themselves out, and a few mild swishes were enough to finish the job.

A week later at Mina, we had a much closer call. The crowds were unusually thick around the three pillars where pilgrims throw stones at the "devil." The steep stairways to the stoning area were so littered with abandoned footwear it was hard to avoid stumbling. In the scramble to get down the stairs in one piece, pilgrims were literally running out of their sandals.

It took us thirty minutes to get within striking distance of the nearest pillar because thousands of pilgrims were shoving in opposite directions at the same time. About half were pushing us aside, determined to depart the same way they arrived instead of advancing toward the other pillars in a continuous flow. Stones were flying everywhere. Most landed far short of the target, showering down on screaming pilgrims pinned against the wall surrounding the pillar and desperate to leave by any route.

Sultan and I got close enough to throw our stones over the sea of bobbing heads; then we stepped aside so Hussain and Ashraf could do the same. A few stones hit the "devil," but most whizzed by and went too far. In trying to avoid hitting the pilgrims in front of us, we threw so hard we struck people on the other side of the pillar.

When it was time to leave, we were as confused as everyone else about what path to take. Only Sultan was tall enough to see over the mass of bodies and waving arms. He spotted an opening to the right and told us to walk in front of him as he shouted directions. For the next ten minutes, he guided us to safety one step at a time, as cool as a rush-hour commuter inching toward his regular train. I was never more than a few inches away from him, close enough to feel his chest against my head, like a baby kangaroo peering out of its mother's pouch.

Ashraf kept up with us, but Hussain disappeared. After an hour and a half walk back to our tent, we were relieved to find him talking excitedly with others in the group. Many were asking him to take their stones so he could cast them on their behalf. They were too frightened and weak to return to the pillars, so we agreed to be their proxies. The next day, we set out early with extra pebbles in hand, making sure to beat the afternoon crowds and return before the crush. Amazingly, no one was killed during the days of stoning that year. Before long, however, death tolls became so alarming that 'ulama in Saudi Arabia and Egypt suggested extending the prescribed hours for stoning so crowds could spread out over the cooler mornings as well as the blistering afternoons.

## Transnational Society Galore

Once we learned to recognize it, we saw our informal team approach replicated all around us. Small groups of five or six are not as obvious as larger units traveling on the same airplanes and hailing from neighboring villages. Yet informal groups are the key to organizing daily life inside all the big delegations clustered around national flags and sporting distinctive uniforms.

Everyone marveled at the regimentation of Singaporeans and the utter disarray of Nigerians. Women from Singapore all wore the same clothing—a white head cover and smock with bright red-and-white flags stitched to their backs so they could spot one another at a distance. Wherever we went, they were the tiniest hajjis in the biggest groups. We never saw fewer than twenty at a time, darting past everyone else and locking arms when necessary to hold their ranks together.

The Nigerians were constantly underfoot. The moment we stepped off the plane in Jeddah, we found them sprawled out on the cool pavement, sleeping soundly while the whole world tried to avoid stomping on their heads. Nigerian men—the most destitute of all pilgrims—were turning the Holy Cities into a giant open-air dormitory, camping out behind the mosques and in the streets, with remains of cardboard boxes as their mattresses. Nigerian women were the most enterprising pilgrims. They set up instant street markets at every turn, laying out colorful cloth and dresses that sold so briskly the police hardly bothered to shoo them away.

Most pilgrims were in between the tight-knit Singaporeans and the free-floating Nigerians. Like us, they improvised their own small solutions, adapting each day as they developed more confidence and learned to expect the unexpected. As we mingled with Bangladeshis and Indonesians, we realized they were unusually adept at creating flexible structures invisible to outsiders.

I discovered the Bangladeshis during an embarrassing encounter in Mina, where their tactfulness saved me from starting a needless quarrel. On a sweltering morning after an hour's wait to use the toilet and brush my teeth, I remembered it was my turn to fetch the tea for my companions. When I finally located the nearest tent where refreshments were sold, it looked like a disaster. About fifty drowsy pilgrims were scattered about waiting for a couple of workmen to boil water. At the back of the tent, three barrel-sized cauldrons sat atop sputtering gas burners no match for the job.

I was resigned to waiting in yet another interminable line, but where was it? When I asked how to queue up, they shrugged their shoulders, saying, "We are all waiting together." Exasperated, I snapped back, "Great, no line. I bet you guys wouldn't know a line if it fell on you."

Instead of responding in kind, they stood up and formed three neat rows— one for each cauldron. In less than a minute, they taught me a double lesson without uttering a word. They were urging me to control my temper so I would not risk a spat that would spoil their hajjs as well as my own. They were also showing me that they were far more organized than I realized. Even if they were not standing in line continuously, they carried an agreed pecking order in their heads and could produce it at a moment's notice.

Indonesian pilgrims are renowned for their tradition of teamwork, which their government tries to harness in official groups lead by hajj bureaucrats. Every planeload of Indonesians is divided into regional units outfitted with distinctive costumes and color-coded suitcases and linked in a single chain of command. The Indonesians stand out not just because of their unique appearance but because of their extraordinary generosity.

One of many examples I witnessed was at the Grand Mosque in Mecca during Friday noontime prayers. At the last minute, Sultan, Ashraf, and I managed to squeeze onto the escalator to the second level and nudge our way toward a railing overlooking the vast courtyard. Nearly all the early arrivals were Indonesians, and they had already packed into the tightest ranks imaginable. Yet as soon as they saw a stream of latecomers, they somehow created whole new rows welcoming anyone who wanted to join them.

That day's sermon seemed to last forever, and everyone was wilting from the heat. An orange watercooler with paper cups was located near the railing, but it was inaccessible to everyone except the hundred or so Indonesians seated around it. A few people in the rear asked for water, and before long Indonesians were passing cups back and forth in all directions, never taking a drop for themselves. The cups were disposable, but most empties found their way back to the cooler and were recycled until the water ran out. Afterward, the used cups were dutifully returned to the dispenser, leaving the wastebasket beside the cooler nearly empty when prayers finished.

Our last days in Mecca were relaxed and leisurely. In the lull before the madness of departure, new hajjis were busy shopping and sightseeing. Others tried to catch up on sleep, hoping to remember the normal rhythm of day and night. Most of us had become complacent tourists; a terrorist attack in the heart of the city was the furthest thing from our minds.

The evening the first bomb exploded, Ashraf and I were walking by one of the main entrances to the central market. We had just stepped out of our hotel to round up cold drinks for our roommates when a sudden roar stopped us in our tracks. We stared upward and to the left, searching for some visual clue of what had happened. Instead, we heard another roar coming from the market—first a dull rumbling, then a steady tremor like an earthquake. Suddenly, tides of people began pouring out of the market into the square. It was a stampede—a human avalanche heading straight at us.

Ashraf and I happened to be standing between two of the tall light towers illuminating the plaza. He jumped a few feet to the right, I scooted to the left, and we crouched behind the thick pillars, hoping they might shield us if we remained perfectly still. For the next fifteen minutes we waited and watched, as thousands of people dashed past us on both sides.

Soon, my mind started tricking me. I was floating safely above the panic, no longer standing in its midst. I was just as terrified as the fleeing crowds, but, unable to run with them or away from them, I imagined myself hovering over them instead.

Miraculously, no one fell, and no one was trampled. Two nights later, another bomb exploded farther away, but this time we were in the hotel lobby seeing off friends whose flight left the next day. Several people were injured in the blasts, but a Pakistani pilgrim was the only fatality. The Saudis arrested twenty-nine Kuwaiti Shi'ites, calling them Iranian-trained saboteurs who smuggled in explosives to spread mayhem during the hajj. Within two months, sixteen were beheaded, and four others received long prison sentences.[8]

Once again, we saw that no government could really protect the pilgrims. They could provide basic services and punish criminals, but the rest was up to us. Even on the final day in Mecca, our group was still learning to pull together against common danger. As my roommates returned from the last circling of the Ka'ba—the "farewell tawaf"—they told remarkably different stories.

After weeks of failure, Sultan finally pushed close enough to kiss the Black Stone, but just a few feet behind him the "brothers" from Ohio lost all their cash to thieves who slashed their clothes and money belts. Back in the hotel, Sultan—fearless and elated—boasted of his feat, giving heart to the hapless brothers, listening intently as they peeked out from their bunk beds, dazed and shaken but unharmed.

# 2

# What Does the Hajj Mean?

Modernist Islamic thinkers see the hajj as a treasure-house of fluid symbols carrying infinite meanings everyone is free to interpret and reinterpret as they choose. Inviting Muslims to think of the hajj creatively is part of modernists' wider commitment to democratizing religious knowledge. In their view, "reading" the hajj's inner meanings is similar to reading any sacred text, including the Qur'an—every mortal mind can grasp a fraction of God's message, but no human authority, no matter how learned and esteemed, can monopolize the discussion or claim the final word.

Modernists argue that the *'ulama* have barely begun to explore the hajj as a symbolic universe, and they portray their own interpretations as speculative or poetic imaginings designed to provoke debate among people from all walks of life. "Rereadings" of the hajj are more daring and explicitly political than treatments of scripture and law—fields more deeply encrusted with dogma, where direct challenges carry far greater danger. Hajj symbolism has always been a reservoir of ancient lore and esoteric knowledge more attractive to mystics and philosophers than to conventional scholars.

Like everyone else, the *'ulama* readily acknowledge that the hajj is filled with hidden meanings no one can understand completely. They regularly debunk practices they regard as superstitious, but they shy away from proposing any set of interpretations as authoritative. The bulk of their hajj writings spell out the steps of a legally valid pilgrimage, including special prayers and salutations for each shrine and station along the way. By stressing the minutiae of ritual performance and discounting the emotional significance of the experience as a whole, the *'ulama* have effectively relinquished a core area of religious interpretation to popular and heterodox approaches.

In every Muslim country, bookshops and sidewalk stalls are packed with two types of hajj commentary—dry as dust manuals of the *'ulama* on the one hand and soaring inquiries into the "secrets" and "mysteries" of the hajj penned by returned pilgrims and lay writers on the other. Modernists have exploited the freedom and popularity of the latter genre to produce some of the most original and synthetic writing in the Islamic world. Their interpretations of hajj symbolism draw on Islam's mystical and philosophical heritages, as well as contemporary Western thinking in the humanities and social sciences.

Three writers have produced widely influential reinterpretations that portray the hajj as a powerful agent of social and political reform: Muhammad Iqbal of India, 'Ali Shari'ati of Iran, and Mohammed Arkoun of Algeria. Iqbal imagines the hajj as resurgence and reconstruction rather than as simple return. More than a spiritual journey preparing individuals for the afterlife, the pilgrimage to Mecca is a collective reawakening that inspires the entire community to reshape itself and reclaim a creative role in history.

In Shari'ati's view, the hajj mobilizes the *umma* and seeks to redistribute power to its weakest members. Pilgrimage is a time for criticizing glaring injustices and protesting the exploitation of interlocking elites in political, economic, and religious life.

For Arkoun, the hajj reflects universal human aspirations that transcend Islam or any religion. The hajj is the highest expression of an Islamic civilization that subsumes every race and culture, but it also embodies the quest for a worldwide civilization embracing followers of all faiths, as well as followers of none.

Iqbal's revivalism, Shari'ati's rebelliousness, and Arkoun's humanism have merged into a modernist stream of hajj interpretation that enjoys mass audiences in dozens of languages and nations. Their views are constantly discussed and debated by a cosmopolitan hajj community that is increasingly youthful, female, educated, urban, and non-Middle Eastern.

Today's hajjis are not the aged and illiterate peasants and tribespeople who might once have accepted a cryptic wisdom that they were undertaking a journey of pure obedience or a dress rehearsal for Judgment Day. More and more, they are sophisticated world citizens firmly fixed on this life, expecting concrete social and political benefits, as well as ultimate spiritual rewards.

## Muhammad Iqbal: Islam in History

In describing the hajj as a "journey of the soul," Iqbal relied on familiar imagery from Islam's most famous mystics and philosophers. Unlike his pred-

ecessors, however, he saw it as a distinctively modern journey signifying progress and choice instead of repetition and predestination. He took Rumi as his
guide and alter ego, embracing a vision of the ineluctable ascent of all creation
toward the Creator but linking it to human will instead of divine dictate.[1]

Part of Rumi's attraction was that he seemed to be an antidote to the
troublesome pantheism of Ibn 'Arabi, the Andalusian mystic Iqbal regarded
as a patriarch of the degenerate and superstitious Sufism of modern times. In
his youth, Iqbal read Rumi and Ibn 'Arabi as echoes of the same ancient
teaching—God exists in everything he creates, and when his creatures draw
near him, they are reuniting with their own divine selves. However, Iqbal came
to see Rumi as singing about the spirit's evolution through a ceaseless striving
for perfection instead of a return to primeval existence.

Iqbal interpreted Rumi's most celebrated metaphor—the sighing reed
flute—as a sign of all-embracing evolution instead of pantheistic return. Separated from the reed bed, the cry of the reed flute expresses creativity as well
as longing. "It stands for Adam who, far away from Paradise and its peace,
began to work and to invent arts and crafts, since only separation makes man
creative and inventive."[2] For Rumi, all change flowed directly from God's grace
and love. For Iqbal, however, human development was a special case, where
will was essential and leadership was decisive.

Not surprisingly, Iqbal reserved the most important role in shaping human
will for the poet himself. The poet not only lauded the soul's upward journey
but also guided it. To signify his own place in history, Iqbal chose a signature
metaphor that became as famous as any of Rumi's—the bell of the caravan to
Mecca, summoning pilgrims to reconnect with their spiritual home and remake earthly society in its image.[3]

By depicting himself as the voice of the hajj caravan, Iqbal claimed descent
from a long line of Indian reformers, including Ahmad Sirhindi, Shah Wali
Allah of Delhi, and Sir Sayyid Ahmad Khan—revivalists who called on the
subcontinent's Muslims to renovate their religion in order to shore up crumbling political power.[4] Iqbal saw the political and spiritual resurrection of the
community as inseparable, arguing that the truth of Islam is proven by the
strength and success of its followers.

Just as Muhammad was the "seal of the prophets," so should the *umma*
be the "seal of nations," the most perfect, all-embracing community. Just as
the prophet of Islam combined several roles—lawgiver, spiritual intercessor,
and state builder—so should poet-philosophers rally stray Muslims to the hajj
caravan and guide them to the sanctuary of the *Ka'ba*.[5] There, at last, they
would become revived not as separate souls but as a unique community with
a fateful mission.

Of course, Iqbal never believed that Mecca could be a model for any modern community. Mecca was an icon of a worldly haven where Muslims could
enjoy peace and security, where they could ward off the dangers of materialism

and ethnocentrism that spread with the intrusion of alien cultures. Muslims could create this Mecca anywhere, but they had to do so by adapting general principles of Islam to current times and specific places, not by squeezing themselves into a straitjacket of preconceived rules.

The core of Iqbal's message is that religion should unleash humanity's potential for growth instead of stifling it. Religion must increase believers' self-esteem—individual as well as collective—and this can only happen if it awakens their inner sense of strength and power. "Religion without power is only philosophy."[6]

His favorite poetic images extol the consolidation of a distinctive personality that becomes ever more certain of its self in striving for higher levels of perfection. The tulip spends early life underground, becoming visible only when its rugged beauty is ready to be appreciated. The solitary pearl takes shape on the ocean floor, where it hardens and gains value instead of merging into a watery void. The aloe wood shows its uniqueness by yielding the sweetest fragrances when consumed by flames—precisely when ordinary plants are annihilated. The firefly illuminates its way with its own light—a light from within signifying what it is and where it wants to go.[7]

In all of creation, however, it is only humanity that embraces development by choice. The jealous Iblis (Satan) was cast from heaven for disobeying God's order that all angels should bow before Adam in deference to humanity's unique capacity to distinguish good from evil. For Iqbal, Adam's descendants outrank even the most faithful angels. Gabriel himself—divine messenger to the prophets—is unaware of our most intimate moments with God, particularly in prayers at the *Ka'ba* and during the hajj.[8]

The bell of the hajj caravan—Iqbal's poetic persona—awakens self-esteem in all humanity and reminds us that we are God's most beloved creatures, endowed with matchless talents and unlimited potential. The bell—like the poet—serves many purposes. It shakes pilgrims out of their slumber, rouses them to action, and guides their quest for spiritual roots. Above all, it makes noise, and this, in turn, should provoke thoughtful people everywhere to make noise as well—to complain, call for change, and demand a better destiny.

Iqbal urges believers to take their complaints and demands directly to God. When we speak "person to person" with God, the dialogue makes us more human as well as more divine. We better understand God's majesty and absorb some of his attributes into ourselves. For Iqbal, the attraction between God and humanity is mutual. Humans are not mere instruments of God's will. We are God's vice-regents on earth, his partners and coworkers, perfecting his creation with our own skills and even influencing his decisions.

> Thou didst create night and I made the lamp,
> Thou didst create clay and I made the cup,
> Thou didst create the deserts, mountains and forest,

I produced the orchards, gardens and groves,
It is I who turns stone into a mirror,
And it is I who turns poison into an antidote![9]

As the completers and improvers of God's work, human beings understand the inexhaustible possibilities of creation, and they deserve the right to ask for a better fate from the infinite destinies still available. Humans can ask God to use them in a way they choose. Humanity should dare to tell God, "We have suited Thee—now suit us!"[10]

For Iqbal, the *Ka'ba* is the unique vantage point where the human enjoys a direct vision of God. In God's own house, every believer shares a glimpse of his face, just as Muhammad did when he ascended to heaven. Visiting the *Ka'ba* is returning to the heart of one's being. Seeing the *Ka'ba* is beholding the unity of God and remembering it is a model for the integrity of the ideal personality, for the solidarity of the ideal community.

Leaving home to make the hajj is like Muhammad's fateful decision to break with his parochial birthplace and establish a universal society transcending kinship, color, and class. The hajj is like daily prayer writ large. Continuous alternation between bowing and standing reminds believers of their esteemed position in God's order—inferior to none but the Creator and equal among themselves.[11]

God's guests can see firsthand that his house is free of idols. But they will also recall the long line of prophets who had to destroy the new crops of false gods that humans kept growing and worshiping in every era. Knowing God's house has been cleansed and repaired many times, pilgrims should be ready to carry on that work in their own lands. According to Iqbal, today's Muslims have two sets of idols to smash: homegrown icons of dogmatism and superstition, as well as imported Western deities of nationalism, imperialism, and materialism.[12]

What Muslims see looking directly at God's house they also see looking directly at his book. If a pilgrim can behold God's face as Muhammad did, then all Muslims should be able to feel his words as though they were revealed to them personally. From whatever direction Iqbal views God, he sees infinite possibilities and eternal change—the famous "principle of movement" he expressed in lectures on *The Reconstruction of Religious Thought in Islam*.[13]

The principle of movement is Iqbal's refutation of the myth of "eternal return"—belief that the spirit attains immortality by reliving the events of creation and dissolving itself in the Creator. Iqbal viewed the notion of eternal return as a dangerous negation of self and life that Muslims inherited from pantheistic Sufis and that Westerners recycled via philosophy, psychology, and comparative religion. To Iqbal, eternal return promised constant rebirth for the soul, but in this world it encouraged only imitation, self-effacement, and passivity.

Iqbal sought immortality not in repetition but in innovation and ceaseless effort. "Heaven is no holiday," he quipped. Iqbal believed the principle of movement was identical to *ijtihad*—independent thinking about religious questions that medieval jurists condemned but modernists are rekindling. When Iqbal admonishes Muslims to "repair their *Ka'ba*," he is telling them to strengthen their personalities and societies—and to reconstruct their religion in accord with reason and science. By ringing the bell of the hajj caravan, the noisy poet is summoning pilgrims to a journey where they must exercise *ijtihad* with every step, confident they will continue the habit of seeing things their own way long after returning home.

## 'Ali Shari'ati: Islam in Revolt

Where Iqbal saw the weakening of faith and community as a pervasive decline with many causes, Shari'ati riveted his attention on a single source of corruption and bombarded it relentlessly. He placed the blame squarely at the feet of the religious establishment—the pyramid of clerics who treat God's word as their exclusive property and distort it to enslave others.

The touchstone for Shari'ati's critique is the distinction between religious message and religious knowledge. Islam's message comes directly from God, whereas knowledge of Islam comes from human beings tied to historical and social conditions. *'Ulama* substitute self-interested knowledge for God's eternal message, pretending there is no difference.[14] Shari'ati insists that Muslims are free to break the clerical monopoly because religious knowledge is man-made and inherently fallible. It is constantly changing and open to advances in other fields where clerics have no expertise and deserve no deference.

A key area where all Muslims can contribute to religious knowledge is the hajj. Performing the hajj is every Muslim's duty; interpreting its meanings is every Muslim's right. Far from being an isolated example of intellectual freedom, the hajj is a prototype for religious knowledge in general. Young people must study religion themselves instead of waiting for their elders to provide pat answers. Just as pilgrims teach one another throughout their journeys, all Muslims should share their religious insights without regard for titles and certificates.[15]

In this spirit, Shari'ati offers his own reflections on the hajj, creating a poetic and political tour de force that remains the most imitated and refuted reading in the world a quarter century after his death. His understanding of the hajj is like no other—precisely the goal he sets for every pilgrim and every thinking Muslim.

Shari'ati tells the pilgrim she is the star of a divinely scripted drama where she plays multiple roles, reenacting heroic exploits of monotheism's illustrious founders, Adam, Ibrahim, and, above all, Hagar. Each character and shrine teaches an essential lesson about the journey of the soul—trusting God's love, battling Satan's temptations, and overcoming our deepest fears. Pilgrims will experience all this emotionally, but they must integrate the fragments into a coherent whole and apply their understandings in daily life.

Every page of Shari'ati's account sparkles with originality. It is impossible to grasp the full measure of his achievement without reading the work from cover to cover and comparing it with half a dozen samples of the standard fare in hajj interpretation. Yet even a casual reader senses that his most striking images are idiosyncratic. The best example is his treatment of Hagar, concubine of Ibrahim and mother of Isma'il. For every other commentator, she is a minor player. In this production, she steals the show.

Shari'ati turns Hagar into an archetype of the outcast spurned by humanity and embraced by God. Every facet of her nature compounds her marginality and speaks of oppression. She is a slave girl—weak, poor, and black. She is a new mother despised by Ibrahim's old and barren wife, whose jealousy forces Ibrahim to abandon mother and infant in the parched Meccan desert, where they struggle for survival.

Hagar does not sit quietly. She is constantly searching, running, wandering. Disturbed and confused at first, she emerges as a mature and responsible woman, relying on her ingenuity and inner strength. Her motives are purely selfish and material. She acts for the sake of this world alone, not for heaven and not for God.

Yet God rewards her efforts many times over. He reveals the sacred well that saves her life. He raises her—the most wretched of mortals—to an exalted place at his side, granting her a final resting place at the foot of the Ka'ba, where she becomes his eternal partner—a "roommate" dwelling with him under the same roof.[16]

Shari'ati explains that Hagar represents far more than the triumph of the meek and the oppressed. He compares her panic and bewilderment to Ibrahim's reluctance to obey God's order to sacrifice their son, Isma'il. Both are haunted by doubts that reflect the contradictory makeup of all humans—our divided nature as mud and the spirit of God. When hajjis reenact the trials of Hagar and Ibrahim, they should feel the same doubt because they never know for certain if God will accept their pilgrimages—if he will decide they have turned away from their lower nature and strengthened what is God-like in their souls.[17]

Shari'ati contrasts Hagar with Ibrahim, portraying them as contradictory poles pulling pilgrims in opposite directions. Ibrahim—architect of the Ka'ba—is uppermost during the *tawaf*, whereas Hagar—discoverer of life-saving Zamzam waters—predominates in the *sa'y*. Shari'ati describes the *tawaf* as devoted to the adoration of God, to submission and love, the afterlife, and the spiritualism of the East. The *sa'y* stands for development of the self, for assertiveness and logic, action in this world, and the rationalism of the West.[18]

Shari'ati insists that Islam incorporates all these attributes and that pilgrims must learn to balance and resolve them. By linking "masculine" characteristics to Hagar's rite and "feminine" characteristics to Ibrahim's rite, he makes both man and woman models of synthesis and equilibrium. If the founders of the hajj could embody a full spectrum of Islamic virtues, then pilgrims who walk in their paths can do the same.

Shari'ati's second act shatters even more stereotypes. He shifts the spotlight from 'Arafat to Mina, from standing to stoning, from quiet contemplation to armed combat. Everyone knows "The hajj is 'Arafat." To miss the Day of Standing is to miss the hajj itself, and no act of restitution can repair the damage. Yet, for this director, it is just the staging area for a long march, throwing two million pilgrims into war with the devil.

Shari'ati imagines the last stages of the hajj as a descent to inferior knowledge based on pure reason, followed by ascent to higher knowledge inspired by pure love. He takes his cue from mystical connotations of the place names in Arabic. 'Arafat ("knowledge") signifies science and rationality, Muzdalifa's environs—*Mash'ar* ("feelings" or "senses")—suggest subconscious intuition, and Mina ("hope" or "desire") recalls selfless love.

Adam descended into sterile rationality after expulsion from Paradise but regained higher consciousness when he and Eve reunited. Pilgrims retrace Adam's fall and ascension by moving from 'Arafat, the farthest point from Mecca, and back to Mina, the nearest point. Echoing Rumi, Shari'ati tells pilgrims they cannot rest too long at any station because their true destination is not the *Ka'ba* or 'Arafat but absolute perfection. Theirs is an eternal journey, requiring ceaseless movement and effort.[19]

When pilgrims arrive in Mina, what awaits them is not blissful love but Satan incarnate, wearing three masks of oppression. As pilgrims cast their stones at three pillars representing Satan, they are also firing bullets at three earthly agents that do his work in every society—the tyrants, exploiters, and hypocrites who corrupt governments, economies, and religions the world over. Shari'ati cautions pilgrims to aim carefully when they shoot so all seven bullets hit the Satans squarely in the face. Wounding them in the belly or legs is not enough, because they are good friends who constantly work together to dominate, impoverish, and brainwash the unsuspecting.

On the first day in Mina, pilgrims stone only one Satan, and during subsequent days they attack all three. That first day, Shari'ati recommends pilgrims imagine themselves shooting the most evil member of the trio so it gets an extra bashing. Which Satan deserves the fiercest beating? Each hajji must decide for herself, depending on her preferred methods for social change, her responsibilities to others, and the social-political system in which she lives.[20]

He admits that during his first pilgrimages, he took it for granted that the clergy were the most despicable Satan. It seemed self-evident that spiritual leaders who sold their faith for wealth and power were the most treacherous and destructive enemies. But during his third hajj, he realized this simply reflected his own experiences and the problems of his society. God never thought it necessary to identify and rank each Satan by name. If the "stage-manager" of the universe avoided doing so, perhaps it is because the three are so closely connected that each represents the other and shooting one is shooting them all.

Shari'ati suggests the most sensible solution is for all pilgrims to pick their own worst Satan. If they live under despotism or militarism, they will probably see the first pillar as political repression. If their greatest struggle is against hierarchy and inequality, it might represent economic exploitation. If they are intellectuals from countries where paganism and polytheism rule under the cover of Islam, they are likely to think as he did during his earliest pilgrimages.[21]

No matter how hajjis characterize the Satans, they must continue fighting long after returning to their homelands. Pilgrims should think as though they were always in Mina, destroying idols and stoning devils, just as Ibrahim did in his lifelong revolt against injustice. Like Ibrahim, they should become God's architects, building Ka'bas in their own communities—creating societies that are sanctuaries of peace, freedom, equality, and love for humanity.

The hajj's greatest mystery comes at its conclusion: "Why does the hajj end in Mina instead of in Mecca and near the Ka'ba?" His answer is simple: So pilgrims can think. He notes that during the final days at Mina there is nothing to do and, most important, no place to shop. Hajjis have no choice but to talk to one another about all they have just done and what it means.[22]

Shari'ati describes the days at Mina as an open-air seminar—an international convention where pilgrims mingle and exchange news about conditions in their countries. Because Mina is the land of all hopes and needs, many hajjis will ask, "What should we do for the community?" Having put themselves in the positions of Ibrahim, Hagar, and Adam, they should realize that the best choice is to continue playing those roles for the rest of their lives. "All these ceremonies were for you to ignore self-service and begin to serve others."[23]

Mina is where pilgrims make their animal sacrifices, commemorating God's willingness to spare Isma'il by permitting Ibrahim to slaughter an animal instead of his son. For Shari'ati, this is the high point of the hajj. Like Ibrahim, pilgrims should be prepared to sacrifice whatever is dearest to their hearts—their "Isma'ils"—in order to show trust in God.

> Who is your Isma'il or what is it? Is it your position, honor, profession, money, house, farm, car, love, family, knowledge, social class, art, dress, name, life, youth, beauty? . . . Imagine . . . there is only one thing for which you can give up everything and sacrifice any other love for its love—that is your Isma'il.[24]

Shari'ati believes that hajjis must be prepared to sacrifice the rest of their lives in the fight for freedom. Even if they attain victory, they must never think the battle has ended, for Satans are most dangerous when their adversaries are complacent. "Numb snakes can wake up and change their colors." Only one seventh of the struggle is needed to achieve victory; the other six sevenths must be devoted to preserving it.[25]

The essence of the hajj is humanity's evolution toward God in life as well as death. Those who think the hajj is pointless and that only daily life has meaning see everything backward. The hajj gives a glimpse of God's abode, whereas life as we live it is the house of man—a prison, slaughterhouse, and brothel that leaves us empty and aimless.[26]

Like all creation, the hajj is brimming with God's signs—with hints and codes revealing his messages for all to see. This is why it is so important for pilgrims to understand the meanings of everything they do in and around Mecca. If they can read the signs (ayat) of God in the hajj, they can read them everywhere, especially in the verses (ayat) of his book.[27] Like the hajj, the Qur'an is a miraculous storehouse of meanings waiting to be unlocked by every "reader," whether or not they have the good fortune to become pilgrims.

Mecca is unique because it "belongs to nobody."[28] Only God owns Mecca. This means all Muslims can visit God's house and learn to rebuild their earthly houses in its image.

Anyone who thinks the hajj is merely about preparing for death is as good as dead already.

They turn their backs to the Ka'ba and face the qibla of their miserable life, saying to themselves "the hell with this world, let's work for the paradise of the hereafter." Feeling happy with the joy of the life after death, they are sound asleep on the warm ashes of the master's kitchen floor and enjoy the leftovers of the plunderer's table.[29]

## Mohammed Arkoun: Islam in Eternity

Arkoun sees the hajj as belonging to all humanity. In his vision, the hajj embodies universal ideals that inspire and transcend every religion.

Arkoun describes the hajj as a pagan Arab rite that was "Islamized" twice—originally in the name of progress and civilization, but then in service of dogma and authoritarianism. The first Islamization was the work of the Qur'an; it breathed imagination into withered Bedouin practices that had lost their ancient meaning and purpose. The second Islamization was the work of legal scholars, who squeezed the life out of the hajj by codifying banal interpretations instead of exploring its multilayered symbols. The Islamization of the Qur'an was "open, semantic, and transcendent," whereas the Islamization of the legists was "closed, literal, and concrete." The first Islamization moved beyond the *existentiel* (spelled with an *e* in French and implying material being in this world) to the *existential* (spelled with an *a* and exploring ultimate spiritual values), but the second reversed direction.[30] The result was an Islam—and a hajj—stripped of its most imaginative heritage, floundering like the Arabs themselves between an idolatrous past and a Qur'anic promise.

Arkoun's goal is a third Islamization—one that surpasses paganism and Arabism, bringing Muslims into harmony with the rest of the world. The hajj is crucial because it embodies competing residues from the previous Islamizations. Modern Muslims have inherited two hajjs in constant conflict—the "spiritual hajj" of the Qur'an and the "codified hajj" of the *'ulama*. In reinterpreting the hajj, Arkoun seeks to revalue the former heritage and devalue the latter.[31]

Much of this reinterpretive labor, Arkoun argues, was accomplished by earlier generations of philosophers, mystics, and lawyers. Even Abu Hamid al-Ghazali (1058–1111), who thought the hajj might have no rational meaning at all, elaborated a tame and conventional reading to rein in a profusion of esoteric treatments. Arkoun is convinced that al-Ghazali's strategy backfired. By authoring a skeptic's account that satisfied neither mind nor spirit, he unwittingly opened the door for more daring thinkers to stretch his ideas in novel directions.

Yet Arkoun has no intention of limiting himself to Islamic sources and methods. Modern Islam can reignite its imagination with fertile sparks from its own tradition, but there is no reason to stop there. Self-sufficiency is neither practical nor desirable. The social sciences and interpretive arts are available to everyone—they are truly human sciences with universal applications, not the property of one civilization or the bane of any other.

Unlocking the mysteries of the "spiritual hajj" will connect Muslims with far more than "their" forefathers and "their" God. It will open them to the same insights other pilgrimages provide all over the world. Arkoun even goes so far as to claim that the hajj is not really unique—essentially, it is just another pilgrimage: "We know that the Hajj is not at all exceptional. In India, the 'Kumbha Mela' also mobilizes millions of faithful who accept countless sacrifices, endure all types of hardships, and confront every danger in striving toward a 'spiritual' ideal."[32]

Viewing the hajj as just another pilgrimage allows Arkoun to see the *Ka'ba* as just another house. It is God's house, but it was built by humans—not once but many times, subject to repeated destruction and requiring constant renovation. God's creation could not be more different. He made the universe once and for all time. But humans have always built God's house imperfectly because they have never been able to understand his blueprint, let alone follow it faithfully and completely.

Because the *Ka'ba*'s architects are mere mortals, it is never more than a work in progress. Humans build their own worlds with no greater skill than they build their *Ka'bas.* They have no choice but to reconstruct both of them over and over, constantly redrawing the plan and reimagining the final product.

Because humanity's spiritual and political labors require infinite imagination, Arkoun argues, the inherent ambiguity of the hajj is one of modern Islam's most valuable resources. The hajj requires everyone to make sense of her personal and unmediated contact with God. This is possible only by encouraging individualistic interpretation, not by enshrining yet another codification.

Arkoun believes that the hajj is the most important opportunity for Muslims to connect with a transsocial and transhistorical community.[33] Reopening the interpretation of hajj symbolism will bring pilgrims in touch with a reservoir of competing views that resonate beyond their own traditions and times. He portrays the hajj the same way philosophers and mystics have long depicted the *Ka'ba*—as a microcosm of the universe, an archeology of monotheism, and a bridge to all that is complete and eternal.

All pilgrims, Arkoun contends, feel a constant tension between the two hajjs—the spiritual and the codified—particularly as younger, more educated people make up a growing share of the crowds year after year. He sees sophisticated Muslims becoming increasingly dissatisfied with clerics who reduce pilgrimage to an arbitrary set of rites—fixed and untouchable, shrouded in commands and taboos that kill the spirit for sake of the law. In reality, the hajj has always performed a host of functions—both profane and sacred—that elude its would-be codifiers. Understanding the hajj requires a multidisciplinary approach to grasp its political, economic, and psychological roles, as well as its religious significance.[34]

Blending symbolic analysis and social science, Arkoun composes an ode to the hajj's multidimensionality and a meditation on its future as the cradle of a "new humanism." The hajj reawakens the "Islamic consciousness," shaking it out of complacency and orthodoxy. Pilgrimage juxtaposes competing views within Islam and opens the heritage to influences from other civilizations. Most important, the hajj can promote creative interactions between religion and all the sciences—natural, social and analytical, and interpretive.[35]

For Arkoun, the new humanist—"the modern man of science"—is like the mystic trying to reconcile myth and logic, art and reason. Modern humanists are in danger of being overwhelmed by an implacable division between dogmatic religion and positivist science unless they provide interpretations of Creator and creation that are both reasoned and inspired. Arkoun's ideal humanist resembles his vision of the modern pilgrim—not just the hajji but any pilgrim. He argues that pilgrims in all religions share the same objectives—a personal connection with the Beloved, a regeneration of the spirit, and a sweeping reinterpretation of life.[36]

Like all Islamic modernists, it is the sweeping reinterpretation that Arkoun values most because he assumes that the hajj stands for Islam at its best and that liberating its idealism serves a wider struggle for freedom and progress. "The Hajj can and must restore the Qur'anic language in its dynamic function of radically contesting inequalities, arbitrary rulers, ideological manipulations, and hierarchies based on group wealth and power."[37] The ideas are vintage Iqbal and Shari'ati, but now they explicitly apply to every faith, particularly to Hindus and Christians, who should also channel their pilgrimages' untapped energies into the worldwide struggle for freedom and justice.

Arkoun argues that the heaviest shackles on hajj interpretation were forged by al-Ghazali—the very jurist Western commentators portray as a leading rationalist who took pains to uncover the inner meanings and purposes of ritual obligations. From Arkoun's perspective, the flaw in al-Ghazali's "reading" is that it extols death over life and submission over freedom. Al-Ghazali is riveted on the terrors of the tomb and the certainty of Judgment Day. Dangers and sufferings along the route foreshadow agonies the pilgrim will experience in his grave between death and resurrection. The brigands and pirates are Munkar and Nakir, two black angels that interrogate the soul inside the freshly buried corpse. The wild beasts are the worms and serpents that will devour its decaying flesh. Every limb of every animal the pilgrim sacrifices at Mina is a limb of his own body he hopes to save from the flames of hell.[38]

According to Arkoun, al-Ghazali's reading might have suited his era, but it suffered the worst fate that can befall any great text: It became suspended in time with no replenishing connection to new contexts that could bring it to life for later generations. Al-Ghazali's deathly imagery was itself interred in the official *manasik*, smothered under endless commands drilling pilgrims on where to walk and where to trot, when to chant together as a single mighty voice and when to whisper privately so none but God can hear.

Meanwhile, Arkoun notes, it was the Sufis and Shi'ite cosmologists who nurtured the spiritual hajj. They split the *Ka'ba* into a thousand pieces, every one a mirror revealing a parallel universe. The geometry of the cube became a mandala unifying matter, faith, and mind. Its four pillars were the physical world—water, fire, air, and earth. The eight corners pointed to the messengers of monotheism—Noah, Ibrahim, Moses, and Jesus surrounding the base and Muhammad, 'Ali, Hussain, and Hasan forming the roof. Planes of the six surfaces stood for the seen and unseen levels of reality, for universal intelligence and love, and for endless time and space.[39]

Compared to Shari'ati's multistage performance, Arkoun's preoccupation with the *Ka'ba* might appear simplistic and outdated. But Arkoun's *Ka'ba* is not the familiar black box of divine inscrutability—cold, empty, and unfathomable. Rather, it is a Sufi inversion of Alice's rabbit hole, where the pilgrim falls out instead of in—escaping tunnels of confusion for a realm of infinite light and meaning.

Arkoun's new humanist is a mystic, a social scientist, and a pilgrim. In a gesture of supreme generosity toward the old-guard 'ulama, he even acknowledges a place for the occasional open-minded lawyer.[40] All have resolved to cast aside the second phase of Islamization—especially its despiritualizing and dispiriting literalism that imprisons the hajj, the Qur'an, and the mind.

## Rebuilding the Ka'ba Is Re-Creating the World

Iqbal, Shari'ati, and Arkoun employ the same building metaphor—humanity as God's architect—yet each has a distinctive view of the task and its prospects for success. Over time, they provide increasingly modest assessments of the human builder's innate skills and ever more demanding inventories of the arts humans have to learn.

For Iqbal, humans can develop into nothing less than a second creator. As the collective deputy of the master builder, humanity continues God's work independently, crafting his raw materials into new products with greater use and value. The earthly architect begins with his own personality, consolidating a self that absorbs as much as possible of its maker's likeness. The self-constructed self rebuilds its community as a house of God, starting in separate nations and fashioning them into a universal family that realizes its destiny to live under a single roof.

Shari'ati's builder knows he must begin with the wrecking ball, demolishing idolaters' temples to clear the way for a new Ka'ba on a firm foundation. Shari'ati insists on surveying his site carefully so no one will underestimate the amount of grubby deconstruction ahead. His architects are seasoned excavators, certain they must destroy today if they want to rebuild tomorrow.

In Arkoun's account, the majestic labor of re-creation looks more like the artless fumbling of home improvement. Humanity never really rebuilds its Ka'bas; it merely keeps remodeling them—tinkering fearlessly and discovering new tricks of the trade as the need arises. But time is running out for do-it-yourselfers. Until they learn the interlacing crafts of humanism, they will ride out looming storms in the same old fix-me-ups that barely sheltered them in more peaceful days.

But there is no question of their interpretations being imported or tailored to agnostic tastes. Some of their views are provocative, disrespectful, and—if taken literally—even blasphemous. Certainly, all three writers spent their lives cultivating exactly this reputation. Yet they speak from deep within an honored heritage of pious dissent that resonates with consciences in all quarters, regardless of class and education. And when they speak the magical language of the hajj, they instantly tap into a worldwide conversation about Islam's most cherished ideals.

# 3

# Pilgrimage and Power

Debates over the politics of pilgrimage revolve around three key questions. Do pilgrimages tend to fall under the control of entrenched authorities—secular and religious—or do they remain independent social movements inherently hostile to hierarchy and hegemony? Do pilgrimages encourage universal and egalitarian identities, or do they harden parochial loyalties already dividing nations, sects, and social groups? And are modernization and globalization destroying pilgrimages or making them more vigorous than ever—reducing them to quasi-secular tourism or turning them into truly worldwide expressions of spiritual revivals?

To a remarkable degree, these debates amount to an ongoing conversation with the legacy of a single man—Victor Turner, the British anthropologist who was the world's leading authority on ritual and the pioneer of comparative pilgrimage studies. Turner argued that pilgrimage carries greater political significance than any other ritual. He never investigated the hajj firsthand, but he believed its far-reaching political implications make it the most important pilgrimage of all.

Turner is best known as the theorist and proponent of *communitas*—an idealistic belief that all human beings are bound together by a fundamental sameness transcending whatever particular cultures teach about differences in our nature and interests. Communitas was the polar opposite of *structure*—the system of rank and status underlying the division of labor in society. The two poles were by no means equal; structure was dominant; and it kept the upper hand by carving out safe times and places where communitas could express itself harmlessly in the language of myth and symbol. Rituals created special conditions so communitas could bolster structure instead of threatening it. Precisely because rituals occur in supernatural circumstances—in a "time out of time"—they can challenge the status quo with coded and stage-managed attacks that dominant elites would otherwise find intolerable.

Turner thought pilgrimage inspired the most intense clashes between communitas and structure. Catholic clergy opposed mass pilgrimages in medieval Europe precisely because they were spontaneous movements of ordinary believers that threatened church authority. Only after the church realized that the power and popularity of pilgrimages were permanent did it embrace them and give them official guidance. Many pilgrimages produced elaborate organizations that paralleled and intersected the church.

Turner was intrigued by the interplay of social interests—religious and secular, mass and elite, national and international—that competed to control pilgrimages across Europe and the New World. He spent years trying to explain how they could spawn so much communitas and so much structure at the same time.[1] Having characterized communitas as antistructure, Turner faced a seeming contradiction: Many pilgrimages retained great autonomy and mass appeal long after creating well-organized institutions of their own.

To resolve the paradox, he abandoned the notion of communitas as antistructure and called it counterstructure. In this view, communitas allows humanist and universal values to challenge dominant institutions without being absorbed by them. Turner even decided that communitas and structure are complementary—basic instincts constantly needing to be balanced and harmonized. To express the ideal synthesis of communitas and structure, he coined yet another neologism—*societas*. Structure represents the human need to conserve, and communitas is the perennial need to grow. Societas combines the two, reconciling our inherently dualistic nature. No matter how much Turner softened his portrayal of the clash between communitas and structure, he never expected the conflict to end. Indeed, he hoped it would intensify as communitas found new channels of expression and ensure a permanent source of creative tension in societies in danger of becoming too rigid and complacent.

Turner was remarkably confident that pilgrimage remains forever irrepressible. "There is something inveterately populist, anarchical, even anticlerical, about pilgrimages in their very essence."[2] He insisted that pilgrimage serves society best by criticizing it instead of reproducing it. Pilgrimage nurtures a special communitas—a constant striving toward transcendent ideals that fill our hearts and souls.

Turner was particularly fascinated by the hajj, which he believed to be the best example of "structured communitas." How is it that the same pilgrimage that is so intertwined with nation-states and entrenched elites is also the pilgrimage confronting them most radically with a contrary vision—that we are all bound together as equal members of a universal human community? How is it that dominant powers ceaselessly impose structure on the hajj, only to find that they are unwittingly inventing new ways for hajjis to experience communitas on their own?

## The Great International Pilgrimage Systems

Although many religions have international pilgrimages with ancient roots and mass followings, the hajj has always been in a class by itself. Compared with the fluid and multilayered pilgrimages of Hinduism, Christianity, Buddhism, and Judaism, the hajj is a model of simplicity. Most pilgrimages are voluntary, but the hajj is a basic obligation the Qur'an explicitly demands of all Muslims who are physically and financially capable.

The hajj must be performed in a single location, at a specific time, and in a prescribed manner. Other faiths grant pilgrims wide latitude in choosing the sacred places they wish to visit, arranging travel around daily responsibilities, and completing ritual duties at their own pace. Hajjis enjoy none of this freedom and flexibility. Many avoid any variation and innovation, determined to follow the example Muhammad established with his own pilgrimages.

Muhammad radically reformed the hajj, breaking its ties to paganism and modeling it on the heroic story of Ibrahim (Abraham), the founder of monotheism, whose unfaltering obedience to God is the overarching inspiration for the hajj and for Islam in general. Muhammad used his last pilgrimage as the setting for the famous "Farewell Sermon" atop the Mount of Mercy on the plain of 'Arafat, where he revealed the final portion of the Qur'an, declaring to hajjis assembled below that he had "perfected" their religion.

Just as Muhammad regarded the restoration of the "authentic" hajj as the capstone of his prophecy, Muslims view the hajj as the most important of Islam's "five pillars" and as the crowning spiritual achievement of their lives. When Muslims undertake the hajj, they are reenacting decisive acts of monotheism's two greatest prophets—the very first and the very last. The drama reminds pilgrims of their bonds with Muslims around the world and with the millions of pilgrims who preceded them over fourteen centuries.

On a deeper level, the rituals transport hajjis as far into the past and future as the mind can conceive. When hajjis circle the *Ka'ba*, they walk in Muhammad's footsteps. They also imitate forms of worship laid down by Ibrahim before the birth of Islam, by Adam before history's dawn, and by adoring angels who circled God's throne in heaven before he created the universe.

Looking to the other pole of eternity, the visit to God's house is a dress rehearsal for Judgment Day. The pilgrim's simple white garb, the *ihram*, is the shroud all souls will wear when they rise from the grave and stand before their Creator at the end of time. In anticipation, many hajjis carefully preserve the towel-like wrappings they wear in Mecca, instructing their families to make them their real burial shrouds so they can appear at the final Judgment just as they did during their most hallowed days on earth.

The hajj is an obligation that can be fulfilled only in Mecca. Unlike Banaras and Jerusalem, Mecca does not stand at the top of a staircase of sacred sites, where multiple pilgrimages confer ascending degrees of grace. The hajj so clearly overshadows all other pious journeys that for Muslims it *is* their pilgrimage system, pure and simple.

Journeys to other sacred places are mere "visits" (*ziyaras*) that can never substitute for a hajj no matter how many times they are repeated. No combination of *ziyaras* can equal a hajj, even if their destinations include the prophet's mosque in Medina, the tombs of the most venerated imams in Iraq and Iran, or the final resting places of the thousands of saints and martyrs all across Asia and Africa.

Not even a visit to Mecca itself can replace the hajj if it falls outside the designated pilgrimage season—the last month of the Islamic calendar, Dhu al-Hijjah. Muslims can make the *'umra*—an abbreviated version of the hajj—whenever they wish, but it will not take the place of a hajj.

Although the *'umra* can be completed in a single day, it requires the same special dress as the hajj and includes the same rites within Mecca. But the *'umra* omits all the key rituals on the city's outskirts—culminating acts that "make the hajj the hajj"—especially the Day of Standing on the plain of 'Arafat and the stoning of the "devil" and animal sacrifice at Mina.

Because the *'umra* mimics famous scenes of the hajj, non-Muslims often refer to it as "the lesser pilgrimage," and even some Muslims harbor the superstition that seven *'umras* are equivalent to a hajj. Nonetheless, an *'umra* is just another *ziyara*—more meritorious than a morning trek to the tomb of a local saint but no substitute for obeying an explicit command of God.

The hajj's exceptional importance in world politics flows directly from its exalted religious status. Firm roots in scripture, combined with an unswerving focus on a single sacred city, promote a global pilgrimage distinguished by unparalleled cosmopolitanism and continuity. Hinduism and Christianity have pilgrimage systems with comparable breadth and vitality and even longer histories of politicization. Yet, because they are so numerous and malleable, Hindu and Christian pilgrimages never acquired anything approaching the hajj's preeminence.

## From Sacred Truce to Global Parliament

Although the hajj is the youngest of the great pilgrimages, it has always been the most politicized. Its political dimensions predated Muhammad by centuries. The spread of Islam merely broadened the scope and deepened the meanings of an annual religious gathering that was already a linchpin of Arabia's political and economic life.

Mecca was the wealthiest of the competing city-states straddling the busy trade routes that link the Mediterranean and the Indian Ocean. Mecca's pre-eminence stemmed from its role as religious hub of a fractious society with no clear political center. Even in polytheistic times, shared veneration of the Ka'ba induced feud-prone tribes throughout Arabia to set aside differences long enough to assemble for their holiest rites.

The heart of the pre-Islamic hajj was Mecca's "sacred truce"—a customary pact declaring the city a safe haven where bloodshed was outlawed during Arabia's most celebrated festival. By preserving Mecca's status as a sanctuary (haram), the tribes shared a vital mechanism for resolving conflicts, sealing their pact each year during the pilgrimage. Creating a secure forum for negotiation and arbitration is a consistent theme of the hajj in ancient Arabia and the Islamic era.

A striking example of this continuity is a famous Muslim parable linking Muhammad to the Ka'ba and portraying him as a skilled mediator before he became a prophet. The people of Mecca had just completed a major renovation of the Ka'ba. The four most powerful tribal confederations of central Arabia were at odds, each claiming the honor to return the Black Stone to its proper location in a corner of the shrine. To avoid violence, the tribes accepted Muhammad's arbitration and vowed to abide by his decision. To their surprise, Muhammad awarded the honor to all the tribes without really giving it to any of them. Rather than engender lasting enmity by declaring a winner, Muhammad asked a chief of each confederation to grasp a corner of a four-sided robe. Then he placed the Black Stone in the center of the cloth and told the bearers to carry it together to the Ka'ba, where he alone fitted the stone in its new setting.[3]

The diplomatic role of the early hajj made it analogous to the Olympic games of ancient Greece. The Olympics also encouraged a broader identity—pan-Hellenism—among evenly matched city-states sharing a common culture yet locked in constant warfare.[4] The comparison is still fitting today. Like the International Olympic Committee, hajj managers are constantly accused of hypocrisy—of indulging the very commercialism, nationalism, and favoritism they are supposed to transcend.[5] Both the hajj and the Olympics must garner support from the same political and economic powers that would be destroyed if their loftiest principles became reality.

Debate over the politics of the hajj is as old as Islam itself. Because Muhammad founded a new state as well as a new religion, there has always been lively interest in how the hajj fits into his dual mission as prophet and political reformer. The debate boils down to competing understandings of Muhammad's intentions.

In making the hajj a pillar of Islam, was Muhammad looking to the past or to the future? Was he pragmatically bending to customs of a deeply conservative society, hoping to win over Meccan oligarchs who nearly destroyed him? Or was he planting the seed of a new society, radically different from anything the world had experienced—a universal and egalitarian community that can grow into an irresistible force if the hajj nurtures its ideals in Muslim hearts around the world?

There is truth in both explanations, and they are by no means mutually exclusive. Nonetheless, Western narrators tend to favor the tale of compromise, whereas Muslims overwhelmingly endorse the revolutionary account, acknowledging that reality is everywhere far from the dream. Westerners see Islamization of the hajj as reinforcing entrenched power, whereas Muslims see it as an idealistic vision of a new order.[6]

## The Dutch Uncle of Modern Hajj Policy

The Westerner who most cogently advanced the conservative explanation of the hajj's origins is Christiaan Snouck Hurgronje—the renowned Dutch Orientalist and colonial officer whose views shaped modern pilgrimage policy, first in Dutch-ruled Indonesia and, long after his death, in independent states throughout Asia and Africa.[7] If Victor Turner saw the hajj as shining communitas, Snouck Hurgronje viewed it as a bulwark of the status quo. Turner thought the hajj embodied irrepressible demands for equality, but Snouck Hurgronje spent his life reassuring nervous elites that they could use it to subjugate Muslims everywhere.

Snouck Hurgronje's confidence about the malleability of the hajj stemmed from his unparalleled knowledge of Islamic history, contemporary Meccan society, and the cultures of Indonesia.[8] He regarded Muhammad's decision to preserve the hajj as a stroke of political genius that accomplished many goals simultaneously.

By centering his new state in Mecca (the city he was forced to flee and conquer) instead of Medina (the city that gave him refuge), Muhammad won over his former enemies and consolidated Islam in Arabia. He also marshaled resources to launch a united force against the greatest military powers of his day, the Byzantine and Persian empires. When Muhammad instructed Muslims to pray in the direction of Mecca rather than Jerusalem, his community could make a double claim: They could be monotheistic without being Jews or Christians, and they could be universalistic without ceasing to be Arab.

Snouck Hurgronje's Muhammad is the soul of realism—a prophet-statesman who preserved the "Meccan Festival" because it was a cherished Arabian heritage that helped mobilize a primitive people "whose conservatism penetrated to the marrow of their bones." His Muhammad—the most political of all prophets—viewed the hajj as "a means and not an end."[9] By wrapping the hajj in Islamic garb, he "accentuated the Arabian character of his religion," making it palatable to a pagan society that worshiped their customs more than their deities.[10] By this account, the hajj was not only inherently political but also inherently conservative.

Snouck Hurgronje spent about a year in Jeddah and Mecca and became the first Western ethnographer of Meccan society and one of the few to photograph intimate scenes of its family life.[11] His observations persuaded him that Europeans greatly exaggerated the city's role as a breeding ground for anticolonial agitation in the Islamic world. He insisted native Meccans were preoccupied with fleecing their pilgrim prey, not with spreading radicalism. The true danger was the network of exiles and students who took refuge in Mecca's many expatriate communities, exploiting the freedom of the hajj to propagandize visitors from their homelands.

Snouck Hurgronje was most critical of Mecca's "Jawa colony"—the settlement of Malay-speaking Muslims who used their commercial and religious connections to undermine Dutch and British rule in Southeast Asia. The greatest threat was not the herd of gullible hajjis but this handful of conspirators who turned their piety into fanaticism and rebellion.

He opposed European calls to cut off the flow of pilgrims and urged colonialists to use their vital interest in the hajj to justify stepping up diplomacy and espionage in the holy city. At his instigation, the Netherlands became the first non-Muslim state to set up a full-service hajj bureau in Jeddah. The ostensible purpose was to protect Indonesian pilgrims from swindlers and predators, but the mission included surveillance of Mecca's Malay community, particularly their political activities and communications with hajjis from Southeast Asia.[12]

Snouck Hurgronje's most important legacy was the "Islamic strategy" he devised to pave the way for colonialism in the Dutch East Indies. For more than thirty years, he fended off the objections of Dutch merchants, missionaries, and generals to build an administration that would "civilize" Islam instead of suppressing it. The crux of his approach was to distinguish between religious and political dimensions of Islam, sponsoring the former and crushing the latter.[13] He called for constant vigilance against pan-Islam, Mahdism, and jihad. Yet he also insisted non-Muslim rulers could win gratitude and acquiescence by supporting cherished institutions, such as religious schools, courts blending Islamic and customary law, and, above all, a well-run pilgrimage to Mecca.

Unlike most Europeans of his day, Snouck Hurgronje believed that the political unity of Islam had ended forever and that there was no reason to fear communications between Muslims of different nationalities. He regarded talk of Islamic revival as Turkish and German propaganda—a "despicable game" that sought "to light the blaze of a Mohammedan religious war on a large scale, and thereby to cause endless confusion in international relations."[14] He scorned the French and British for backing rival candidates for a caliphate that had no real power and in Indonesia little popularity.

While other colonial powers banned the hajj or strangled it with red tape, the Dutch sponsored pilgrimages at record rates. In the 1880s, only 4,000 Indonesians made the pilgrimage each year. By World War I, the number was 30,000, and on the eve of the Great Depression it surpassed 50,000. The upsurge was a direct result of Snouck Hurgronje's efforts as advisor for native and Arabian affairs in Netherlands India from 1889 to 1906 and as tutor to a new generation of colonial officers at the University of Leiden until his death in 1936.[15]

Snouck Hurgronje always contended the specter of the "fanatical hajji" was a phantom that Dutch politicians used to bully colleagues who knew nothing about Indonesia into endorsing anti-Islamic policies. He responded that the vast majority of hajjis returned home exactly as they departed—not as rebels but as "sheep." Any effort to suppress pilgrimage was unnecessary and doomed to backfire.[16] Snouck Hurgronje counted on the presumed passivity of ordinary Muslims to give the Dutch time to implement a paternalistic policy of "association"—nurturing a loyal cadre of European-educated Indonesians who would push Islam to the margins of an increasingly secular society. He believed it was best to let the hajj die a natural death, a victim of its own excesses and the irresistible lure of Western culture.[17]

In fact, Snouck Hurgronje grossly underestimated the power and political skills of Indonesia's Muslims, especially their ability to mobilize modern parties and mass movements. In the end, his immense knowledge of Islam and admiration for its civilization were no match for his sense of cultural superiority and historical inevitability. No matter how much he lauded parallels between Dutch liberalism and Islamic idealism—their dreams of racial equality, individual freedom, and universal peace—he never doubted that Europeans and not Muslims would shape the values and institutions of international society.[18]

## Empire and Nation: Managing the Common Heritage of Islam

Snouck Hurgronje's hajj policies gained wider acceptance in independent states that arose after his death than they ever enjoyed among his peers in Europe. Facing the resurgent Islam that Snouck Hurgronje had discounted, rulers in the new nations adopted his strategy of seizing pilgrimage before opponents could turn it against them. In one country after another, state sponsorship grew into regulation, control, and monopoly.

Compared with their former colonial masters, politicians who guided the nationalist movements of the Third World had greater respect for the hajj as a perpetual repository of universalistic ideals. Even if only nominal Muslims, they realized Snouck Hurgronje missed the point when he saw the hajj as reflecting Muhammad's ambitions instead of God's commands. The great nationalist leaders of the post–World War II era—Nasser of Egypt, Sukarno of Indonesia, Adnan Menderes in Turkey, Tunku Abdul Rahman of Malaysia, and Ahmadu Bello in Nigeria—understood that in the popular imagination the hajj has always been the most powerful reminder that Islam is a single community of believers distinguished by their degree of piety and not by their origins.

Nationalist politicians also realized the hajj would never be fully compatible with their own determination to wield sovereignty in separate societies. No matter how much Islam adapted to disparate cultures, the hajj would always be a countervailing force, pulling Muslims toward a common identity transcending legal boundaries and political allegiances. Nothing makes Muslims more mindful of God's indifference to their differences than the sight of pilgrims from every race and class performing the same acts of worship at the same time and place. No other experience so openly invites them to question how well their existing institutions—international and domestic—live up to God's standards. And no other experience so readily inspires self-criticism and demands for social change.

Muslim nationalists share Snouck Hurgronje's fascination with the political uses of the hajj. But they are much closer to Victor Turner in interpreting pilgrimage as a humanistic vision with worldwide appeal—a vision that inevitably contradicts parochial identities, including nationalism. Snouck Hurgronje never outgrew his amazement that a set of incomprehensible rites, beginning as little more than a tribal picnic, could blossom into the world's most poignant expression of transnational community. Because Muslim politicians assume the hajj was created by God and the prophets rather than by the Bedouin, they see no anomaly in its blend of Arabian roots and universal reach.

Before and after the creation of independent nation-states, Muslim leaders competed to gain political advantage from the hajj. Yet even when it turns violent, rivalry is tempered by subtlety and calculated ambiguity, particularly in asserting claims of sovereignty over the pilgrimage and the cities of Mecca and Medina. The king of Saudi Arabia scrupulously limits his title to "Custodian of the Two Holy Cities," stressing the gravity of his responsibilities and not the supremacy of his command. In projecting authority through innuendo and symbolism more than law and might, the Saudis echo the many dynasties that collectively managed the hajj for more than a millennium. Constant maneuvering to control the pilgrimage was a politics of prestige more than a politics of power. Sultans and emirs enhanced their legitimacy by subsidizing and protecting the hajj, not simply by flexing military muscle.

Even under the Ottomans—the most modern and centralized of all Islamic empires—the Hejaz remained a land of insolence, too important to be ignored yet too remote to be subdued.[19] Like all Ottoman vassals, the sharif of Mecca knew that the sultan's power shrank exponentially with distance from Istanbul. And no one was more cunning and venal in exploiting that weakness than Mecca's ruling families.

Pageantry and tribute were as important as the show of force. Great powers in the Islamic world tried to outdo one another in assembling the biggest hajj caravans and sending the most generous tokens of patronage. Their benefi-cence was ostentatious and widely distributed—endowments for Mecca and charities for its residents, stipends and bribes for its officials, and protection money to buy off Bedouin raiders who devastated even the best armed caravans crossing their domains.[20]

Two donations acquired unique importance as icons of imperial preemi-nence. The *mahmal* was a ceremonial litter filled with silks and jewels, carried atop a colorfully adorned camel. The centerpiece was a precious box, often containing nothing more than a Qur'an presented to the people of Mecca as testimony of a sultan's devoted protection. The *kiswa* is the large black cloth— covered with Qur'anic verses magnificently embroidered in golden thread— that is draped over the Ka'ba. Each year, a new *kiswa* is unfurled at the begin-ning of the hajj season, and the old one is cut into pieces that distinguished pilgrims receive as treasured souvenirs.[21]

Presenting the *mahmal* and *kiswa* was a royal prerogative, jealously guarded by regimes that outfitted their caravans as though mobilizing for war. Mamluk sultans of Egypt claimed the exclusive right to send the *mahmal*, but rival offerings also came from rulers of Syria, Iraq, and Yemen. When the Ottomans became the hegemonic power in the Hejaz, they often permitted *mahmals* from other regions, as long as they deferred to the stronger caravans from Istanbul and Damascus.[22]

With the rise of nation-states, Saudi Arabia gradually decided to end these prerogatives. After a skirmish between Saudi and Egyptian troops during the hajj of 1926, *mahmals* were banned. To underline their self-sufficiency, the Saudis began manufacturing *kiswas* on their own soil, ending six centuries of Egyptian privilege in "dressing" Islam's most sacred shrine.[23]

The system of nation-states still has not resolved disputes over who should administer the hajj. Now as before, all claims of sovereignty are contested and conditional at best. Premodern dynasties may have described the Holy Cities as another fiefdom or province, but they behaved as though entrusted with a commons that is the shared heritage of all Muslims. Today as well, Islamic states debate Saudi Arabia's claims over the hajj with the same vigor that the international community contests issues such as sharing the oceans, guarding the biosphere, and exploring outer space.[24]

More than ever, Muslim rulers understand that hajj management must be a truly international effort. Forced to restrain political rivalries within a com-mon set of religious commitments, they increasingly turn to international law. Fashioning flexible rules and processes they can respect and periodically re-

negotiate, they have built the world's first international regime explicitly devoted to pilgrimage.

Their regime relies more on customary international law than on formal
treaties and strict compliance. They are less concerned with transparency and
uniformity than with consensus and fairness. Because the hajj is just one of
many fields where they must cooperate, they are usually willing to compromise
today and renegotiate tomorrow.

By using the Organization of the Islamic Conference as an arena for multilateral negotiations, they have created a hajj regime that adjusts the international balance of power in favor of non-Arab nations. Blending religion, law,
and power, they draw simultaneously on Islamic tradition and the current
thinking of international lawyers and social scientists. Their efforts will shape
the future of the world's greatest pilgrimage.

# 4

# The Growth of the Hajj

*Global and Regional Trends*

The explosive growth of the hajj is a very recent phenomenon. Before the 1950s, the number of overseas pilgrims rarely topped 100,000, whereas nowadays it never falls below a million. In the nineteenth century, steamships and railroads made pilgrimage faster and safer than ever. Yet, at the same time, the Islamic world was falling under the control of European imperialism. Colonial powers discouraged the hajj both at its sources and at its center. They restricted travel in the lands they administered while forcing the Ottomans to accept an international health regime that quarantined thousands of pilgrims suspected of carrying infectious diseases.[1]

The controls and disruptions of colonialism neutralized the revolution in transportation and communications, holding pilgrimage at modest levels throughout the first half of the twentieth century[2] (Figure 4.1). Every time the hajj appeared ready to take off, it collapsed because an extended international crisis made travel costlier and more dangerous. The history of the hajj before the 1950s is a series of small peaks and deep troughs, marked by the two world wars and the Great Depression. As soon as each crisis ended, the pent-up demand of Muslims forced to delay their travel quickly drove the hajj back up to its previous high point.

The turning point was the end of World War II. An early casualty of decolonization was the European-sponsored system of health controls that checked pilgrimage in South and Southeast Asia. As Saudi Arabia consolidated control over hajj management, newly independent nations in Asia and Africa began promoting pilgrimage instead of stifling it. In most of the Muslim world, independence

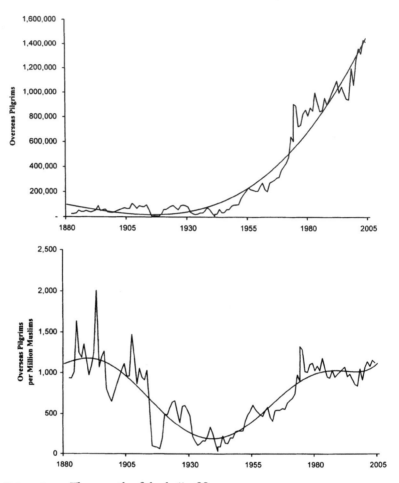

FIGURE 4.1 The growth of the hajj, 1882–2004

was coupled with economic development, allowing the hajj to recover and surge ahead at a record pace, decade after decade.

Hajj growth suffered recurrent setbacks during regional wars, but these were milder than the global shocks before 1945. Nearly all the recent disruptions in hajj traffic resulted from short-term crises involving a handful of countries. The major examples are the Suez War of 1956, the war in Yemen during the early 1960s, the Arab-Israeli War of 1967, the Indo-Pakistani War of 1971, the Iran-Iraq War during the 1980s, and the East Asian financial meltdown of 1998. Each event temporarily slowed hajj growth because it involved populous countries that usually send large delegations of pilgrims to Mecca. But since the 1970s, the hajj has expanded to include a much wider range of countries, making the pilgrimage as a whole less vulnerable to disruptions in any nation or region.

Since 1945, hajj growth has been continuous and spectacular. Nonetheless, it has moved in clear cycles—slower in the 1960s, faster in the 1970s, and slower again in the 1990s (Figure A4.1). The down cycle of the 1960s reflects the earlier predominance of pilgrims from Arab countries and the protracted rivalry between Egypt and Saudi Arabia. Nasser flirted with the idea of turning the hajj into a platform for his brand of Arab nationalism, but the Saudis used it to rally an "Islamic" counteralliance against him.

The hajj contracted briefly while Egypt and Saudi Arabia fought their proxy war in Yemen during the early 1960s. Egyptian and Yemeni pilgrims consistently ranked among the three largest contingents, and their dwindling numbers weakened the hajj in general. Before long, the Saudis drove the Egyptians not only from the battlefields of Yemen but also from the plain of 'Arafat.

Egypt virtually withdrew from the hajj until Nasser's death in 1969. Nasser's hajj ambitions clearly backfired, making the Saudis more determined than ever to exert exclusive control over symbolic assets within their territory. Realizing that socialist Egypt had less influence over pilgrimage than it enjoyed under the monarchy he had destroyed, Nasser opted for no influence at all.

The greatest spurt in hajj growth came after the Arab-Israeli War of 1973 and the subsequent spike in petroleum prices. This is when King Faysal was at the peak of his power.[3] Adding Saudi economic leverage to Egyptian military strength, he induced the industrialized nations to broker a land-for-peace settlement between Israel and its neighbors. Faysal's manipulation of money, personal diplomacy, and religion temporarily transformed Saudi Arabia from the head of a pack of Bedouin monarchs into the preeminent power in the Muslim world.

Faysal based his Islamic foreign policy on petrodollars and the Organization of the Islamic Conference (OIC), as well as the hajj. His reign coincided with the spread of inexpensive air travel throughout Asia and Africa—a development that made the pilgrimage larger and more diverse than at any time in history. When Faysal assumed the throne in 1964, overseas pilgrims averaged about 250,000 per year, with only a quarter of them arriving by plane. By the time of his assassination in 1975, the number had swelled to 900,000, and nearly 60 percent traveled by air (Table A4.1).

The biggest surge was outside the Arab world, where Faysal courted Muslim leaders by inviting them to make the hajj as his personal guests. It became common for countries to send 100,000 pilgrims or more in a single year. Pakistan neared the mark in 1973, and Turkey broke it in 1974, 1975, and 1976. Soon, the list included North Yemen (which merged with South Yemen in 1990), Nigeria, and Iraq, with Egypt, Iran, and Indonesia close behind (Table A4.2).

Growth slackened under Faysal's successors, especially after 1988, when the OIC adopted quotas pegging each country's delegation to its population. The system froze per capita pilgrimage at the same level it reached when Faysal was killed—1,000 pilgrims per million Muslims, amounting to 1 million pilgrims in 1990 and 1.3 million by the year 2003.

King Fahd reined in the pilgrimage to cope with crushing crowds and, more important, to fend off an Iranian-led campaign to replace Saudi sovereignty over the hajj and the Holy Cities with an international regime run by all Islamic countries. Realizing that collective hajj management was inevitable, the Saudis embraced a system that allowed them to administer the decisions of the OIC—the international organization that Faysal had created.

The quotas were designed to grapple with political disputes and logistical problems, but the results have been disappointing in both spheres. By the 1980s, the sheer size of the hajj was a mortal danger. In the past, pilgrims died en masse on the route to Mecca from disease, banditry, and exhaustion. Now, they fly to Saudi Arabia in comfort and safety only to perish in the sacred rites themselves. Nearly every year witnesses a new disaster—fires in the massive tent city at Mina, human stampedes at the tunnels and pedestrian bridges leading to the *jamarat* (the stone effigies of Satan), terrorist bombings near Mecca's main market, and riots in the very center of the Grand Mosque.

No matter how much money and technology the Saudis threw at the problem, the body counts continued to rise. Saudi officials began to suffer casualty fatigue, speaking as though it were a good year if they lost scores of lives instead of hundreds or thousands. Most of the casualties were from Indonesia, Malaysia, Pakistan, and India—countries that enjoyed long friendships with Saudi Arabia but expressed deep resentment over the perceived incompetence and callousness of Saudi security.

The new hajj regime is more effective in managing political conflicts than in controlling crowds. Even though the hajj reforms originally ostracized revolutionary Iran, they eventually allowed Iranians to reenter the mainstream of Islamic diplomacy. The Saudis sought support for a quota system so they could prevent the Iranians from flooding the hajj with massive delegations of 150,000 people, whose demonstrations spread dissent among pilgrims from other countries. Iran protested the quotas—boycotting the hajj from 1988 through 1990—but after Ayatollah Khomeini's death and the Gulf War against Iraq, Iranians moved to reconcile with the Arab monarchies they had tried to subvert.

A key step in the rapprochement was a bargain in 1997, when Iran accepted the quotas in return for the election of its new president, Ayatollah Khatami, as leader of the OIC, which supervises the hajj regime. Khatami's ascendance dramatized the internationalization of the hajj. After decades of insisting on unfettered sovereignty over the pilgrimage, Saudi Arabia showed it was willing to share decision making with even its most powerful adversary.

The Saudis could not have mustered the diplomatic support they needed to parry Iran's assault on the hajj without accepting a new system of international administration. That reform gave great weight to many non-Arab countries with no direct stake in the Saudi-Iranian dispute. After 1987, Turkey, Indonesia, Pakistan, Malaysia, and Nigeria became more prominent in both the hajj and the OIC. These countries backed Saudi Arabia's efforts to cut Iran's contingent, but, as soon as Khomeini passed away, they fashioned compromises over the numbers and behavior of Iranian pilgrims, encouraging Tehran to normalize its relations with the rest of the Muslim world. By 1997, the same hajj regime that was devised to isolate Iran made special concessions to back Ayatollah Khatami as he struggled to break the radical clergy's grip on power.

As the hajj becomes more inclusive and internationalized, it also becomes a barometer of the shifting balance of power among Muslim nations. Eighty percent of all Muslims live in the non-Arab countries of Asia and Africa—once regarded as the periphery of the Islamic world. Many of these countries have emerged as leading centers of economic development and political power. They acknowledge Saudi Arabia as the spiritual center of Islam, but they view themselves as the pacesetters in trade, culture, and diplomacy. For Muslims in Istanbul and Karachi, in Jakarta and Kuala Lumpur, in Lagos and Dakar, it is the Saudis who are marginal to modern Islam.

Today, when these metropolises speak of an Islamic periphery, they are referring to predominantly Christian and Buddhist regions where Muslim minorities still struggle for recognition—Europe and the Americas, Australia and South Africa, China and Russia. Pilgrims from these countries attract great attention in Mecca because they belong to communities where Islam is relatively young or where it has a long history of persecution. Non-Arab pilgrims are particularly pleased to meet hajjis from distant regions of the Muslim world. The presence of Muslim minorities demonstrates that Islam is a universal faith transcending ethnic and racial boundaries.

Most hajj managers agree that pilgrimage quotas should be relaxed for Muslim minorities because of their symbolic importance and because they usually lack the government assistance that helps defray expenses for hajjis elsewhere. Often, the quotas for Muslim minorities are pegged to their countries' total populations instead of to the far smaller numbers of Muslims. In wealthier nations such as Singapore, the United Kingdom, and South Africa, per capita hajj rates are several times higher than the international average.

Despite this consensus over the smaller minorities, the quota system provokes constant complaints about discriminatory enforcement. When the quotas were still being introduced, Turgut Özal tried to delay their application to Turkey. Banking on his personal relationships with the Saudi royal family, Özal requested an exemption for Turkish pilgrims in 1990, but the Saudis refused, and Turkey had to cancel reservations for 120,000 hajjis.[4]

Although Saudi Arabia rejected preferential treatment for friends in Turkey, it was eager to make special arrangements for foes in Iran. In order to ease Iran's return to Mecca, the Saudis agreed to ignore political gatherings among Iranian pilgrims as long as they were indoors and confined to their own delegation.[5] During the Iranian parliamentary campaign of 2000, the rules were bent even further. Iran received a bonus in its quota of about 40 percent—from 65,000 to 92,000—to boost Ayatollah Khatami's popularity in the last weeks before the election.[6]

The most serious quota problems are in religiously mixed societies such as Malaysia, Nigeria, and India. In these countries, Muslim leaders often claim entitlements to higher quotas because of special needs to bolster Muslim solidarity in political systems explicitly based on religious and ethnic power sharing. Under these circumstances, any effort to set hajj quotas sets off a chain reaction of debates over delicate national pacts regulating the balance of power between rival communities and within them. Inevitably, these pacts embody privately negotiated compromises that violate conventional notions of "secularism" and "Islamic government." Tampering with the hajj is easily seen as tampering with the national pact itself—with the unavoidable danger of unleashing new rounds of violence and partition.

Malaysia's hajj board, Tabung Haji, pools the savings of special pilgrims' bank accounts in an investment fund that promotes Muslim-run enterprises in an economy traditionally dominated by Chinese and Europeans. Because a cap on pilgrims also curbs Malay capitalism, Malaysia bitterly objects to the quotas, even though its hajj allocation is twice what it would be if its non-Muslim communities were excluded from the arithmetic.

To make matters worse, the quotas do not really limit Malay pilgrimage. When Tabung Haji announces that its annual quota is filled, thousands of Malays travel to the Philippines, where they pay $1,000 or more for forged documents allowing them to pose as Filipino pilgrims.[7] In Malaysia, quotas merely force pilgrimage into illegal channels, siphoning funds from banks and industries the government created to employ Muslims.

Nigeria's quota is based only on its Muslim population, and even that was greatly understated in the 1991 census. Nigeria is a remarkable case where both the national government and the Saudis actively discourage pilgrimage. Saudi Arabia became particularly annoyed with Nigerian hajjis for involvement in illegal immigration, drug trafficking, and prostitution. During the 1980s and 1990s, Nigeria's dictators and technocrats also wanted to cut hajj services and subsidies in the belief that they wasted foreign exchange and provoked Christian militants to claim Nigeria was becoming an Islamic state. Muslim generals even decided to create a state-sponsored Christian pilgrimage to neutralize accusations of religious favoritism.

When Nigeria returned to democracy under a Christian president in 1999, the pendulum swung in the other direction. One of Olusegun Obasanjo's earliest decisions was to double the size of the hajj. Just as his Muslim predecessors squeezed the hajj to mollify Christian opponents, Obasanjo revived it to reassure predominantly Muslim states in the north that they would not face reprisals from a southern Christian.

India's hajj took off in the 1990s, as economic development allowed more Muslims to travel and Hindu nationalism spurred them toward a counterdisplay of communal solidarity. By the year 2000, the Indian hajj was bigger than Pakistan's—a startling reversal of the lead Pakistan had held since the 1950s. India's hajj grew so quickly that local pilgrimage managers actually requested a reduction of their quota from 91,000 to 66,000 so they could organize state boards to cope with the demand.

While pilgrimage directors were asking for a breathing spell, many 'ulama insisted the government sponsor all 120,000 pilgrims that India was entitled to under the new hajj regime. 'Ulama promised to launch mass protests if New Delhi refused, warning that looting and riots would break out unless the quota was raised to its maximum.[8]

## The Expansion of a Worldwide Pilgrimage System

Geographically and culturally, today's hajj is nearly universal. The highest per capita hajj rates are still in countries closest to Mecca, particularly in the Arabian Peninsula and the Fertile Crescent (Figure 4.2). But air travel allows Muslims in dozens of countries to participate with equal frequency, even though they live thousands of miles from the Middle East.

The contemporary hajj is a planetary network that encompasses most lands from London to Cape Town and from Trinidad to Mindanao. The newest branches are the Americas, where Muslims are still a tiny fraction, and the former communist bloc, where religious travel was virtually impossible before the 1990s.

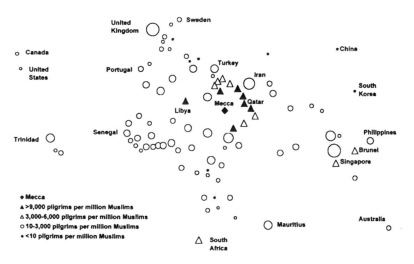

FIGURE 4.2 Worldwide pilgrimage rates, 1961–1987

After World War II, the hajj spread in a multistep process, with different regions participating at each stage. Even after several decades, diffusion is far from complete. Global maps of hajj activity reveal extraordinary breadth and striking inequality (Figure A4.2 and Table A4.3). During the 1950s, centers of hajj participation were compressed in the western portion of the Arab world between Syria and Yemen. A few outlying centers existed in Senegal, South Africa, and Malaysia, but they seemed remote and disconnected from the Middle Eastern core. By the end of the 1960s, a host of newly independent countries filled in the western and eastern quarters of the network, and a northern quarter emerged in Western Europe.

In the 1970s and 1980s, countries with rising hajj activity formed distinct clusters in several regions. Nearly the entire African continent became dotted with local clusters that converged from North Africa, West Africa, and the Indian Ocean. One of the largest groupings arose in Southeast Asia, including Malay-speaking countries, Indonesia, the Philippines, and Australia. The United Kingdom developed into a pole of hajj activity that sits astride a chain of European centers that stretch from Stockholm to Lisbon. By the end of the 1980s, North America and the Caribbean Basin defined the outer limits of a steadily expanding world network.

Growth and diffusion were accompanied by long-term shifts in pilgrims' ethnic and cultural backgrounds. While African pilgrims remained a steady 5 to 10 percent of world totals, the balance between Asian and Arab hajjis seesawed many times (Figure 4.3). Just after World War II, the greatest number came from Asia, but Arabic-speaking countries soon took a sizable lead. During the 1960s, the two groups were about equal, and the Arab advantage reap-

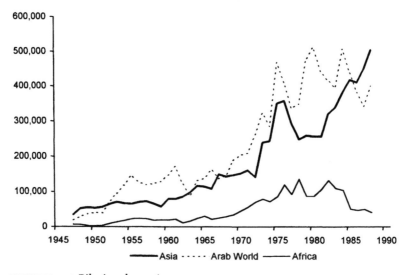

FIGURE 4.3 Pilgrims by region

peared with the surge of the 1970s. Then, the number of Asian pilgrims exploded, and, by the end of the 1980s, they once again formed the greatest contingents.

The role of the Arab world shrinks even more if we discount the extreme case of North Yemen—Saudi Arabia's poor and populous southern neighbor, where, until recently, tens of thousands of migrant workers and tribal peoples crossed porous borders to perform the hajj every year. Excluding North Yemen, the balance between Arab and Asian pilgrims is very close (Figure A4.3). The Arabs' advantage is slim, and Asians gradually recovered the lead they held before 1953. Striking shifts occurred both within the Arab world and among the subregions of Asia (Table A4.4). The center of gravity of Arab pilgrimage moved from east to west—from the wealthier Fertile Crescent and Arabian Peninsula toward the larger and poorer nations of the Red Sea and North Africa.

By the 1980s, Red Sea countries were the leading source of Arab pilgrims, and far away North Africa was just as important as the Fertile Crescent and the Arabian Peninsula. The steady development of the North African hajj contrasts with sharp oscillations in other Arab regions. The most unstable area was the Red Sea, where persistent ups and downs in Egyptian-Saudi relations were quickly reflected in the pilgrimage.

Much of the volatility in Arab pilgrimage stems from Saudi Arabia's unusual role in inter-Arab politics. As the strongest state in the Arabian Peninsula, Saudi Arabia always has rocky relations with neighbors who resist Saudi hegemony by allying with great powers in search of a foothold in the Persian Gulf. For their part, the Saudis have fought Egyptian, Syrian, Libyan, and Iraqi efforts to dominate the Arab world. This dual diplomacy—asserting hegemony locally while combating it regionally—has led Saudi Arabia into confrontations with states in every Arab region that produced at least temporary setbacks for the hajj in each case.

In Asia, regional patterns have been much more stable. Most of the time, the leading area has been West Asia (Turkey, Iran, and Afghanistan), with South Asia and Southeast Asia close behind. Compared with the Arab world, pilgrimage in Asia has been more closely tied to long-term economic development than to short-term political events. Nonetheless, here, too, the hajj grew fastest when political manipulation was obvious—in Turkey under the right-wing governments of Süleyman Demirel, Necmettin Erbakan, and Turgut Özal, in Pakistan during the rule of Zulfikar Ali Bhutto, and in Iran after the Islamic revolution.

Asia's growing prominence is clear when we compare long-term changes in the per capita pilgrimage rates of the major regions. Even before the quota system was adopted, regional gaps were already narrowing. In West Asia, hajj rates rose to the same level as in the Arab world. In South and Southeast Asia, growth was slower but more uniform, surpassing the rate for Africa. Regional convergence was particularly strong after 1980, when oil-producing states lost ground to countries with more diversified industries and exports.

## Regional Shifts in the Arab World

In the richest Arab countries, pilgrimage rates fell long before oil revenues dried up (Figure A4.4). As the hajj attracted massive crowds from distant and unfamiliar cultures, Mecca became less attractive to residents of the Persian Gulf sheikhdoms. People in these countries were accustomed to making the hajj at their leisure, and many came every year. For those who still wanted to visit the Holy Cities annually, it was a simple matter to adapt by replacing the hajj with the 'umra—a shorter and less arduous pilgrimage that can easily be scheduled outside the frantic hajj season.

After 1960, hajj rates declined nearly everywhere on the Arab side of the gulf. The only exception was a brief upturn in Bahrain's pilgrimage after 1980, when much of the local Shi'ite majority responded to Iran's call to turn the hajj into a protest against Bahrain's Sunni rulers. The center of hajj activity on the Arabian Peninsula shifted to the poorer and more insular countries of the south—to North Yemen and to Oman, where a young sultan was just beginning to open his country to the modern world.

In the Fertile Crescent, pilgrimage was tied to petroleum revenues. After 1980, hajj rates fell in oil-producing states such as Iraq and Syria, as well as in economies that depended on foreign remittances and investment, such as Lebanon, Jordan, and Palestine. In terms of their propensity to participate in the hajj, the order of Fertile Crescent countries hardly changed. Syria and Lebanon were about average for the region as a whole, while Jordan surged ahead and Iraq lagged behind.

In Jordan, the Hashemite royal family that ruled over Mecca and Medina in Ottoman times saw the hajj as a way of reinforcing their link with the Prophet's family and homeland.[9] Half a century after the Saudis drove the Hashemites out of Arabia, Jordanian Muslims continued to make the hajj twice as often as their neighbors. Although the same family ruled in Baghdad until 1958, Iraq's hajj is consistently the weakest in the Fertile Crescent.

Shi'ite Muslims—the majority in Iraq—complain that the Saudis discriminate against them by restricting their visits to hallowed grave sites in the Hejaz. Shi'ites who fear being mistreated in Mecca can defer the hajj until conditions improve and in the meantime make lesser pilgrimages to Kerbala and Najaf—renowned shrines in their own country that attract Shi'ite worshipers from all over the world.[10]

The Palestinians were the only nationality in the Fertile Crescent that experienced abrupt changes in their pilgrimage habits. Before the 1967 War, Palestinians made the hajj as frequently as Jordanians, but afterward, under Israeli occupation, they trailed even the Iraqis.

Whenever possible, Saudi officials continued to classify all hajjis from prepartition Palestine in the same category, regardless of whether they lived under Jordanian rule on the West Bank, under Egyptian control in the Gaza Strip, or in other countries as permanent residents or citizens. Hence, even the small number of Palestinian pilgrims recorded after 1967 overstates the hajj from historic Palestine. The situation improved during the 1980s, when Israel allowed residents of the West Bank and Gaza Strip to make the hajj via Jordan. By the 1990s, they also opened the door for Muslims living inside Israel's original borders.

Compared with Palestinians, the Lebanese rebuilt their hajj with relative ease after a series of political upheavals. Lebanon's hajj closely tracked Syria's except for sharp downturns with the factional fighting of 1958, the outbreak of the civil war in 1976, and the Israeli invasion of 1982. Each time, the Lebanese pilgrimage bounced back to its previous level. The long-term drop in Lebanon's hajj resulted from the same economic problems that affected its neighbors rather than from domestic turmoil.

While hajj rates declined in the Gulf States and the Fertile Crescent, they steadily increased in the western half of the Arab world (Figure A4.5). In the Red Sea countries, growth was uniform, but in North Africa there were much larger disparities between nations. Sudan and Egypt usually outpaced Djibouti and Somalia, but all Red Sea states hovered near the international average.

In North Africa, Libya's enthusiasm for the hajj is unparalleled. Its closest rival is Algeria, another major oil producer with a pilgrimage that follows the volatile international market. Yet Libyan hajj rates are seven times higher than Algeria's—a level more typical of an Arabian sultanate than of a former European protectorate the Italians once regarded as their "fourth shore." Libya's leadership in pilgrimage is rooted in a long tradition of religious nationalism that precedes the discovery of oil by decades and owes little to the regime of Muammar Qaddafi.

Modern Libya was born out of generations of anti-imperialist struggle led by the Sanusi religious brotherhood—an Islamic reformist movement that originated in Mecca about the same time as the Wahhabis. By grafting religious militancy onto tribal cohesion, the Sanusis wore down better armed invaders and established a nation-state that constantly reminded its citizens of their special connection to the Holy Cities.

Even after Qaddafi overthrew the monarchy, he sought to exploit the religious aura it bequeathed to Libyan nationalism, and this led him to become a zealous defender of the pilgrimage. When Qaddafi challenges Saudi Arabia's exclusive right to control the hajj, he is not only asserting his own grandiose ambitions but also echoing a popular Libyan view that their ties with Mecca are at least as strong as those of the Saudis.

For non-oil-producing countries in North Africa, hajj activity varies according to income per capita and distance from Mecca: Tunisia is the leader and Mauritania the laggard. At this end of the Arab world, the hajj is stronger than in the poorer parts of Asia and Africa but not as strong as in the non-Arab countries that have overtaken North Africa in economic development.

## Asia: The Interplay of Development and Communalism

In Asia, pilgrimage activity mirrors economic differences between regions and within them. Hajj rates are highest in Southeast Asia and lowest in South Asia, with West Asia falling in between (Figure A4.6). Economic factors are particularly important in Southeast Asia, where differences in hajj activity mimic widening gaps in living standards.

Singapore and Malaysia consistently outdistanced their neighbors in pilgrimage, just as they have in economic development.[11] The most dramatic contrast is between Brunei—the tiny oil-rich kingdom on the northern shore of Kalimantan—and Myanmar, the repressive military state formerly known as Burma.

The sultan of Brunei used a fraction of his personal fortune to shower his subjects with welfare programs, amusement parks, and free hajjs, hoping to prop up a ruling family whose corruption in business and private life exceeded even the low standards of the Suhartos in Indonesia.[12] Myanmar's Muslims suffered the opposite fate. To deflect popular rage over their economic failures, Myanmar's generals unleashed a campaign of persecution that drove the bulk of the Muslim minority to refugee camps in Bangladesh.

In Southeast Asia's divided societies, politics is as important as economics in understanding the radically different ways pilgrimage developed. Where Muslims are pivotal to the political process, the hajj thrived regardless of whether they comprise a clear majority, as in Indonesia; a dominant faction, as in Malaysia; or a protected minority, as in Singapore. Where Muslim minorities are marginal and rebellious, as in Thailand and the Philippines, hajj rates plummeted no matter which way the economic winds were blowing.[13]

The interplay of economic development and communal politics is equally decisive for South Asian pilgrimage. The new nation of Pakistan was so depleted by ethnic and partisan conflict that its hajj rate trailed India's two decades after partition, even though Pakistan was born an "Islamic state" and India was ruled by secularists. The Pakistani pilgrimage soared with the outpouring of religious nationalism after the loss of Bangladesh, but it tapered off under Zia-ul-Haq's dictatorship and crash-landed during the economic crisis of the 1990s. By 2000, India's economic success allowed Hindu nationalist governments to become stronger hajj patrons than the Muslim League politicians who pushed Pakistan to the edge of bankruptcy.

Politics is the key reason for the extreme instability of pilgrimage in Turkey and Iran. Since 1960, Turkey's hajj has gone through three wrenching cycles of boom and bust with little connection to economic trends. Instead, oscillations coincide with the parade of civilian and military governments taking turns in implementing contradictory religious policies. Every time right-wing politicians came to power, they poured public funds into the hajj, hoping to solidify support among Muslim voters. Whenever the military seized power, they slashed pilgrimage services, claiming they violated Ataturk's commitment to secularism and Westernization.

The most dramatic example of hajj policy in disregarding economic reality was postrevolutionary Iran. Under the shah, Iran's pilgrimage grew in step with oil production, as in most petroleum-exporting countries. The shah's technocrats made sure hajj growth was restrained, tracking gradual increases in the number of barrels exported instead of the meteoric rise in revenues. The Islamic revolution severed the connection between planning and pilgrimage, doubling the hajj precisely as Iran's industry was being devastated in the war with Iraq. For the ayatollahs, recasting the hajj as a movement of militants seemed an ideal formula for consolidating the revolution and spreading it abroad. For a decade, Iran was the only country in the world where soaring pilgrimage accompanied economic collapse instead of development.

## Africa: Two Coasts and Two Hajjs

In sub-Saharan Africa, hajj rates have usually been close to the international average. These countries account for about 10 percent of the world's Muslims, and in most years they make up the same proportion of all pilgrims. But the hajj is much stronger in West Africa, where Islam was spread widely by indigenous peoples, than in East Africa, where it is still identified with coastal enclaves tied to Arabia and South Asia (Figure A4.7).

Disparities in hajj rates are far greater in East Africa than in West Africa. The gap between Nigeria and Senegal is minute compared with the chasm separating South Africa from Ethiopia. The West African pilgrimage covers a larger territory and a wider array of ethnic groups and social classes.

In much of Africa, the hajj is extremely dependent on the fate of specific commodities in the international marketplace. In many countries the path of the hajj is identical to the path of the price for a single export—gold in South Africa, oil in Nigeria, and groundnuts in Senegal.

African hajj trends also reflect the degree to which governments can regulate commodity markets and cushion consumers against disruptions. The relative stability of pilgrimage in Senegal was a consequence of the Socialist Party's determination to protect its core constituency of peanut farmers from deterioration of the terms of trade for their cash crop. Subsidizing the groundnut economy meant diverting resources from the overcrowded cities and running up foreign debt. Nevertheless, the government continued the subsidies to prop up rural purchasing power and to win over popular Sufi orders that controlled votes in the countryside. For decades, Presidents Leopold Senghor and Abdou Diouf guaranteed the marabouts (Sufi leaders) steady revenues and stable pilgrimages. Hajj policy and agricultural policy intertwined to keep the Socialists in power, while fueling the bitter urban opposition that finally defeated them in the 2000 elections.[14]

Unlike Senegal, governments in Nigeria and South Africa could never defend their economies from the shocks of the oil and gold markets. In both countries, pilgrimage thrived on a precarious prosperity that brought great rewards and greater unpredictability. Nigeria's Muslim community controlled the northern half of the country and most top military posts. They created a system of state-funded pilgrims' boards providing basic services and subsidies even during periods of recession.

But South Africa's Muslims are a tiny minority of "coloureds" clustered in Cape Town and Durban—descendants of Malay exiles banished by the Dutch and of indentured laborers the British imported from India.[15] With little influence over either black or white politics, Muslims in South Africa were forced to finance the hajj almost exclusively from private resources, even after the fall of apartheid. Whereas hajj rates are stable in Senegal and turbulent in Nigeria, they have been utterly tumultuous in South Africa.[16]

In West Africa, there is an interesting contrast between the Sahel (the arid swath hugging the southern edge of the Sahara) and the Atlantic coast. Pilgrimage is much stronger in the Sahel, despite lower living standards and constant susceptibility to drought. In Chad and Burkina Faso, where most Muslims are poor farmers, hajj rates are four times higher than in Liberia and Sierra Leone, where they are fairly prosperous urban minorities.

For most of the twentieth century, millions of pilgrims from the Sahel moved back and forth to Mecca along vast overland routes stretching from the Niger basin through Sudan and Ethiopia. Often, their journeys lasted years, as they stopped to work in permanent pilgrims' settlements that sprang up to accommodate migrants from all over West Africa who were moving in both directions. Even after air travel made distance from Mecca seem irrelevant, the Sahel states still had higher hajj rates than their Atlantic neighbors. Land links between West Africa and Arabia have withered, but they left an enduring legacy of enthusiasm for pilgrimage in societies they touched the most. Today, West Africa is the only part of the world where proximity to Mecca remains a better predictor of hajj activity than per capita income.

In East Africa, the hajj is far weaker, even though Muslims there are more prosperous and live on Mecca's doorstep. Many Muslims in this region are descendants of Indian immigrants, including Shi'ite followers of the Agha Khan. They commonly adhere to strict tithing traditions, focusing on their own communities rather than on the wider Islamic world. Compared with the Muslims of West Africa, they have better opportunities to perform the hajj, but they have shown little interest in pursuing them.[17]

Pilgrimage in East Africa also faces daunting political constraints. Muslims here are racial and religious minorities often regarded as carpetbaggers with a neocolonial stranglehold over local economies. Even those with modest wealth are vulnerable to chauvinist governments that profit from their business connections while turning them into scapegoats.

East African Muslims cope with these dangers in some countries but not in others, and their contrasting fates are clearly visible in divergent patterns of hajj participation. In Kenya and Mauritius, where immigrant businesses and nationalist politicians cooperate, pilgrimage has grown steadily. In Tanzania, however, the hajj never recovered from the communal violence that accompanied independence and the overthrow of the Arab sultanate in Zanzibar.

For the Muslims of Uganda, Idi Amin paved the way to quick riches, only to bring wholesale deportation in the end. Amin tried to buy converts to Islam by showering them with government jobs and free hajjs. After his fall, he found safe haven in Saudi Arabia, but Muslims were expelled in a backlash against everything foreign and Islamic.

### Tomorrow's Hajjis: Newcomers and Latecomers

The new frontiers of the hajj are Europe, the Americas, Australia, and former communist countries (Figure A4.8). London has become the hajj capital of Europe. After the rapid influx of immigrants from Commonwealth countries, Britain's hajj took off in the 1970s and 1980s. By the year 2000, the United Kingdom regularly sent 20,000 people to Mecca each year, prompting the British to open the first European consulate in Jeddah to deal exclusively with pilgrims' affairs.[18]

Previously, the focus of European hajj activity was Belgrade and Sarajevo rather than London. President Tito sponsored the hajj to strengthen alliances with Muslims at home and abroad. The hajj bolstered a separate Bosnian political identity against the ambitions of Serbian nationalists, and it was a gesture that enhanced Yugoslavia's prestige in the nonaligned movement. By sending pilgrims to Mecca and theology students to Cairo, Tito showed Third World audiences that his socialism had no connection to the religious persecutions they witnessed in the rest of the communist bloc.[19]

Compared with Britain, France's hajj has barely begun. Even though they lived in one of Europe's most open and prosperous societies, French Muslims made the pilgrimage only a bit more often than Bosnians and Kosovars before the breakup of Yugoslavia. Muslims in France have not yet attained anything approaching the social acceptance and political recognition that they achieved in Britain twenty years ago. While British Muslims created a host of voluntary organizations that enjoyed access to state agencies, France's Muslims were battling racist politicians and hostile security forces.[20]

Britain, France, and Yugoslavia show that hajj strength is closely related to the degree of religious tolerance European societies extend to Muslim minorities. Wide variations in tolerance reflect religious traditions in the host countries far more than the characteristics of their Muslim populations. For the Muslims of Europe, both social acceptance and hajj activity are greatest in the Protestant north, weaker in the Catholic southwest, and weakest in the Orthodox southeast. Since 1970, the hajj has expanded to most of Scandinavia while shrinking in Iberia and the Balkans.

In the Americas and Australia, hajj growth started late but climbed steeply after 1980. The hajj rates of Canada and Australia quickly rose to the international average, and well-to-do Indian migrants in Trinidad became the unchallenged pilgrimage leaders of the Western Hemisphere.

Muslims in the United States are just beginning to join the pilgrimage network, despite the many travel agents offering hajj packages in every big city. The deviance of the United States is likely to diminish as immigrants become better established and as more African American Muslims join the Islamic mainstream. In the meantime, hajj rates in the United States will probably continue to trail the rest of the industrialized world.[21]

The lands where the hajj remains least developed are the nations of the former communist bloc, especially Russia,[22] Central Asia,[23] and China.[24] In the 1990s, all these countries began sending token delegations to Mecca to rebuild their international reputations after decades of religious oppression. Yet in every case, governments moved at a snail's pace out of fear that political opponents would manipulate an uncontrolled pilgrimage.

Because none of these countries approves more than a few thousand hajj applications per year, about 10 percent of the world's Muslims are still effectively barred from the pilgrimage. Nor is there much likelihood that these states will liberalize their policies in the foreseeable future. With Moscow combating separatists in Chechnya and Dagestan, with the Central Asian republics fending off infiltration from Afghanistan and Iran, and with Beijing crushing revolts in Xinjiang, Mecca will probably remain beyond the reach of these Muslims for years to come.

## Competing Explanations of Hajj Participation: Seasonal and Sociological Models

There are many explanations for wide variations in hajj activity over time and across countries. What are the best models in predicting hajj participation, and how well do they stand up in different times and regions?

Two of the most popular explanations have nothing to do with economics, culture, and politics. They focus on cyclical changes in climate and on a random event in astronomy. Many people assume the size of the hajj is a seasonal phenomenon—that pilgrimage swells when Saudi Arabian temperatures moderate and dwindles when heat is most oppressive.

Because the pilgrimage period is determined according to a lunar calendar, the hajj rotates through all seasons. From the standpoint of those following the Julian calendar, every year the hajj begins eleven days earlier than it did the previous year. In this manner, the hajj works its way "backward" through the solar calendar, completing a thirty-three-year cycle before beginning on the same day once again. Given the murderous summer sun in Saudi Arabia, it is natural to expect pilgrims to modulate travel to avoid the summer whenever possible.

The astronomical factor is far less predictable than the weather. Many Muslims believe the hajj carries special blessings when the Day of Standing at 'Arafat—the high point of the pilgrimage—falls on Friday. Some people even claim this is a "Greater Hajj" (Hajj al-Akbar), when pilgrims reap spiritual rewards a hundred times greater than normal. This view is common throughout the Muslim world, but it is particularly popular in South and Southeast Asia.

The problem is that no one can know in advance the exact day of the week when the hajj will begin. Some years, the odds are fifty-fifty that the Day of Standing will be on Friday, but it could just as well fall on Thursday or Saturday. It all depends on the sighting of the new moon that marks the beginning of Dhu al-Hijja, the month when the hajj occurs—and that is never known until after pilgrims have already confirmed their travel plans.

During the twentieth century, hajj trends confirmed neither the climactic hypothesis nor the astronomical hypothesis[25] (Figure A4.9). Sometimes pilgrimage declined with rising temperatures, and sometimes it rose. Likewise, falling temperatures coincided with larger crowds in some years and smaller than usual crowds in others. Before 1945 and after 1965, there is some evidence that pilgrimage and temperature moved in opposite directions, as the hypothesis of seasonal cycles predicts. But in the intervening years, when the hajj was bouncing back from the shocks of war and depression, the largest crowds came in the hottest months, and the smallest were in the coolest months.

As for the greater blessings of Friday at 'Arafat, there is no hint that the day of the week makes the slightest difference in turnout. Among the sixty-two hajjs between 1928 and 1987, the Day of Standing fell on Friday eleven times. Out of these eleven occasions, the hajj was larger than usual only three times (1955, 1978, and 1983). On the other hand, pilgrimage was merely average in five of these years (1935, 1942, 1947, 1950, and 1958), and on three occasions (1963, 1968, and 1971) it was much smaller than usual. A Friday at 'Arafat did nothing to increase attendance.

Nor does it matter if we include years when pilgrims might have made unlucky guesses about a possible Hajj al-Akbar—hoping to be at 'Arafat on a Friday but ending up there a day early or late. Thursdays and Saturdays were just as irrelevant as Fridays. Even if a popular preference for the Hajj al-Akbar survives, it has no discernible influence on aggregate behavior.

Social scientific explanations of hajj activity focus on economics, geography, and religion. Pilgrimage is costly, time-consuming, and physically demanding. The vast majority of Muslims will never be able to afford it. Islamic scholars are nearly unanimous that no one should make the hajj if it will cause hardship for oneself or one's family. In practice and in principle, the hajj is not an absolute obligation—only a highly desirable duty for those financially and physically capable of making the journey in reasonable safety and comfort.

Of course, every pilgrim knows that Mecca attracts the destitute and infirm in droves and that many long for the opportunity to end their days in "God's house" and enter paradise instantly. These might be the most committed pilgrims of all, but they must summon energy and resources that elude most believers.

For centuries, the most formidable obstacle to pilgrimage was geography. Distance magnified the duration and expense of the journey while multiplying dangers—shipwreck, plague, pirates, Bedouin raiders, and simple exhaustion. In distant regions, greater hardship was itself regarded as an incentive to undertake the pilgrimage because added sacrifice supposedly earned extra blessings. Hajjis from Spain, West Africa, India, the Malay world, and China were deeply admired as intrepid and devoted pilgrims, both in their own lands and along the route to Mecca.

Today, people often lament that air travel and packaged tours remove too much pain from the hajj, turning it into just another shopping spree. In fact, the enormous death tolls during recent pilgrimages show that hajjis still face many of the old dangers, as well as new ones that never existed before. Sunstroke and dehydration are as pernicious as ever, and even more lives are lost to stampeding crowds and exploding stoves. Most of the truly life-threatening situations now appear in Mecca itself rather than on the way. Nowadays, survival depends less on the length of the journey than on the class of accommodations and medical services hajjis can afford in the Holy Cities.

A time-series analysis of international data on hajj participation shows that the relative importance of economics, geography, and culture changed markedly between 1961 and 1987[26] (Table A4.5). Results vary somewhat with the specific countries examined, but overall trends are extremely clear. The strongest predictor of hajj activity is per capita income, and the weakest is distance from Mecca.

The most decisive change was the evaporation of distance as an obstacle. In the early 1960s, when about 75 percent of all pilgrims traveled by sea and land, distance was a formidable deterrent. Less than thirty years later, the major barrier was simply the price of an airline ticket and hotel reservation. As Muslim communities sprang up in Europe, the Americas, and Australia, they joined the international hajj network, but not as quickly as one would expect from their high incomes.

Many Muslims argue that the hajj can flourish only in an environment that allows Islam to thrive as well. They assume that predominantly Muslim cultures will place a higher value on pilgrimage than societies where Islam is a small or disfavored religion. When Muslims are a majority or an influential pressure group, they might also be able to generate support for programs that subsidize the hajj, making it accessible to people who could never go if they had to rely on their own assets. In this view, the relative size of the Muslim population itself affects the degree to which Islamic organizations can mobilize resources on behalf of the pilgrimage.

The relative size of the Muslim population became increasingly important for hajj activity worldwide but not in the Asian and African countries where most pilgrims live. In terms of pilgrimage, the political and organizational weakness of Muslim minorities clearly diluted the benefits of greater wealth. On a global scale, the mere fact of living in a predominantly Muslim society became an increasingly powerful predictor of hajj activity from 1960 onward, and by 1975 it was as important as per capita income.

In the established Muslim communities of Asia and Africa, hajj rates were much less sensitive to whether they were majorities or minorities. Compared with Muslims in predominantly white Christian or communist countries, constraints on their pilgrimage prospects were more economic than cultural or political. In Asia and Africa, per capita income constantly outpaced other predictors of hajj participation.

Income is even more important if we exclude the countries of the Arabian Peninsula. The link between pilgrimage and prosperity is based on far more than the concentration of wealth in a handful of city-states bordering Saudi Arabia. As economic development spreads through Asia and Africa, it enables more Muslims to make the hajj. But uneven development also accentuates disparities between nations and classes that can afford the rising costs of pilgrimage and those that cannot.

The effect of income inequality is most severe in the non-Arab countries of Asia and least severe in West Africa. In Asia, wealth so thoroughly supplanted distance from Mecca as the major determinant of pilgrimage that geography hardly matters any more (Figure A4.10). Traveling eastward from Turkey and Iran, hajj rates slump in South Asia but quickly rise again in Malay-speaking societies straddling the trade routes between the Indian and Pacific Oceans. Largely because of growing Malay prosperity, Asia is the only region where a Muslim's likelihood of making the hajj actually *increases* with distance from the Holy Cities.

Conversely, West Africa is the only region where geography matters as much as ever (Figure A4.11). For these countries, hajj participation still reflects historic ties with Arabia forged by generations of migrant-pilgrims who lived and traveled along overland routes to the Red Sea. West Africa's pilgrimage rates steadily diminish with distance from Mecca, even though air travel replaced most overland traffic three decades ago.

International flights from this region are among the most expensive in the world. Along the Atlantic coast where costs are highest, some governments offered discounted fares on national airlines. But state intervention occurred only in Senegal, Gambia, and Guinea—where Muslims are a majority—and not in Liberia, Sierra Leone, and Guinea-Bissau, where they enjoy less political influence.

## The Growing Yet Unequal Role of Female Pilgrims

Female participation is a special dimension of pilgrimage that demonstrates the enduring power of culture. Hajj growth has been accompanied by a steady rise in the proportion of women pilgrims. In the early 1960s, only 30 percent of all hajjis were women; three decades later, they made up 45 percent of the total. Even though the gender gap narrowed globally, it survives in many large and culturally divided countries. In many nations, regional disparities in female pilgrimage reflect virtually separate societies with incompatible views of the value and freedom women deserve.

Worldwide, the percentage of women pilgrims rises along with increases in national hajj rates (Figure A4.12). But the connection is weak, and we cannot assume that expanding opportunities to make the pilgrimage translate into more opportunities for women. Economic development improves everyone's chances of traveling to Mecca, but males benefit more than females.

The role of women is strongest in Southeast Asia, the Fertile Crescent, and East Africa. As early as the mid-1970s, women were the majority of pilgrims from Malaysia, Thailand, Singapore, Lebanon, Palestine, Bahrain, South Africa, Mauritius, Madagascar, and Chad. Male domination is strongest in southern Arabia, West Asia, and southern Europe. Women made up less than 20 percent of pilgrims from North Yemen, Afghanistan, Bangladesh, Yugoslavia, Portugal, and Spain. Fewer than 30 percent of hajjis from Ethiopia, Central Africa, Sierra Leone, Turkey, Greece, Canada, and the United States were female.

Female participation is closely tied to family structure, immigration, and poverty levels. Women hajjis are rarest in tribal societies, especially southern Arabia and the mountain lands between eastern Turkey and western Pakistan, where seminomadic life is common. Women are often the majority of pilgrims in the agrarian and seafaring societies of Southeast Asia, where female inheritance is widely protected by local custom and where men and women frequently alternate as head of the household. Contrasts between nomadic and seafaring cultures are unusually clear—as though they were pure types of contradictory ideals of patriarchy and egalitarianism permeating family life in the Islamic world as a whole.

Large-scale immigration can either encourage or suppress women's participation. When Muslim immigrants are mainly guest workers living apart from their families or first-generation communities, female pilgrims are rare. Until the 1990s, this was the predominant pattern in most of Europe, the Americas, and Australia. However, women often are 50 percent of the pilgrims from well-established overseas communities of Muslims, such as the Indians of East Africa and the Caribbean. Women are also the majority of pilgrims among Lebanese and Palestinians—nationalities with high migration by businesspeople and professionals, who commonly retain dual residency and make the hajj as citizens of their native countries.

Economic conditions influence women's chances of making the hajj just as much as men's chances, but in a different way. In poorer countries, everyone goes on the hajj less frequently, but women are more likely not to go at all. In most countries, men prefer to make the pilgrimage with their wives. But if finances make that impossible, men often make a solo hajj in hopes that their wives will be able to go later. Of course, when a family's economic prospects are poor, the husband who seizes his chance to make the pilgrimage now is effectively destroying his wife's ability to do so in the future. When it comes to family decisions about the hajj, poverty creates a moral economy that puts women and children last.

As women come close to forming half the world's hajjis, the most striking gender gaps are no longer between nations but within them. Some of the greatest increases in female participation occurred in Pakistan, Turkey, and Indonesia, where Benazir Bhutto, Tansu Çiller, and Megawati Sukarnoputri, respectively, paved the way for Muslim women to lead mass parties and democratic governments. Yet even in these countries, women's progress in pilgrimage has been extremely uneven—well above the international norm in a few districts but far below it in many others (Table 4.1).

TABLE 4.1 The growth of female pilgrimage (females as a percentage of total pilgrims)

| | 1968–1975 | Later Rates | | Regional Disparities |
|---|---|---|---|---|
| | | Percent | Years | |
| World | 34.5 | 43.0 | 1993 | Southeast Asia 46.7, Africa 38.8, South Asia 34.9, Arab World 34.5, West Asia 26.8, Europe 20.1 |
| Malaysia | 53.7 | 55.4 | 1991–1995 | n. a. |
| Indonesia | 43.7 | 52.3 | 1985–1989 | Sulawesi 63.8, Sumatra 56.6, Maluku 51.0, Java 49.5, Nusa Tenggara 35.0 |
| Nigeria | 38.1 | 42.0 | 1999 | Lagos 50.7, Kaduna 38.9 |
| Pakistan | 34.8 | 41.2 | 1985–1988 | Punjab 46.4, Sindh 43.4, Frontier 28.3, Baluchistan 17.7 |
| Turkey | 26.7 | 45.7 | 1990–1993 | Western Anatolia 51.2, South East 41.1, Black Sea 35.9, North East 29.0 |

Politicizing the Hajj: Guests of God or Guests of the State?

Although the hajj has always been political as well as religious, its merger of power and faith is more conspicuous today than ever before. The hallmark of the modern hajj is that it is an affair of state. Every detail is planned and regulated by governments and international organizations that are pursuing special interests at home and around the world. Every government with a sizable Muslim population has promulgated a hajj policy in the hope that new services will win over grateful pilgrims and new restrictions will ward off potential troublemakers.

Eventually, every government learns that controlling the hajj carries great dangers and uncertain benefits. Pilgrimage management is an inherently risky undertaking precisely because Islam gives no one the authority to stand in the way of a believer who wishes to visit "God's house."

All aspects of pilgrimage policy are under constant public scrutiny, and even supporters of the government are quick to protest measures that appear unduly restrictive or discriminatory. Attacks on the shortcomings and abuses of hajj management keep the flames of political opposition burning, even under the most repressive regimes where other criticism is crushed without hesitation. Skirmishes over the hajj provide ready ammunition for wider power struggles rooted in religion, party, ethnicity, class, gender, and age. Those who control the state can wield the hajj as an instrument of power and prestige, but they cannot prevent others from wielding it with similar success.

Politicization of the hajj is most notorious in precisely those countries that pioneered modern pilgrimage administration. State intervention in the hajj is a gradual process that leads imperceptibly from subsidy to regulation, from guiding private markets to creating public monopolies, from creeping bureaucratization to empire building and outright nationalization.

Over time, hajj agencies accumulate enormous power and wealth. They command large budgets and staffs, they control or replace thousands of private businesses, they manage huge investment funds with interests in every economic sector, and they ally with politicians and interest groups in broad coalitions across parties, ministries, and local governments.

Above all, pilgrimage managers have the power to innovate and discriminate. They have virtually reinvented the way Muslims experience the hajj. In one country after another, they enveloped pilgrimage in detailed rules, often with more zeal for surveillance than service.

Hajj officials tried to streamline the rituals in Mecca and Medina by discouraging customary devotions they see as hampering the orderly flow of worshipers. Pilgrim guides and police are constantly telling the crowds to keep moving and to avoid ancient but unnecessary practices such as kissing the

Black Stone, halting at the spot where Ibrahim's footprints appear on an ancient rock, and praying at the tombs of Muhammad and his companions.

Traditionally, pilgrims spent several months in the Holy Cities, where they mingled freely with Muslims of all races and nations. Today, pilgrimage is abbreviated to what bureaucrats clinically term "the hajj exercise"—a mass airlift of well-screened and often well-heeled tourists herded under one roof and extracted from Saudi Arabia as quickly as possible before they have a chance to create mischief.

The power to discriminate is subject to more abuse and criticism than the power to innovate. Hajj agencies determine who performs the pilgrimage and who profits from it. Hajj directors are invariably political appointees, and most are career politicians in their own right, with client networks and voter constituencies just as powerful—and just as demanding—as those of any cabinet member. When it comes to showering their home districts with inflated quotas and padded contracts, pilgrimage directors are no different from transport ministers or budget committee chairs; each knows instinctively that "all politics is local."

Political manipulation of the hajj is most intense during election campaigns. Ruling party leaders target hajj services to reward loyal supporters while reaching out to swing voters. The geographic and social distributions of pilgrims are excellent signs of a regime's strategy of domination—its assessment of groups that form its core constituency and of weak points needing special care.

As election time approaches, the press is always filled with exposés about corrupt hajj officials and horror stories about pilgrims who were swindled by unscrupulous tour operators. The opposition parties are sure to demand a thorough investigation, claiming such reports give only a glimmer of the rampant injustice and inefficiency in hajj administration. A vulnerable hajj director is a prime target for opposition leaders. If he is an appointed official as in Turkey, they try to drive him from office with accusations and rumors. If he is a member of Parliament as in Malaysia, they will spare no expense to defeat him in his home district.

Modern pilgrimage management has spread throughout the Islamic world, but a handful of countries led the way and advised dozens of nations seeking to learn from their experiences. Malaysia and Pakistan were the first to establish centralized and well-funded hajj bureaucracies. During the 1960s and 1970s, they set the international standard in pilgrim education, medical services, and subsidized air travel. Soon afterward, Turkey and Nigeria developed flexible monopolies that preserve roles for private enterprise and local power brokers. They showed that governments bound by explicitly secular constitutions could still launch ambitious hajj programs if they spread the benefits widely among voters and campaign contributors.

In the 1990s, Indonesia adopted elements from all these models, creating the world's largest pilgrimage agency in Asia's most corrupt dictatorship. With a booming economy and a population of 200 million, Indonesia was the greatest beneficiary of quotas pegging pilgrimage delegations to census results. The chance to bask in the hajj came in the nick of time for Suharto. As he quarreled with army commanders who were the backbone of his regime, Suharto reinvented himself as "Pak Harto"—the hajji president and pious father figure, dispensing nearly as much wealth to the new Muslim middle class as his real children stole from the treasury.

Each of these countries made a unique contribution to technical and political aspects of hajj management, and they continue to be international models.[27] Younger hajj agencies elsewhere regularly send observers to these veteran organizations to keep abreast of best practices and current debates. In Kuala Lumpur, Malaysian hajj officials introduced me to colleagues from Uzbekistan and Turkmenistan who were just setting up their own operations. The Central Asians explained that, after leaving Malaysia, they also intended to visit Islamabad and Ankara.

The technical innovations spread quickly and widely. Pakistan created the first computerized system for processing hajj applications, including online registration and airline reservations for Internet users. Indonesia developed a complex set of international leases, assembling the world's largest fleet of rented aircraft for each hajj season and disbanding it for the rest of the year. Cost-conscious bureaucrats are rapidly drawn to these technologies and practices, and they become more common every year.

The most intriguing hajj schemes are also the riskiest because they experiment with social change. Besides regulating pilgrimage, they tackle chronic problems such as rivalries between state and private enterprises and conflicts between Muslims and non-Muslims. Malaysian technocrats built an entire banking system around hajj savings accounts by using the funds as investment capital for new Muslim-owned industries that challenged the traditional dominance of Chinese and foreign cartels. Turkey's right-wing parties set up a bargaining process that allows hajj managers and private entrepreneurs to divide up the pilgrimage business and periodically renegotiate market shares. Nigerian generals even transformed their pilgrims' board into an interdenominational agency that aids Christians traveling to Jerusalem and Rome, as well as Muslims going to Mecca.

Pilgrimage agencies are also important instruments of foreign policy. All the countries that pioneered hajj management aspire to be grand players on the world stage. Pakistan dreamed of leading a Muslim League of Nations or an Islamic Commonwealth. Even when such projects were financed by Arabian oil, they gave Pakistani intellectuals a sounding board for plans to reshape international economics and law according to Islamic principles. In a country where religious and national identities are indistinguishable, all Pakistani governments have believed that they must cultivate a global reputation for defending Islam and linking it to modern science. Leading the way in hajj administration is just as important as driving the Russians from Afghanistan, developing an "Islamic bomb," or fathering "Islamic economics."

Pilgrimage promotes religious diplomacy even in Turkey, the secular and Western model that is the supposed antithesis of Pakistan and Iran. Turkey repeatedly positions itself as a pivotal broker between Europe and the Islamic world, telling countries in both camps they need a trusted intermediary to overcome their historic enmities and conflicting civilizations. Turkey's leaders are well aware that the struggle between Western and Islamic identities can tear their country apart. Yet they also know that influence in the Muslim world increases their leverage in every capital between Washington and Beijing. Today, even secular Ataturkist parties endorse a state-supported hajj because it strengthens ties with a host of non-Western countries Turkey needs as markets and allies.

Nigerian politicians have always regarded pilgrimage as a means to advance their ambitions abroad. The founders of Nigeria's hajj administration were diplomats and businessmen who hoped Middle Eastern investors would help turn their country into the powerhouse of Africa. Christian leaders attacked the pilgrims' boards as foreshadowing an Islamic state. The ruling generals discovered that the best way to quiet Christian complaints was to give them a pilgrimage of their own—even if sending pilgrims to Jerusalem meant reestablishing relations with Israel. Yet Nigeria waited until 1996 before recognizing Israel so it would be following Arab states instead of leading them. For the generals in Abuja, balancing rival claims of Christian and Muslim pilgrims made sense only if it served their foreign policy instead of disrupting it. A Christian pilgrimage that placated critics at home would have little value if it alienated powerful friends abroad, especially friends they had to face each year in Mecca.

Countries with strong pilgrimage administrations were in the best position to take advantage of the hajj's growing importance in world politics. When Saudi Arabia and Iran made the hajj the crux of their power struggle, both sides needed to find third-party mediators. This enhanced the influence of non-Arab states with wide experience in pilgrimage affairs, particularly Pakistan, Malaysia, Turkey, Indonesia, and Nigeria. These are the countries that paved the way for the hajj reforms of the 1980s and for Iran's subsequent integration into the new international regime supervising pilgrimage.

These nations also have a common interest in a new balance of power in the Islamic world. Before the Iranian-Saudi confrontation, Islamic international organizations were still dominated by a handful of Arabian kingdoms and preoccupied with inter-Arab quarrels. The bigger states of Asia and Africa were indifferent to Islamic diplomacy. Frustrated in the OIC, they bypassed its largely symbolic process in favor of regional organizations focused on economic and security interests instead of religion.

The Islamic revolution in Iran revived the role of non-Arab states in the OIC. Saudi Arabia was desperate for help in fending off Iranian demands for internationalization of the hajj and the Holy Cities. But the Saudis soon realized that their allies had demands of their own: more power in both the new pilgrimage system and the OIC. Many states were willing to breathe new life into the OIC so it could do what no Saudi ruler dared to do unilaterally—close the door on the flood of Iranian agitators who were turning the pilgrimage into an annual confrontation.

In return, they insisted that the OIC put an end to the overrepresentation of Arabs in the hajj. Eighty percent of all Muslims live outside the Arab world, and 40 percent are citizens of the five non-Arab countries with the strongest hajj agencies. The new pilgrimage regime gives non-Arab states the same proportional representation in the hajj that they would like to enjoy throughout the OIC.

By limiting the access of Iranian pilgrims, they increased access for themselves. Making the OIC the ultimate authority in hajj affairs gave non-Arab members the same influence in Islamic diplomacy that Turkey already wielded in the North Atlantic Treaty Organization, that Indonesia and Malaysia held in the Association of Southeast Asian Nations, and that Nigeria had in the Organization of African Unity.

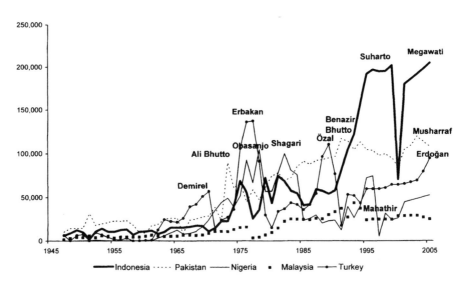

FIGURE 4.4 Hajj growth in Indonesia, Pakistan, Turkey, Nigeria, and Malaysia, 1947–2004

It is the pilgrimage agencies of the most experienced countries that make the new hajj regime possible. By capping the number of pilgrims and shortening their time in the Holy Cities, they enable Saudis to cope with an explosive situation that every year threatens to spin out of control. These agencies are the key enforcers of unpopular quotas and multiyear waiting periods for applicants who already performed the hajj and want to go again. They provide the training programs and legal opinions that allow Saudis to alter Islam's most hallowed rites when they imperil security and safety.[28]

Pilgrimage agencies even promote other religious journeys as alternatives to the hajj. Most governments encourage the private sector to develop the 'umra business as a niche market, and Indonesia supports a Jordanian project to make Jerusalem a thriving center of Islamic pilgrimage. All these efforts translate into reduced pressures on Saudi Arabia and enhanced power for states with strong pilgrimage agencies.

Although hajj agencies share common structures and operations, each pursues special policies designed to reflect and change its environment. Similar facades mask different motives and interests. The global convergence of bureaucratic style and language is often outweighed by profound national contrasts in skills and resources.

All of today's leading pilgrimage bodies grew out of religious upsurges orchestrated by ambitious heads of state who staked their political lives on attracting mass support as champions of the hajj (Figure 4.4). Popular reaction to their efforts has varied enormously from country to country. Even when politicians succeed in reshaping pilgrimage to their liking, the public responds with as much denunciation as gratitude.

Symbolically and emotionally, the hajj is so great that even sincere efforts at improvement can spark anger—and hardly anyone believes pilgrimage management is apolitical. Most Muslims are justifiably skeptical of any government body that tampers with religion, whatever its motives. Worse yet, hajj agencies are usually nested inside older state bureaucracies well known for favoritism and cronyism in managing a wide range of religious activities.

# 5

# Pakistan

*"Why Would Our Hajjis Vote against Us?"*

A deep irony runs through Pakistan's pilgrimage. Zulfikar Ali Bhutto did more to encourage the hajj than any other ruler in the nation's history. In just six years, from 1972 through 1977, Bhutto sent about 400,000 pilgrims to Mecca—almost as many as all his predecessors combined. Nonetheless, the beneficiaries of Bhutto's hajj reforms were not the voters who brought him to power in 1970, and, when both his government and his life were in danger, they never lifted a finger in his defense. Indeed, many of the districts where Muslims most eagerly took advantage of new pilgrimage opportunities were the same areas where mass demonstrations helped topple Bhutto in 1977 and where people quickly fell in line behind the dictator who presided over his execution two years later.

In retrospect, it is tempting to conclude that Bhutto simply expected too much from the hajj. More puzzling, however, is the continued devotion of his heirs to the original plan of embracing pilgrimage for political gain. After assuming her father's mantle, Benazir Bhutto led the Pakistan People's Party (PPP) in four national elections, winning in 1988 and 1993 but losing in 1990 and 1997. In every election, the district-level vote for the PPP was negatively related to hajj participation.

Despite these discouraging results, the People's Party still tries to mobilize the country's largest hajj contingents whenever it controls the federal government. Undaunted, Benazir Bhutto and her advisors insist that, sooner or later, Muslim voters will reward them at the polls for championing huge and costly pilgrimages that are organized and subsidized by the state.

Why did Zulfikar Ali Bhutto bet so heavily on the hajj? Why did his strategy fail? And why do his followers cling to a legacy that seems to serve their rivals' interests more than their own?

The hajj was, in many ways, an asset for Bhutto both at home and abroad. It helped him shed his early image as a socialist firebrand and recast himself as the spokesman of a homegrown Islamic egalitarianism that was compatible with the traditional values of the masses. Pilgrimage also paved the way for Bhutto's famous alliance with King Faysal of Saudi Arabia and for visits to three dozen Muslim countries when Pakistan desperately needed foreign backing to overcome the humiliating loss of Bangladesh.[1]

But many of Pakistan's religious leaders viewed Bhutto's appropriation of the hajj as a grab for power. Most of the politically active 'ulama believed Bhutto supported Islamic institutions only because he wanted to dominate them. As his government nationalized hundreds of banks and businesses, they feared it was planning to force them into the same kind of straitjacket by placing their shrines, mosques, and schools under a central Ministry of Religious Affairs. For Pakistan's religious establishment, Bhutto's new hajj administration was a raiding party, probing their flanks and signaling the state's intention to strike at the heart of their wealth and power.

Bhutto's enemies fought back with astonishing force. 'Ulama associations closed ranks with right-wing parties, poured thousands of religious students into the streets, and launched a nationwide agitation bankrolled by business groups who were fed up with harassment from PPP cronies and bureaucrats. Fearing he would fall short of the two-thirds parliamentary majority he needed to amend the constitution at his pleasure, Bhutto panicked and rigged the 1977 elections.[2] Unable to quell the outpouring of rage that followed, he asked the army to impose martial law. At that point, Bhutto was at the mercy of General Zia-ul-Haq, who saw the PPP's efforts to establish its own militia as a threat to the armed forces and the civil service elite—the "steel frame" of career administrators that seems determined to rule the country no matter which party wins at the polls.

After the military deposed and executed Bhutto, Zia inaugurated a decade of authoritarianism around a stream of pseudo-Islamic reforms that used religion to justify crushing dissent and concentrating wealth. Zia put great effort into buying off the religious establishment, but he gave little attention to the hajj, which, in his judgment, wasted hard currency that was better spent on defense and development. As economic conditions improved in the 1980s, Zia turned up the flow of pilgrims, particularly those who could purchase their dollars and Saudi riyals overseas instead of in Pakistan.

Under Zia, the hajj became a badge of social mobility and political connection.[3] Like prosperity and power in general, the pilgrimage shifted steadily toward Punjab, especially the booming towns of the northeast that hug the Grand Trunk Road between Islamabad and Lahore. In contrast, the poorer regions of Baluchistan and rural Sindh—the People's Party's stronghold—saw hajj participation sink to a fraction of its level under Bhutto. By the time of Zia's death in 1988, the district map of pilgrimage exposed a deeply fractured nation where inequalities between ethnic and linguistic communities were hardening into castelike divisions.

One of Benazir Bhutto's earliest reforms after being elected prime minister was to reinstate her father's liberal hajj policies. Although her first government lasted only two years, it mobilized more than 100,000 pilgrims in 1990, surpassing the elder Bhutto and pressuring the PPP's opponents to match its performance when they came to power. Benazir's greatest rival in hajj promotion was Nawaz Sharif, the head of the Pakistan Muslim League, who alternated electoral victories with her while fighting his own battles with the generals who tried to run the country from behind the scenes. Even though the People's Party took the lead in politicizing the pilgrimage, it was Nawaz who reaped the greatest rewards at the polls.

Nawaz's core constituency rested in the flourishing cities and towns of Punjab. A wealthy Lahore industrialist who served as Zia's handpicked chief minister of Punjab, Nawaz was closely identified with the revival of Pakistan's private business sector and with the economic surge that pushed his native province far ahead of other regions. Punjabis are a narrow majority of the nation's population—about 55 percent—but they account for nearly two-thirds of the actual votes cast.

All pilgrims are potential voters, but the relatively affluent Punjabis benefited more than anyone else from the growing opportunities to visit Mecca. Well-to-do Punjabis who already possessed the resources to travel abroad were the same voters who gave rising pluralities to Nawaz's coalition of conservative and religious parties. Large pilgrimages helped to strengthen Nawaz's grip on the Punjabi electorate—and, through them, on the central government—no matter which party claimed credit for expediting the journey.

Yet, even in Punjab, most voters are merely aspiring hajjis. Millions of Muslims can realistically expect to become hajjis only if the government underwrites a generous package of services and subsidies, including large quotas, ample foreign exchange, and discounted accommodations. These incentives are especially important for prospective pilgrims who are women or who live in rural areas, because they are the first to suffer when hajj policies become more restrictive and the most likely to benefit when they are relaxed.

Female and rural voters are also the segments of the Punjabi electorate that are least likely to have formed a stable attachment to any political party.[4] For several years, both Benazir and Nawaz read the same public opinion polls identifying these groups as swing voters. Although many of these polls were conducted by Nawaz's advisors, it was the PPP that was most heartened by the results.

Because many uncommitted voters in Punjab are also marginal pilgrims,

Benazir's backers felt they had a golden opportunity to undercut Nawaz on his home turf. The People's Party and the Muslim League fought their closest electoral battles in about ten Punjabi districts where the margin of victory was no more than 5 percent. In tight races, PPP leaders believed their promises of liberal hajj policies could woo just enough swing voters to tip the balance.

For the PPP, remaining competitive in Punjab is a matter of life or death. Without a credible chance to win in Pakistan's pivotal province, Benazir would be left with little more than her traditional base in rural Sindh. Reduced to a permanent minority, the People's Party would face enormous temptation to become a party of regional protest. Benazir would be hopelessly squeezed between hard-liners in the central government who fear a full-blown secessionist revolt and Sindhi radicals who portray the political wreckage of the Bhutto family as proof that no southerner will ever be allowed to govern a Punjabi-dominated country.

After Pakistan's return to democracy in 1988, Benazir's Punjabi strategy paid off more often than not. The People's Party managed to build a broad coalition combining longtime pockets of strength in the cities with newer support from religious and linguistic minorities in southern and western Punjab. These gains were temporarily erased after Benazir was driven from power in 1996, but her followers quickly regrouped after General Pervez Musharraf overthrew Nawaz in 1999.

People's Party leaders refuse to be labeled as regionalists or to write off any province as beyond their reach. On the contrary, Benazir's advisors relish upsetting rival party bosses in their home districts. The PPP is particularly determined to attract pious voters in the Muslim League's backyard, and it is convinced that pilgrimage is a natural bridge to that constituency.

The larger question is not whether the PPP will bounce back but whether Pakistan can survive the passions that every party is fanning with sectarian and ethnic appeals. The hajj is merely one of the most visible battles between weak parties and well-entrenched interest groups for control over the entire spectrum of Islamic symbols and institutions. Each of these battles aggravates long-standing divisions between language groups, economic interests, and geographic regions. No matter which side prevails in any particular area of Islamic policy, the constant intersection of religious and social antagonisms exaggerates the country's weaknesses and threatens to tear it apart.


The Islamic State and the Struggle for Power

Pakistan was born an Islamic state, but its citizens spent the next half century arguing about what that means in practice.[5] Conflicting visions of Islamization mirror the interests of the power brokers who dominate the debate—soldiers, landowners, intellectuals, and 'ulama, as well as the ethnic groups that spawn them. Participants in the discussion display a disarming blend of idealism and cynicism. A friend who is a fairly traditional religious scholar once gave me a copy of an article he had just published in a popular journal. The essay was entitled "Islamic Methods of Islamization." When I asked if he was suggesting Pakistanis had devised some "non-Islamic" methods of Islamization, he answered, "Of course. Everything we've ever tried fits that category."

Pakistanis express great ambivalence about the nexus of religion and politics in their nation's development. They consider themselves fortunate that Islam endowed them with a unique identity and an opportunity to pioneer experiments that can inspire Muslims around the world. Yet they also complain that Pakistan's leaders pay less attention to "genuine Islam" than to spouting self-serving platitudes their own followers deride as "rhetorical Islam." Pointing to the gap between Islamic ideals and Islamic ideology, many Pakistanis argue that their propensity to frame political questions in religious terms is not a special strength but their Achilles' heel. A common lament is that Pakistan began as a society where religion counted more than anything, but that it is now an explosive collection of clans and sects where everything else counts more than religion.

Islam is politicized by a tug-of-war between the state and powerful religious groups such as 'ulama associations, Sufi landowners, and the Jamaat-i-Islami (Islamic Association). The hajj is one of the most valued prizes in the struggle, particularly for government leaders, who enjoy a clearer advantage over entrenched interests in this arena than in others.

Islamic groups can influence state authority in every sector where they claim a vital interest, including constitution drafting, the rights of non-Muslim minorities, Islamic research and publications, pious endowments, mosques, religious schools, and charitable contributions. But in pilgrims' affairs, successive governments advanced from regulation to sponsorship and direct control with no serious resistance.

When Pakistan's hajj policies change, it is not because rulers are trying to appease mullahs and extremists. Pilgrimage managers modify policy because each government has its own priorities and strategies for garnering popular approval. Different regimes regularly reverse one another's decisions on key hajj issues such as the size of the pilgrimage, costs of subsidies and services, and representation of regions and social groups. Yet no matter what formula Pakistani politicians select, they apply it directly by reaching out to prospective pilgrims rather than to the religious figures who claim to speak for them.

Control of the pilgrimage does not give control of the pilgrims or their votes. Many Pakistanis contend that, in an Islamic state, all rulers have a duty to provide efficient hajj services, no matter what political or economic system they espouse. When public opinion raises the bar to this level, even generous pilgrimage policies fail to engender gratitude. Besides, for voters motivated by religion, the hajj is only one of many questions demanding attention. Pilgrimage might be more salient for middle-of-the-road voters with weak religious and partisan loyalties than for committed followers of social movements with ambitious agendas.

Although governments met little resistance in taking over the hajj, in most other areas of religious life, asserting state control is more difficult. Each regime developed a different set of Islamic reforms and a distinctive style of managing religious leaders it regarded as useful or troublesome. In one field after another, the state challenged traditional scholars, mystical leaders, and radical reformers who sought to turn religious resources into political power and succeeded in many ways. Islamic groups became so dependent on official aid and so divided by factional rivalries that they regularly embrace expanding state controls instead of resisting them.

But assaults on religious leaders also made them more aggressive and imaginative adversaries. As their power contracts, they wield it more effectively and more destructively by forming alliances and unleashing street violence to offset their fragmentation and weakness in elected assemblies.

Four groups dominated the debates that created the Islamic state.[6] Most British-educated intellectuals, who led the early parties and formed the first governments, were allied with Pakistan's founding father, Muhammad Ali Jinnah. They favored a parliamentary regime inspired by vague Islamic principles that would be freely interpreted by elected lawmakers. This group also attracted Islamic modernists who answered Muhammad Iqbal's call for a religious reformation by seeking to revive the independent reason and democracy they saw as the core of Islam's original teaching.

Two opposing groups favored a theocratic vision. Most *'ulama* defended the continuing relevance of rulings handed down from classical and medieval jurists. They sought to translate these scattered precepts into coherent codes that would be the law of the land. Relying on their expertise in interpreting Islamic law, the *'ulama* claimed primacy in the bodies that created Pakistan's constitution and legal systems. Their rival and most powerful ally was the Jamaat-i-Islami, a radical reform movement drawing strength from urban middle-class followers of Maulana Maududi. Unlike the *'ulama*, the Jamaat-i-Islami found Islamic law not in inherited opinions of religious scholars but in direct study of sacred texts at the root of the faith—the Qur'an and the Sunna (customs and sayings) of Muhammad and his companions. Although Maududi's group proclaimed independence from tradition, they insisted on reading religious texts so restrictively that, in practice, they usually sided with the *'ulama* against secularists and modernists. As British-educated politicians gained the upper hand, the *'ulama* and the Jamaat-i-Islami became increasingly defiant. Instead of lobbying constitutional commissions, they turned to mass agitation. Hoping to maneuver weak governments into siding with an unpopular minority, they campaigned against the dissident Ahmadi sect, founded in the late nineteenth century, and demanded that the state declare it a heresy.

The Ahmadis were vulnerable because they questioned the completeness of Muhammad's prophecy and because they were concentrated in relatively affluent trades and professions. Many *'ulama* leading the anti-Ahmadiya riots had opposed Jinnah's demand for a Muslim state because they feared they would be unable to control it. In targeting the Ahmadis, they shrewdly sought to regain supporters they alienated before partition. Siding with persecution discredited the religious right, but their violence was fatal to Pakistan's new democracy. As civilian governments clashed with extremists, General Ayub Khan set up a martial law administration that became a full-fledged military government in 1958.

More than any other Pakistani ruler, Ayub confronted religious authorities head-on. He pushed aside most conventional *'ulama* in favor of handpicked intellectuals and technocrats whose interpretations of Islam complemented his own programs of rapid economic development. In religious reform, Ayub was a model of the rationalizing soldier. While implementing the new law on pious endowments, he placed hundreds of mosques and shrines under state ownership, pressing them into double duty as adult literacy centers and agricultural extension sites.[7]

After Pakistan's defeat in the 1965 war with India, Ayub's penchant for religious innovation drew attacks from traditionalists that helped dig the grave of his wounded regime. An early lightning rod was the Islamic Research Institute, an official group of scholars advising the government on whether its programs were compatible with Islam. This was precisely the power the *'ulama* fought so hard to reserve for themselves in the bitter debates that preceded Ayub. The institute's director, Professor Fazlur Rahman, had to flee the country when angry mullahs put a price on his head for defending bank interest and encouraging independent interpretations of the Qur'an. Soon, Ayub himself was the target of mass revolts stemming from grievances that went far beyond the elite's religious quarrels. Pent-up demands for democracy in West Pakistan and for independence in East Pakistan drove Ayub from power in 1969 and quickly overwhelmed the younger officers who tried to replace him with General Yahya Khan.

When another military defeat gave birth to Bangladesh, Zulfikar Ali Bhutto took over the government. Unlike the autocratic Ayub, Bhutto preferred to sidestep the *'ulama* whenever possible and appease them if necessary. He did his best to convince common people he was a pious Muslim—no matter what they heard about his left-wing ideas or his drinking and womanizing. Besides acting as Pakistan's greatest hajj promoter, Bhutto restored famous Sufi shrines, prepared an authoritative edition of the Qur'an, and sent migrant workers to the Middle East. Despite these gestures, Bhutto never felt his Islamic credentials were enough to stand up to religious extremists. In drafting the 1973 constitution, he gave them symbolic victories: proclaiming Islam the state religion and requiring the president and prime minister to be Muslims.

Then, in 1974, Bhutto caved in to the hard-liners who led renewed attacks on the Ahmadis.

All of Pakistan's governments, civilian and military, had rejected the 'ulama's efforts to declare the Ahmadiya a non-Muslim sect. Nonetheless, Bhutto agreed to change the constitution once again to avoid the accusation that he was protecting infidels simply because they voted for his party and financed his campaigns. From that time on, when Bhutto boasted of his "services" to Islam, he often mentioned his anti-Ahmadiya measures in the same breath with work on behalf of the hajj and Islamic diplomacy.

Unlike Ayub, who disdained the traditionalists, and Bhutto, who feared them, Zia-ul-Haq was a master at playing them against one another. Zia wooed the 'ulama with subsidies and jobs while exploiting their mutual jealousies. The centerpiece of his Islamic reform was a plan to divert the mullahs' revenues to the state and dole them out to a loyal flock of preachers, students, and bureaucrats. Zia transformed zakat from discretionary charity to a mandatory tax. Instead of making donations to local religious leaders of their choice, Muslims were expected to pay fixed amounts to regional boards controlled by Islamabad.[8]

Zia passed out money to needy students in religious schools, but only if their institutions adopted changes in curriculum and staffing that most 'ulama had resisted for years. To sweeten the pill, Zia promised that madrassa diplomas would be regarded as equivalent to public school diplomas for purposes of government employment. As a result, religious school enrollment exploded in the 1980s, flooding the job market with graduates who discovered that Zia gave no guarantee that the state could cover their salaries.

Zia's brand of Islamization was a three-way bargain that pulled bureaucrats and religious leaders into his orbit. He benefited by placing a veneer of legitimacy on a military dictatorship that grew more repressive as it sacrificed equity to growth. The bureaucracy gained control over funds and policies that had escaped state regulation for decades. The 'ulama and the Jamaat-i-Islami traded autonomy for financial aid and for the opportunity to count themselves among the state's valued partners instead of remaining impotent critics.

Zia's Islamization nurtured political alliances that outlived him, giving the People's Party's enemies remarkable organizational continuity under both military and civilian governments. Zia inherited his Islamic support from the Pakistan National Alliance—the rightist coalition that led the anti-Bhutto uprising in 1977—and many Zia appointees were businessmen and politicians who had suffered from Bhutto's bureaucrats and thugs. When democracy returned in 1988, dozens of Zia protégés joined Nawaz Sharif's Muslim League and went on to serve in parliaments and cabinets over the next two decades.

## Pilgrimage in an Ethnically Divided Society

Hajj growth closely tracks the power struggles and ideological shifts that shaped and demolished Pakistan's political regimes. Before 1970, pilgrimage fluctuated erratically[9] (Figure 5.1). Modest surges were followed by abrupt declines coinciding with the heaviest blows to the new state: the outbreak of anti-Ahmadi rioting, the declaration of Ayub's military government, and the 1965 war with India.

The PPP's victory in the 1970 elections was a watershed in hajj development. Pilgrimage shot up immediately, rocketing to its highest levels during the national despondency that followed the loss of Bangladesh.

The early 1970s were the years of Bhutto's widest foreign travels and his most frantic efforts to create an Islamic persona. The peak of hajj activity overlapped preparations for the 1974 Islamic summit in Lahore, where Bhutto gloried in hosting Muslim heads of state under the wing of Saudi Arabia's King Faysal. Bhutto reciprocated by renaming Pakistan's third largest city Faisalabad in the king's honor and by sending training missions to Saudi Arabia to bolster his armed forces.

This was also the time when Bhutto gave Pakistan one of the world's most modern systems of pilgrimage management. He set up a separate hajj directorate in the Ministry of Religious Affairs that provided funds for a central, computerized process of pilgrim selection, as well as a training institute to ensure that Pakistan's enormous delegations would be orderly and respectful when they reached the Holy Cities. Bhutto's achievements are especially dramatic when viewed in terms of per capita hajj activity rather than absolute

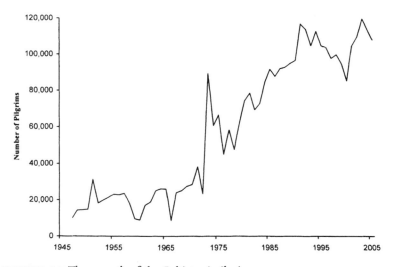

FIGURE 5.1 The growth of the Pakistani pilgrimage, 1947–2004

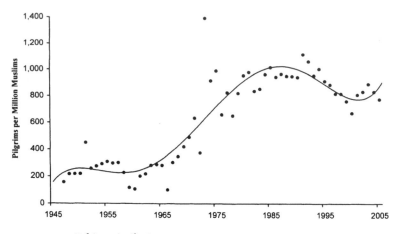

FIGURE 5.2 Pakistani pilgrimage rates, 1947–2004

numbers of pilgrims (Figure 5.2). Hajj rates under Bhutto were three to four times higher than under his predecessors. When Bhutto fell from power, hajj growth slackened and did not recover until long after his death.

Zia cut back on pilgrimage costs by adopting a two-tiered selection system that penalized applicants who bought their foreign exchange from the central bank. Zia eased these restrictions only in the final half of his reign, when the economy was in full swing. Even then, pilgrimage rates barely equaled 1970s levels. Benazir Bhutto's first government quickly surpassed Zia's hajj efforts, but no Pakistani ruler has ever matched her father's record mark of 1973. Although Zia-ul-Haq invested far less in the hajj than Zulfikar Ali Bhutto, his impact was equally profound. Whereas Bhutto revolutionized hajj organization, Zia quietly reshaped the social roots of the Pakistani contingents.

One of the few ways Zia advanced social equality was by narrowing the gender gap among Pakistani pilgrims[10] (Tables A5.1 and A5.2). Nationwide, the proportion of female hajjis increased only about 5 percent during the 1980s, but the worst interregional disparities shrank substantially. The greatest gains for women occurred in the most isolated districts—interior Baluchistan and the mountainous tribal areas along the Afghanistan border.

Generally, however, Zia's hajj reforms decisively favored the strong over the weak. In addition to raising the cost of foreign travel, Zia also abolished Bhutto's quota system for selecting applicants by region rather than by their ability to pay. Under Zia, the hajj mirrored Pakistan's growing inequalities. Because economic development became more concentrated geographically, pilgrimage also reinforced gaps that were harming relations between regions and ethnic groups.[11]

Geographic trends in pilgrimage changed enormously between 1970 and 1990[12] (Figure 5.3). During Zulfikar Ali Bhutto's administration, no region

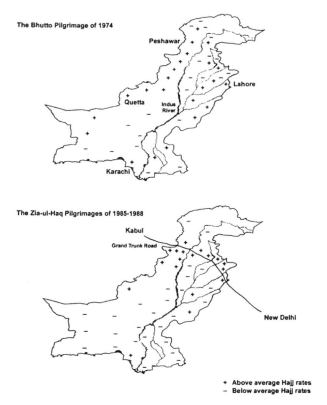

FIGURE 5.3 Geographic patterns of hajj participation under the Governments of Zulfikar Ali Bhutto and General Zia-ul-Haq

dominated the hajj. Zones of strong and weak pilgrimage cut across provincial boundaries, highlighting differences between Muslims living close to Pakistan's porous international borders and those residing in more isolated parts of the interior. Under Bhutto, the hajj was popular along the entire corridor of districts neighboring Afghanistan and Iran, as well as in the eastern areas close to India. Pilgrimage was least popular in the Indus River valley, particularly in districts straddling the river's weak lower branch (Figure 5.4).

By the end of Zia's reign, the country was split starkly between north and south. The chief axis of hajj participation shifted to the Grand Trunk Road between Peshawar and Lahore. In nearly every district along this commercial artery, pilgrimage growth outpaced advances in Pakistan as a whole. In the south, however, only a handful of districts retained strong pilgrimages. The cities of Karachi and Quetta stood out like hyperactive islands in a sea of indifference toward the hajj. Their sole companions were Multan and Bahawalpur, headquarters for some of Pakistan's strongest 'ulama and Sufi organizations.

| NORTHWEST FRONTIER | PUNJAB | SINDH | BALUCHISTAN |
|---|---|---|---|
| 1 Chitral | 17 Attock | 36 Jacobabad | 47 Zhob |
| 2 Dir | 18 Rawalpindi | 37 Sukkur | 48 Quetta |
| 3 Swat | 19 Jhelum | 38 Larkana | 49 Chagai |
| 4 Hazara | 20 Gujrat | 39 Dadu | 50 Loralai |
| 5 Malakand | 21 Gujranwala | 40 Thatta | 51 Sibi |
| 6 Mardan | 22 Sialkot | 41 Nawabshah | 52 Kacchi |
| 7 Peshawar | 23 Sheikhupura | 42 Khairpur | 53 Kalat |
| 8 Kohat | 24 Lahore | 43 Sanghar | 54 Lasbela |
| 9 Bannu | 25 Sargodha | 44 Tharpakar | 55 Makran |
| 10 Dera Ismail Khan | 26 Jhang | 45 Hyderabad | 56 Kharan |
| | 27 Faisalabad | 46 Karachi | |
| TRIBAL AREAS | 28 Sahiwal | | |
| 11 Mohmand | 29 Multan | | |
| 12 Bajur | 30 Bahawalnagar | | |
| 13 Kyber | 31 Bahawalpur | | |
| 14 Kurram | 32 Mianwali | | |
| 15 N. Waziristan | 33 Muzaffargarh | | |
| 16 S. Waziristan | 34 Dera Ghazi Khan | | |
| | 35 Rahimyar Khan | | |

FIGURE 5.4 The districts of Pakistan

The core zone of weak pilgrimage in the lower Indus Valley expanded in several directions. Taking in virtually all of Sindh and Baluchistan, it also reached into the southern portion of Punjab, where the upper branches of the Indus River come together.

It was in rural districts, rather than the cities, that Zia's favoritism toward Punjab was most obvious (Figure 5.5). Economic growth in rural Punjab was more sustained and widespread than in the villages and small towns of other regions. Under Ayub Khan, rural Punjab had already developed a strong class of small owner-cultivators, and Zia's planners gave them free rein to build larger, more efficient enterprises.[13]

Government development projects and steady remittances from migrant workers in the Persian Gulf countries helped transform the Punjabi country-side. Investment spurred capital-intensive agriculture, linked buzzing regional markets with new roads and vehicles, and touched off a construction boom that choked towns with more earth-moving equipment than they could handle.

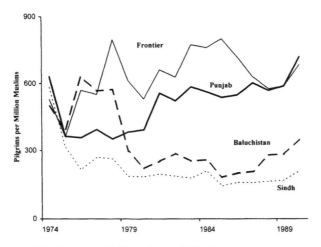

FIGURE 5.5 Pilgrimage in Pakistan's rural districts, 1974–1990

By 1990, Punjabi farmers and townsfolk were making the hajj even more frequently than the pious Pashtuns of the North-West Frontier Province (NWFP).

To a lesser degree, the Frontier also prospered under Zia. Several districts bordering Afghanistan profited from the long war against the Soviet-backed regime in Kabul. Many of the two million Afghan refugees who poured through this region came with enough money and connections to set up their own businesses and to claim a share of the arms- and drug-smuggling businesses that free-roaming Pashtun tribes have carried on for decades.

But benefits from the Frontier's wartime windfalls never matched the lasting and widely distributed gains of Punjab's green revolution. While hajj rates climbed steadily in the Punjabi countryside, they rose and fell in the NWFP with little net gain. At the time of Zia's death, rural populations in the two provinces supported the pilgrimage with nearly equal strength.

The biggest losers of the Zia years were the villages and tribes of interior Sindh and Baluchistan. The PPP's most reliable base, rural Sindh, became Pakistan's rarest source of pilgrims. By 1988, when Benazir Bhutto was first elected prime minister, rural hajj activity in her home province was languishing at about the same level it had reached in Pakistan as a whole in 1958.

Baluchistan's pilgrimage contracted even more abruptly. Zulfikar Ali Bhutto had tried to crush Baluchi nationalism by dismissing the provincial assembly and dispatching three army divisions against rebellious tribes in central Baluchistan.[14] Yet Bhutto also encouraged strong pilgrimages from northern and western Baluchistan—areas populated mainly by Pashtuns, along with Punjabi- and Urdu-speaking settlers. Zia did not resume large-scale military operations in rural Baluchistan, but he neglected the region to the point that even non-Baluchi communities had to tighten their belts and postpone their hajjs.

Under Zia, nationalist protest picked up momentum among native Sindhis and Baluchis, as both peoples felt the state was turning them into dispossessed minorities in their homelands. The chasm between rural pilgrimage in Punjab and the Frontier versus Sindh and Baluchistan poignantly illustrated Zia's redistribution of power and wealth among regions and ethnic groups.

When democracy returned, grievances stemming from these inequities were aired openly, aggravating communal conflicts that were already inflamed by long religious quarrels. Nowadays, it is commonplace for Sindhi and Baluchi nationalists to claim they are fighting the same sort of state-sanctioned racism that destroyed Native Americans and other indigenous peoples.[15]

Punjab's steady advance is also evident from pilgrimage trends in the big cities (Figure 5.6). Among the four largest Punjabi cities, pilgrimage is particularly strong in the national capital of Islamabad-Rawalpindi, where soldiers and civil servants receive special hajj leaves and subsidies. The hajj is much weaker in Multan, where city life quickly blends into a poor village hinterland.

Pilgrimage grew more rapidly in the new, mid-sized industrial centers clustering around the Grand Trunk Road than in the old metropolises of Lahore and Faisalabad. Northeastern Punjab is filled with hundreds of factories turning out everything from Sialkot's precision surgical instruments to Gujranwala's not-so-durable green washing machines. Throughout urban Punjab, rising income and status quickly translated into bigger apartments filled

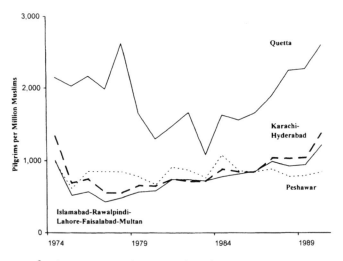

FIGURE 5.6 Pilgrimage in Pakistan's urban districts, 1974–1990

with new furniture and appliances, as well as family visits to the Holy Cities.

By the mid-1980s, hajj growth in Punjabi cities outpaced increases in Peshawar, the capital of the North-West Frontier Province and Pakistan's historic center of Islamic higher education. The war in Afghanistan brought the same economic windfalls to Peshawar that appeared in neighboring districts along the border. But Peshawar also had to carry a greater share of wartime burdens because it was the center for treating the wounded and settling the homeless.

The flow of support from Islamabad and abroad never made up for Peshawar's inadequate infrastructure. Long before the war, city leaders complained that the central government was ignoring their need for housing, schools, roads, and clinics. Overwhelmed by added stress to their weakest points, many Peshawar residents expressed resentment toward Islamabad as well as toward the refugees.

Pilgrimage growth in urban Punjab most resembled the soaring rates of Karachi and Hyderabad, the southern metropolises that attracted the largest concentration of Urdu-speaking immigrants (muhajirs) from India. The first generation of muhajirs were far more prosperous and educated than the native Sindhis among whom they settled, and they quickly assumed the roles of the Hindu merchants and landlords who fled after partition. During the last two decades, Urdu speakers have seen their local preeminence disappear as other ethnic groups poured into urban Sindh and as rival muhajir militias decimated their own community in multiple civil wars.[16]

Loss of status triggered a profound change in muhajir identity. Formerly they viewed themselves as the educated, pious elite that conceived the dream of Pakistan and uprooted their families to make that dream come true. In contrast, the children and grandchildren of the original muhajirs are more apt to see themselves as an underprivileged ethnic minority battling for the same state recognition accorded to the largest indigenous communities. Despite their vastly different experiences and self-perceptions, both generations of muhajirs have maintained strong attachments to the hajj. Even while Urdu speakers lost influence in Sindh and in the nation as a whole, they preserved a leading position in the pilgrimage.

The only urban center that consistently supported a stronger hajj than Punjab was Quetta, the remote capital of Baluchistan. Quetta is a former British garrison town guarding the Bolan Pass and the overland trade routes from Afghanistan and Iran. Quetta's residents mockingly describe their city as "the Hong Kong of Pakistan"—the country's only true free port, where the flow of consumer goods is abundant as long as the government is wise enough to ignore massive smuggling that earns foreign exchange while easing pent-up middle-class demand.

Because of its boomtown reputation, Quetta attracts settlers from every part of Pakistan. The largest communities are Pashtuns, Punjabis, and *mu-hajirs*, but no group is a majority. In fact, Quetta is one of the few districts in all Pakistan where no linguistic group can claim dominance, either numerically or politically. Aside from occasional clashes with Shi'ite protesters encouraged by proximity to Iran, Quetta seems like a model of tolerance compared with the carnage ravaging the much larger melting pot of Karachi.

Behind Quetta's casual multiculturalism and its free enterprise mania is a web of government patronage linking the Pashtuns of Baluchistan to the top levels of the hajj bureaucracy in Islamabad. The civil servant who runs the pilgrimage directorate is a powerful man—in both physique and personality—who is also a Pashtun from Quetta. Aside from his official staff, he employs a number of fellow townsmen who are fervent supporters of the Pashtun nationalist movement that is gaining ground in northern Baluchistan.

One of the more devoted members of his retinue was determined to instruct me on the continuing Anglo-American plot to conquer the Pashtun nation by dismembering its lands in Afghanistan and Pakistan. While we were lunching on kebab one day, he unfolded a paper napkin and drew a map of what he hoped would soon become an independent nation of Pashto speakers. Like most Pashtun nationalists these days, he called the territory Pakhtunkhwa, a term suggesting something like "the place of the Pashtuns" instead of the explicit claim to statehood conveyed by the older word, Pakhtunistan, which the central government regards as seditious irredentism.[17]

I often heard Pashtuns disagree about the specific territories they visualized as making up Pakhtunkhwa. In Peshawar, most party leaders expressed a minimalist view that Pakhtunkhwa should simply become the new name of the North-West Frontier Province. For them, it is enough that the existing region be known by an indigenous title instead of a colorless expression left over from colonialism.

The Awami National Party and its ethnocentric rivals in the Pakhtun Khawa Milli Awami Party (PKMAP) have more ambitious goals. They see a name change as just the first step toward carving out a larger unit that will annex northern Baluchistan to the current NWFP. Their objective is to unite all predominantly Pashtun districts in a single province that will be surpassed in size and power only by Punjab. Many describe this territory with the slogan "from Bolan to Chitral," meaning all the lands between Quetta and Pakistan's northern borders with China and Tajikistan.

Even these maximal versions of Pakhtunkhwa are modest compared with the grand design the hajj director's associate sketched for me around the corner from the Ministry of Religious Affairs. His plan does not stop at adjusting district and provincial boundaries; it reshapes international frontiers in a manner that challenges Pakistan and the whole edifice of multiethnic states tottering throughout South and Central Asia.

## Multiple Determinants of Pilgrimage: Ethnicity, Economic Development, and Party Vote

Regional conflicts in Pakistan reflect the cumulative effects of ethnic, economic, and political differences. All these factors influence hajj participation. When we compare the geographic areas dominated by Pakistan's five major ethnic groups, it is clear that pilgrimage varies just as widely as other indicators of social and political organization[18] (Table A5.3).

Ethnicity is one of the most powerful predictors of hajj activity in Pakistan (Figure A5.1). When we classify the country's sixty-two districts according to the dominant languages of their residents, it is clear that speakers of Pashto and Punjabi sent more than their share of pilgrims to Mecca between 1974 and 1990. Speakers of Sindhi and Baluchi-Brahvi sent far less than their share. Urdu-speaking districts were slightly above the national average, and Siraiki-speaking areas were about even with the country as a whole. Differences between ethnic groups' hajj levels were at least as great as the differences between provincial rates.

Pilgrimage is also linked to many measures of economic development[19] (Table A5.4). The hajj is weakest in areas with large concentrations of agricultural workers. The depressing effect of agriculture is remarkably consistent nationwide, despite wide local variations in cultivation. Pilgrimage is no higher in rice-and sugar-growing regions than in the cotton and wheat belts. Capital-intensive agriculture produces only slightly more hajjis than traditional methods. Pilgrimage increases where farmers invest in tractors and tube wells but not where they rely heavily on fertilizer and irrigation.

Land ownership is one of the few agricultural characteristics that helps distinguish rural populations with different propensities to make the hajj. Concentrated landholding dampens pilgrimage, but farm size is less critical than whether cultivators own the land they work. The hajj thrives where owner-operators abound, and it languishes where tenant farming is the rule. Individual ownership encourages pilgrimage among farmers across the board, regardless of province or ethnicity. Pashtun farmers in the arid zone south of Peshawar make the pilgrimage more often than their northern kinsmen in the fertile lands of Mardan and the Swat Valley, who must often choose between tilling big family estates or seeking work abroad. Punjabi peasants who scrape out a living in the rocky hills of Attock and Chakwal produce far more hajjis than their neighbors in the open fields of Sargodha and Jhang. Even in feudal Sindh, where tenancy still binds entire villages, rural pilgrimage is strongest in the east bank district of Khairpur, where reclaimed lands have been distributed widely.

Outside the agricultural sector, service-oriented economies stimulate pilgrimage more than manufacturing centers. The hajj is particularly popular where government is a large employer—in Islamabad-Rawalpindi and the four provincial capitals, as well as near military bases. Some of the highest hajj rates are in areas hosting the biggest concentrations of troops.

· Many forms of education and mass communication encourage pilgrimage, especially high school enrollment and television ownership. During the 1980s, the importance of literacy in Urdu and English rose steadily, but the specific ability to read portions of the Qur'an in Arabic emerged as one of the best predictors of hajj activity. Qur'anic literacy correlates strongly with pilgrimage for women as well as men and for rural residents as well as urbanites. The connection is unusually strong for females in the rural and semiurban districts of Punjab. Even though these women report much lower rates of Urdu and English literacy than males, they generally know how to read the Qur'an, and they make the hajj just as frequently as men.

Urbanization has improved as a determinant of pilgrimage, but it has never kept up with broad measures of public health and transportation, such as the number of hospital beds and motor vehicles. Like most dimensions of modernization in Pakistan, hajj growth reaches well beyond the largest cities. Pilgrimage activity is particularly striking in medium-sized towns and district capitals, where urban and rural societies constantly intersect. The small-town milieu that is most conducive to pilgrimage combines expanding economic opportunity and social mobility with enduring attachment to religious traditions. In one town after another, construction crews are hard at work on the unmistakable landmarks of the pious middle class: multistory Islamic schools, shiny neighborhood mosques, and freshly painted storefronts filled with gear and clothing for next year's hajjis.

Whenever Pakistanis are able to vote in free elections, support for the major political parties correlates with pilgrimage[20] (Table A5.5). Ever since 1970, the People's Party vote has been inversely related to the hajj, although Benazir Bhutto has fared somewhat better than her father. After Zia's death, the political benefits of pilgrimage shifted from the small religious parties to Nawaz Sharif's Muslim League. Districts with high hajj activity retained a slight bias against the People's Party, but they are more pro-Nawaz than anti-Bhutto.

In the 2002 elections, religious parties did exceptionally well in the Frontier and Baluchistan. But they swept districts with both high and low hajj activity, demonstrating regional resentment toward the military government rather than a realignment of Muslim voters. Musharraf forced both Benazir and Nawaz to remain in exile abroad, creating a vacuum the small parties skillfully exploited to vent popular anger against Islamabad's cooperation with American actions in Afghanistan. Nationally, Benazir's party polled nearly as many votes as Musharraf's allies, even though she never set foot in the country.

Together, these three factors—party vote, ethnicity, and economic development—explain about half the variance in hajj rates (Table A5.6). All three variables carry about equal weight. Sometimes ethnicity is a bit stronger and party vote is a bit weaker, but the differences are slight and suggest no stable rank order. Each factor makes a distinct contribution to pilgrimage that cannot be attributed to the others.

## Pilgrimage and the Dream of an All-Pakistan Party

Today more than ever, religion and ethnicity are the dominant forces driving electoral competition in Pakistan. Every party builds its core around a language group or sect, with a clear center of gravity in a particular territory. No party has been able to reach far beyond its communal base to recruit reliable support from a cross-section of voters in different regions. The growing vigor of communal identities benefits a number of parties, large and small, but its primary casualty is the Pakistan People's Party. While Nawaz Sharif's Muslim League tightened its grip on the Punjabi majority and a host of splinter groups found firm niches among aggrieved minorities, the PPP suffered a serious setback in its long-term ambition to build Pakistan's first truly nationwide party.

The PPP leaders have always been keenly aware of their need for a national campaign strategy. The Bhutto stronghold in rural Sindh is simply too small and too poor to serve as the cornerstone of a central government. Even if all of Karachi's voters are included, Sindh alone accounts for only about one-fifth of the total electorate. The People's Party can rule only by building a multiethnic coalition that draws voters away from powerful local parties, especially in Punjab and the Frontier. Coalition building, in turn, requires broad ideological appeals that can attract swing voters in every province. Both Zulfikar Ali Bhutto and Benazir Bhutto chose a vague blend of socialism and Islam as the prospective glue for a mass party with a mild left-of-center image. This would be a formidable sales job for any political organization, but it is particularly challenging when the popular imagination views the party's first family as feudal dynasts accustomed to living by their own rules. Marshaling state resources behind a massive pilgrimage was a masterstroke for the Bhuttos in several ways.

The Hajj Directorate provided a splendid example of the expanded services that People's Party election manifestos asked the government to undertake throughout the economy. By personally identifying the Bhuttos with the pilgrimage, party strategists cast the glow of socialism and Islam on a powerful landholding family far more renowned for its shrewdness in business than its piety. The PPP's hajj subsidies gave wavering voters an added incentive to defy local bosses and helped create swing districts in what were once enemy bastions.

Although hajj promotion has been a common theme of PPP strategy since the 1970s, Benazir uses the symbolism of pilgrimage more skillfully than her father did. The elder Bhutto followed the conventional path of presenting the hajj as a unifying force that would help assemble the widest possible collection of voters from all ethnic groups and sects. Benazir explicitly links pilgrimage with the weak and downtrodden against the privileged. Zulfikar Ali Bhutto relied on the hajj to create a mass party and, then, to rally a country that seemed to be falling apart. Benazir used the hajj to pull one group after another out of her opponents' orbit and draw them into an alliance of protest movements under the People's Party banner.

Benazir relied on the hajj to reassure skeptical Muslims that the PPP is a God-fearing party they can embrace. But she also appealed to the millions of aspiring pilgrims who feared they might never be able to go to Mecca because they were ignored by Zia and his pro-business successors. For each minority, the People's Party portrays liberal pilgrimage policies as proof of its commitment to helping outsiders become insiders. Whereas Zulfikar Ali Bhutto used the hajj to place himself in the political mainstream, Benazir uses pilgrimage to help a wide range of aggrieved groups enter the social and economic mainstream.

Under Benazir, the People's Party has been particularly active among four groups: Pashtuns in and around Peshawar, the Siraiki-speaking community in southern Punjab, Shi'ites in central Punjab, and women in northern Punjab. The hajj is important to all of these people, even though the Pashtun and Punjabi districts in the north have much higher pilgrimage rates than the Siraiki and Shi'ite areas of the central Indus Valley[21] (Table A5.7 and Figures 5.7 and 5.8).

When the PPP aggressively promotes pilgrimage, it is showing Muslims that the party shares their basic religious values. Benazir and her colleagues also want to foster an inclusive and egalitarian hajj spirit, with a special appeal to voters suffering discrimination because of their ethnicity, sect, or gender. The People's Party views the hajj as a conventional form of patronage and welfare, but pilgrimage also serves a radical strategy of opening doors to new protest movements based on language, class, and gender.

## Southern Pashtuns

The PPP has been on the attack in the North-West Frontier Province for several years. Instead of merely forging alliances with small, locally dominant parties, People's Party leaders have challenged powerful elites head-to-head on their own turf. Gradually, the PPP grew to have the widest reach in the Frontier's fragmented political landscape.

When Benazir was elected prime minister in 1988, her colleagues won control of the provincial government. The PPP became the second strongest party in several districts and frequently embarrassed local religious and tribal

FIGURE 5.7 Pakistani districts with high hajj participation, 1974–1990

leaders (*maulvi* and *khans*) who regard their assembly seats as family patrimony.

The PPP's point man in the Frontier was Aftab Sherpao, one of the largest landholders of Charsadda in the rich, sugar-growing plain just north of Peshawar. The Sherpaos are neighbors and bitter rivals of Wali Khan, head of the Awami National Party (ANP) and son of Abdul Ghaffar Khan, a legendary Pashtun tribal chief who was an early opponent of Pakistani statehood. Aftab's older brother, Hayat, was a rising star of the PPP who helped Zulfikar Ali Bhutto block Wali Khan from seizing the provincial governments of the Frontier and Baluchistan. Hayat served as Bhutto's appointed governor of the North-West Frontier Province, but in 1975 he was killed in a guerrilla bombing at Peshawar University that PPP supporters still describe as an assassination ordered by Wali Khan. Awami Party followers refute the claim, countering that Bhutto himself wanted Hayat out of the way because he was a looming competitor.[22]

When Aftab assumed his brother's mantle, the family feud provided fresh ammunition for the interlocking clan and party divisions that run through Charsadda and surrounding villages. The degree of politicization in these communities is extraordinary. Most homes and shops display flags proclaiming the

Chitral

Mohmand

S. Waziristan

Jhang

Sibi
KACCHI
Kharan
Kalat
JACOBABAD
LARKANA     Sukkur
LASBELA   DADU     Khairpur
Makran
Sanghar
Tharpakar
THATTA

— Hajj Rate < 200 per year
- Hajj Rate < 350 per year

FIGURE 5.8 Pakistani districts with low hajj participation, 1974–1990

occupants' party allegiances as though they were rooting for rival teams in World Cup cricket or football playoffs. All major parties are represented, but the PPP and ANP are the clear favorites.

Benazir added fuel to the conflict by campaigning at Aftab's side before the 1990 voting. She even agreed to run for a Peshawar seat in the district right next to Sherpao's at the same time she stood for election in her hometown of Larkana. Sherpao had a chance to repay the gesture a few years later, when Benazir feared her career was coming to an end. After she was dismissed from power for the second time and trounced in the 1997 elections, Benazir offered to resign as party leader, claiming that the army would never accept a Sindhi prime minister. At the next PPP national convention, Sherpao summoned a grand show of support for Benazir, rousing delegates to insist she be declared the party's president for life.[23]

I met Aftab Sherpao through a mutual friend, a Peshawar lawyer named Qazi Anwar who served as his attorney general when the PPP ran the provincial government. We talked at Sherpao's guesthouse on a Friday afternoon in late summer, while outside about fifty villagers returned from the midday prayer and began queuing up for their weekly audiences with the benefactor who tended to their family problems.

When Sherpao told me about the PPP's commitment to the hajj and its contribution to the party's electoral success, I was skeptical. He insisted on taking credit for the record-breaking hajj of 1990, when Pakistan sent more than 100,000 pilgrims to Mecca. Although that year's hajj occurred shortly after Nawaz replaced Benazir in Islamabad, it was the PPP government that had done all of the work before stepping down. "That was *our* hajj, and those were *our* hajjis," he boasted.

Puzzled at his good cheer after he had just been thrown out of office, I asked, "In that case, why did so many of your hajjis vote for your rivals?" In disbelief, Sherpao turned to Qazi Anwar and demanded, "Where? Where did that happen?"

I gave several examples of districts, including some in his own province, where high pilgrimage went hand in hand with a low vote for the PPP. But Sherpao's confidence was unshaken. Unwilling to accept a conclusion that seemed utterly counterintuitive, he asked in gentle protest, "Why would our hajjis vote against us?"

It was only later—when I left the guesthouse and passed the long line of pious petitioners hoping to see their *khan*—that I realized how odd my question must have seemed to a lord of the valley. Perhaps it was self-evident to him that what worked at the personal level would also work in mass politics— that one kindness would quietly invite another, creating a self-sustaining flow of favors and fealty. Sherpao probably assumed that the prospective hajjis the PPP was trying to influence were like the country folk who patiently waited to press his hand that day. In his mind, they "belonged" to him, and it was only natural for him to expect they would belong to his party as well.

People's Party leaders in Peshawar do not have to go far to find evidence that their religious and nationalist opponents dominate the Pashtun areas where pilgrimage is most popular. Year in and year out, some of Pakistan's highest hajj rates appear in three districts immediately south of Peshawar: Kohat, Bannu, and Dera Ismail Khan. The Frontier is the cradle of Pakistan's Sunni religious elite. No other region nurtures so many eminent preachers and scholars. In per capita terms, this southern pocket of the Frontier consistently ranks among the nation's top producers of religious school graduates.[24]

The southern Pashtuns also form the core of one of Pakistan's strongest religious parties, the Jamiat-i-Ulama Islam (JUI). The JUI is led by conservative *maulvis* from the Deobandi school, the country's predominant Sunni faction, which originated in prepartition India and spread all the way to Kabul. *Maulvis* enjoy greater political prominence south of Peshawar because of their traditional role as peacemakers among the many tribes that quarrel over land and transit rights along the border.[25]

Tribal leaders here are relatively weak compared with the northern *khans*, who control far more fertile estates. In a rugged milieu where secular leaders possess impressive firepower but only modest authority, religious figures can be credible arbitrators precisely because they lack the power to enforce their decisions. In these arid and mountainous zones, *maulvis'* limited access to land and weapons broadens their influence instead of curtailing it.[26]

The People's Party does not hesitate to challenge the *maulvis* on their own ground. The two parties often run close races in all the districts between Peshawar and Quetta. In 1990, a PPP candidate even upset the leader of the JUI, Maulana Fazlur Rahman, in his home district. The *maulvis* have had little success in creating a national presence for the JUI, and the popularity of Pashtun nationalism makes it hard for them to hold on to their traditional niches. The People's Party applies constant pressure on the *maulvis* to prove that no district is really safe for any party.

Like the *khans* of Charsadda, the *maulvis* of Bannu and Kohat are learning that "their hajjis" have many choices at the polls. Even for pious voters, religion is not always the most important campaign issue. The PPP will never persuade Pashtun voters that it best represents their religious preferences. But the party's strong record in supporting pilgrimage makes it easier for its candidates to shift the argument away from religion to other issues, where their candidates can expect a more sympathetic hearing. When Benazir's colleagues can highlight their views on economic equality and foreign policy, they have a better chance to identify with local grievances instead of looking like agents of impious outsiders who are manipulating the region for their own benefit.

Benazir's search for support from particular ethnic and religious groups is even more pronounced in Punjab. Although her opponents never tire of labeling the PPP a "Sindhi" party, it pulls most of its votes from Punjabis. In most elections, the People's Party was more representative of Punjab than Nawaz's Muslim League. Whereas the PPP vote is evenly spread across towns and villages throughout the province, the Muslim League draws disproportionate support from big cities and the prosperous north. Because Punjab's economic imbalances overlap with divisions of language, sect, and gender, the PPP is able to capitalize on the discontent of the region's key minorities. As the leader of disadvantaged southerners rallying against the privileged north, Benazir demonstrated that Punjab is still wide open to any party with a truly national vision. Her "southern strategy" targeted vast areas of Punjab, beginning just across the boundary with Sindh and winding up the Indus Valley as far as Islamabad itself.

## Siraikis

The People's Party made inroads in a pivotal language and ethnic group that claims to be Pakistan's oldest indigenous community—the Siraiki speakers of southern and western Punjab. Although Siraikis boast an ancient pedigree, their political consciousness is recent and modest compared with other ethnic groups clamoring for privileges. Siraiki is the fourth most common language in Pakistan after Punjabi (48%), Pashto (13%), and Sindhi (12%). It is the mother tongue for 10 percent of all Pakistanis and about 15 percent of Punjab's population. Siraikis are more numerous than the combative Urdu-speaking *muhajirs* (8%), who seek recognition as Pakistan's fifth "native" society, and more than twice the size of the rebellious Baluchi-Brahvi group (a mere 4%) that receives wider attention because of its many uprisings against the central government.

Siraikis jelled into a voting block only in the last decade. The main impetus for their awakening was a rival language movement of Punjabi speakers centered in nearby Lahore.[27] As Punjab's primacy became obvious, educated Punjabis began shifting their attachments from Urdu and its association with pan-Indian Islam toward their own vernacular. Punjabi appeared along with Urdu in schools and universities, radio and television, and the huge film industry based in Lahore. The Punjabi revival reflected the assertiveness of Pakistan's dominant ethnic group and a general decline of literary languages in favor of "national" vernaculars in Pakistan and throughout South Asia.[28]

Siraikis are newcomers to Pakistan's language wars, and their entrance is particularly jolting to the old stereotype that they are merely Punjabis with a southern accent. Compared with the other ethnic movements, Siraikis are a model of moderation. Their demands are cultural and economic rather than territorial. They are not separatists longing for statehood but Pakistani nationalists trying to improve their lot in a contentious society, where a convincing display of ethnic solidarity is virtually a precondition for counting in the balance of power.

For all their talk of cultural distinctiveness, Siraikis are fervent advocates of national integration. They link their identity more to language than race, and their language is rooted in ancient Indus Valley civilizations that occupied Pakistan's heartland. They often describe Siraiki as a pre-Aryan tongue that grew up in the city-states of Mohenjodaro, Harappa, and Taxila—Pakistan's most celebrated archeological sites and pillars of pride for all citizens. By this account, *all* other Pakistanis are *"muhajirs"*—immigrants—regardless of whether their ancestors came before or after partition.

Siraikis are especially eager to portray their culture as a bridge between the two superpowers of the Indus Valley—Punjabis and Sindhis—who have come to view one another as implacable foes. The image of Siraiki culture as a vital hinge holding together a hostile north and south includes religious life. Siraiki is described as a regional lingua franca that unites trade routes and pilgrimage centers crisscrossing the central Indus Valley. Its major literary texts are collections of mystical poetry, and its oral tradition is a treasury of Sufi folk songs.[29] Both types of works are famous for preaching brotherly love among all sects and races. The early sponsors of Siraiki literary societies were shrine keepers supervising the tombs of Sufis that attract millions of pilgrims from all over Pakistan, especially in Multan—the "city of saints" and southern Punjab's biggest urban center.[30]

As the supposedly unifying forces of Pakistani society—Urdu, the army, civil service, and universities—become preserves of particular ethnic groups, the mystical strain in Islam has enjoyed a surprising resurgence among urban intellectuals who once regarded it as superstition. Siraiki leaders frequently stress their historical connection with Sufism, appealing to all Pakistanis who want Islam to be a healing force instead of just another cause of division.

The tombs of Multan have always been multicultural pilgrimage sites where many sects and races converge to seek therapeutic interventions and blessings. Since the days of Ayub Khan, the state has lent new respectability to the shrines by toning down their rituals and regulating their finances.[31] Siraiki leaders embraced this standardized mysticism as a way of enhancing their image among educated Pakistanis.

As Siraiki consciousness grew, it spoke with a sharper tone of protest. Its cutting edge is university students and professionals who claim Punjabis monopolize the best jobs, even where Siraikis are the majority. Siraiki students demonstrated in several Punjabi universities against discrimination by teachers and employers. Siraiki graduates demand hiring quotas in the civil service and more Siraiki programming on television and radio. Their frustrations in the cities make educated Siraikis natural bridges for People's Party candidates seeking entry to the towns and villages of southern Punjab.

The PPP connects with radical Siraikis in Multan, a city that has long resented being the stepchild of Lahore. For an urban center of its size and renown, Multan is astonishingly backward in economic development and public services. Even though it is the only major city between Lahore and Hyderabad, Multan is more a living museum than a regional capital.

Arriving from Lahore, visitors step into another culture and another century. Multan complains that Punjab's provincial government cheated it twice over: by forcing talented people to move to the north and by giving the city's best jobs to Punjabi-speaking immigrants. People's Party candidates are logical beneficiaries of anti-Punjabi feeling because it is closely associated with the Sindhi fusion of cultural and economic protest sweeping Benazir's home province.

Although the Muslim League enjoys an advantage in Punjab as a whole, the PPP holds an edge in five contiguous districts where Siraikis are concentrated. Their candidates have won seats in Rahimyar Khan and Dera Ghazi Khan, where Siraikis are about 70 percent of the voters, and in Multan, where they make up at least half the rural population. The major holdouts are Muzaffargarh and Bahawalpur, where big landholders overshadow all the parties. Muzaffargarh regularly elects independent deputies, leaving Bahawalpur as the only southern district landing in the Muslim League column.

Bahawalpur is Multan's longtime rival and a center of early, "prepolitical" Siraiki activity. It is a former princely state that lobbied for special status after partition so it could overtake Multan as the unofficial capital of southern Punjab. The nawab of Bahawalpur patronized the first literary projects of Siraiki societies but not demands for Siraiki instruction in public schools or efforts at political organization.

When middle-class Siraikis became more assertive, they shifted the movement to Multan and allied with the People's Party. Bahawalpur's elite opted for a counteralliance with Lahore and the Muslim League. Siraiki politicians who thought their synthetic culture could narrow the gap between Punjab and Sindh found their own region torn apart by partisan struggle.

Multan and Bahawalpur also compete as pilgrimage centers. The two share a rare distinction: They are favorite destinations for pilgrims within Pakistan, and they also send big hajj contingents to Mecca. Sufi shrines here encourage both types of pilgrimage rather than one at the expense of the other. Sufis commonly hold special ceremonies during the hajj season, and many undertake a ten-day fast to participate vicariously in the rites at Mecca.[32]

Zulfikar Ali Bhutto tried to strengthen connections between the hajj and local pilgrimage by smoothing conflicts between popular mystics and the 'ulama. Bhutto reduced the authority of the hereditary pirs that profited from the shrines, but he wanted the public to see the state as strengthening the shrines themselves. Bhutto required major shrines to display official histories that ignored living Sufis while giving flowery biographies of the founding saints, lauding them not as miracle workers but as illustrious scholars trained in Mecca.

Benazir continued her father's appeal to popular Islam and economic grievance, but her success owed more to economics than to religion. In terms of the political effects of pilgrimage, the Siraiki region follows the same pattern as Punjab in general—hajj activity is more closely connected to the Muslim League than to the PPP. The People's Party's gains were greater in the backward rural areas of Dera Ghazi Khan and Rahimyar Khan than in urban centers, where pilgrimage is far more popular. The most prolific source of Siraiki hajjis, Bahawalpur, is the Muslim League's most stalwart supporter in the region.

Although Siraiki culture has been associated with regional and international pilgrimage for centuries, there is no evidence that Siraikis have any greater predisposition for pilgrimage than other Pakistanis. Their hajj rates are close to or slightly below the national average, corresponding to their intermediate position between the prospering north and the languishing countryside of Sindh and Baluchistan. Among Siraikis, variations in hajj activity can be explained by the usual factors of economic development and political sponsorship without resorting to local lore about a distinctive mystical personality. Nonetheless, People's Party candidates find that liberal hajj policies win them considerable sympathy among Siraiki voters, who resent being taken for granted by Punjabi politicians.

## Shi'ites

Just north of the Siraiki region, the People's Party's became embroiled in violent quarrels between Shi'ites and Sunnis. Shi'ites are about 20 percent of Pakistan's population. Although they live in every part of the country, they are particularly numerous in three areas. Isma'ili Shi'ites (often known as "Seveners" because they follow Isma'il, the older son of the sixth imam) cluster in small sects, including disciples of the Agha Khan. Isma'ilis are concentrated in Karachi's merchant classes and in the remote districts of Gilgit and Baltistan near the border with China. Pakistan's largest Muslim minority is the Ja'fari Shi'ites (known as "Twelvers"), who live in the countryside of central Punjab between Islamabad and Multan. Twelvers belong to the same Shi'ite school prevailing in Iran and Iraq. Punjabis frequently study in those countries and keep Pakistan well connected to the activism and internationalism permeating mainstream Shi'ism.

After the Islamic revolution in Iran, clashes between Shi'ites and Sunnis increased throughout Pakistan, as Tehran and Riyadh showered money and arms on militants in both camps.[33] The Punjabi district of Jhang became an early battlefield and a key target of People's Party campaigners. Jhang was the incubator for a generation of Sunni and Shi'ite extremists, who replicated their organizations and activities all over the country. One example was the notorious Army of the Prophet's Companions (Anjuman-e Sipah-e Sahaba), paramilitary Sunni zealots who gunned down marchers in Shi'ite mourning processions (azadaris) they condemned as insulting the early caliphs.[34] Many Jhang residents accused the Punjab provincial government of encouraging Sunni extremists to forestall a Shi'ite drift toward the People's Party.

The Shi'ites were galvanized by a new breed of religious leaders who rejected the passivity of the landlords and shrine keepers who dominated local politics. Jhang and its northern neighbor, Sargodha, account for 20 percent of all graduates of Shi'ite religious schools in Pakistan.[35] They were in the forefront of young Shi'ites urging their people to arm themselves and create a political movement.

When the founder of the Army of the Prophet's Companions was assassinated in 1990, Jhang was engulfed in militia reprisals and unsolved arsons. Attacks on Shi'ite passion plays escalated into open warfare with heavy weapons that drove thousands from their homes.

Shi'ite affinity for the PPP stems more from political convenience than religious commitment. The Bhutto family is of Shi'ite stock—Zulfikar is the name of 'Ali's sword—but they have always kept their sectarian affiliations ambiguous and unadvertised. Many Shi'ites regard Benazir as a "secular" leader, and they support her simply because she seems less threatening than her rivals. Even though her father is remembered as siding with the anti-Ahmadi persecutions, Shi'ites commonly view Benazir as the Pakistani politician least likely to embrace Sunni exclusivity. It is precisely because Sunni extremists savagely attack the People's Party for being "anti-Islamic" that many Shi'ites welcome an alliance with Benazir.

The Shi'ite-PPP union is fruitful in terms of pilgrims as well as voters. During the 1990 elections, when Benazir was crushed in the rest of Punjab, Jhang alone gave the PPP three of the fourteen seats it carried in the province—it was the only Punjabi district where the People's Party controlled the parliamentary delegation. Just before the 1990 election, thanks to the first Benazir government, Jhang's hajj contingent jumped from about 800 to more than 1,300, surpassing its previous high point (reached just after Khomeini came to power) but still far below the rate for Punjab as a whole. Even a friendly administration in Islamabad could raise hajj activity only so far in a backward rural society, where wealth is concentrated in a handful of families.

Shi'ite agitation soon spread northward from Jhang and Sargodha to Jhelum, located on the outskirts of the nation's capital. Here, sectarian conflict sharpened with the rise of mechanized farming and modern factories. Small farmers and wage laborers were pushed into the cities, where they found that Sunni employers reserved the best jobs for their own people. Residents returning from the Persian Gulf with added cash brought ambitions that undercut traditional hierarchy in both sects.

In the towns, Shi'ite mourning processions denounced Sunni efforts to dictate Islamic law in Pakistan and called on the Saudis to give up control over the hajj and the Holy Cities. By turning religious celebrations into mass protests, Shi'ite leaders paved the way for predictable battles with police and Sunni extremists, who stalked these demonstrations all over the country.

One of the hottest flash points is also a star producer of pilgrims. The district of Chakwal is a fast-growing textile center just south of Islamabad, where the craggy hills of the Salt Range open to the central cotton belt. Sectarian divisions have colored family, business, and political life in this area for generations, but bitterness rose sharply after the Iranian revolution and Zia's project for mandatory *zakat* collection by the state.

In 1983, Chakwal's Shi'ites attracted nationwide ridicule when a local *sayyid* (member of a "noble" family claiming descent from Muhammad) announced that his daughter was receiving revelations from the hidden imam.[36] Following her visions, about forty believers traveled to Hawkes Bay in Karachi, where they locked one another in trunks and threw them into the Arabian Sea, expecting to be miraculously transported to Iraq for a visit to Imam Hussein's tomb in Karbala. Half of them drowned, but the other half were celebrated as bereaved survivors of martyrs who laid the affliction of Pakistan's Shi'ites before the world.

After the Hawkes Bay incident, Chakwal became a magnet for every sectarian group seeking the political limelight. Pakistan's largest Shi'ite organization, the Movement to Implement the Ja'fari Religious Law (Tahrik-e Nifaz-e Fiq-e Ja'fariya), had just split into two factions. Both wings descended on Chakwal to debate one another and to drum up support for an independent Shi'ite party. Shi'ite processions in Chakwal turned into full-scale riots that journalists and politicians likened to larger disturbances in Lahore, Multan, and Karachi.[37]

The rise in violence came just as prominent Sunni groups also stepped up activities in the area. Chakwal became a frequent destination for members of the Jamaat-i-Islami youth organization and the Anjuman Sipah-i-Sahaba. Chakwal Shi'ites even drew attacks from the new Zia Foundation, created to continue the late president's religious work and supported by his son, Ijaz-ul-Haq, who became a Muslim League deputy from nearby Rawalpindi.

Much of the sectarian confrontation in Chakwal was organized not by outsiders but by local businessmen. One was a prominent Sunni leader who was having second thoughts about his actions when I visited his hometown. He was a young textile engineer who had recently succeeded his father as head of a big Sufi order.

We met at the brotherhood's main mosque and school, a lavishly decorated complex that already dominated the town square and was being expanded with revenues from busy factories the entrepreneur-sheikh managed on behalf of the fraternity. As he introduced me to his students and staff, the young man explained the problems he faced in juggling his multiple roles.

He was eager to go to the United States for graduate work but worried about leaving while sectarian relations were deteriorating. He acknowledged the brotherhood's desire to employ only Sunni workers, yet he realized such practices were causing bloodshed, and he wanted to find a fairer approach. As an engineer, he knew that he needed to prepare himself to manage a modern industry and that this preparation would probably take him abroad for at least a few years. But as a spiritual leader, it was equally important for him to remain close to his community so he could control its radical fringes.

The combination of new wealth and old quarrels has lifted Chakwal to just behind Islamabad as the busiest hajj center in all of Punjab. As in nearby Jhang, both prospering Sunnis and protesting Shi'ites drove pilgrimage to new heights year after year. Yet in many ways Chakwal is the mirror image of Jhang. Jhang is poor, agricultural, and largely Shi'ite. Although its hajj rates are rising quickly, they are still only half the Punjabi average. Chakwal is prosperous, industrial, and Sunni. Hajj rates there are more than twice as high as in the rest of the province.

Jhang and Chakwal are also diverging politically. Whereas the People's Party made enormous headway in Jhang, the Muslim League held its own in Chakwal. Chakwal owes much of its current prosperity to Zia and his successors. It was during Nawaz Sharif's tenure as provincial governor that Chakwal emerged from the shadow of Jhelum to become a separate district. Chakwal has two seats in parliament. One is a swing seat that goes to deputies from both the PPP and the Muslim League. The other is a sinecure for one of the oldest relics of the Zia dictatorship, a retired general who won every election with backing from the Muslim League.[38]

Jhang and Chakwal typify the rapid mobilization and countermobilization of Shi'ites and Sunnis in central Punjab. In both areas, soaring hajj rates are a sign of growing affluence and a symptom of deepening confrontation. Each sect promotes pilgrimage to rally the faithful and flex its muscles against the other.

The People's Party and the Muslim League compete in sponsoring the hajj, just as they compete in denouncing one another for playing sectarian favorites and allowing the Saudis and Iranians to do the same. Pilgrimage helps build new coalitions, but they behave more like armies than voting blocks.

## Punjabi Women

Competition between the People's Party and the Muslim League is most intense in northeastern Punjab, especially in the fast-growing towns between Islamabad and Lahore. In all of Pakistan, this area comes closest to supporting a two-party system where key contestants are also the dominant players nationally.

Margins of victory are slim for both parties, so small voting shifts can produce wide swings in the balance of power in parliament and the provincial assembly. Partisan combat regularly breeds violence, whether the elections are national or local. During any election season, the regional press is filled with reports of political murders, vote fraud, and court-ordered recounts.

In this pivotal region, four contiguous districts stand out as perennial battlegrounds and as hot spots of pilgrimage: Jhelum, Gujrat, Gujranwala, and Sialkot. All these areas have flourishing economies and hajjs that are unusually strong, even by Punjabi standards. They are the only districts in Pakistan where the majority of pilgrims are women. This corner of Punjab is also notable for high rates of female literacy—in Arabic as well as Urdu and English.

This constellation would seem to be ideal for the Muslim League. Industrializing towns, prospering middle classes, Punjabi ethnic dominance, conservative Sunni families that can afford to send their women to private Islamic schools and to Mecca—all are classic ingredients of electoral success for Nawaz and his followers. In fact, the two major parties are surprisingly equal in these districts. The People's Party does somewhat better in Gujrat and Jhelum, whereas the Muslim League has an advantage in Gujranwala and Sialkot. Yet, the margins of victory are usually narrow, and the results often depend on which side grabs the ballot boxes first. An even split is hardly the clear-cut outcome PPP supporters desire, but it is an excellent showing for a supposedly "secular" and "Sindhi" party trying to stay alive in the "Muslim" League's Punjabi heartland.

In this part of Punjab, Benazir Bhutto could claim considerable success in overcoming the stereotypes her rivals used against her in the province as a whole. Much of Benazir's popularity here stemmed from her appeal to pious Punjabi women who, regardless of their families' partisan ties, could see her as they see themselves—educated, open-minded, and filled with confidence about building careers and overcoming sexism.

In the electoral debacle of 1997, the PPP lost every parliamentary seat in Punjab—all 117 of them. Humiliated by her husband's scandals, by political quarrels with her mother, and by accusations of complicity in her brother's assassination, Benazir offered to resign as party leader. She claimed the same "Punjabi establishment" that killed her father was determined to destroy her as well and that the PPP could survive only by replacing her with a leader from Punjab.[39]

If Benazir believed her own rhetoric, she greatly underestimated her attractiveness to a critical portion of the Punjabi electorate. The party leaders who encouraged her to persevere understood that she poses a challenge to Punjab's politicians that neither her father nor any Punjabi male could equal. For although Benazir's enemies portray her as a corrupt Sindhi "feudal," their female relatives and neighbors think of her as a modern Muslim woman whose struggles parallel their own.

Benazir has never lost her image as a scrappy underdog taking on entrenched interests whose power far exceeds anything she can muster. Despite her privileged upbringing and her leadership of two governments, Pakistanis view Benazir as a deeply tragic figure—a permanent outsider who throws herself against the status quo with a combination of courage and vulnerability that surprises her foes and admirers alike.

Before she was convicted of financial wrongdoing, Benazir enjoyed a considerable reservoir of popularity, thanks to her father's murder and the special animus many in the army and civil service hold toward the Bhutto family for persistently attacking their authority. Beyond this, Benazir attracted an extra measure of sympathy as a symbol of protest because she is a talented woman obstructed by powerful men.

Nawaz was just as powerless as Benazir, even when heading the government. Pakistan's economy and politics were locked in a stalemate no prime minister could overcome. International donors insisted on free market reforms, but there was no constituency for them. Defense spending was untouchable, and landowners vetoed agricultural taxes. Business expected subsidized energy and transport, and the working poor could cripple any government that threatened cheap food or public employment.

Any prime minister had to share power with nonelected presidents and armed forces chiefs contemptuous of all politicians. Pakistan's prime ministers are, at best, partners in a troika where every member tries to outmaneuver the others. Even when Benazir and Nawaz managed to influence presidential succession, their own candidates still tossed them out of power and put them in the docket for corruption.

Despite their shared frustrations, Benazir and Nawaz are generally seen as personifying contradictory social forces. In the popular script, Nawaz is the tool of the establishment, and Benazir is the voice of the voiceless. Such stereotypes create openings for the People's Party in many parts of Punjab considered preserves of the Muslim League.

Northern Punjab is the core of Pakistan's burgeoning women's movement and of human rights groups that urge provincial governments to punish the widespread abuse and murder of young women.[40] Leaders of these groups are educated Muslim women who, like Benazir, are daughters of the elite but committed to defending women who cannot defend themselves.

One issue, above all, pitted Punjabi women against the Muslim League bosses who dominated local government: the rise of "kitchen killings" in which young wives are burned to death by gas stoves that explode in their faces yet miraculously injure no one else.[41] A typical case would feature a recently married woman who has just given birth to her first child. Especially if the baby is a girl, the husband's relatives will demand an additional dowry from the bride's family—a water buffalo and a refrigerator, for example. If the woman's family objects or drags its feet, she is beaten or burned. If the demands remain unfulfilled, the bride is incinerated in her own home. Even if the woman survives long enough to receive medical attention, she is so terrified that her in-laws will harm her infant that she refuses to admit the obvious foul play to the authorities.

Punjabi women's groups launched street demonstrations and court battles to force the government to intervene. The best they could accomplish was a weak measure allowing doctors and police to record dying declarations from victims willing to implicate their relatives.

Feminist organizations also protested the outbreak of a new type of sex crime—politically motivated rape. In parts of rural Pakistan, sexual humiliation of women is a weapon of feuding clans and families retaliating against affronts to their honor. During the last decade, similar attacks targeted the wives and daughters of politicians, including two highly publicized assaults on members of the People's Party.[42] If these "political rapes" were intended to intimidate potential PPP supporters, they clearly backfired. Sex crimes against the women of the only party led by a woman created far more outrage than fear. For female voters already angry at the Muslim League's indifference to the wave of stove murders, partisan rape made Benazir an even more attractive choice.

Benazir's popularity among Muslim women was a notable exception to the shifting social base of People's Party support in Punjab. In 1970, Zulfikar Ali Bhutto swept Punjab's most developed districts but lagged behind in the central and southern countryside. Under Benazir, the tables reversed: The Muslim League became the more urban party, whereas the PPP picked up new strength in the rural areas. Nonetheless, People's Party candidates continued to run well in northern Punjab, where Muslim women are gaining strength in professional and public life.

Although the Muslim League is regarded as the mouthpiece of urban Punjab's pious middle class, Benazir's party enjoys nearly equal support in districts where about half the hajjis are women. Both major parties do well where Punjabi women have high literacy rates in Arabic. Pilgrimage and reading knowledge of the Qur'an help the PPP among urban women and help the Muslim League among rural men. Yet no party can claim a lock on Punjab's religious voters, whether male or female.

## The Social Effects of Political Pilgrimage

The hajj aids Pakistan's politicians in many ways, but how does their pilgrimage management affect the country? On balance, there have been two small contributions outweighed by an enormous cost.

Partisan competition over Pakistan's hajj helped broaden religious debates instead of leaving them in the hands of extremists who reject any middle ground. Pakistan's pilgrimage has never been a preserve of the right or a target of contemptuous secularists. Because Pakistani modernists never yielded Islam to the mullahs, they still speak with authority on religious issues where open-minded Muslims see room for disagreement.

Being ahead of the competition on the hajj helps religious moderates defend more contentious proposals, such as reforming Islamic law, trimming the power of the *'ulama*, and protecting minority rights. Identifying with the hajj allows Pakistani progressives to participate in a semicivil debate about building a state that is more humane and Islamic, whereas their secular counterparts in Turkey are still grappling with the unsettling discovery that they live in a society of believers.

As for the second contribution, Pakistan's hajj has not become a state-controlled cash cow, as in Indonesia. Pakistani politicians prevented an already overprivileged army and bureaucracy from squeezing the hajj for profit and power. Pakistan's government has taken over most of the hajj business, but no one runs either the government or the business for long. Indeed, post-Zia Pakistan probably offers a preview of what lies ahead for the Indonesian pilgrimage after Suharto.

In both Pakistan and Indonesia, grassroots organizations fashioned pilgrimage networks to exchange patronage for votes—only to see their creations commandeered by military dictators. When Benazir first took power, one of her earliest moves was to reclaim control of the pilgrimage agency her father had established. Indonesia's Islamic politicians were making similar demands long before Suharto's demise. Their campaign to denationalize the hajj business Suharto took from their predecessors is quite similar to the People's Party's protective—almost proprietary—attitude toward the Pakistani pilgrimage.

Unfortunately, these gains are offset by an aggravation of ethnic and sectarian tensions that are incompatible with the essence of the hajj and perhaps with Pakistan's survival. Pakistan's hajj is still entwined with communalism in ways that push social tensions beyond the breaking point. Widening gaps in hajj activity do not simply mirror the nation's divisions; they exacerbate them.

After seizing power in 1999, General Musharraf tried to steer clear of favoritism in pilgrimage operations, at least temporarily. At first, he ran the hajj strictly by the book, letting the number of pilgrims rise close to the maximum allowed by international quotas and scrupulously apportioning provincial participation according to population size. However, when Islamic opposition parties won the 2002 elections in the NWFP and Baluchistan, Musharraf quickly changed course. Like every other Pakistani ruler—military and civilian—he used the pilgrimage to appeal for ethnic and regional support. By 2004, Muslims living near the turbulent border with Afghanistan were greatly overrepresented in the hajj and those near the Indian border were clearly underrepresented, particularly in Nawaz's stronghold of Lahore.[43]

Religious differences in Pakistan amount to far more than the subtle shading in pious temperaments that lets Anatolian subcultures imperceptibly blend into one another. Nor are disagreements among Pakistani Muslims as benign as the mystical versus modernist tendencies in Indonesia, where friendly neighbors admonish one another about the relative merits of making a second pilgrimage instead of making donations to a mosque or school.

In Pakistan, the hajj is a metaphor of economic and political struggle between rival regions and ethnic groups. It is yet another weapon in the battle rather than a respite from the war.

# 6

# Malaysia

*The Broken Piggy Bank*

No leaders in the Muslim world have displayed more imagination in harnessing pilgrimage to the pursuit of power and wealth than Malaysia's. They have carefully nurtured Malaysia's hajj agency into an internationally applauded experiment to spur modern capitalism with the aid of traditional religious values. Pilgrimage not only fosters economic development but also helps centrist Malay politicians dominate their Chinese partners in the ruling alliance and weaken the appeal of radical Islamic rivals.

However, the very political prominence that allowed the hajj agency to thrive for nearly forty years is crippling it today. The organization has become such an effective instrument of the ascendant Malay elite that it now exacerbates the same conflicts of race, class, and region that plague the nation as a whole.

## The Hajj Market Turns Bearish

The Tabung Haji—an American English equivalent would be "the Pilgrimage Piggy Bank"—began as the dream of a Malay economist who wanted to give elderly farmers a way of saving for trips to Mecca so they would not have to sell their lands and return home as paupers. In a series of well-known articles published in the 1950s, Professor Ungku Aziz proposed that while poor Muslims watched their yearly deposits accumulate, fund managers would invest the capital in new Malay-owned businesses that might one day challenge Chinese and foreign control of the economy. He envisioned the enterprise as a form of interest-free Islamic banking, where depositors and lenders share profits and sometimes ownership with borrowing businesses.[1]

The pilgrimage fund was launched in 1963, and in 1969 it merged with the older hajj welfare board to form the nucleus of Tabung Haji. The organization meshed perfectly with the new economic policy designed to redress Malay grievances that had triggered the race riots of 1969. Before long, the pilgrimage fund blossomed into one of Malaysia's most diversified holding companies. Today, Tabung Haji's corporate headquarters are perched atop a sleek skyscraper the agency built for itself just off Jalan Ampang, the upscale shopping boulevard winding along the western leg of the Golden Triangle in downtown Kuala Lumpur. A tapered, concave cylinder that seems to soar far beyond its thirty-five stories, the landmark is an endearing star of popular television commercials running throughout Ramadan and the hajj season. Computer graphics slowly rotate a three-dimensional likeness of the tower and magically morph it into a desktop coin box, leaving a slit in the roof where viewers can imagine tossing in their loose change.

In fact, Malaysian Muslims entrust the pilgrimage fund with much more than pocket change. More than four million Muslims—about half the adult Malay population—are depositors of Tabung Haji. Their savings exceed 10 billion Malaysian ringgit (around $2.64 billion), most of which is invested in thirty subsidiaries and joint ventures. These holdings are spread among all of Malaysia's major industries, including rubber, palm, and cocoa plantations, food products, real estate, construction, textiles, clothing, cement, building materials, chemicals, fertilizers, electronics, telecommunications, publishing, advertising, and pharmaceuticals.[2]

Tabung Haji has lost most of the luster that surrounded its creative beginnings. Although the rest of the Muslim world still views it as a pacesetter in hajj management, Malaysians began losing their fascination with the agency long ago. When the Tabung Haji headquarters first opened for business, it dominated the skyline as the tallest building not just in Malaysia but in the Islamic world. Nowadays, it is barely noticeable in aerial photographs of the city, overshadowed by more than a dozen steel and glass towers of the banks, hotels, and office centers that belong to far weightier players in Malaysian capitalism. The top floor of the Tabung Haji building still offers spectacular views of the mountains to the northeast, but even they seem tainted in the eyes of the pious bureaucrats working there. When I marveled at the unobstructed view of the Genting Highlands resort area in the neighboring state of Pahang, one of my hosts quickly reminded me that I was not seeing the complete picture. "That's not a good place for Muslims," he cautioned. "There's a casino up there where gambling is still legal."

Before long, I heard government opponents throughout Malaysia making almost identical criticisms of Tabung Haji itself: It is not a good place for Muslims to put their money because the state gives it to private speculators who gamble with the people's savings.[3] For years, Tabung Haji officials refuted such claims, insisting that all investments were managed by a permanent finance committee staffed solely with senior civil servants and Islamic scholars. But in 2002, the agency was rocked by a major scandal that seemed to vindicate the worst allegations of financial mismanagement.

Tabung Haji admitted it had violated its own rules by turning over $52 million to private fund managers who lost at least $20 million of it in high-risk ventures, including foreign currency trading.[4] Financial scandals are not exactly earthshaking news in Malaysia, but even the pro-government press was filled with outrage. Everybody agreed that Tabung Haji must be held to a higher standard than other investors because its funds are not an ordinary pool of savings but a sacred trust that every Muslim counts on. With newspaper editorials describing the loss not simply as incompetence but as a betrayal of the state's commitment to Islam, Prime Minister Dr. Mahathir Muhammad and his deputy, Abdullah Badawi, personally pledged to clean house at Tabung Haji and to sue the investment firm for restitution.[5]

Even before it drew the attention of prosecutors, Tabung Haji was facing many obstacles that threatened its growth and very survival. Although aggregate returns on investments rose steadily, yield was mediocre by the standards of Malaysia's burgeoning capital markets. During the 1990s, Tabung Haji's annual dividends fell to about 6 percent—well below returns from private enterprises, particularly those benefiting from foreign investment and technology.

In recent years, only the National Workers' Pension Fund has posted lower earnings than Tabung Haji. Poor performance by the workers' fund prompted a nasty exchange of insults between Prime Minister Mahathir and angry union leaders, who accused the government of using retirement savings for sweetheart loans to cronies in the ruling party. Mahathir snubbed the unionists' requests for an audience and scolded them as ungrateful troublemakers. At first, he passed them off to his former deputy and heir apparent, Anwar Ibrahim, who kept canceling their meetings until the row dropped out of the headlines. But during the meltdown of Asia's financial markets in 1997 and 1998, Anwar himself led the attack against using public funds to bail out sinking Malay businesses.

Tabung Haji is experiencing a far more damaging wave of protest from its own depositors. Prospective hajjis can respond to weak earnings in less clamorous yet far more effective ways than workers. Increasing numbers of depositors simply avoid making large advance payments; they put their money to more profitable use until a year or two before they intend to go to Mecca. Then, they deposit the equivalent of several installments in a Tabung Haji account just in time to qualify for the discounted package tours. Such "free-rider" hajjis boost the agency's short-term profits from travel services, but they undercut its already sagging role as a national entrepreneur.

An even greater danger for Tabung Haji lies in the limits on the number of pilgrims it can send to Mecca. The international quota system abruptly froze Malaysia's hajj market, choking the agency's biggest revenue stream before its other investments matured to the point where they can take over in fueling future growth. Knowing that quotas would quickly produce shortfalls in financing, Tabung Haji fought a hard but losing battle to wring exemptions and delays from Saudi Arabia in implementing the system. During the early 1990s, the Saudis agreed briefly to a unique regional quota for all of Southeast Asia so Indonesia's neighbors could share the unused portion of its enormous allotment of 180,000 pilgrims. This allowed smaller and wealthier countries such as Malaysia, Singapore, and Brunei to continue sending pilgrims at rates far exceeding the global guideline of 1,000 hajjis per one million people.

By 1993, however, Suharto expanded the Indonesian pilgrimage so quickly that it was nearing the numerical limit, and Jakarta withdrew from the pact. That year Saudi Arabia insisted on applying the quotas to Malaysia and Singapore for the first time. The Saudis substantially softened the impact by permitting both countries to size their delegations according to total population figures rather than their Muslim populations—only 55 percent in Malaysia and a mere 17 percent in Singapore. This concession left Malaysia with a rate of hajj participation that was still twice the international norm.

Nonetheless, about 40 percent of Tabung Haji's business vanished overnight. After peaking at more than 43,000 in 1992, the Malaysian pilgrimage fell to 24,000 in 1994 and 25,000 in 1995[6] (Figure 6.1).

Malaysia reluctantly obeys the quotas, recognizing them as a binding collective decision of the Organization of the Islamic Conference. At the same time, Tabung Haji continues pressing the Saudis for new concessions to ease

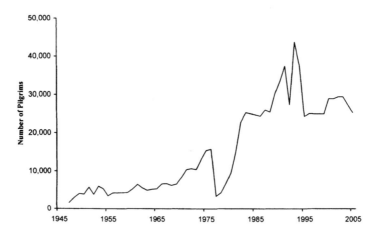

FIGURE 6.1 The growth of the Malaysian pilgrimage, 1947–2004

its economic setbacks. Malaysian pilgrimage managers try to avoid public quarrels that might jeopardize their working relations with Saudi officials, but they fear Saudi Arabia is too willing to sacrifice Malaysia's interests in order to coax Indonesia into an alliance against Iran.

Visitors to Tabung Haji's headquarters see a poignant expression of their unhappiness with Saudi Arabia in the grim rooms set aside to memorialize Malaysian pilgrims who perished in the Mu'aisim Tunnel disaster of 1990. The 1,426 hajjis crushed in the tunnel stampede included about 150 Malaysians. Photos of their mutilated corpses rest behind a long row of black curtains that normally conceal the view from unsuspecting eyes. Escorts draw the curtains, turn their heads away from the pictures, and recite a quiet prayer. Then, they softly explain that the mangled and severed body parts were retrieved from mountains of human remains that Saudi bulldozers haphazardly threw up near the tunnel entrances.

After failing to persuade Saudi Arabia and Indonesia to provide a way around the quotas, Tabung Haji leaders tried to shore up their position with a new law designed to give them a tighter monopoly over pilgrimage traffic. Realizing they could no longer avoid smaller pilgrimages, they sought exclusive control of what remained. New amendments to the Tabung Haji Act require all pilgrims to enroll directly with the government's program or with a small consortium of approved travel agents. These measures were doomed to failure from their inception. They are openly flouted throughout the country, and it is hard to imagine they will ever be enforced effectively. They are a futile attempt to support in law a state monopoly that long ago disappeared.

Tabung Haji has built one of the most modern and profitable pilgrimage administrations in the world. Yet, it also has fostered one of the largest streams of illegal pilgrims—Muslims who insist on observing the hajj as their ancestors did, even if this means defying both Malaysian and Saudi Arabian authorities. Travel agents and hajj officials estimate that Malaysia sends at least 10,000 fugitive pilgrims to Mecca each year, meaning that one of every three Malaysian hajjis is illegal.

Most fugitive pilgrims go to Saudi Arabia a few months before the hajj season, usually for the fast of Ramadan. They enter the country with visas not for the hajj but for the 'umra, the "smaller pilgrimage" to Mecca that can be performed any time of year. Then, instead of returning home, they overstay their visas, hiding in the homes of Malay residents of Saudi Arabia, in out-of-the-way lodgings provided by travel agents, or in the flood of foreigners that overwhelms Mecca just before the hajj. Normally, these gate-crashers run little risk in either Mecca or Malaysia. They do their best to stay out of sight, and Saudi authorities tend to ignore them unless they run into trouble. If they are unlucky enough to get caught, the police simply make them leave the country. If they are destitute or ill, the Saudis may even pay for their return trip.[7]

Malaysian officials publicly deplore these practices, but they do little to prevent them or to punish those apprehended. After all, under the new quota system, every illegal pilgrim creates room for someone else Tabung Haji would otherwise have to turn away. Besides, the government can argue that the very magnitude of the fugitive traffic proves Malaysia has legitimate grievances against the current system.

Tabung Haji's decline is a result of several factors—economic, cultural, and political. The government tries to discourage repeat pilgrimages by imposing a surcharge on those who obtained hajj visas in the past. The penalty increases according to the number of previous trips to Mecca, adding up to a sizable tax even for pilgrims willing to play by the new rules. Another disincentive is the very system of installment payments that once made Tabung Haji so attractive. Now that its accounts are paying below-market dividends, pilgrims are reluctant to tie up their money, especially when most private travel agents require no advance deposits for their services, legal or not.

No matter how reasonable the price, many Malaysians demand more from their experiences in the Holy Cities than package tours can offer. For at least a century before Tabung Haji's creation, Malay pilgrims were well known for combining arduous ocean voyages with extended periods of residence in the Hejaz. Mecca hosted a large community of Malay-speaking pilgrims who remained there to study and work, to raise families, and sometimes to die. In the last twenty years, this leisurely style of pilgrimage has given way to rapid, standardized trips that reduce hajjis' time away from home and homogenize their exposure to the Holy Cities and to one another.

Malaysians demonstrated remarkable resistance to the "modernization" of pilgrimage. Between 1975 and 1980, Tabung Haji quickly shifted virtually all of Malaysia's pilgrim traffic from steamships to airliners. By this time, most other countries already had completed similar changeovers and were doubling or tripling their pilgrimage business. In Malaysia, however, many people feared the government was replacing popular traditions with restrictive practices motivated by greed and politics. During the first year of the transition, the Malaysian pilgrimage fell from 16,000 to only 3,500 and did not recover until the next decade. Some of the setback stemmed from temporary hitches in the changeover from sea to air travel and from shortages of foreign exchange when tin and rubber prices slumped on the world market. But Tabung Haji's growing power also provoked religious critics, who encouraged Muslims to boycott the agency. Conservative religious leaders predicted that pilgrims would actually miss spending long weeks at sea. They feared that jet travel left no time for the shipboard lectures and group discussions that gave previous generations of Malays the spiritual preparation they needed for a successful hajj.

Tabung Haji answered these attacks by launching new predeparture courses to teach prospective pilgrims about the requirements and meanings of the hajj. They developed intensive three-day training sessions for groups of 100 to 150 pilgrims and offered them in about 180 sites throughout the country.[8] Yet, as the government assured critics it was not turning pilgrimage into mass tourism, the new courses themselves spawned even greater controversy.

Before becoming prime minister, Mahathir was entangled in a well-publicized spat over Tabung Haji's unorthodox training methods. In 1975, while serving as minister of education, Mahathir unleashed a vigorous counterattack against university students who criticized the government for defaming Islam. Student groups in London and Kuala Lumpur accused the ruling party of desecrating Muhammad's birthday celebrations with processions that included effigies of the Prophet. Mahathir insisted that the students were spreading malicious rumors. Mahathir explained that the alleged incidents really concerned representations of the *Ka'ba* that Tabung Haji was using in its new classes. One of the highlights of the program is a simulated circling of the *Ka'ba*, complete with future pilgrims in *ihram* dress walking around a portable model of God's House. According to Mahathir, the students knew the truth but cooked up their story to sabotage the government's hajj campaign.[9]

Such confrontations enhanced Mahathir's reputation as a pugnacious leader. By cracking down on unruly campuses and revoking the scholarships of political troublemakers, he gave Malaysians a foretaste of how he would soon govern the entire country.

## A Demographic Profile of Malaysian Pilgrims

Once Tabung Haji completed the transition to air travel in the 1980s, pilgrimage rates rose again. Malaysians adapted to the new system and welcomed its greater comfort and safety. However, despite a rapid increase in the number of hajjis, their social backgrounds changed little. Compared with pilgrims from other countries, Malaysian hajjis remain disproportionately female, young, and middle class.[10]

Female pilgrims have been the majority of Malaysia's delegation for more than three decades (Table A6.1). Between 1968 and 1975, when women accounted for only 35 percent of the world's hajjis, they had already surpassed 53 percent in Malaysia. Since 1979, their share has remained remarkably consistent, averaging 55 percent and never falling below 53 percent.

Malaysian pilgrims are also quite young (Table A6.2). Most are in their fifties, and a similar number are in their thirties and forties. On the other hand, elderly pilgrims are rare. Only about 7 percent are seventy or older.

Pilgrims' occupations have shifted slightly, reflecting the economy's gradual movement from agriculture and public employment toward private services (Table A6.3). The most striking switch was the steady decline of farmers in favor of the self-employed. Civil servants never rose above 13 percent, and smaller groups such as pensioners, traders, and workers hardly changed at all.

The largest category is housewives, averaging about 35 percent of the total. At least 20 percent of all Malaysian pilgrims are women employed outside the home. The actual share of working women is probably much higher because many wage earners are also likely to identify themselves as "housewives," particularly when reporting personal information to a religious agency.

In contrast to minor changes in gender, age, and occupation, abrupt shifts occurred in geographic origins (Table 6.1 and Figure 6.2). Since the 1960s, rapid pilgrimage growth has reflected widening gaps in the economic, religious, and political characteristics of Muslims in different states. In the more modern and prosperous west coast region between Kedah and Johor, the hajj flourished until Malaysia was forced to adopt quotas during the 1990s.

In the poorer and more isolated states, pilgrimage is just beginning to take off, or it has already slipped out of the government's control. In the remote eastern regions of Pahang, Sarawak, and Sabah, pilgrimage has always lagged behind the national average. Where Islamic opposition groups are strongest— in the northern states of Kelantan, Terengganu, and Perlis—Tabung Haji confronts a mounting flow of clandestine pilgrims who openly flout its monopolistic pretensions.

TABLE 6.1 Regional distribution of Malaysian pilgrims, 1969–1995 (average annual number of pilgrims per million Muslims)

| State | 1969–1970 | 1971–1975 | 1976–1980 | 1981–1985 | 1986–1990 | 1991–1995 | 1969–1995 |
|---|---|---|---|---|---|---|---|
| Perlis | 1,116 | 1,659 | 1,252 | 2,881 | 3,762 | 2,707 | 2,767 |
| Kedah | 2,007 | 2,129 | 1,067 | 3,228 | 3,561 | 3,174 | 2,586 |
| Penang | 1,414 | 1,850 | 1,028 | 2,404 | 3,215 | 3,438 | 2,315 |
| Perak | 1,103 | 1,418 | 848 | 2,051 | 3,037 | 2,926 | 1,985 |
| Selangor | 1,166 | 2,865 | 1,433 | 2,975 | 3,391 | 3,072 | 2,630 |
| Negeri Sembilan | 1,560 | 1,887 | 1,197 | 3,242 | 4,437 | 3,556 | 2,767 |
| Malacca | 1,846 | 2,287 | 1,528 | 4,400 | 5,317 | 4,069 | 3,396 |
| Johor | 1,007 | 1,512 | 1,075 | 2,354 | 3,100 | 3,073 | 2,133 |
| Pahang | 1,090 | 1,209 | 724 | 1,661 | 1,964 | 1,847 | 1,452 |
| Terengganu | 1,593 | 1,911 | 1,348 | 4,203 | 2,864 | 2,027 | 2,406 |
| Kelantan | 3,187 | 2,984 | 1,340 | 3,746 | 2,518 | 1,324 | 2,442 |
| Sabah | 1,108 | 1,478 | 474 | 1,284 | 1,286 | 1,161 | 1,134 |
| Sarawak | 1,260 | 1,645 | 653 | 2,142 | 2,236 | 2,236 | 1,744 |
| Malaysia | 1,518 | 1,968 | 1,067 | 2,717 | 2,920 | 2,515 | 2,184 |

FIGURE 6.2 The states of Malaysia

## The Mahathir-Daim-Anwar Regime and the Decline of the "Malay Way"

Tabung Haji's checkered performance in the states parallels the shifting fortunes of the ruling party, the United Malays National Organization (UMNO).[11] When Mahathir became prime minister in 1981, he frequently aggravated factional conflicts in the Malay community and in his own party. His career unfolded around bitter battles in which he championed the Malay middle class over the aristocracy, private enterprise against the public sector, and a pro-Islamic regime instead of a secular state.[12] Each struggle degenerated into personal feuds that left resentments smoldering years after policy differences were settled.

Mahathir's appetite for confrontation was an abrupt departure from traditions of secretive bargaining between ethnic elites who pledged to restrain their communities. Lee Kuan Yew, who became president of independent Singapore, dubbed him the "Malay ultra" when he spurned Lee's call for a "Malaysian Malaysia," where race would carry neither privilege nor stigma.[13] By the time Mahathir subdued his rivals in UMNO and humiliated his handpicked successor, Anwar Ibrahim, there was nothing left of the once cherished "Malay way"—the code of deference and mutual accommodation that muted conflicts for earlier generations.[14]

A decade before he became prime minister, Mahathir accused Malaysia's founding fathers of selling out to Chinese and British business interests. Taking on Tunku Abdul Rahman, the head of the independence movement, he charged that UMNO neglected the rights of *bumiputras* ("sons of the soil")—indigenous Malay Muslims who occupied the peninsula before British colonialists imported Chinese and Indians to work the plantations and tin mines. Mahathir was particularly irked by UMNO's complacency over the unequal division of labor between races reflected in Abdul Rahman's admonition to "Let the Chinese be traders and the Malays be politicians."

His revolt against Tunku Abdul Rahman was the opening shot in a long effort to break the power of the Malay nobility. Both men came from the northwestern state of Kedah, but they represented different classes and generations.

The Tunku skillfully interwove Malay nationalism with Britain's economic interests and the sultans' political prerogatives. Insisting that the Chinese would be politically unreliable no matter how many millionaires they produced, he convinced the British that the only stable government would be one dominated by Malay politicians and Malay princes. His bargaining position was greatly strengthened by the key role of Malay fighters in the colonial forces that put down the mainly Chinese communist insurgency of the 1950s.

In contrast, Mahathir was a small-town doctor with no aristocratic ties who was educated locally rather than in England. The Mahathir family home in Alor Setar is just across the river on the edge of town, and its humble surroundings are worlds apart from the princely mansions and gardens that grace the city center.

In the government of Tun Abdul Razak, Mahathir was a star among the young technocrats driving the social reforms of the 1970s. As minister of finance, he created several state-run trusts that took over foreign companies on behalf of the Malay community. These firms became corporate incubators for politically connected Malays who filled overlapping directorates in countless enterprises, public and private. Mahathir allies took up positions in UMNO's Fleet Group—the holding company that showered new Malay businesses with government loans and licenses.

Mahathir appointed Daim Zainuddin, a wealthy industrialist who also came from Kedah, to all the top economic posts in the party and government. By 1985, Daim headed his own corporate network as well as the ministry of finance, the UMNO treasury, and the Fleet Group.[15] Daim led privatization programs allowing a small group of companies to acquire properties the state supposedly held in trust for all Malays.

In their eagerness to cultivate Malay millionaires, Mahathir and Daim provoked intense struggles within UMNO. In 1987, Mahathir was nearly overthrown by rivals condemning the privatizations as giveaways to Daim's cronies, who kicked back huge campaign contributions to keep Mahathir in power. The insurgents won a stunning court ruling that declared UMNO illegal and ordered it to divest its commercial empire. UMNO had to spin off assets, but they went to new conglomerates owned by proxies and party figureheads. Each month, Malaysians learned new details about the "money politics" that tainted UMNO's fratricidal leaders, even as it helped them cling to power.[16]

One of UMNO's most costly projects was the North-South Expressway running all the way from the border with Thailand to the Singapore causeway. Built by United Engineers, a private company passed around by various UMNO affiliates, the expressway was the greatest stimulus to regional integration that any Malaysian government has undertaken.[17] Opposition parties spent years exposing the string pulling that surrounded the contract, but eventually the superhighway wound its way through the home districts of every UMNO kingpin between Alor Setar and Johor Bharu.

Reports that the ruling party was "for sale" flew during the battle to select Mahathir's successor as UMNO president and prime minister in 1993.[18] The victor, Anwar Ibrahim, was the former leader of radical Islamic students in Angkatan Belia Islam Malaysia (ABIM, "The Islamic Youth Movement of Malaysia"). Just months after Mahathir took power, knowing Anwar was on the verge of joining UMNO's religious opponent, Parti Islam SeMalaysia (PAS, "The Islamic Party of Malaysia"), he asked Anwar to head the UMNO Youth Group.[19]

Everyone understood that Anwar was being groomed for a top position. After serving as youth minister and agriculture minister, he took over education and then finance, the same posts Mahathir held before becoming prime minister. Soon Anwar was also Daim's favorite as heir apparent because he could calm foreign investors who feared Malaysia was falling into the hands of fanatics.

Anwar had a long list of opponents—those he inherited from Mahathir and those he acquired on his own. Islamists viewed him as a hypocrite who sacrificed his dream for an Islamic state to serve a regime that made only empty gestures of faith. Secularists saw him as an upstart exploiting religion to grab power for newly enriched business elites.

Anwar's "American-style" campaign for UMNO's deputy presidency was expensive and divisive. He unseated a much older leader from Malacca, Abd Ghafar Baba, who was one of Mahathir's strongest allies in trimming royal powers and putting down party revolts.[20] Anwar claimed his enemies were trying to turn Ghafar Baba against him, leaving him no choice but to seize the top positions for his own people. UMNO partisans touted the showdown as a display of party democracy, but Anwar was denounced for spending millions to buy a newspaper and television station so he could mount a steady stream of personal attacks against his rivals.

Anwar Ibrahim's rise sharpened debates over the future of Islam in Malaysia. Mahathir claimed state support for moderate Islam yielded vital benefits—checking religious fanaticism and spurring the economic growth that allows a pluralistic society to survive. But his critics argued that he made Islam the keystone of a "Malay first" policy that demanded racial hegemony as the price for social peace.

The social compact fashioned by Mahathir, Daim, and Anwar inspired scant enthusiasm among either Malays or non-Malays. It is a bargain that is viable only if an expanding economy lulls Malaysians into ignoring its inherent inequities and abuses. The obvious fragility of such an arrangement explains why Malaysians are so preoccupied with business rumors and consumer fads. Any sign that the "Malaysian miracle" is faltering stirs resentment between ethnic communities and within them. Pride in tolerance and prosperity is constantly balanced against fear that everything could unravel the moment foreign trade and investment turn sour.

Both Muslims and non-Muslims suspect their government is less interested in modernizing Islam than in twisting it into an ideology of profiteering authoritarianism. Mahathir blurs distinctions between Islam and Confucianism by exhorting Malays to emulate their wealthy Asian neighbors instead of religious zealots in the Middle East or consumer zealots in Europe and North America. His "Look East" policy is filled with polemics and stereotypes—the disciplined productivity of Japan, Taiwan, and South Korea versus the hedonism of the West.

"Looking east" implies many things in Malaysia, but it really means looking backward more than forward. An eastern focus tells upwardly mobile Malays that their culture is compatible with modern capitalism. The government constantly reminds them that Islam encourages hard work and frugality and that it provides the moral rudder they need to navigate the temptations of success. Yet by portraying Malaysian Islam as a hybrid "Asian value system," Mahathir encourages conformity and patriarchy over innovation and freedom. The Look East campaign is the centerpiece of a counterattack against Westerners who criticize Malaysia's political repression and racial discrimination.[21]

Accusing the West of neocolonialism, Mahathir insists that Asians have their own models of democracy and human rights that stress respect for authority and tradition. Unfortunately, his sermons on cultural relativism are little more than rationalizations for his own use of quotas, censorship, and "expedited justice."

A "more Confucian" Islam is unlikely to improve Malaysia's race relations or its commerce in the Pacific basin. But it does strengthen intolerant and undemocratic religious currents UMNO has battled for decades—puritanical groups advocating the adoption of Islamic law and its imposition on non-Muslims. Mahathir prevented coordination among these movements by crushing fundamentalist societies such as Darul Arkam and offering powerful posts to scores of student leaders.[22] Yet just when these threats seemed neutralized, religious militancy reemerged in PAS, where a new generation of leaders learned to cooperate with the Chinese opposition.

## The Anwar Fiasco: Othman Fights Back and Mahathir Bows Out

The financial crisis that shook Asia in the late 1990s did not devastate Malaysia's economy as much as its neighbors', but it plunged the elite into a tragicomedy of mudslinging and self-destruction. By unleashing a torrent of lurid accusations against one another, Mahathir, Daim, and Anwar—the three most powerful men in the nation—discredited themselves and the institutions they devoted their lives to nurturing.

Mahathir and Daim scrambled to cope with a sinking ringgit and mounting bankruptcies and to avoid a prolonged recession that would let foreigners gobble up Malay industries in a fire sale. Rejecting the unanimous advice of economists and international lenders, they decided to lower interest rates and increase public spending.[23]

In contrast, Anwar feared that a bailout of pampered Malay millionaires would come at the expense of ordinary workers and consumers. As minister of finance, he argued that complying with foreign demands for tighter credit and spending was in the interest of the majority, no matter how much panic it created among cronies of the ruling party. Mahathir and Daim wanted to relax collections on nonperforming loans, but Anwar tightened them by declaring defaults after three months instead of six.[24]

Anwar's economic reasoning was impeccable, but his political timing could not have been worse. Just a month after Suharto was toppled in Indonesia, Anwar's supporters used the annual UMNO convention to attack the government for corruption and nepotism. Fearing that Anwar was about to launch the same sort of reform movement sweeping Indonesia, Mahathir ordered a preemptive strike.[25] In the prime minister's eyes, his heir apparent had become too apparent, too soon.

Mahathir fired pro-Anwar editors at two leading Malay-language newspapers.[26] Then he reopened an investigation into supposedly groundless accusations that Anwar was carrying on multiple sexual adventures and using his office to cover them up. Responding to tips from Anwar's "victims," police raided an apartment allegedly used for the assignations and seized a semen-stained mattress for DNA testing. Soon the world learned that the "real" Anwar was a sodomite and adulterer who had forced himself on his adopted brother, his (male) speechwriter, his (male) secretary's wife, his wife's (male) driver, and his wife's (female) secretary.[27] Mahathir claimed he had spoken with Anwar's supposed sex partners and that he believed their confessions. But Mahathir never explained why he rejected their later charges that the statements were false and had been extracted with police intimidation.

In September 1998, Mahathir sacked Anwar, describing him as "morally unfit" to hold office, let alone to become prime minister. Mahathir forced Anwar's associates out of the Finance Ministry and reappointed Daim as his chief economic advisor. Daim then approved low-interest loans from pension funds to bail out several failing companies, including a firm belonging to one of Mahathir's sons.[28]

Malaysians responded to Mahathir's mini-coup with the largest and most violent protests since the race riots of 1969. Anwar took to the campaign trail, calling for a Malaysian version of "people's power" and *reformasi* at mass meetings in Malacca, Johor, Penang, Kedah, and Kelantan.[29] In Kuala Lumpur, a crowd of 35,000 demonstrated outside the National Mosque and swelled to 50,000 by the time it clashed with police in Merdeka Square.

In late September, Anwar was arrested, beaten during interrogation, and put through a seven-month show trial that mimicked the private degradations he supposedly inflicted on others.[30] His wife, Wan Azizah Wan Ismail, took his place at the head of a burgeoning opposition alliance—the Barisan Alternatif—that prepared to challenge the Barisan Nasional in the coming elections. Wan Azizah's new Keadilan (Justice) Party adopted a black-and-white eye as its symbol, reminding voters of the black eye that the police gave Anwar while he was blindfolded and celebrating the sudden popularity of his ophthalmologist wife, a mother of six.[31]

The Anwar trial produced the inevitable conviction but at great cost to the entire political establishment. During cross-examination, a director of the intelligence service left no one unscathed. He admitted knowing that Daim instigated the accusations against Anwar and that Anwar used strong-arm tactics in persuading the witnesses to recant. For good measure, he even acknowledged his own willingness to lie under oath if his superiors so ordered.[32]

In the run-up to the 1999 elections, the governing party stumbled repeatedly. While Wan Azizah was closing deals for a multiracial alliance with opposition leaders in PAS and the Democratic Action Party, Ghafar Baba flew to Jakarta to patch up quarrels with Indonesia's new rulers, who made no secret of their sympathy for Anwar. Instead of reassuring the Indonesians, Ghafar Baba insulted them, saying that although homosexuality was perfectly acceptable in their culture, it was a crime in Malaysia.[33] Nothing could have better convinced Suharto's long-suffering successors that Malaysia was battling a political generation gap exceeding even their own.

Mahathir fared no better when he tried to shore up his prestige by making an election-year hajj—his first since 1974. Within days of his return from Saudi

Arabia, he was hospitalized with a lung infection.[34] Instead of persuading skeptical Malays he was building an Islamic government, he gave the succession problem heightened urgency precisely when UMNO seemed most determined to tear itself apart.

The election itself was a near disaster for UMNO. For the first time, they failed to win a majority of the Malay vote. Four members of Mahathir's cabinet were defeated, including Abdul Hamid Othman, the minister of religious affairs and director of Tabung Haji. PAS won control of the parliamentary delegation from Mahathir's home state of Kedah and the state house in Terengganu, where the federal government had rushed to open a new international airport so local hajjis could fly directly to Mecca without passing through Kuala Lumpur. Even where UMNO candidates held on, they often scraped through by the skin of their teeth. The number of safe districts dwindled, and in five states Malays split down the middle between the ruling party and Islamic rivals. UMNO could hardly claim to speak for Malays when across the nation its share of the Malay vote plummeted as the proportion of Malay voters increased[35] (Figure A6.1).

The only solace for the Barisan Nasional (BN) was a backlash of Chinese and Indian voters, who defected from the Democratic Action Party for becoming too cozy with the Islamic opposition. Yet their return to the BN could not compensate for the massive flight of Malays fed up with the Anwar fiasco and the deep-seated corruption it exposed. The ruling coalition held on to its two-thirds margin in parliament but only because a quarter of the seats were now located in remote districts of Sarawak and Sabah, where regional parties supported any government in Kuala Lumpur that gave them development funds.

Mahathir tried to rebound from these electoral and economic shocks by relying more than ever on appeals to religion and race. He promoted his religious advisor, Abdul Hamid Othman, and demoted his economic architect, Daim Zainuddin. It made no difference that Othman had just lost his seat in parliament while Daim had managed to hang on to his. Mahathir viewed Othman as the more valuable asset because he could defend the government's Islamization policies and counterattack PAS spokesmen trying to avoid concrete discussions of the "Islamic state" they hoped to build. Conversely, the prime minister saw Daim as a liability because of his prominence in the Anwar "lynching" and his penchant for chasing wealth instead of displaying piety. Thus, Othman's star rose in domestic and international circles while Daim eventually resigned, leaving Mahathir to act as his own finance minister.[36]

Soon after the election setbacks, Mahathir and Othman boosted Malaysia's role in Islamic diplomacy by hosting a series of international conferences.[37] Othman gathered representatives from fifty countries for an international seminar on hajj management.[38] The Organization of the Islamic Conference held its annual foreign ministers' meeting in Kuala Lumpur, where Mahathir delivered an impassioned keynote warning that unless Muslims adopted advanced technology they would become colonies of industrialized countries. The world's most powerful nations, he insisted, are hostile to Islam and would do everything possible to prevent Muslims from achieving economic freedom.[39]

Malaysia's role became even more important when the foreign ministers failed to agree on a new secretary general for the OIC. Malaysians had to broker a compromise between rival Arab and Asian factions by arranging for one Moroccan diplomat to replace another in exchange for a pledge that the job would rotate to an Asian in the following term.

Mahathir made it clear he was looking forward to chairing the 2003 OIC Summit Conference in Kuala Lumpur, where he expected to shine over heads of state from fifty-seven Islamic nations. In June 2002, a weary Mahathir jolted UMNO with the news that he wanted to resign as prime minister, agreeing to stay on only until the Islamic summit, when he would hand over power to his new deputy, Abdullah Badawi.[40]

After Othman lost his home district to PAS, he became much bolder in attacking them on the national stage. He launched the first state-sponsored radio station devoted to Islamic programming and threatened to crack down on illegal hajjis, who are overwhelmingly PAS constituents. In a swipe at the prudish new PAS regime in Terengganu that was promising to segregate the sexes in public, he said the federal government would issue special identity cards to married couples so religious zealots could not challenge their right to be together outside the home.[41]

Othman's most provocative campaign tried to persuade Malays that, thanks to UMNO, they already lived in an Islamic state. To prove his case, Othman asked the director of al-Azhar University in Cairo to dispatch a team of experts who would inspect Malaysia's religious programs and certify them as an authentic Islamic government.[42] Othman was well aware of al-Azhar's tarnished reputation among Egyptian Muslims because of its habitual submissiveness before a string of authoritarian regimes dating back to the colonial era. Nonetheless, he was determined to give PAS leaders a taste of their own medicine by invoking the authority of the very institutions that trained them. Like most of UMNO's religious bureaucrats, Othman had studied in Malaysia and Europe—not in the venerable madrassas of the Middle East and South Asia. By appealing to al-Azhar, he sought not a pedigree he never valued but a wedge that would set the traditionalists against one another in Malaysia and internationally.

Othman also challenged PAS's leading ideologue, Hadi Awang, to join him in television debates, where they would go head-to-head in explaining their visions of Islamic rule.[43] Awang refused the bait, but when PAS spokesmen made approving remarks about Osama bin Laden and the Taliban, Othman leaped at the chance to brand them as extremists.

By relentlessly hammering the "Islamic state" controversy, Othman dissolved the opposition coalition Wan Azizah had cobbled together with Chinese and Islamic parties. Leaders of the Democratic Action Party became so alarmed about PAS's intentions that they demanded an ironclad guarantee that non-Muslims would be exempt from future Islamic legislation. When PAS dragged its feet, its Chinese and Indian partners walked out of the alliance.[44] Convinced that UMNO was regaining the ground it lost in the Anwar affair, Othman led a ruling party chorus urging Mahathir to call early elections, whether or not he headed the ticket himself.

## Pilgrimage and the Deepening of Regionalism

Tabung Haji is vulnerable to the conservative religious views sweeping both the government and its opponents. UMNO's Islamic rivals attack Tabung Haji because of its leadership in creating a dubious brand of Islamic capitalism. As Mahathir's stature grew, Tabung Haji also became an inviting target for enemies wishing to associate it with the favoritism and corruption that pervaded his regime.

The pilgrimage agency's entanglement with UMNO's problems is clear in the enormous regional disparities of the Malaysian hajj, which are closely tied to gaps in economic development, racial composition, and partisan loyalties. Between 1960 and 2000, hajj participation skyrocketed, with the greatest surge beginning just as Mahathir took power[45] (Figure 6.3). Oddly, however, nearly every region deviated from this nominally "Malaysian" pattern. In about half the states, hajj rates were always much higher or much lower than in the rest of the country. In the other half, pilgrimage fluctuated so abruptly that local tendencies flatly contradicted the national trend.

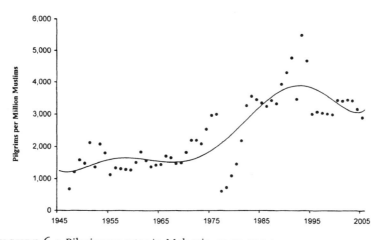

FIGURE 6.3 Pilgrimage rates in Malaysia, 1947–2004

Hajj rates are particularly high in four states along the west coast: Malacca, Negeri Sembilan, Selangor, and Kedah (Figure A6.2). Once regarded as ruling party bastions, these states demanded more and more resources from beleaguered governments trying to fend off both Malay and Chinese opponents.

After 1969, state-sponsored pilgrimage helped UMNO shore up support in core constituencies shaken by racial tensions and Islamic radicalism. Tabung Haji promoted the hajj most vigorously where UMNO was most threatened, in Malacca and Negeri Sembilan. Where UMNO was able to reestablish its dominance more quickly—in Kedah and Selangor—hajj growth was slower yet well above the national average.

Using pilgrimage as political patronage has a long history in Kedah, the home of both Mahathir and Daim Zainuddin, as well as the long-time director of Tabung Haji, Abdul Hamid Othman. In the state capital of Alor Setar, Tabung Haji's office building sits aside not one but two UMNO headquarters. All three structures host an assortment of government and commercial tenants, allowing visitors to flow seamlessly between party, state, and business.

At the entrance to the Tabung Haji office in Alor Setar, I met a cheerful young man escorting a frail companion down the stairs.

"Are you going on the hajj?" he asked teasingly.

"No, not now," I explained. "I went a few years ago."

"Me, too," he said. "This is my uncle. I brought him to town so he could make his last payment. He wants to go next year." The old man beamed with pride, leaving the talking to us. "When did you go?"

"In 1989," I recalled.

"Oh," he said approvingly. "You were very fortunate. I went the next year— at the time of the tunnel disaster. But I was never in danger. I didn't stay in the camp with the other pilgrims. Tabung Haji put me in a new hotel in the center of Mina so I didn't have to walk far to do the stonings. Now they're making the same arrangements for my uncle."

The young hajji was a local engineer, well dressed and well spoken. The pilgrim-to-be was a pensioner with arthritis. Neither expressed the slightest criticism of the government's hajj operations, even though the nephew's fate might have hung on a booking agent's whim. On the contrary, both were clearly grateful for the opportunity to fulfill a lifelong dream in relative comfort and safety. Nor did it concern them that the uncle's opportunity came so much later in life than the nephew's. If anything, they seemed to think the disparity showed how admirably the system was working by rewarding achievement before seniority.

Selangor's hajj grew at a pace similar to Kedah's. But hajj rates rise and fall more abruptly in Selangor than elsewhere because of the high concentration of civil servants in the federal territory surrounding Kuala Lumpur. Although the government used to provide leave and discounts to public workers making the pilgrimage, it slashed these incentives when the quotas began to bite in the 1990s. Even young managers in Tabung Haji's headquarters told me they had not yet made the pilgrimage because they lacked the rank and experience required under the new system. Paring down the civil service's pilgrimage benefits reflects political as well as budgetary considerations. The government prefers to see the quotas' burdens fall disproportionately on its own workers in the capital rather than on independent voters in swing districts.

Malaysia's highest pilgrimage rates consistently appear in Malacca and Negeri Sembilan, neighboring states that lie just south of Selangor. This region is highly pluralistic, both racially and politically, causing recurrent headaches for the Barisan Nasional. Inland towns such as Alor Gajah, near the border between Malacca and Negeri Sembilan, are filled with memorials to the struggle against the British, with Islamic secondary schools, and with travel agencies specializing in hajj and 'umra. UMNO enjoys an advantage among voters here, but their support has never come cheaply. Tabung Haji chose to locate its regional headquarters in Alor Gajah instead of in the busy state capitals of Seremban and Malacca City. Alor Gajah lies right on the North-South Expressway, flanked by the railroad to north and a new airport to the south. Along with waves of state-financed infrastructure, private investments poured in to create thousands of jobs in tourism, light industry, and rubber processing.

After 1980, while hajj growth was slowing down in the nation as a whole, it surged ahead in Penang, Perak, and Johor. Before Mahathir took power, hajj rates in these states lagged behind the rest of the country, but today all three are national leaders. Penang in the north and Johor in the south are Malaysia's strongest regional poles of economic growth. They are the chief beneficiaries of efforts to spread industrialization up and down the west coast instead of concentrating it further around Kuala Lumpur.[46] In Penang, Perak, and Johor, UMNO tried to strengthen itself by creating greater economic opportunities in Malay communities whose votes it once took for granted. In these states, rising pilgrimage and higher UMNO vote counts reflected a bigger and more prosperous Malay middle class.

Anwar Ibrahim represented a Penang district that clearly illustrates the confluence of UMNO support with heightened economic and religious activity. Anwar's constituency, Permatang Pauh, is a thriving Malay neighborhood on the Penang mainland—a region the British once called Wellesley Province. After generations in the shadow of the far wealthier Chinese on Penang Island, mainland Muslims cashed in on new investments by state and federal governments. After 1980, the Malays of Penang had the fastest growing pilgrimage in the nation. They were always loyal UMNO followers, but when Anwar was still in power, they gave the ruling party greater majorities than Malays in any other state, reaching 88 percent in 1995.

The most unusual pattern of hajj growth appears in the northern states of Kelantan, Terengganu, and Perlis[47] (Figure A6.3). These are the only areas where official hajj rates have actually fallen in recent years. The trend in Kelantan is particularly striking. When Tabung Haji took over the pilgrimage, Kelantan had the country's highest rates of participation, despite its economic backwardness. The more UMNO governments consolidated their control over the hajj, the more the people of Kelantan bypassed Tabung Haji in favor of private and illegal alternatives.

After Mahathir came to power, Kelantan's official hajj rate collapsed—not because local Muslims went to Mecca less frequently but because they circumvented new directives they found objectionable on both religious and political grounds. Tabung Haji's records suggest that Kelantan's pilgrimage rate is now the lowest in all of peninsular Malaysia, matched only by remote Sabah, which has always been at the bottom of the heap. In fact, hajj officials and travel agents in Kota Bharu, the state capital, note that Kelantan sends more pilgrims than ever to Mecca but that only about one-third of them conform to Malaysian and Saudi Arabian regulations.

One-third is also the proportion of the statewide Malay vote that went to UMNO candidates in the elections of 1990 and 1995. Not surprisingly, while two-thirds of the pilgrims avoid Tabung Haji, about two-thirds of the Muslim voters also support the leading Malay opposition parties. The Kelantan branch of PAS, the strongest in the nation, has turned the state government into a powerful critic of Kuala Lumpur's alleged economic corruption and religious laxity.

PAS does not openly flaunt its sponsorship of illegal pilgrimage, but it makes no effort to conceal the connection. The party owns a large office building and shopping mall in downtown Kota Bharu. The complex houses PAS's headquarters, as well as two extremely successful businesses: al-Jihad Bookstore, the city's largest supplier of Islamic publications, and the Ibn Battuta Travel Agency, the private company with the biggest share of pilgrimage traffic after Tabung Haji itself.

The Kelantan trend foreshadowed similar reversals for Tabung Haji in neighboring Terengganu and in the northwestern state of Perlis. In Terengganu, official hajj rates began to fall a few years later than in Kelantan. Then, around 1990, Perlis followed suit. In both states, downturns in legal pilgrimage paralleled electoral advances by UMNO's rivals. In 1999, Terengganu became the second state to elect a PAS-led government, and it seemed that Kedah and Perlis might be poised to become the third and fourth.

When I described the government's statistics on the Terengganu hajj to one of that state's leading travel agents, she showed a brief flash of anger and then burst into laughter.

"Impossible," she exclaimed. "We are the real Muslims in Malaysia. Those people in Kuala Lumpur are all show-show. They're too busy gambling and partying in discotheques to know what's happening up here." Like her colleagues in Kota Bharu, she insisted that Terengganu sends as many pilgrims as ever to Mecca and that the number is rising steadily because of greater revenues from the local oil industry.

Malaysia's lowest rates of pilgrimage have always appeared in the vast forest zones of Pahang, Sarawak, and Sabah. Pahang's mountains and jungles are the most beautiful and least accessible regions of peninsular Malaysia. Pahang's hajj has improved steadily with new investment in the sprawling port city of Kuantan, but it still trails far behind the country as a whole.

Sarawak and Sabah lie across the South China Sea on the northern coast of the island of Kalimantan, which they share with Brunei and Indonesia. Sarawak and Sabah are far from the mainland, with racial and religious mixtures that differ greatly from the rest of the country. Most residents here are indigenous peoples who practice Christianity and various folk religions in addition to Islam.

Pilgrimage in Sarawak is rising closer to the national average, and it has outpaced Pahang since the early 1980s. Only about 30 percent of Sarawak's residents are Muslims, but three-quarters of these are Malays. On the other hand, Sabah's pilgrimage has always been the most laggard in the nation, and it shows no sign of changing. Muslims form a majority in Sabah, but they are overwhelmingly non-Malay. Today, the pilgrimage rate in Sabah is about what it was in the rest of Malaysia thirty years ago.

## The Changing Socioeconomic and Political Bases of Pilgrimage

Tabung Haji's managers have presided over important long-term changes in the social, economic, and political bases of Malaysia's hajj[48] (Table A6.4). Since 1969, the most active centers of pilgrimage have shifted from homogeneous Malay communities to cosmopolitan areas where Muslims live alongside Buddhists, Confucians, Hindus, and Christians. The hajj is now most popular not where Malays are an unchallenged majority but in racially mixed states where they comprise only 40 to 60 percent of the population.

Compared with the pilgrims of the 1960s, today's hajjis are less likely to come from poor villages than from well-off farming communities and fast-growing towns. By 1980, pilgrimage became closely connected to most measures of economic development, including urbanization, per capita income, and industrialization. The most powerful predictors of the hajj are the indicators of broad improvements in rural and small-town living conditions, such as literacy, secondary education, access to fresh drinking water, and falling age dependency ratios.

Since Tabung Haji's ascendance, the partisan dimensions of pilgrimage have changed just as dramatically as its cultural and economic bases[49] (Table A6.5). Connections between pilgrimage and votes for the major political parties have reversed completely since the 1960s. Electoral support for the Barisan Nasional was *inversely* related to hajj participation until the mid-1970s. The negative connection weakened during the 1980s and became positive only in the 1990s. Pilgrimage's relation to votes for the opposition parties reversed as well. The trend for PAS is the mirror image of the trend for the Barisan Nasional. The trend for the DAP, on the other hand, tracks the ruling coalition, as they compete more fiercely in states with large Chinese populations. These changes are national in scope rather than merely reflecting the deviance of a few states or regions. In Malaysia as a whole, hajj activity became increasingly linked to racial and religious diversity, economic development, and—until the backlash against Anwar's sacking—to support for the Barisan Nasional.

Nevertheless, a closer look at the 1999 elections reveals a gloomier assessment of UMNO's overall hajj strategy. Comparing the 1999 vote with hajj participation over the entire lifetime of Tabung Haji, all the opposition parties enjoyed at least moderate support in areas with strong pilgrimage, whereas the ruling party had little to show for its decades of investment (Table A6.6). Rural and east coast Malays, who made up a large share of pilgrims before Tabung Haji's quasi monopoly, supported PAS. Urban and west coast Malays, who became the clients of Tabung Haji, supported Wan Azizah, while their non-Malay neighbors backed her partners in the Democratic Action Party. Comparing the two multiracial alliances, the news for Malaysia's hajj establishment was even more disturbing. The Barisan Alternatif ran well in all areas with strong pilgrimage traditions—whether because of Tabung Haji or in spite of it—whereas the Barisan Nasional vote was greatest where hajj activity was weakest.

Voter defections from the Barisan Nasional followed a remarkably consistent pattern nationwide (Figure 6.4). Desertion from the ruling coalition rose hand-in-hand with the popularity of the hajj. The only states where the Barisan Nasional increased its share of the vote were Sabah and Sarawak—culturally distinct areas where pilgrimage has never taken off. On this evidence, it appears that the more desperately the government tries to control pilgrimage, the more they alienate Muslim voters and even the hajjis.

Even if Tabung Haji seems to be crumbling as quickly as every other UMNO pillar, it is important to acknowledge how well it served the Malay establishment in its heyday, particularly under Mahathir. Barisan Nasional politicians showed remarkable success in winning back the key west coast states that were their Achilles' heel during the racial unrest of 1969. The most important battleground was in four swing states where Malays are about half of the population: Malacca, Negeri Sembilan, Selangor, and Perak. In all these states, voters rejected the ruling alliance in 1969 but provided some of Mahathir's largest margins of victory in 1995.

This dramatic improvement resulted primarily from growing support among Malays rather than Chinese. After 1969, UMNO's share of the Malay

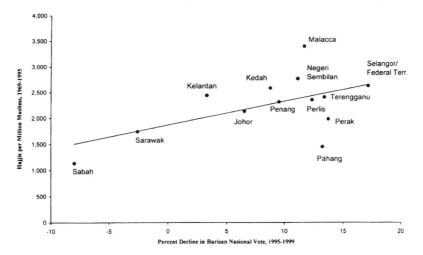

FIGURE 6.4 Hajj participation and Barisan Nasional electoral losses,
1995–1999

vote in these states rose from barely half to about three-fourths. UMNO's most
striking turnaround occurred in Malacca, where its share of the Malay vote
shot up from the lowest in the nation in 1969 (35%) to the second highest in
1995 (82%). In 1969, Malacca's Malays were deeply divided. UMNO and PAS
split 70 percent of the vote about evenly, and the remainder went to small
leftist parties. Malaccan Malays were voting not like their neighbors in other
ethnically mixed states but like the insular Muslim communities far to the
north and northeast. UMNO's rescue operation in Malacca included an impressive package of economic, political, and religious initiatives designed to
bring the state back into the shaken ruling coalition. Government and foreign
investment flowed into construction, tourism, textiles, rubber, and electronics.

Tabung Haji was vital to the government's courtship of Malaccan Muslims.
By the mid-1970s, Malacca overtook Kelantan as Malaysia's leader in pilgrim-
age per capita, and it never relinquished that position. Under Mahathir, Tabung
Haji raised more money per capita in Malacca than in any other state. In return,
Malacca's Islamic charities and associations consistently received the country's
highest *zakat* contributions from Tabung Haji.

After acquiring a reputation as the nation's most Islamically oriented voters, the Kelantan electorate became the most fragmented of all the Malay communities. Kelantan's voters rejected Mahathir, but they split evenly between
PAS and the defectors from UMNO who named their party Semangat '46
("The Spirit of 1946") in order to identify with the early struggles of Malay
nationalism. Even though PAS headed the state's coalition government, it was
still too weak to force through controversial religious reforms, such as Islamic

criminal penalties and dress codes. In fact, the Kelantan of 1995 closely resembled the Malacca of 1969—politically divided, economically laggard, and
religiously quarrelsome. UMNO leaders not only repelled PAS's thrust into
the west coast but also managed to weaken the Islamic opposition in its heartland.

In both states, the hajj flourished because of sharper struggles between
Malay factions. Yet, the pilgrimages of Malacca and Kelantan diverged more
and more each year, embodying the broader division between Malaysia's competing hajj systems—the stagnant, official pilgrimage versus the thriving, clandestine hajj. One hajj system passes through Kuala Lumpur; the other shuns
it. One includes the beneficiaries of racial quotas and privatization; the other
appeals to those who believe such policies merely alienate Malays from one
another and from their traditions. The official hajj strives to be cosmopolitan,
up-to-date, and open-minded; the clandestine hajj prefers to be authentic, old-
fashioned, and correct.

## Playing It Safe: The Retreat from Innovation

The conflict between these diverging hajjs has already influenced the government's own programs for educating prospective pilgrims. Tabung Haji's training courses and publications have always highlighted the economic, social, and
political benefits of pilgrimage for Malaysians and for Muslims the world over.
Like the colorful lectures and slide shows Indonesian hajj officials present to
audiences in every province, Tabung Haji's booklets echo modernist and mystical themes reminiscent of popular authors like Muhammad Iqbal and 'Ali
Shari'ati. [50]

In contrast to the stuffy guidebooks of the old-fashioned sheikhs that detail
requirements of each ritual, Tabung Haji's materials invite pilgrims to think
about the meanings of the hajj as a whole and its broader implications for
social action. Tabung Haji's writers devote entire chapters to explaining the
wisdom (hikmah), mysteries (rahasiya), and philosophy (falsafah) of the pilgrimage, stressing the value of equality, independent thought, international cooperation, and economic development.

Nonetheless, Tabung Haji's prepilgrimage television shows are preoccupied with the most routine questions of ritual propriety. These programs are
as lifeless as any of the manuals churned out by traditionalist sheikhs and
bureaucratic committees. Each evening, viewers are presented a half-hour dialogue between a Tabung Haji official and a religious scholar, who march
through a catechism of hypotheticals: "What should a woman do if she unin-
tentionally exposes part of her arm while circling the Ka'ba?" "At Mina, what
if you throw six stones at once and then throw one more instead of throwing
the seven stones separately?" "When praying at the Prophet's tomb, will rela-

tives and friends receive more benefit if you mention them individually and by name, or can you simply ask that they be blessed as a group?"

Although these broadcasts provide some useful information, their primary objective is to avoid any misstep that would offend the government's Islamic critics—even at the risk of putting viewers to sleep or driving them to other channels. Tabung Haji grows particularly sensitive when the press carries rumors that Iran is introducing Shi'ite teachings into Malaysia or that terrorists are living among the Pakistanis and Indonesians working in Kuala Lumpur. All these countries are hajj hotspots, and Malaysian authorities see them as potentially subversive.

The modernist and entrepreneurial impulses that once made Tabung Haji such an intriguing experiment are under attack from several directions. Pilgrimage quotas and financial scandals have demoted Tabung Haji to a second fiddle in economic development. The clandestine hajj has undercut its role in dispensing patronage for the ruling party. Worst of all, the government itself now views Tabung Haji's history of religious innovation as a liability instead of an asset. Facing constant charges that the state's sponsorship of Islam is both too aggressive and too shallow, the government is reining in the creative thinking that gave birth to Tabung Haji in the first place.

## Religion, Race, and Chain-Reaction Revivalism

Tabung Haji's eclipse is symptomatic of a general deterioration of religious discourse in Malaysia—the tendency for debate over Islam to aggravate conflicts of race and class. This trend was especially vivid in the mid-1990s, when the festivities of Ramadan and the Chinese New Year fell in the same season. Weeks of dual celebrations between January and March showed that Malaysia's government and business leaders can be extremely imaginative in promoting racial harmony—and that they will need to marshal every resource at their disposal in the years ahead.

The problem is not that Malays have failed to prosper. The New Economic Policy that put Tabung Haji at center stage helped an entire generation of Malays to rise in government service, the professions, and private enterprise. Malays no longer occupy the bottom rung on the economic ladder. Today, urban Malays are far better off than new immigrants from other Asian countries, and they are nearly as successful as native-born Malaysians of Indian descent.[51]

Yet even well-to-do Malays complain that no matter how high they rise, the Chinese will always rise higher and that the country's fate is still in the hands of foreigners who regard Malays as inferior. In addition, Malays in the lagging regions feel ignored by UMNO-led governments. For them, UMNO has created divisions among Malays just as deep as the gaps between the races.

Malays' social advancement is evident in the prevalence of foreigners in jobs requiring strenuous labor. It was mainly Pakistanis and Indians that built the Petronis Twin Towers, which, as Malaysians unfailingly remind visitors from Chicago, are now the *two* largest skyscrapers on earth. Employers often complain that foreign workers demand higher wages in Malaysia than elsewhere because they know how much Malays disdain manual labor. Malaysian politicians fear the tight labor market has attracted too many foreigners, aggravating racial tensions that are already at the flash point. The government even threatened to construct a huge fence along Malaysia's northern border to stem the flow of fugitive job seekers from Thailand, Burma, and Bangladesh.

It is far more difficult to combat immigration from the south and east, particularly by Indonesians, whose national language is a dialect of Malay. Chit Kow, the working-class section of Kuala Lumpur where anti-Chinese riots broke out in 1969, has changed from a Malay slum into an Indonesian market town. During the day, Chit Kow is the transfer center for minibus traffic choking the city from end to end. At night, its side streets are a haven for thousands of young Indonesian men—mostly illegal workers and hawkers—who run an elaborate underground economy.

The government's campaign to promote the Malay language has heightened resentments among non-Malays, particularly Indians. Requiring competence in Malay for advancement in public employment and education has diminished the linguistic edge Indians once enjoyed from greater exposure to British education. Although Malay is the language of state, English is the language of business and the tongue citizens of different races use to scream at each other in public. In this arena, at least, Malaysians of Indian background retain a decided advantage over their fellow citizens.

Young educated Chinese generally know enough Malay and English to communicate with anyone. On Jalan Petaling, in the heart of Kuala Lumpur's Chinatown, I attended a New Year's celebration and dragon dance that included Malaysians of all races and foreign guests from several countries. The street party was hosted by Chinese business leaders and politicians, whose trilingual stump speeches included expansive ad libs in Malay and English.

Malays already realize their linguistic advantage might be short-lived. In Kelantan, I discussed the interplay of language, race, and religion with a prospective hajji and retired army officer who spent years fighting the Chinese communist insurgents.

"Do Malays make an effort to learn Chinese?" I asked.

"Very rarely," he admitted with regret. "But the Chinese students learn Malay better than we do. And if they wanted, they could learn more about Islam than we know, too."

My friend was joking about the possible "threat" of Chinese conversions to Islam, but he put his finger on one of the most sensitive issues dividing today's Malay politicians: Is Islam a universal faith that should embrace all

Malaysians, or does it define Malays as a separate race and culture? For Muslims to whom race is truly irrelevant, the prospect of well-educated Chinese converts is alluring, not threatening.

Until recently, most Malays regarded both Islam and the Malay language as markers of racial and national identity. But a new generation of Malay-speaking Chinese is weakening the salience of language as a racial marker. As the distinguishing power of language diminishes, religion acquires an even greater power to magnify or moderate racial tensions.

Ironically, the "traditionalists" of PAS are promoting the universalistic view of Islam, whereas the "modernists" of UMNO are clinging more than ever to the nationalist and racial view. The young leaders who took control of PAS in the 1980s assure Chinese voters that their version of an Islamic state will respect non-Muslim businesses, schools, and sanctuaries. They denounce the government for encouraging Malay chauvinism, characterizing affirmative action policies as examples of ethnic exclusivism ('asabiyya) that contradicts Islam's transcendence of race and nationality. PAS's criticisms recall the views of former student leaders who condemned racial quotas but then accepted posts in the government. Indeed, many of the party's current leaders were members of Islamic student groups who refused to follow Anwar Ibrahim into the UMNO ranks.

UMNO treats PAS's attempts to forge a multiracial opposition as a betrayal of Malay solidarity. UMNO candidates frequently warn Malay voters that an opposition victory will put an end to special entitlements such as scholarships, loans, and subsidized pilgrimages. For the government, supporting Islam is a way to reinforce Malay ethnic identity and correct the injustices of colonialism. For the opposition, however, equating religion and race merely allows a privileged segment of Malay society to dominate a permanently divided country.

About half the Malay voters choose to stay with UMNO's communalist approach to Islam. By persuading insecure bumiputras they can prosper only with preferential treatment, UMNO deflects recurrent challenges from PAS and other Islamic movements. The ruling party tries to keep the upper hand by reminding Malays how much it has done for Islam and how effectively it contains religious extremists who jeopardize their economic future.

But UMNO's assertive communalism also heightens racial and religious consciousness among non-Muslims. Many Chinese and Indians sense that Muslims are becoming less tolerant, and they fear the danger will increase if Islam acquires more state sponsorship, no matter which Malay party prevails. Consequently, Malaysians of all races are increasingly determined to preserve their distinctive religious and cultural heritages. By exploiting Malaysia's Islamic resurgence, the government has unwittingly kindled similar revivalist movements among Buddhists, Hindus, and Christians.

As these groups collide, the state is drawn into bitter quarrels over language instruction, temple and church building, and proselytizing—controversies where politicians of all communities know that compromise is essential but where they fear being denounced as sellouts. Malaysia's business and party elites are deeply ambivalent about representing religion and race. The same leaders who worry that cultural heritages will wane if they are not constantly reinforced also fear that racial antagonisms will explode unless they are skillfully managed.

Ambivalence toward religion and race permeates Malaysia's dual celebration of the Chinese New Year and the end of Ramadan. The holidays' symbols are deliberately blurred to suggest a single national festival continuing for nearly two weeks. Everywhere banners and ads present traditional seasons' greetings side by side in Chinese and Malay—Gong Xi Fa Cai ("A Prosperous New Year") in red letters and Selamat Hari Raya Idul Fitri ("A Blessed Fast-Breaking") in green.

Muslims exchange "New Year's" greetings, even though the Islamic New Year is still two months ahead. Malay children receive gifts of "Ramadan money" just as Chinese toddlers receive "New Year's money," though not in the same bright red envelopes. On the feast days, "open house" receptions encourage neighbors of all races and creeds to exchange family visits and swap special dishes.

Malays like to emphasize that the end of Ramadan is a time to wipe the slate clean in personal relationships by asking for pardon (maaf) from anyone they might have offended in the previous year. Malaysians who promote the dual-celebration approach want to build upon this process of mutual pardoning—transforming it from an act of obeisance that Muslim children pay to their elders into a national display of atonement by citizens who might otherwise have little interaction with people of other races and religions.

Foreign corporations are enthusiastic sponsors of the dual celebrations. During my visit, Rothman and Marlboro funded complementary advertising campaigns highlighting the broad overlap of Chinese and Malay cultures in dance, music, handicrafts, sports, and martial arts.

One of the most popular ads portrayed a Chinese drummer and a Malay drummer standing face to face, separated only by the man-sized instruments each was pummeling furiously. Both men were young, powerfully built, and seething with aggression. Depending on the viewer's angle of vision, their smoldering eyes were either fixed on the drums between them or glaring straight at one another.

# 7

# Turkey

*The Belated Quest for Religious Tolerance*

Since Turkey became a democracy in 1950, the hajj has blossomed into an emotionally charged symbol of conflict between a Muslim society and a supposedly secular state. Modern Turkey is heir to a cosmopolitan empire and a nationalist revolution in which generations of Westernizing reformers steadily reduced the power of Islamic leaders and institutions. Today, whether they aim at manipulating religion or repressing it, at preserving Islam or reinterpreting it, Turkey's politicians universally describe their policies as a continuation of secularist ideals promulgated by Ataturk and pioneered by the Ottomans.

Although secularism is a widely shared value in Turkey, there is no consensus on its meaning. Turkey's secularism has always been hotly contested, open to periodic redefinition in law and practice. When Turkish politicians battle over the pilgrimage, their attacks take on an added ferocity, slashing across the party and ideological lines that frame routine squabbles about mosque building, religious education, and dress codes. Ongoing debate over the hajj illustrates the malleability of Turkish secularism and its endless capacity to divide the nation.[1]

In Turkey's towns and villages, people see the rapid growth of the hajj as a sign of the expanding freedom and prosperity they have enjoyed since Ataturk's authoritarianism gave way to democracy. For the peasantry and the provincial middle class, opportunities to make the pilgrimage are a welcome end to what they long regarded as punitive restrictions on the freedom to worship and travel. In their view, Turkey's state-supported hajj is a proud emblem of popular sovereignty and social mobility—a stunning turnabout in policy that confirms the common citizens' power over elected officials and over their own fate. For religious groups and parties trying to win the support of both pious and nominal Muslims, the pilgrimage's new legitimacy carries an added importance. A strong hajj demonstrates the continuing vigor of religion among the masses as it reconnects Turkey to the global culture of Islam after three generations of foreign policy attuned to Western Europe.

Against the tide of pro-hajj sentiment, much of Turkey's Westernized elite still condemns the pilgrimage. Although their numbers are relatively small, they include many of the country's most powerful military commanders, university professors, and industrialists. For them, a thriving hajj signifies a relapse into the decay they thought Ataturk had uprooted once and for all. To the Westernizers, pilgrimage is an unpardonable waste of national wealth, a cynical lure for the votes of pious rustics, and a rallying point for fanatics from all corners of the Islamic world who want to destroy Ataturk's revolution. In these circles, the hajj is the shameful face of Turkey—ignorance and superstition, demagoguery and subversion—all the most embarrassing features they desperately want to change.

During most of the last fifty years, Turkey has been governed by right-wing parties eager to soften the antireligious implications of Ataturkism by funding an array of Islamic activities as though they were conventional social services. Yet, even pro-Islamic parties avoided openly embracing the hajj until the mid-1960s. Turkey created a central system of pilgrimage management only in 1979, when the Directorate of Religious Affairs (Diyanet İşleri Başkanlığı) finally began to coordinate the patchwork of ministries and private companies that had carved out overlapping corners of authority and profit. Since then, all the right-wing parties have accused one another of packing the hajj agency with their followers and squeezing it for commercial and political gain.[2]

Because of Ataturkist hostility and rightist bickering, Turkey created one of the most volatile pilgrimages in the world—and one of the most politicized. Turkey's hajj evolved in abrupt waves and cycles. Its periodic booms and busts stand in sharp contrast to steady increases in other indicators of socioeconomic and religious development, but they coincide precisely with elections, coups, and cabinet reshuffles.

For decades now, virtually all Turkish governments and parties have endorsed state aid for religious activities and organizations. Although any official support for Islam remains controversial, no other state-funded religious program has soared and crashed as often as the hajj, and none has mirrored politics as faithfully.

Despite continuing polemics, state-run hajj programs gradually acquired legitimacy and institutional roots. The hajj agency has grown into an unusually popular part of a state bureaucracy that, in an era of privatization, is increasingly ridiculed. Beginning as just another public service office in the Directorate of Religious Affairs, pilgrimage managers eventually formed a special bureau under the director and the prime minister. A string of executive orders gave it a virtual monopoly over the hajj business and a leading role in inter-ministry committees that coordinate every detail of pilgrim administration.[3]

Year after year, hajj officials broadened their economic reach and public profile. Today, they comanage a multimillion-dollar religious foundation (Türkiye Diyanet Vakfı) and negotiate collective agreements with the association of private travel agents (Türkiye Seyahat Acenteleri Birliği). Recently, they also started organizing off-season visits to Mecca ('umras), which used to be a preserve of private firms.[4]

A turning point for public acceptance of state-supported pilgrimage came in 1988, when Turgut Özal became the first prime minister to perform the hajj while in office. Özal and his family led one of the largest pilgrimage delegations in Turkey's history—more than 100,000 people, including several hundred members of parliament and top civil servants. The press roasted the Özals for flaunting their piety. The front page of Cumhuriyet, the leading left-wing paper, featured two unflattering photos of the prime minister side by side—a tubby Turgut with his belly spilling over snugly wrapped white ihram towels and a dapper Turgut struggling to button a skin-tight double-breasted jacket.[5] Some of the tabloids ran file photos of his wife, Semra, decked out in a gaudy cocktail dress and puffing one of her favorite cigars. The opposition press made sure no one overlooked the connection between the prime minister's hajj and his brother's business interests in Saudi Arabia or its coincidence with Turgut's own plans to dump the floundering Motherland Party and step up to the presidency.

Yet the Özals' embarrassment barely touched the hajj agency. Indeed, the system performed so well that its leaders became overconfident. The Saudis told the Turks they would begin enforcing the new quota system in 1990, when Turkey would be limited to only 55,000 pilgrims. Nevertheless, flushed with success, Turkish hajj managers gambled they could extract a one-year exemption. Ignoring Saudi directives, they set out to top the "Özal hajj" of 1988 by registering 120,000 pilgrims. Hajj officials claimed Turgut Özal himself told them to approve all applications and leave him the task of obtaining the extra visas from King Fahd. At the eleventh hour, Saudi Foreign Minister Prince Faysal flew to Ankara and personally informed now President Özal that the Saudis meant what they said all along: They could make no special arrangements violating the quotas, and Turkey was the only country seeking preferential treatment.[6]

The government had created a disaster. It was forced to cancel bookings for all overland travel to Mecca and managed to reroute only 15,000 people by air. Enraged applicants marched on the offices of the Motherland Party and the Directorate of Religious Affairs across the country. All the opposition parties demanded the resignation of the director of religious affairs, and Özal's leading foe, Süleyman Demirel, called for the entire government to step down. Over the next few months, the state had to refund $30 million in prepaid expenses to nearly 100,000 citizens.[7]

Although the "hajj scandal" of 1990 tarnished a handful of politicians and bureaucrats, it revealed widespread support for the pilgrimage system. Criticism focused on political abuses and administrative snafus, yet the reforms aimed at strengthening the hajj agency instead of abolishing it. Even leftists acknowledged that a publicly funded pilgrimage was here to stay and the best strategy was to run it as professionally as possible.

The most surprising aspect of the hajj scandal was its banality. After decades of posturing by crusaders for "religious freedom" and self-anointed guardians of "secularism," one of the hottest issues of religion and politics sounded like a tiresome quarrel about administrative law: "How can we balance bureaucratic independence with political accountability?" "Should hajj affairs be run from the prime minister's office or a regular ministry subject to legislative oversight?" "What about a semipublic entity midway between the civil service and a private foundation?" It was as though Turkey's leaders had concluded that mobilizing the state on behalf of Islam's most exalted ritual was no different from fine-tuning a central bank, a national airline, or a public broadcasting service.

Then again, a bit of boredom could be just what the doctor ordered in a nation that often seems poised for civil war because some of its university students insist on wearing headscarves and growing beards. Perhaps Turkey would be better off if its politicians thought of the hajj as a struggling railroad that ought to run on time instead of as a needless loyalty test between God and country.

The rationality and open-mindedness that have crept into hajj debates demonstrate how far younger Turks have progressed in reevaluating stereotypes about the connection between religion and politics. Both Ataturkists and Muslims are eager for fresh thinking about secularism and realize that Turkey has already redefined its practice to the point where corresponding changes in theory are long overdue.

Behind the shouting over the role of Islam, a great deal of learning is occurring among educated Turks from all religious backgrounds. Middle-class youth in the big cities who were weaned on secularism are learning that their parents and grandparents were less interested in separating religion and politics than in establishing state control over Islam to break its hold on society. Younger Ataturkists are realizing that their pious classmates and coworkers from the provinces are a far cry from the "fanatics" and "counterrevolutionaries" their history teachers described as implacable enemies of the republic. Many in this generation are calling for a flexible brand of secularism better suited to current conditions than the anticlerical views of authoritarians who had to build a nation from the ruins of empire. This breed of Ataturkist is urging nominal Muslims and nonbelievers to avoid alienating Turkey's Islamic movement and to draw it into dialogue while it is still diverse and open to moderation.

Similarly, Muslim activists are trying to shape a movement faithful to universal Islamic principles but able to survive with modern realities. Because formal Islamic education was virtually nonexistent in Turkey for two generations, the new era of democracy and prosperity spawned a multiplicity of religious views unfettered by traditional authority. Younger Muslims show far less respect for patriarchy and pedigree than for higher education and knowledge of modern science. They prefer leaders who are not religious functionaries but professional politicians trained in engineering, medicine, and economics. They study the Qur'an not to parrot it but to interpret it in light of their own experience and to exchange their insights. They want to reconnect Turkey with the rest of the Islamic world, but they also devour anything in Western languages about feminism and environmentalism.

Although it may be too early to speak of a full-fledged convergence of Ataturkists and Muslims, there are unmistakable steps in that direction all across the country. Some extraordinary gestures toward reconciliation occurred during October 1998, as Turkey prepared to celebrate the seventy-fifth anniversary of the republic. In the town of Sincan, close to Ankara, a well-known artist stunned old-fashioned secularists by unveiling a bust of a smiling Ataturk standing with open arms and welcoming a group of adoring children.

Two years before the unveiling, Sincan was the scene of a fateful confrontation between the military and radical Islamists. After the mayor allowed Iranian sympathizers to hold an evening-long demonstration, the army sent dozens of tanks rolling through the town square in a show of force against religious extremism, foreshadowing the overthrow of the pro-Islamic Refah Party government in June 1997.

Sincan's new city council was eager to demonstrate that the town had fully adapted to the purge, and they commissioned a new bust of Ataturk to commemorate the restoration of secular rule, both locally and nationally. But the artist did not present them with the icon they expected. When they threatened to prosecute him for insulting Ataturk, he told them there was no reason to keep portraying the nation's father as a menacing authority figure. "I cannot create a lifeless form," he said. "Ataturk was not a scowling person cut off from society. My goal is to show Ataturk lovingly embracing all the people of Sincan. It is a beautiful thing to represent the Ataturk who lives in our hearts with a smiling face."[8]

At the same time, tens of thousands of Muslim students marched in about twenty cities to protest the ban on headscarves in universities and state offices. In several towns, they stopped traffic by forming human chains that signified resistance to all shackles on the freedom of thought. In Istanbul, they shut down the Bosporus Bridge, delaying runners in an intercontinental marathon trying to finish their race on the Asian side.[9]

Their theatrical originality appropriated the Ataturkists' own symbols. Alongside the conventional posters of Ataturk, they carried photos of his wife, Latife, wearing the same type of headdress prohibited today. In some towns, marchers proceeded to the local Ataturk memorial, where they stood in silent respect and sang the national anthem with all the reverence of devoted school-children and soldiers.[10]

## The Hajj and Turkish Democracy

The fluctuation of Turkey's hajj is an uncanny barometer of shifts between democracy and dictatorship. Someone with no knowledge of Turkish history could almost guess when the country was ruled by elected governments or military regimes by glancing at oscillations in the annual number of pilgrims[11] (Figure 7.1). The peaks are high points of multiparty pluralism; the valleys signal coups and transition governments backed by the armed forces.

Every surge in pilgrimage coincided with the ascendance of a strong party leader who campaigned as the champion of the Muslim majority in the pro-vincial towns and villages: Adnan Menderes in the 1950s, Süleyman Demirel in the 1960s, Necmettin Erbakan in the 1970s, and Turgut Özal in the 1980s. The hajj's setbacks came with military interventions that overthrew civilian governments three times in twenty years: coups against Menderes in 1960 and against Demirel in 1971 and 1980.

All the conservative parties have included propilgrimage policies as part of their appeal to religious voters. Yet the hajj took off only after the military

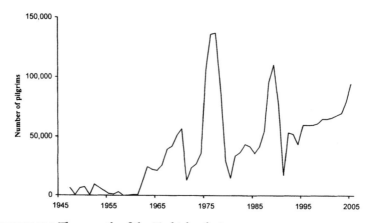

FIGURE 7.1 The growth of the Turkish pilgrimage, 1947–2004

destroyed the Democratic Party and threw right-wing forces into permanent disarray. Pilgrimage languished while Adnan Menderes mustered powerful majorities under a single banner, but it flourished when his coalition split into rival groups that fought over the same supporters without ever reassembling a dominant party. Although military interventions discouraged the hajj in the short run, they helped spur it in the long term by spawning a flock of conservative parties with greater incentives to court religious voters.

Weak parties and unstable governments are the most enduring legacy of Turkey's juntas. When the military and intellectual elite realized rural voters would never elect Ataturk's would-be successors in the Republican People's Party, they imposed a string of reforms aimed at throttling the party system. Each junta added more rigid safeguards against the "tyranny of the majority." Proportional representation paved the way for splinter parties and coalitions to replace two-party democracy. Established parties were repeatedly banned and forced to reinvent their leadership and alliances with voluntary associations. Under the 1982 constitution, active-duty officers even gained the right to make policy in a National Security Council that put military commanders on a par with top cabinet ministers.

Unlike recent right-wing politicians, Menderes did not need to promote a massive pilgrimage for political gain. The parliamentary majorities that tempted him to gag his Ataturkist opponents also emboldened him to set strict limits on the hajj when he thought they were necessary.

Between 1950 and 1954, the Democrats increased the pilgrimage from about 6,000 to 12,000 people. But by 1955 Menderes was under pressure to conserve foreign exchange, and soon he had to accept a tough stabilization program from the International Monetary Fund. Antihajj sentiment appeared among Westernized urbanites who could no longer buy hard currency for European sojourns and among Istanbul importers who were the Democratic Party's biggest financiers. A pro-Democratic newspaper in Istanbul even called on the Directorate of Religious Affairs to relieve Turks of the duty to perform the hajj at a time when the country could not afford the imported medicines and supplies it needed to care for earthquake victims.[12]

Menderes responded with several half-measures that pleased no one. First, he tried stealth and deception. All preparations for the pilgrimage were put off until the last minute. Travel agents never knew whether to book passage by sea or air. Foreign exchange prices and quotas were closely guarded secrets. The press was filled with rumors of disease and profiteering in Saudi Arabia, suggesting the hajj might be canceled at any time.

The Democrats were desperately trying to cut demand for pilgrimage without openly issuing regulations that would anger pious supporters. By making it impossible for aspiring hajjis to plan, Menderes hoped to nip pilgrimage traffic in the bud while avoiding explicit prohibitions on religious travel.

When these tactics backfired, the Democrats tried to choke the hajj with red tape. A cascade of regulations forced pilgrims to obtain written permission from multiple agencies. They had to verify round-trip transportation, foreign exchange purchases, financial support for nontraveling dependents, vaccinations, medical fitness, completion of military service, payment of outstanding debts, and clean criminal records.[13] Each approval required a stack of documents and affidavits that would discourage healthy and well-educated applicants, let alone the semiliterates who tended to make pilgrimages late in life. After years of wishing for more state intervention in hajj affairs, prospective pilgrims were now pleading for less.

Imposing conditions that no one could fulfill left the government with nearly total freedom to ignore them when it was politically expedient. The Democrats did not enforce the new regulations until they won the 1954 elections. Then, they slashed the yearly number of hajjis from 9,000 to 1,000.

Determined pilgrims who could afford air travel still made their way to Beirut and applied for visas there. Just before the 1957 elections, the Democrats let traffic along this clandestine route swell to twice the size of the official hajj. That year, the Saudis recorded 3,199 pilgrims from Turkey, even though Ankara authorized only 1,175.

As the economy deteriorated, Menderes finally issued the pilgrimage ban he had struggled to avoid. Since the early 1950s, hazelnut cooperatives in the Black Sea provinces had helped stave off the move by pledging hard currency from their exports to a special account reserved for the hajj. By the end of Menderes's rule, even that was not enough. In 1958 and 1959, the only Turkish hajjis were those already outside the country or those who could slip across the southeastern border and take their chances as fugitive pilgrims.

The abuses and hardships of the 1950s persuaded the Democrats' successors that they needed a more coherent pilgrimage system. Experience convinced them that discomfort and destitution would not deter Muslims from fulfilling a clear religious obligation, no matter how quaint or irrational it appeared to the enlightened classes. Indeed, many Turks believed that adversity enhanced the spiritual value of their journeys, and they were more than willing to endure whatever indignities their officials devised. Turkish hajjis returned home with countless stories about how miserably their conditions compared with those of Muslims from other countries, where state pilgrimage boards helped citizens every step of the way. "Why," they asked, "should Turks have less assistance than people from far poorer nations such as India, Pakistan, Malaysia, Indonesia—and even Nigeria?"[14]

Although the Justice Party victory of 1965 put the Menderes coalition back in power, right-wing governments waited another decade before entrusting hajj management to the state bureaucracy. As a staunch supporter of free enterprise, Süleyman Demirel preferred to channel pilgrimage profits to private firms. The Justice Party formed ad hoc committees to ensure that public officials facilitated the hajj instead of stifling it, but there was no central authority in charge.

In parliament, Demirel's colleagues were equally divided between those wanting the Directorate of Religious Affairs to assume these duties and those who doubted the agency could ever outgrow its historic antagonism to Islam. Conservative politicians did not wholeheartedly embrace the idea of a national pilgrimage system until they accomplished far-reaching changes in bureaucratic recruitment and religious education.

Demirel presided over a profound transformation of the directorate's mission and staff. More than anyone else, he reshaped the directorate from an instrument of state control to a dispenser of social services. The drafters of the 1961 constitution encouraged this shift by explicitly legitimizing the directorate's role. They clearly sought a more even balance between promoting religious activity and regulating it. There was sharp disagreement about how far a "secular" state should go in supporting religion, but the jurists let elected parliaments adjust the details according to changing conditions.

In 1965, the Justice Party, by expanding the duties of the Directorate of Religious Affairs, paved the way for rapid increases in its budget and personnel. The agency acquired greater powers to manage the tens of thousands of mosques springing up in hamlets and villages all over the country and staff them with qualified preachers. The controversial law also instructed the directorate to "enlighten society on the topic of religion" and "manage the beliefs, practices, and moral principles of Islam."[15] This was a clean break with the secularism that confined religion to matters of personal conscience. Henceforth, the state would compete directly with private groups and foundations that had always provided the bulk of religious guidance.

The Directorate of Religious Affairs tightened its hold over the two pillars of Islamic training: the İmam-Hatip schools and the Qur'an courses. The İmam-Hatip schools offer secondary education combining state-approved Islamic instruction with the science and humanities curriculum of general high schools. The 1965 law that reorganized the religious bureaucracy spurred enrollment in Islamic secondary schools by requiring the directorate to staff its cadres with graduates from the İmam-Hatip schools and the Divinity Faculty of Ankara University. Previously, most religious functionaries had only a primary school education or a diploma from one of the thousands of Qur'an courses sponsored by Sufi brotherhoods or local philanthropists.

After the 1971 coup, the military government nationalized Qur'an courses and ordered the directorate to purge their teachers and lay down a common curriculum. From that point onward, most Qur'an course teachers also had to be İmam-Hatip graduates. The Directorate of Religious Affairs soon became the manager and employer for a network of religious schools running from grade six through the university level.

İmam-Hatip schools entered the educational mainstream with surprising speed. Although they were conceived as technical schools for religious functionaries, they grew into a popular alternative for university-bound students aiming for jobs in business, government, and the professions. In 1973, the ratio of İmam-Hatip students to general secondary students was about one to twenty. By 1995, it was one to eight.

The most striking change in religious education is the steady rise in female enrollment (Table A7.1). In just two decades, the proportion of female students in religious high schools jumped from nearly zero to about 40 percent—the same rate as in the older and larger system of general secondary schools. What started as a narrow track for poor village boys seeking a meager state salary snowballed into the system of choice for conservative parents from many regions and classes who wanted their daughters to continue studies free of the distractions coeducation presents.

A string of coalition governments during the 1970s increased state aid for religion far beyond the levels the Justice Party initiated. These governments included two right-wing parties that vigorously competed with Demirel for the Muslim vote: the National Salvation Party (Milli Selamet Partisi), led by Necmettin Erbakan, and the National Action Party (Milli Hareket Partisi) of Alparslan Türkeş. Some of the most pro-Islamic policies appeared during two brief administrations in 1974 and 1978, headed not by rightists but by Bülent Ecevit of the Republican People's Party (Cumhuriyet Halk Partisi). Ecevit steered Ataturk's decrepit party leftward to build a social democratic movement that identified with working people and not just the educated elite still convinced of its inherent right to rule. Ecevit's populism promoted a softer view of secularism that threw all the conventional ideologues off balance. Rather than cling to the old Ataturkist strategy of trying to undercut Islam, Ecevit encouraged strains of piety he regarded as liberal and humane. He was particularly sympathetic to eclectic Sufi teachings that ignored conflicts between sects and minimized differences between believers and nonbelievers. Throughout the 1970s, Demirel and Ecevit took turns pasting together coalition cabinets that augmented state support for religious activities.

These were the years when the Directorate of Religious Affairs grew into a hybrid that broke all prior assumptions about secularism in theory and practice. The directorate operated simultaneously as the official regulator of Islam and as a lobby for public assistance to politically connected religious groups across the country. A turning point came with the "socialist-Islamist" government that Ecevit and Erbakan formed in 1974. Erbakan proposed making the directorate's presidency a lifetime appointment—a move that critics compared with reviving the Ottoman office of Şeyhülislam, with all its trappings of ecclesiastic hierarchy and privilege.[16]

Although Erbakan lost that battle, he won many others. İmam-Hatip school graduates gained parity in public employment and university admissions. They took over most jobs in the directorate's Ankara headquarters and its provincial branches, where they replaced an older generation of semieducated clerks and teachers. Enrollment in Islamic academies and Qur'an courses swelled, producing a steady flow of candidates for all universities and technical schools. The religious bureaucracy became a full-service operation, running a network of mosques, schools, and offices that reached into every district[17] (Figure 7.2).

Erbakan and Ecevit also laid the foundation of centralized hajj management. They presided over the first pilgrimage in Turkey's history to top the 100,000 mark. When Demirel returned to power in 1975, he went further, sponsoring three massive pilgrimages in a row—136,000 in 1975, 137,000 in 1976, and 91,000 in 1977. During this period Turkey was the world's undisputed leader in pilgrimage, accounting for 14 percent of all overseas hajjis. The closest competitors were the Nigerians (9%) and North Yemenis (10%), but even they exceeded 100,000 pilgrims only once each.

As pilgrimage boomed, the Directorate of Religious Affairs emerged from its shadowy role as the de facto coordinator of hajj services to lead an annual

| THRACE | CENTRAL | MEDITERRANEAN |
|---|---|---|
| 1 Edirne | 20 Ankara | 45 Antalya |
| 2 Kırklareli | 21 Çankırı | 46 İçel |
| 3 Tekirdağ | 22 Çorum | 47 Adana |
| 4 İstanbul | 23 Amasya | 48 Hatay |
| | 24 Tokat | |
| AEGEAN | 25 Yozgat | NORTH EAST |
| 5 Çanakkale | 26 Sivas | 49 Kars |
| 6 Balıkesir | 27 Kayseri | 50 Ağrı |
| 7 Manisa | 28 Nevşehir | 51 Erzurum |
| 8 İzmir | 29 Kırsehir | 52 Erzincan |
| 9 Aydın | 30 Niğde | 53 Tunceli |
| 10 Muğla | 31 Konya | 54 Bingöl |
| | | 55 Muş |
| WESTERN | BLACK SEA | |
| 11 Bursa | 32 Kocaeli | SOUTH EAST |
| 12 Bilecik | 33 Sakarya | 56 Malatya |
| 13 Eskişehir | 34 Bolu | 57 Elazığ |
| 14 Kütahya | 35 Zonguldak | 58 Maraş |
| 15 Afyon | 36 Kastamonu | 59 Gaziantep |
| 16 Uşak | 37 Sinop | 60 Adıyaman |
| 17 Denizli | 38 Samsun | 61 Urfa |
| 18 Burdur | 39 Ordu | 62 Diyarbakır |
| 19 Isparta | 40 Giresun | 63 Mardin |
| | 41 Gümüşhane | 64 Siirt |
| | 42 Trabzon | 65 Bitlis |
| | 43 Rize | 66 Van |
| | 44 Artvin | 67 Hakkâri |

FIGURE 7.2 The provinces of Turkey

religious festival that became an undeclared national holiday. By the end of the decade, the directorate managed every aspect of the hajj business as a state monopoly, controlling market entrance and dictating terms of trade.

All the governing parties helped fashion the new pilgrimage apparatus, but Erbakan's preeminence and persistence were unequaled. Although Erbakan headed none of the coalition cabinets, his followers drafted the reorganizations, staffed the new bureaus, and pressed the other parties—on the left, as well as the right—to expand their powers and resources. Erbakan's role is particularly impressive when we compare governments in which he was a junior partner with administrations that other conservatives ran singlehandedly. Controlling for population growth, the peaks of hajj activity in the 1970s dwarfed all the highpoints under Menderes, Demirel, and Özal (Figure 7.3).

Adnan Menderes is often portrayed as the demagogue who opened the floodgates of religious exploitation in Turkish politics. Yet Menderes made only a modest contribution to rebuilding the pilgrimage, which he quickly perceived as undermining his main goal of stimulating private business. Demirel and Ecevit were the prime ministers who put the government in charge of the hajj business, but it was Erbakan who drew up the reforms and drove his partners to sign them.

Turgut Özal became the "Hajji Prime Minster" who publicized the pilgrimage while using it as a springboard to the presidency. Özal simply took advantage of the cumulative efforts of his predecessors. He helped rebuild the

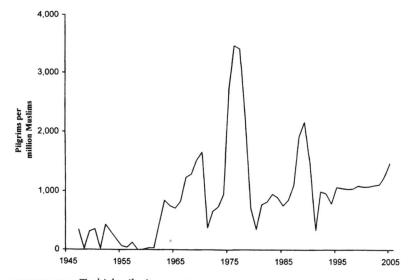

FIGURE 7.3 Turkish pilgrimage rates, 1947–2004

hajj after the 1980 coup, but his major innovation was renegotiating a larger share of the hajj traffic for private travel agents who felt the government had nationalized the most profitable segment of the market.

Özal riveted popular attention by making a single hajj in office. But Erbakan holds the personal record for multiple pilgrimages by a Turkish party chief—twenty-six, according to a 1998 announcement by the Virtue Party (Fazilet Partisi).[18]

Today, the Directorate of Religious Affairs is an unassuming office building in the shadow of Ankara's most controversial landmark—the Kocatepe Mosque and Shopping Center. The Kocatepe complex is a massive monument, holding Ankara's central house of worship, as well as a full complement of well-stocked stores, including a gigantic underground supermarket that swallows most of the city block beneath the mosque itself. After twenty years of quarreling over a host of ultramodern designs, the religious bureaucrats picked the most retro-looking plan imaginable—a Byzantine mother-dome with terraces of progressively smaller domes cascading downward on all sides.

The architects who developed the early prototypes wanted to show the world that the Turks are the most modern Muslims in history. They all submitted futurist visions as daring as any of the trendy mosques in Southeast Asia or the Persian Gulf. But the right-wing governments that built the compound had a different message in mind—and a different audience. They wanted to remind the nation's capital—especially the Ataturkists—that modern Turks are also Muslims who have inherited a glorious past.

Kocatepe is a spiritual-material union par excellence—the Lord above, the market below, the state across the street. In the same spot, Muslims pray, trade, and lobby without breaking stride.

## The Many Facets of Islam in Turkey

The religious controversies shaking Turkey spring from long-standing cultural and regional divisions that intensify as migration and mass communication throw people from different worlds into constant contact. The hajj reflects these divisions in many ways.

Differences in hajj rates highlight areas where religious organization is particularly strong or weak. In addition, the regional mix of male and female pilgrims indicates whether local Muslims encourage parity or inequality between the genders. Because the hajj is such an important component of status, it is a sphere where women's access reveals broader social and economic opportunities.

Comparing hajj participation with other religious activities paints a picture of the ways popular piety expresses itself from region to region. In combination with mosque building, Islamic education, and voting for pro-Islamic candidates, the hajj highlights multiple Muslim subcultures that crisscross one another, blending on some axes and clashing on others.

## Pilgrimage and Regionalism

Based on average pilgrimage rates for all sixty-seven provinces between 1979 and 1993, Turkey's regional divisions run along two major lines: a dominant cleavage separating east and west and a secondary split between north and south[19] (Table 7.1). Year in and year out, western and central Anatolia produce two to three times as many pilgrims per capita as eastern Anatolia. Similarly, hajj rates are nearly twice as high along the Black Sea coast as in the Mediterranean area.

A more precise view of regionalism emerges when we examine hajj rates province by province (Figure 7.4 and Table A7.2). Turkey's "hajj belt" is a solid band of thirteen contiguous provinces covering the western Anatolian hinterland. It resembles a thick, crescent-shaped arch with Bursa as its northwestern tip, Konya as its southerly center, and Kayseri as its eastern edge.

Connected to this core zone are several secondary areas of high pilgrimage. One lies along the highway from Ankara to Samsun on the central Black Sea coast. Bursa and Konya also have neighbors with strong pilgrimages: Çanakkale and Balıkesir on the Aegean coast and Isparta, Burdur, and Denizli near the Mediterranean.

A remote pocket of hajj activity appears on the Black Sea's far eastern shore in Trabzon, Rize, and Gümüşhane. In this corner of the Black Sea, mountain villages and towns are still quite isolated from the rest of the country. Although these are Turkish-speaking communities, many preserve older dialects of Greek, Georgian, and Laz, along with strict adherence to conservative Islam.[20] Turks from other regions are well aware that "Black Sea people" retain a dis-

TABLE 7.1 Turkish pilgrimage rates by region, 1979–1993

| Region | 1979–1984 | 1985–1989 | 1990–1993 | 1979–1993 |
|---|---|---|---|---|
| Thrace | 635 | 1,245 | 697 | 855 |
| Aegean | 497 | 998 | 379 | 633 |
| Western Anatolia | 1,155 | 1,883 | 895 | 1,328 |
| Central Anatolia | 881 | 1,773 | 984 | 1,206 |
| Black Sea | 642 | 1,286 | 597 | 845 |
| Mediterranean | 294 | 674 | 437 | 459 |
| North East | 287 | 633 | 383 | 428 |
| South East | 360 | 808 | 350 | 507 |
| Turkey | 617 | 1,240 | 645 | 832 |

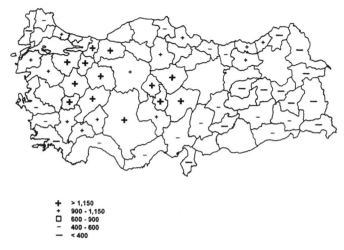

+    > 1,150
+    900 - 1,150
□    600 - 900
-    400 - 600
—    < 400

FIGURE 7.4 Turkish pilgrimage rates by province, 1979–1993

tinctive subculture, even though they are far better at mimicking its features than defining them. All the stereotypes agree the Black Sea is a bastion of Islamic traditionalism, but—as far as the hajj is concerned—only three easterly districts deserve the reputation.

Provinces with unusually low levels of hajj activity cluster in the east. They lie along two nearly perpendicular lines intersecting near Lake Van. One line runs the length of the eastern border, from Artvin and Kars in the north to Hakkâri in the south. The second stretches westward, connecting Van and Bitlis with Bingöl and Tunceli. The zone of weak pilgrimage extends well beyond the east to encompass the entire southern rim of the country. Low hajj rates predominate all along the Mediterranean shore and halfway up the Aegean coast. Moving clockwise from Artvin in the northeast, a long band of weak hajj activity passes through almost every border and coastal district as far as Izmir in the far west. Pilgrimage is weak even near Turkey's European border, particularly in the provinces of Thrace just next to Greece and Bulgaria.

Most striking is the dramatic dichotomy between the Anatolian heartland of the Turkish-speaking, Sunni majority and all other areas populated by any sizable linguistic or sectarian minority. Today's hajj belt is surprisingly similar to the remnant of Anatolia the European powers intended to leave for Turkey after they destroyed the Ottoman Empire in World War I. Pilgrimage is weakest in nearly all provinces surrounding this historic core—in precisely those outlying zones that were to be carved into postwar protectorates and ministates linked to Britain, France, Italy, Greece, and Russia. In effect, today's high pilgrimage area is the truncated Turkey that Europe wanted to create by fiat in 1920 with the Treaty of Sèvres. The surrounding regions of low pilgrimage are the lands that Ataturk and his colleagues regained through arms and diplomacy with the Treaty of Lausanne in 1923.[21]

The regions that produced the most pilgrims during the last two decades also provided the key armies and battlefields in Turkey's war of independence eighty years ago. Indeed, the province of Kütahya—which boasts the highest hajj rate in the country—was the site of the decisive campaign where Turkish forces finally broke the Greek lines and turned the tide of the war. Regions where pilgrimage remains weak also mounted famous rebellions against the young republic. The eastern province of Tunceli consistently trails every other district in pilgrimage. It has a long history of warfare against the central government and against neighboring tribes that allied with Ottoman and republican officials.[22]

The hajj belt is the crossroads for diverse political and religious organizations with strong roots in the towns and villages of the Anatolian interior. Rivalries and shifting alliances between these movements drive religious policy in Ankara and the nation. Although they compete vigorously for votes and money, they all pull in the same direction when it comes to lobbying for government support of the pilgrimage.

Three kinds of groups are particularly entrenched in this region: right-wing parties dividing up the old Menderes coalition, survivals of the Ottoman Sufi orders (tarikats) that recently resurfaced after decades of underground activity, and a handful of Islamic modernist groups that sprang up in the republican era.

All of Turkey's conservative parties enjoy support in the hajj belt. Among high pilgrimage districts, each party has carved out a stronghold—Demirel's followers in the extreme west, Özal's party in the north, and Erbakan to the east. Despite their differences, all share descent from the Democrats and the Justice Party, and they compete for the same voters. In critical elections, when lines between friend and foe are unusually clear, a single party can rally a conservative majority by standing as the spokesman for all factions. After the army deposed Menderes, the adoption of proportional representation made this difficult. Nonetheless, Demirel accomplished it in 1965 and 1969, when socialism was in full swing, and Özal did it in 1983, when the outgoing junta tried to strong-arm voters into swallowing its handpicked candidate. In all these electoral showdowns, voters in the hajj belt closed ranks behind the conservative victors.

The lands between Bursa and Kayseri have formed the backbone of organized Sufism since early Ottoman times. Once again, Kütahya and its neighbors stand out from the pack.[23] It was Sufis from this area who first translated Rumi's works into Turkish, beginning the local practice of making the hajj with the Qur'an in one pocket and a Turkish version of the *Mesnevi* in another. Kütahya remained a Sufi center until the early days of the republic. The historian İsmail Hakki Uzunçarşılıoğlu describes half a dozen mystical orders as active in the area all the way up to the 1924 decree that supposedly banned them.[24]

The revival of the *tarikats* sparked an explosion of Islamic associations and foundations that poured contributions into mosque building, school construction, and scholarships. Nakşibendi groups have been particularly bold in expressing their political ambitions. Under Özal and Erbakan, they formed strong factions inside the Motherland Party and the Welfare Party. After the 1995 elections, about 100 members of parliament—nearly 20 percent of all deputies—were affiliated with a Sufi organization.[25]

Two modernist movements benefit from Sufism's diminished prestige among educated youth and women, especially in the western half of the hajj belt. Most important are the followers of Bediuzzaman Said Nursi—a fiery Kurdish revivalist the republicans exiled to western Turkey, where, even when imprisoned, he attracted a more influential audience than he ever could have found in the east.[26] From the 1930s until his death in 1960, prosecutors pursued Said Nursi from Isparta to Kastomonu and back again, accusing him of preaching against secularism. Each time he was acquitted, boosting demand for handwritten copies of his sermons that disciples spread throughout Anatolia. "Nurcus," as his followers are called, have broken into factions, but most share a boundless enthusiasm for proving Islam's compatibility with modern science and an affinity for the Justice Party–True Path Party as the rightful heir to Menderes's "Democratic mission."[27]

The other modernist group is descended from Süleyman Hilmi Tunahan, an enigmatic *hoca* (religious teacher) who turned Qur'an study into a national passion by persuading thousands of businesses to finance his web of schools and dormitories so Turkey's children would not forget how to read God's word.[28] "Süleymancıs" have business and party connections intersecting those of Nurcus and Nakşibendis from one end of the hajj belt to the other. Whereas most religious groups develop stable relations with a favorite party, Süleymancıs have built passing alliances with all conservative politicians, depending on who seemed most likely to control the government. For Süleymancıs, shifting loyalties are a sign of vulnerability. Desperate to hold onto the educational movement they launched and still subsidize, Süleymancıs must constantly find a counterweight to the Directorate of Religious Affairs, which, since 1971, has run the Qur'an courses and staffed them with graduates of the İmam-Hatip schools instead of Süleymancıs.[29]

The thriving network of towns and provincial capitals stretching from Bursa to Kayseri is not only the heartland of the hajj but also the chief beneficiary of Turkey's success with democracy and capitalism. Here more than anywhere else in Turkey, Islam's prominence signifies a diffusion of wealth and power. In these districts, Islam is a rallying point for rising social groups flexing their political muscle and demanding deference to the rural and small-town voters who are the majority.

Across western Anatolia, the pilgrimage boom is a capstone to the social transformations of the last half century. For these Muslims, the hajj summarizes many achievements simultaneously: the prosperity of the provinces, unswerving support for conservative parties that dominate parliament, greater freedom to practice religion in public, and a chance to translate new wealth into social status.

The geographic distribution of the pilgrimage confirms the progress of the Turkish-speaking Sunni majority, but it also reminds us Turkey is a land of many minorities that have been less fortunate. Some geographical differences in hajj activity reveal subtle variations in subcultures that blend into one another imperceptibly.

Travelers moving north, south, or west from Ankara notice countless changes in dialect and dress, in customs and cuisine, in music and dance, especially as they approach the three coasts. There are also gradual shifts in preferences for the right-wing parties, for mystical or modernist Islam, for building mosques or building schools.

Traveling eastward from Ankara is a different experience altogether. Moving toward the Arab, Iranian, and Caucasian borders, declining hajj rates are rooted in far deeper differences in family structure, ethnicity, and sect. Three groups are particularly striking for their weaker participation in the hajj: women, Kurds, and Alevis.

## Pilgrimage and Gender

When it comes to the relative balance between female and male hajjis, the chasm between east and west is stark and seemingly unbridgeable (Figure 7.5).

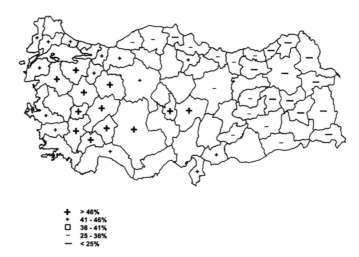

```
+   > 46%
+   41 - 46%
□   36 - 41%
-   25 - 36%
—   < 25%
```

FIGURE 7.5 Percent of female pilgrims by province in Turkey, 1979–1993

The west-central provinces lead the nation in pilgrimage precisely because their delegations to Mecca include large numbers of women. In fact, women are the majority of pilgrims in some provinces in the western part of the hajj belt, and the numbers are evenly split in many others. The western trend in favor of female pilgrimage extends even to the Aegean and European regions. Though the hajj lags behind the national average, women in these regions account for more than 40 percent of all pilgrims.

By contrast, in eastern Turkey, less than one hajji in four is female. In some districts near the border, women pilgrims are negligible: 15 percent in Van and Ağrı, 14 percent in Bitlis, 11 percent in Artvin and Hakkâri. Black Sea provinces display the most contradictory pattern—very high rates for males versus very low rates for females. The Black Sea coast forms a solid band of male-dominated pilgrimage from Zonguldak eastward. Pronounced imbalances between the sexes make the Black Sea seem like a long extension of the impoverished east rather than a pious cousin of the Anatolian heartland. Even in the northeastern districts where the hajj is exceptionally strong, women are only 19 to 30 percent of all pilgrims. On the other hand, the Mediterranean region, which possesses only half the Black Sea's hajj rate, shows no sign of a gender gap.

Divergent patterns of regionalism for female pilgrimage and total pilgrimage suggest different causal explanations. Although overall participation in the hajj varies according to a mix of factors—economic, cultural, and political—the balance between men and women is closely tied to economics alone. Economic development goes hand in hand with gender equality across the country. Women hajjis are predominant in the prosperous west, less frequent in the poorer center, and rarest in the backward east.

Below a certain economic threshold, Turkish hajjis are overwhelmingly male. In the hajj, as in most spheres of Turkish life, men go first. If family resources are adequate, females accompany their fathers, husbands, and sons to Mecca. Otherwise, men go by themselves.

The Black Sea is a striking case where economics and culture reinforce one another to produce a gender bias that is extreme even by Turkish standards. "Black Sea culture" undoubtedly possesses characteristics that boost pilgrimage for males—a high respect for religious learning, an eagerness to travel far from home, and a willingness to let women support the family—and the same characteristics also discourage female pilgrimage by secluding women in the name of male honor and binding them to menial labor.

Regardless of whether Turkey's multiple gender gaps are primarily economic or cultural in origin, they are becoming increasingly politicized, especially among religious voters. Many conservative politicians have begun altering their electoral strategies to accommodate what they perceive as different regional attitudes toward gender.

In 1993, leadership fights arose in two right-wing parties when Turgut

Özal died and Süleyman Demirel retraced his path from the prime ministry to the presidency. Eager to strengthen its advantage with educated women in western Turkey, Demirel's True Path Party chose a little-known female economist from Istanbul, Tansu Çiller, as the new party chief and head of government. At about the same time, power in Özal's Motherland Party passed to Mesut Yılmaz of Rize, who represented the rising influence of Black Sea business.

Both parties stressed gender issues as though they were compensating for their convergence in economic policy. Demirel's small-business supporters accused Mrs. Çiller of embracing Özal's radical free market views, just as his own party was beginning to disavow them. Çiller's backers responded that her appeal to educated women would make it difficult for Yılmaz to compete with her, no matter what economic program he proposed.

Çiller's partisans had good reason to bank on her advantage in tapping the conservative female vote. Both Istanbul and Rize have high rates of pilgrimage, but Istanbul's hajjis are twice as likely to be female—44 percent versus 19 percent. When Çiller and Yılmaz faced off for the first time in the 1995 elections, they polled nearly equal numbers of votes nationally, but she trounced him throughout western Turkey, losing decisively only in Yılmaz's Black Sea strongholds.[30]

## Pilgrimage as a Special Dimension of Religiosity

How does the regional distribution of pilgrimage compare with trends for other types of religious activity? Hajj participation does not coincide exactly with any other dimension of religiosity, but there are wide variations in the degree of overlap or divergence.

Pilgrimage most resembles the patterns for urban mosques and enrollment in Qur'an courses[31] (Figure 7.6). Urban mosques are most numerous at the heart of the hajj belt in western and central Anatolia. Qur'an courses are widely scattered along the Black Sea and through the central interior.

The zones of mosques and Qur'an courses intersect in the middle of Anatolia, and, added together, they give a good approximation of the hajj belt's total reach. Of course, managing mosques and supervising Qur'an courses are routine duties of the Directorate of Religious Affairs. In viewing the web of pilgrims, mosques, and Qur'an courses, we are also observing the effective reach of the religious bureaucracy and its connections with local Islamic associations.

There is less overlap between pilgrimage and enrollment in İmam-Hatip schools, and there is hardly any coincidence between hajj and votes for the Welfare Party—the most religiously oriented of the right-wing parties. Support for both the İmam-Hatip schools and the Welfare Party is far more concen-

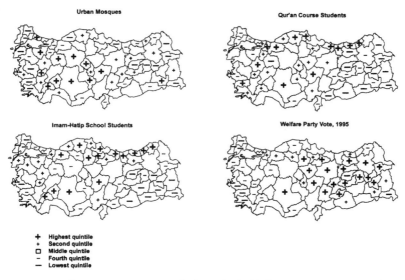

FIGURE 7.6 Regional patterns of religiosity in Turkey

trated than hajj participation. These are the dimensions where Islam in Turkey is most colored by peculiarities of local culture.

Islamic secondary education is popular everywhere along the Black Sea coast. For many years, young men from villages and small towns in this area have been overrepresented in religious occupations throughout Turkey. Black Sea migrants are famous for specializing as itinerant *medrese* teachers, minaret builders, and muftis. Their influence in Ankara has risen since the 1960s, when İmam-Hatip school graduates began filling most of the central posts in the Directorate of Religious Affairs. Some of the most powerful directors of religious affairs have been well-known Islamic scholars from the Black Sea. Sait Yazıcıoğlu, who served under Turgut Özal, hailed from Of, a town near Trabzon renowned for its dogmatic *hocas* and ubiquitous hajjis. Lütfi Doğan, who guided the directorate in the 1970s, became a Welfare Party deputy from Gümüşhane-Bayburt, a rugged alpine region of unforgettable beauty where Saturday morning mosque courses are crammed with straight-backed village kids learning to read the Qur'an.[32]

The tendency to express Islamic solidarity at the polls is also distinct from hajj activity. Support for the Welfare Party is concentrated in the eastern half of Anatolia—precisely where the pilgrimage has always been weakest. It seems odd that the party that worked the hardest to bring modern hajj management to Turkey reaped so little electoral benefit from its efforts, but Erbakan's party succeeded so well in legitimizing the new pilgrimage system that it was no longer a distinctive part of its platform. All the conservative parties and even many leftists now endorse a national pilgrimage. If the hajj is still a contentious issue, it is not a life-or-death struggle about secularism but a haggle over administrative competence and political spoils. Besides, the Welfare Party and its successors have many fish to fry, including grievances more economic than religious.


## The Social and Political Bases of Pilgrimage

The strongest correlates of hajj participation are other types of religious activity, particularly areas where the Directorate of Religious Affairs holds sway[33] (Table A7.3 and Figure A7.1). Qur'an courses, Islamic associations, and urban mosques lead the field. The urban bias of pilgrimage is evident in the weaker role of the İmam-Hatip schools and rural mosques. Poor village communities are far more likely to invest their surplus in mosques than in pilgrimages, especially for females, who fall further behind in hajj as rural mosques proliferate.

Many measures of development and rising living standards encourage pilgrimage, but in nearly every case they have a greater impact for women than for men. Per capita income, literacy, and telephone usage are the strongest economic correlates of hajj participation. Pilgrimage rises with industrial and service workers and falls with agriculture.

The type of land tenure prevailing among farmers is important for pilgrimage rates of rural women. Female hajjis are common in regions where agriculture is highly commercialized. Independent farmers renting additional land to supplement income from their small plots are most likely to take their female relatives along on pilgrimage. Women pilgrims are rarest where landholding is highly fragmented or where rural society is deeply split between big estate owners and peasants working other people's land as either wage laborers or sharecroppers.

Language and ethnicity are just as important as economic factors. The gap between Turkish speakers and Kurdish speakers is profound. Cultural and economic divisions are so closely intertwined that it is often impossible to say where one ends and the other begins. Kurds make the hajj less frequently not because of any inherent predisposition against pilgrimage but because they usually lack the income and influence that pave the way for Turks.

Districts with sizable Arabic-speaking populations also have low hajj rates, though nowhere near the depressed levels of the Kurdish regions. A Slavic-speaking ancestry has no influence on overall hajj participation, but it is the only minority heritage clearly favoring female pilgrimage. In terms of their propensities to make the pilgrimage, the major ethnic groups form a familiar hierarchy: Arabic speakers are less alienated than the Kurds, and Slavic immigrants are not as well integrated as native Turks.

The political rewards of hajj sponsorship are indisputable[34] (Table A7.4). The more enthusiastically the right-wing parties embraced the pilgrimage, the more faithfully Muslim voters embraced their candidates. Demirel played this card more effectively than Menderes, and Özal played it best of all. By the 1990s, the link between pilgrimage and conservative politics was so well established that all the rightist parties shared the benefits. The True Path Party ran stronger where women hajjis prevailed, the Welfare Party and the Motherland Party were more attractive to men, and the National Action Party did well with both genders.

Right-wing candidates received solid support from high pilgrimage areas when they were united in a single party as in 1950, 1969, and 1983. In 1995, none of the conservative parties swept the field, but the right as a whole continued to dominate provinces with high hajj rates. In 1999, the National Action Party carried the hajj belt, and in 2002 the same constituency lined up behind the new Justice and Development Party of Recep Tayyip Erdogăn that replaced Erbakan's banned movement. Only one party thrives in regions of low hajj participation—the pro-Kurdish People's Democratic Party, whose leaders are usually under arrest or prosecution for alleged ties to guerrillas.

Politics, culture, and economics all contribute to hajj participation in Turkey. Assessing their relative importance is difficult, but a rough idea emerges when we control for rural per capita income and the proportion of Turkish speakers (Table A7.5). Three political-organizational factors stand out: Qur'an courses, urban mosques, and votes for the Republican People's Party. The strongest (negative) party connection to pilgrimage appears for the left-wing group closest to the Alevi minority, a community well known for indifference to the hajj.

More important than all the political parties in predicting hajj rates are Qur'an courses and urban mosques—the factors that, in addition to pilgrimage itself, best reflect the growing strength of the religious bureaucracy. After decades of standing in the shadow of the politicians who nurtured it, the Directorate of Religious Affairs has acquired a life of its own. Right-wing parties accept the directorate as a friendly pressure group, and, on the left, only the Republican People's Party still regards it as a true breach of secularism.


## Islam and Turkey's Rebirth as a World Power

Even though military commanders and politicians clash repeatedly over the role of religion in domestic politics, they agree about the utility of Islam in broadening Turkey's influence internationally. Civilian and military leaders are still a long way from working out durable pacts on the daily practice of secularism and democracy at home. But, in the last twenty years, they have developed a common belief that history is again presenting Turkey with irresistible opportunities to project power in many parts of the world simultaneously.

The common thread in these possibilities is Turkey's Islamic heritage. Religious attachments that bedevil Turkish leaders domestically give them an inherent advantage in dealing with half the states of Asia and Africa.

The collapse of the Soviet Union, the persecution of Muslims in the Balkans, the discovery of Caspian oil, warfare in the Caucasus and Persian Gulf, and the scramble for footholds in Central Asia all loosened the tethers that once tied Ankara so firmly to Washington and Berlin. Today, when Turkish politicians and businesspeople look abroad, they see so many open doors they hardly know which to enter first. After decades of disassociating themselves from global ambitions that vexed the Ottomans, Turkey's leaders are conducting a far-flung diplomacy in every capital between Brussels and Beijing.[35]

Turks never believed that their friendship was appreciated by the West. Time and again, they felt humiliated by what they perceive as endless American and European scolding over everything from Cyprus and arms shipments to human rights and customs duties. The European Union pushed Turkey's application for membership from the head of the line to the back of the line and, then, out of the line altogether.

Nowadays, Turks of all political orientations argue that they must make new friends if they are ever to gain the respect of old ones. However much they disagree over domestic policy, Turks yearn for new alliances that will make their country a valued leader instead of an eternal supplicant.

Three men have dominated the debate over how Turkey should recast its foreign policy: Kenan Evren, Turgut Özal, and Necmettin Erbakan. All had bold—even grandiose—visions of Turkey as a pivotal player in the fluid balance of power they expected after the Cold War.

Each man tried to strengthen Turkey's leverage with the West by building closer ties to an array of Third World nations with which Turks might rely on cultural and religious affinities to smooth their way in business and diplomacy. By trial and error, they created a new diplomacy—a sort of "de Gaullism on the Bosporus"—that compensates for souring relations with NATO and the European Union by strengthening ties to the Islamic and Turkish-speaking worlds.

The most unlikely member of this trio was General Kenan Evren, the leader of the 1980 coup and the first Ataturkist ruler to explicitly invoke Islam at home and abroad. Evren was convinced that political violence in Turkey stemmed from the younger generation's corruption by left-wing propaganda. He insisted the state could restore social peace only by creating an educational system that instilled discipline and morality. Even as the Islamic revolution unfolded next door in Iran, he argued that socialism was the cause of Turkey's anarchy and that religion was the antidote. Throughout the 1980s, as head of the military junta and then as president, General Evren reinvented Ataturkism by merging governmental and religious authority in ways no civilian politician could have dared.

During the preparation of Turkey's new constitution, Evren gave wide publicity to right-wing professors and technocrats touting a blend of nationalism and religion known as the "Turkish-Islamic synthesis." By fusing Ataturkism and Islam in a transparently authoritarian creed, they infuriated both religious and nonreligious Turks who had welcomed the 1980 coup as a deliverance from years of urban terrorism. Nonetheless, Evren carried on an extended flirtation with the "synthesizers," intent on translating their views into policy.[36]

Evren's neo-Ataturkism permanently altered the Turkish practice of secularism in two ways—by adopting compulsory religious education and by placing Turkey at the center of Islamic diplomacy. The junta first considered religion classes that would survey ethical principles of many faiths without favoring any. But the Directorate of Religious Affairs prepared the textbooks and course outlines, suggesting a semiofficial version of Islam would be the standard diet. Henceforth, the directorate devoted more of its rising publication budget to convincing young people that Ataturk was a faithful Muslim chosen by God to defend his religion as well as his motherland.

Shortly after the resumption of civilian rule, Evren became the first Turkish president to participate in the summits of the Organization of the Islamic Conference (OIC). In 1984, he flew to Casablanca for a meeting of the OIC's highest decision-making body, the Heads of State Conference.[37] Evren's attendance was a great coup for the OIC.

Turkey was a leading opponent of an Islamic international organization when King Faysal proposed the idea in the 1960s. Now, the blessing of a former Turkish general eased the entrance of secular regimes like Indonesia and Nigeria, where military rulers were still skeptical about the OIC. By the end of the 1980s, Turkey, Indonesia, and Nigeria were no longer bystanders in Islamic diplomacy. Indeed, their growing weight in the OIC allowed the Saudis to push through sweeping reforms of the hajj regime that Riyadh could not have achieved alone.

Egypt and Iran also welcomed Turkish prominence in the OIC. Hosni Mubarak was just beginning to repair Egypt's ties with Arab and Islamic countries that had denounced Anwar Sadat's "sellout" in the Camp David Accords. Egyptians were delighted to receive another powerful Muslim country that recognized Israel. Iran also relied on Turkey to break its diplomatic isolation. Iran boycotted the Casablanca Conference to protest Iraqi aggression and Saudi attacks on Shi'ite pilgrims. Yet before the summit, the Iranian foreign minister flew to Ankara to seek Evren's assurance that Turkey would kill any effort to censure Iran during its absence. In the longer term, Tehran also saw Turkey as a valued mediator that would dilute Arab and Saudi power in the OIC.

Compared with the tight-lipped Evren, Turgut Özal was disarmingly candid about making Islam an instrument of foreign policy. Just after winning the

1983 election, Özal told foreign journalists: "There is a large group of Islamic countries. Once they looked on the Ottoman Empire as the leader of the Islamic World. We shall lead these countries and this will make us more important to the West."[38]

Özal's critics accused him of stressing religion to obscure the pain his free-market reforms inflicted on the masses and the new fortunes they showered on his supporters. In defense, he insisted Turks had to raise their morals as well as their incomes to avoid the social decay that unbridled materialism had unleashed on the West. By combining liberal capitalism with an Islamic renaissance, he was preparing the country for a new era of global prominence—"the Turkish Century."

Özal's genius was his ability to portray Turkey's economic opening as a bonanza for both East and West. The key was diversifying foreign trade and investment so a stronger Turkey would appear to serve capitalism and Islam at the same time. Under Özal, Turkey's trade with the Middle East surpassed its trade with Western Europe for the first time. Swapping engineering services and skilled labor for oil, Turkey dealt freely with many powers that were hostile to one another, including Iran and Iraq, as well as Saudi Arabia and Libya.

Meanwhile, Özal was careful to mend fences in the West, firming military ties with the United States to offset Turkey's economic spats with the European Union. During the first Gulf War, Özal joined the American-led alliance despite objections from public opinion and his own generals. He faced down vocal opposition to the war to convince Americans that Turkey was more indispensable than ever for protecting Western interests in the Islamic world.

Özal often relied on religious connections to open doors in international business and politics. When he permitted Saudis to open Islamic investment companies in Turkey, he also got them to pay the salaries of preachers that the Directorate of Religious Affairs sent to Germany to combat Iranian propaganda among Turkish migrant workers. Özal's close connections with Nakşibendi mystics helped his forays into the newly independent states of Central Asia, where Turkey was countering overtures from Russia and Iran. Just before he died, Özal completed an exhausting tour of Central Asia, where he argued that Muslim Turkey was their natural bridge to Western liberalism, both economically and politically.[39]

Although many claim that Turkey's religion and culture impede its entry to Europe, the United States sees those very characteristics as beneficial in penetrating Asian markets beyond its grasp. Washington encourages Turkish ambitions in Central Asia to prevent Russia and Iran from monopolizing access to oil and natural gas around the Caspian Sea, particularly in Azerbaijan, Kazakhstan, and Turkmenistan. Three American presidents have sought to convince an international consortium of energy companies to fulfill Özal's dream of building a pipeline between Baku and Turkey's Mediterranean coast. The Turkish route is longer and more expensive than alternative pipelines to the Black Sea or the Persian Gulf, but Washington and Ankara insist the West needs multiple outlets to deny its enemies a stranglehold on Caspian oil.[40]

By the time Necmettin Erbakan became prime minister in 1996, Turkey's rapprochement with the Muslim world was in its second decade, and its involvement in Islamic diplomacy was routine. Nonetheless, during the single year he held power, Erbakan stirred up more fuss over foreign policy than Özal and Evren combined. His most audacious suggestion was that Turkey should take the lead in organizing an Islamic Common Market and an Islamic Defense Pact. Although Erbakan described these as substitutes for the European Community and NATO, he quickly shifted gears, arguing that Turkey could reach out in new directions without renouncing its commitments to the West. Erbakan even endorsed Turkey's defense agreements with Israel to avoid a confrontation with the military. He disapproved of the pact with Tel Aviv, but he understood its value in deterring Syrian mischief and hedging against a possible U.S. arms embargo.

Erbakan undercut these conciliatory efforts with calamitous forays in personal diplomacy. The controversy surrounding Özal's pilgrimage to Mecca was trivial compared with the uproar over Erbakan's visits to Iran and Libya. Özal could claim his hajj was an act of personal devotion and a friendly move toward a Western ally. Erbakan had no such defense. The Tehran trip was his first overseas appearance as prime minister, and it seemed calculated to bury Washington's faltering campaign to isolate Iran.[41] If the Americans could not keep NATO's poorest member in line, they could hardly expect Germany and Japan to forgo ventures even more lucrative than the oil deals Erbakan signed with the mullahs. Erbakan's visit to Tripoli was far worse. Khaddafi welcomed Turkey's president but insulted its military and political establishment, calling them puppets of American imperialism. When Erbakan returned home, he was denounced for standing in silence as Khaddafi turned his goodwill gesture into a farce.

On the day the military toppled him in June 1997, Erbakan was in the midst of his most ambitious international project. In Istanbul, he hosted the charter conference for the nucleus of an Islamic Common Market. Three participants—Turkey, Iran, and Pakistan—were already partners in a regional market tracing its origins to the U.S.-sponsored Central Treaty Organization (CENTO) of the 1950s. The new group included five more countries—Nigeria, Egypt, Bangladesh, Malaysia, and Indonesia—with a potential market of 800 million people from West Africa to Southeast Asia.[42]

The Istanbul assembly convened when Turks were still digesting the news that nearly every country in Eastern Europe had moved ahead of them in the queue for membership in the European Union. Just as Brussels was shunning Turkey for the likes of Estonia and Slovenia, Erbakan was determined to show that Ankara could be the capital of an Islamic Union three times the size of the EU. Erbakan dazzled the conference with high-tech projects for building aircraft, helicopters, automobiles, and computers. He envisioned an elaborate division of labor, with Turkey taking the lead in industrialization, Iran in tele-communications, Malaysia in banking, and Nigeria in energy. Egypt would focus on foreign trade, Pakistan on agriculture, Bangladesh on rural develop-ment, and Indonesia on human resources.

The meeting was equally newsworthy for those who were not invited to Istanbul. It excluded all the Arabian oil emirates that usually bankrolled Islamic economic organizations. Except for Egypt, not a single Arab country was rep-resented. The "Developing Eight," as the group was called, challenged both the European Union and the Organization of the Islamic Conference. The largest non-Arab members of the OIC—once regarded as the "periphery" of Islam—were signaling that they were now the major centers of Muslim wealth and power. When the armed forces deposed Erbakan on the fourth day of the con-ference, Saudi Arabia dutifully lamented the assault on Turkish democracy. But none of Erbakan's Arabian allies expressed the slightest disappointment when Turkey's new government shelved his plans for greater cooperation be-tween Muslim states.

## Ataturkism with a Smiling Face

Although Erbakan's ouster was a setback for religious activists, it did not re-verse Islam's advance. Erbakan was always a polarizing figure, and Muslim leaders often cringed at his bluster even when they sympathized with his pol-icies. The generals who overthrew him became equally provocative when they threatened to block the new Virtue Party from forming a government, even if it won future elections. Critics of the military worried that the generals might follow the same bloody course as the Algerian commanders who touched off civil war by denying power to a victorious Islamic party. It seemed the top officers wanted everyone to fear the worst so swing voters would avoid the Virtue Party or stay away from the polls altogether.

Yet military antipathy toward the Islamic movement does not prevent in-dividual soldiers from reaching out to Muslims willing to meet them halfway. In awkward interactions with pious civilians, Turkish officers frequently show far more tact and tolerance than their detractors realize. About a year after Erbakan's resignation, an air force commander displayed those virtues in abun-dance toward a Muslim lady at a socially mixed ceremony in Ankara.[43]

General İlhan Kılıç was greeting guests at a reception on an airbase when Fatma Çelenkoğlu approached to pay her respects. Mrs. Çelenkoğlu wore a head cover more concealing than the simple scarf Turkish women usually don in public. It protected her hair and neck, and its long ends were tucked into the top of her dress so the covering would not come undone. Her headdress was precisely the sort of "turban" strict secularists regard as a sign of rebellion and are determined to ban from universities and state facilities. In the presence of photographers and nervous onlookers, General Kılıç asked Mrs. Çelenkoğlu to open her scarf and retie its ends under her chin. Mrs. Çelenkoğlu complied, wondering what all the fuss was about yet not wishing to offend her illustrious host.

Besieged by reporters, she explained that she had accompanied her son and husband from Adapazarı, a conservative market town at the eastern edge of Istanbul's sprawling industrial corridor. The family was invited to the base so the son, Yasin, could accept an award he won in a national art competition the air force sponsored for secondary school students. Oblivious to the controversy swirling around her, Mrs. Çelenkoğlu assured the journalists, "We don't belong to any group that would be considered 'radical.' All the women in my family dress this way."

Things were far more difficult for the general, who was on the spot in many ways. He was one of the nation's most powerful soldiers, but the Çelenkoğlus were still his guests at a gathering that was supposed to make the air force a part of everyday life for ordinary citizens. Worse still, the awards were being distributed in the midst of a larger celebration of the air force's eighty-seventh anniversary. The hall was filled with retired and active-duty officers who had just watched General Kılıç kiss the hand of Turkey's first female fighter pilot. Within minutes, the general had to honor two women whose contrasting "uniforms" and life choices summed up the fractured legacy of Ataturk's cultural reforms. The air force brass was playing to too many audiences at once, and it was impossible to please them all.

General Kılıç did his best to square the circle. When reporters asked if he disapproved of Mrs. Çelenkoğlu's "turban" on military premises, he put things in perspective. "We are trying to create a modern Turkey," he explained, "but we have no problem with head-covering. Our sisters who work in the fields of Anatolia wear scarves tied under their chins. So do our Black Sea sisters who carry wood on their backs. We have no negative feelings toward them. Let them cover themselves in the market and in private workplaces, but not in state offices. After all, we too are the state."

Like many Ataturkists, the general wants an amicable solution to religious differences, but he fears his side may already have retreated too far. His reactions to Islam are based more on appearances and intentions than on ideology. His comfort with pious Muslims depends on their willingness to respect his notions of propriety, especially in official settings.

Having acquiesced in the steady erosion of taboos against religious expression in so many areas of public life, Ataturkists need to accentuate certain limits to reassure themselves they still exist somewhere. Hence, the extreme preoccupation with the "how" and "where" of religiously inspired dress, as well as the constant suspicion that it is a display of power more than faith.[44]

Drawing protective boundaries around certain types of religious expression helps nominal Muslims and nonbelievers feel they are upholding secularism in principle even as they relax it in practice. Sometimes, it is difficult to understand why secularists draw lines more firmly in some places than in others. Yet the specific boundaries are less important than the tacit agreement that they should be negotiable instead of imposed by either side.

For older Ataturkists like General Kılıç, desire for a flexible secularism is often implicit in personal behavior. Young Ataturkists are challenging stereotypes about religion head-on. Several journalists, academics, and professionals have written best sellers urging colleagues to thoroughly rethink their views of Islam and their daily relations with Muslims. The common theme is that their generation must develop a pragmatic secularism accommodating profound changes since Ataturk's death, particularly the need for open expressions of religious and cultural diversity in a liberal democracy.

Writers such as Gencay Şaylan, Ruşen Çakır, Nilüfer Göle, and İştar Tarhanlı have criticized the military's heavy-handed approach to religion. They attack generals like Kenan Evren, who manipulated Islam, as well as the newer crop of commanders who stepped up the suppression of religious groups in the 1990s. From different perspectives, each sends Ataturkists the same jolting message: "Devote more effort to learning about Islam in Turkey instead of trying to use it or crush it."

They call on their generation to reeducate themselves about the Islamic movement and draw its leaders into a common defense of civil liberties and social justice. They urge secularists to shed their image as elitists who see religion as a badge of ignorance and superstition. In their view, Ataturkists can wield influence only if they take educated Muslims seriously and persuade them that compromise is the best way to settle their differences.

Appealing to Ataturkists' enlightened self-interest, each author highlights an aspect of the Islamic movement that is compatible with modernism and democracy. Ataturkists are introduced to bridge groups with ideals and frustrations not so different from their own. Readers quickly learn that, if treated with tact and respect, the Islamic movement can develop into a friendly adversary and, in time, a strategic ally.

Şaylan holds out the tantalizing prospect that, by allowing Muslims to build an independent force, Ataturkists can weaken the right without abandoning democracy. He claims that Muslim voters are tired of being taken for granted by right-wing politicians and that their desire for separate parties is a sign of growing confidence and maturity. Şaylan argues that Turkey's Muslim leaders are enthusiastic capitalists with no interest in an Iranian-style theocracy that would cut them off from global markets. Ataturkists can continue their clichéd attacks on religion—and cement Islam's alliance with their enemies— or they can create incentives for restive Muslims to avoid the political fringes and move to the center. But Şaylan warns democratically minded Ataturkists that they cannot hope to tame the Islamic movement unless they acknowledge that educated Muslims are equally dedicated to reason and pluralism.[45]

Ruşen Çakır takes a more reassuring tone, arguing that Ataturkists and Muslims share common experiences and overlapping interests. He notes that many Islamic activists were inspired by leftist students who shook up society in the 1960s and by postmodernist critics of the West such as Ivan Illich, R. D. Laing, and E. F. Schumacher. Çakır believes Ataturkists have a golden opportunity to engage Muslim leaders in constructive dialogue because they constantly argue with each other and desperately want to preserve the freedom to interpret Islam in divergent ways. He notes that the most influential Muslim writers are natives of provincial towns and villages who attended a university in the big cities, where they were forced to reinvent their personalities and adapt to modern institutions. Çakır believes Ataturkists should display a similar open-mindedness toward religious Turks, who often know more about urban life than sheltered city dwellers know about the provinces, where Islam is as strong as ever.[46]

In Nilüfer Göle's portrait of women in the Islamic movement, Turkish feminists discover countless examples of struggle and idealism that could have come from their own lives. Hard-line secularists expecting to catch a glance of the Islamic "other" soon realize that they are looking squarely at themselves. Göle shows that when young women adopt Islamic dress, they usually do so for their own purposes rather than to please the overbearing men who try to control them. Letting her interviewees tell their own stories, she makes it clear that Muslim women wear headscarves and overcoats for the same reason nonreligious women avoid plunging necklines: They want men to treat them with respect. Islamic dress is certainly a radical challenge to the status quo but not in the way Ataturkists assume. The target is not an abstract secularism but the palpable sexism uniting most Turkish males, regardless of religious and partisan differences.[47]

İştar Tarhanlı's critique of Ataturkism is the most provocative imaginable. She argues that Ataturkists have never supported a secular system, and it is high time they joined in creating the real thing. Tarhanlı reminds Ataturkists that *they* constructed the state apparatus that nurtures the Islamic movement with increasing grants of authority and funds. The same agencies Ataturkists once used to squelch counterrevolution now help hundreds of religious groups to colonize the state. An expert in administrative law, Tarhanlı claims that most state religious services are illegal, including the hajj agency. In 1979, Turkey's Constitutional Court struck down the statute that expanded the powers of the Directorate of Religious Affairs, and governments filled the gap with a stream of executive orders instead of coaxing another law out of badly fractured parliaments. Sooner or later, the whole mess will have to be renegotiated, and party leaders will be stuck with the question they love to dodge: "How can

Turkey's rulers deliver services Muslim voters take for granted while preserving the façade of official neutrality that secularism requires?"[48]

## Privatization: Clients and Rivals of the Religious Bureaucracy

Nowadays, the most frequent answer is privatization. Allowing Islamic organizations to provide services with their own funds has a double appeal. It takes advantage of the enormous resources Muslim groups have amassed while lightening the burden on citizens who don't want their taxes financing the Sunni establishment. In Western Turkey, local associations and charitable foundations can manage on their own. Private contributions pour into groups for building mosques, schools, and clinics, as well as helping pilgrims and preachers. Most would gladly forgo state assistance if it ended meddling in their activities by bureaucrats.

Privatization is not the natural choice for groups accustomed to using the religious bureaucracy as a political weapon. Ataturkists relied on the directorate to control Islam, and Muslim leaders viewed it as a direct tap into the treasury. The directorate prospered because its managers manipulated both sides with remarkable skill. Depending on who was in power, pious bureaucrats could present their expanding activities as containing Islam, promoting it, or both. By sending a dual message, the directorate maintains at least lukewarm support from clienteles that disagree with one another. Hard-line Ataturkists look to the directorate for supervision of Qur'an courses, İmam-Hatip schools, and Islamic publishers. Their notion of secularism requires an official watchdog protecting the national interest, not a referee standing on the sidelines.

Muslim groups believe the state has a solemn obligation to maintain places of worship and staff them with qualified preachers. This is particularly important in remote provinces where voluntary associations are not strong enough to make self-reliance realistic. In those regions, people want the directorate to stop censoring the sermons Muslims hear at local mosques and to care more for the people who worship in them. Yet, like the Ataturkists, they also expect the directorate to represent them inside the state itself.

Hajj administration could be one of the first areas of reform. Many groups—Islamic and secular—already see benefits in privatizing pilgrimage. Strict Ataturkists would have the satisfaction of knowing that Turkish hajjis were bearing their own costs. The ballooning class of religious professionals would lose the revenue stream they now control single-handedly: The Religion Foundation of Turkey. Nothing worries secularists more than the prospect of an Islamic bureaucracy with the prestige and resources of the Ottoman 'ulama. Diverting profits of the hajj business from ambitious clerics might be the most effective precaution prosecularist Turks can take.

Religious bureaucrats also face powerful resentment in the business community—the major financier for all right-wing parties. Travel agents are enthusiastic advocates of privatizing religious services. Small firms struggle to stay in business from one year to the next, and often it is the pilgrimage that makes the difference. For them, the hajj is a lucrative market the state is entitled to regulate but not monopolize.[49]

The travel agents' approach is pragmatic and flexible. They readily adapted to government intervention in the 'umra because they could pass on the costs of regulation to customers without handing over extra profits to the state. Private business would be delighted to have a similar arrangement for the hajj, but they are realists willing to bargain step by step toward a more even division of the market. They know religious bureaucrats worked for years to consolidate power and wealth—and they are prepared to do the same in reversing the process.

# 8

# Indonesia

*Greening the Pancasila State*

In just three decades, Indonesia has moved from the fringe of the
Islamic world to center stage. An island society long regarded as indifferent to imported "Middle Eastern" religion has become a model
of deepening Islamization. A secular state that once banned any hint
of "political Islam" is now fostering some of the world's most vigorous debates about Islamic democracy. A warring assortment of
tribes and sects, absorbed in an endless struggle to become a nation,
has emerged as the world's fourth largest market and a pivotal
player in Islamic diplomacy.

In 1991, President Suharto made his first pilgrimage to Mecca.
Suharto's hajj was a grand spectacle that both symbolized and accel-
erated profound changes in his country and his regime. Accompanied by his wife and his closest business associates, the president
led an entourage of soldiers and officials in a performance of state
theater aimed at both Indonesians and foreigners.

Suharto's domestic audience was the electorate and the military.
The president was preparing to campaign for a fifth term in office.
Annoyed with ambitious soldiers and technocrats who were questioning his capacity to rule, he was eager to show would-be rivals
that he still enjoyed a mass popularity they could never match.

For years, Suharto turned a deaf ear to religious advisors who
told him a presidential pilgrimage would help rebuild bridges with
the Islamic community and dispel nagging rumors that he was
not really a practicing Muslim. Now, as he considered the prospect
of drawing millions of Muslim voters away from the weak opposi-

tion parties, a timely hajj seemed like the perfect warm-up for the campaign trail.

International developments led Suharto in the same direction. He was receiving urgent appeals from Saudi Arabia's rulers for help in fending off attacks on several fronts. The Saudis were still reeling from criticism over the al-Mu'aisim Tunnel disaster of 1990, when more than 1,400 pilgrims—mostly Indonesians and Malaysians—were crushed to death. Outrage over the carnage was fueling Iranian-led demands to replace Saudi Arabian sovereignty over the Holy Cities with an international administration. Reports of Saudi callousness in retrieving the victims' remains caused many Indonesians to call for reforms in hajj management. Eager to patch up relations with Indonesia, the Saudi government invited Suharto to lead his country's contingent on the very next hajj, adding that Indonesians would even be welcome to bring their own military escorts.

Just as Suharto was considering Riyadh's proposal, Iraq invaded Kuwait and threatened the Saudi oil fields. The Gulf War brought thousands of non-Muslim troops to Saudi territory, and many remained there long after the liberation of Kuwait. Saudi Arabia's critics began asking how anyone could expect the royal family to protect the Holy Cities when they seemed incapable of protecting themselves without American soldiers on their soil.

As the Saudis were still coping with the aftermath of the Gulf War, Suharto finally agreed to make the hajj—a decision that helped Saudi Arabia reassure skeptics that pilgrims would be safe. In fact, Suharto's journey increased pressures on Saudi Arabia to move ahead with one of the most controversial proposals for hajj reform—the new quota system that allocates hajj visas according to each nation's population size. Indonesia was the greatest beneficiary of this system because it had more room for pilgrimage growth than any other country. Saudi Arabia was already committed to implementing the quotas, but it was hearing strong objections from Indonesia's smaller neighbors, particularly Malaysia and Singapore, which knew their delegations would be frozen or reduced. Immediately after Suharto's pilgrimage, the Saudis began rigorously enforcing the quotas, and the Indonesian pilgrimage soared.

Ever since, Indonesians from all regions and ethnic groups have made the hajj in record numbers. Today, Indonesia sends more pilgrims to Mecca than any other country in history has sent—about 200,000 annually, accounting for nearly 20 percent of all overseas hajjis. As in the past, most Indonesian pilgrims come from Java, the most populous island, but the highest rates of participation are on Sumatra, Kalimantan, and Sulawesi—the "outer islands" where Islam's roots are deepest. Under Suharto, the "hajj gap" between Java and the rest of the country steadily narrowed. Before 1990, hajj rates in the outer islands consistently ran two or three times ahead of those on Java. Nowadays, however, even Java's *abangan*—the millions of "statistical Muslims," once portrayed as irrepressible mystics and spirit worshipers—have joined the resurgence of mainstream Islam sweeping the archipelago.

Ironically, the aged dictator who presided over the surge in pilgrimage was the very man who spent his first twenty years in power crushing all independent efforts to politicize Islam. Suharto abolished the powerful parties that dominated the Sukarno era, particularly the communist and Islamic movements that the army held responsible for years of turmoil and bloodshed. His New Order tried to depoliticize society by turning the rural population into a "floating mass" that was forbidden contact with any party between elections except for the government-sponsored apparatus, Golkar.

Suharto also forced all parties and mass organizations to endorse his personal interpretations of Pancasila as the "sole basis" of the political system. Pancasila had been Indonesia's official ideology since 1945, when Sukarno propounded it to paper over cracks in the nationalist movement. It had always been an eclectic blend of the "five principles" (*panca sila*) that Sukarno described as the core values of Indonesian culture: belief in God, democracy through consultation and consensus, national unity, humanitarianism, and social justice.[1] Unlike his predecessor, Suharto relied on Pancasila to narrow discourse rather than broaden it. Any political dissenter could be accused of being "anti-Pancasila." Suspected communists and Muslim extremists were especially vulnerable, but, after the communists were exterminated in the mid-1960s, it was religious critics who ran the greatest risks. When the president told Indonesia's associations to declare that Pancasila was the only possible foundation of the state, he was effectively demanding an open admission from Muslim leaders that the dream of an Islamic state was dead.

Nonetheless, by the late 1980s, Suharto's alliances shifted dramatically. As his relations with the military deteriorated, Suharto reversed his strategy of depoliticizing Islam by seeking support from a new generation of Muslim leaders who had prospered under his economic policies. Under the New Order, thousands of young Muslims, educated in Indonesia and abroad, rose to prominence in government, business, and the professions. Expecting this growing middle class to remain pliable and dependent, Suharto was willing to expand their influence in public life. Government funds flowed into a wide range of Islamic activities, including pilgrimage, religious education, proselytizing, mosque building, charitable services, publishing, and broadcasting. Suharto also responded to Muslims' concerns about issues far beyond religious policy. He embraced many of their proposals to aid native entrepreneurs, to curb the power of army officers and Chinese tycoons, and to give Islamic groups more political leeway—even allowing them a voice in selecting his cabinet and vice president.

At first, Suharto's change of heart seemed to serve him well. Support for Islam boosted his popularity, producing greater landslide victories for Golkar and sending his presidency into its fourth decade. Enhancing Islam's power also deepened fissures in Indonesia's diverse Muslim community. By offering religious leaders more freedom and largess, Suharto sought to prevent any of them from turning into a potent opposition.

The flexible president found that many of his former Muslim critics were eager to forget the past and make themselves available for manipulation. When religious leaders were accused of being co-opted, they replied that Suharto did more to strengthen Islam than all the guerrillas and politicians who battled in vain for an Islamic constitution.[2] Suharto's Muslim supporters insisted that they were changing the Pancasila state far more than it was changing them. Acting from inside the government, they claimed they were recasting the policies and lifestyles of the elite, whereas Islamic militants merely frightened the public and strengthened their enemies in the army. Among Muslim leaders, the strongest disagreements arose not between regime supporters and opponents but between aspiring allies vying to deliver government assistance for their followers and for Islam in general.

Suharto patronized all of Indonesia's powerful Islamic groups. His greatest beneficiaries were the reformist Muhammadiyah ("The Followers of Muhammad") with its network of schools and clinics in every major city, the traditionalist Islamic teachers (kiais) of the Nahdlatul Ulama ("The Reawakening of Religious Scholars") concentrated in rural Java, and the newer Indonesian Association of Muslim Intellectuals (Ikatan Cendekiawan Muslim se-Indonesia) based in Jakarta and headed by the president's friend and advisor, B. J. Habibie. Suharto encouraged competition between and within these groups by allowing their leaders to air controversial opinions on nearly all issues, as long as they endorsed Pancasila instead of an Islamic state.

After his pilgrimage, Suharto made it easier for cooperative Muslim leaders to claim partial victories in opening up political discourse, especially when he revived some of the flexibility that had typified Pancasila in Sukarno's day. Sukarno was fond of saying that he conceived a "monotheistic state" as a unique compromise between equally unacceptable demands for secularism on one hand and an Islamic republic on the other. Suharto reinterpreted Pancasila as though it was a total triumph for the secularists. Yet after 1985, when he won the long battle to make Pancasila unassailable, he, too, became eager to refute accusations that it was anti-Islamic. Suharto began to describe Pancasila as an "open ideology" that welcomes multiple interpretations.

Muslim leaders responded by resuming debates that divide Indonesians today as much as when they arose at the beginning of the twentieth century. Should Muslims develop a more "Indonesian Islam" uniquely adapted to local conditions, or should they create a more "Islamic Indonesia" that looks to the international Muslim community for leadership as well as support? Should religious groups use the state to build an Islamic society, or should they nurture pious citizens, hoping they will eventually demand an Islamic government?

Should Muslims rally around an Islamic party, or can they work through any association that turns public policy in a proper direction?

Competing Islamic factions advance contradictory answers to these questions with full knowledge of their profound implications for Indonesia's future. Each group fashions alliances with Suharto's heirs and enemies in democratic tests of strength that Indonesians welcome and dread at the same time.

One of the most attractive battlegrounds for Muslim politicians is the hajj. Like Pancasila, Suharto put the hajj in play as a legitimate subject for political debate—and manipulation. All the major Muslim leaders have made the hajj— some of them several times—and all have written about their experiences in ways that are calculated to market their political personas. In the post-Suharto era, debates over the hajj and its meanings are a microcosm of power struggles in the world's largest Islamic movements.

## Nationalizing the Hajj

The spectacular growth of Indonesia's pilgrimage occurred only after Suharto took it out of the hands of private business and turned it into a state monopoly. Under Sukarno, the hajj was run by hundreds of merchants and travel agents tied to the big religious parties. They relied on steady contracts from the Ministry of Religious Affairs, which set the pilgrimage quotas, and on friendly members of parliament, who helped arrange subsidized fares and exchange rates for approved companies.[3]

Politicians in Masjumi, the coalition of Islamic parties that led Indonesia's early governments, competed to divert hajj revenues to their clients. In 1952, when the Nahdlatul Ulama (NU) temporarily lost control of the Ministry of Religious Affairs to rivals in the Muhammadiyah, they walked out of Masjumi and formed their own party. From that point onward, the NU traded unswerving support of Sukarno for a secure hold on religious patronage. When Sukarno became annoyed with Masjumi's demands for Islamic legislation and regional autonomy, he regularly counted on the NU for Muslim backing in governments dominated by secular and Javanese parties.[4]

The NU stuck by Sukarno when he assumed dictatorial powers, when he outlawed Masjumi, and even when he pressured Muslim politicians into sharing power with the communists. In return, Sukarno allowed the Ministry of Religious Affairs to become an NU fiefdom. By 1965, it had grown into the largest civilian agency in the government, dispensing millions of dollars for hajj services, school construction, and salaries.[5]

However, during the Sukarno years, the hajj remained a modest matter. Shortages of foreign exchange and confrontations with Muslim opponents discouraged governments from increasing their investment in what many politicians and intellectuals regarded as extravagant religious tourism. From 1950 to 1965, Indonesia's pilgrimage hardly grew at all, usually ranging between 8,000 and 12,000 people and never exceeding 15,000 (Figure 8.1). Under Sukarno, Indonesia had one of the lowest hajj rates in the world—about 130 pilgrims per million Muslims. This was far below its neighbors in Southeast Asia, including Thailand and the Philippines, where Muslims are only about 5 percent of the population.

When Suharto came to power, he quickly reshaped both the pilgrimage system and the Ministry of Religious Affairs. Beginning in 1968, the government virtually nationalized the hajj industry. State agencies replaced small private firms as the main providers of transport, lodging, and information. The takeover was aided by timely publicity about the mismanagement of hajj trust funds, including charges that the NU was diverting monies to its party branches. The new hajj regime centralized authority and resources in the Ministry of Religious Affairs, but the NU no longer controlled it.

From 1971 onward, Suharto picked modernist scholars and senior bureaucrats to head the ministry instead of the usual cast of conservative 'ulama. These ministers filled their staffs with graduates of the new State Institutes of Islamic Studies, which offered broader training than the old-style boarding schools (*pesantren*) run by NU stalwarts. As the religious bureaucracy diversified, NU followers had to share power with better educated modernists who frequently combined religious studies with degrees from national and foreign universities. Although *pesantren* graduates continued to fill the ministry's middle ranks, most of the top jobs went to modernists with stronger language skills in both Arabic and English.

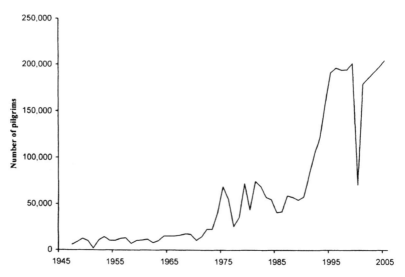

FIGURE 8.1 The growth of the Indonesian pilgrimage, 1947–2004

Political trends gave the modernists an added edge in the state religious apparatus. Suharto made it clear that he would never permit old Masjumi leaders to create a successor party. This left younger modernists the stark but easy choice of taking comfortable civil service jobs or languishing in the phony "Islamic" parties.

Whereas Masjumi sympathizers joined the regime in hopes of changing it from within, NU leaders took up the thankless task of playing a loyal opposition.[6] In 1973, the NU became the major partner in the Development Unity Party (Partai Persatuan Pembangunan, the PPP) created by a state-ordered merger of four weak Muslim factions. NU members in the Ministry of Religious Affairs quickly discovered that their leaders had saddled them with yet another handicap in their losing race against the modernists.

Suharto forced all civil servants to join the pro-government party, Golkar. If they were already affiliated with an opposition party, they had to leave it or give up their government jobs. At first, the religious bureaucracy was exempted from the decree, but soon it was enforced there as well. NU employees in Religious Affairs complained that the "monoloyalty" requirement had a particularly perverse effect for them because it punished followers of a legal party while ignoring sympathizers of rival groups that were formally banned.[7]

By the time the religious bureaucracy was poised to guide the hajj's rapid takeoff, it was far from the enclave of patronage that Sukarno tolerated. Suharto not only gave his pilgrimage agency a legal and commercial monopoly but also made sure its staff was politically reliable. Gradually, the hajj bureau and its parent ministry were transformed from top to bottom. They recruited from a wider range of social and educational backgrounds, they adopted the same routines as the rest of the civil service, and they answered to handpicked directors who were always known as president's men.

When I first visited the Ministry of Religious Affairs, the offices of the Hajj Directorate were humming with final preparations for the pilgrimage. I quickly met two young hajj officers who introduced me to several of their colleagues. All were recent graduates of the state Islamic institutes, and all were on the advance team just about to leave for Jeddah. One of them spoke a bit of English, and two others spoke excellent Arabic they had learned during several stays in Saudi Arabia. I had just arrived from Malaysia and was adapting my budding Malay to Bahasa Indonesia. Three languages were more than enough for us to enjoy a lively conversation that included six or seven hajj workers, as well as a steady stream of visitors who popped into their offices all afternoon.

After a couple of hours, my young hosts introduced me to one of their supervisors—a dignified man with an Egyptian surname, dressed in a *peci* cap and batik shirt, who seemed to have little in common with his more animated coworkers. When he stepped out of the room to deal with an emergency, the young men suggested that it would be wiser for me to bypass the old-fashioned midlevel managers and meet the people at the top. They sent me to Director of Hajj Research and Public Affairs Bambang Pranowo.

When I entered his huge office on the upper floor, Bambang was running to a television interview to explain how the agency was coping with the flood of new pilgrims. The government was being skewered nearly every day in the press and in parliament because of complaints about red tape, overbooking, and fare increases.[8] Bambang was pushed into the limelight because the minister of religious affairs—hoping to dodge the bad publicity—told journalists to take their questions directly to the hajj bureau.

"Tomorrow is a bad day, too," Bambang said. "I have an all-day meeting about globalization. All government bureaucrats are required to attend. Can you come to my house on Sunday at seven o'clock?"

"A.M. or P.M.?" I asked.

"Oh, A.M.," he answered with a smile. "We'll have all morning together. Write down my address," he said, handing me an enormous pen painted with the stars and stripes of the American flag. "It's from your country," he assured me.

Bambang lived at the end of a cul-de-sac in a simple neighborhood in south Jakarta. His was the nicest house on a peaceful street, where I passed several chickens but no foreigners. He greeted me in his sweatsuit after a morning run and took me into a spacious sitting room, where we had tea and biscuits with his wife and teenaged daughter. They took turns filling me in on their hometown in Central Java, their time in Australia (where Bambang earned his doctorate in anthropology), and the daughter's plans to attend business school in the United States.

When Bambang began discussing his work, I realized that Indonesia's hajj was being managed not only by pious bureaucrats but also by some highly skilled social scientists. He explained that he and his colleagues were convinced that much of the hajj's success depends on the small, tight-knit groups that Indonesian pilgrims create to look after one another. When I noted that his explanation conformed perfectly to my own experiences, he acknowledged that Indonesian bureaucrats were simply trying to build on what their hajjis had already been doing for generations before the state got into pilgrimage on a grand scale.

In Bambang's view, the agency's most important innovation was formalizing the group networks and making them the backbone of the Indonesian system. For every planeload of pilgrims—480 people on the largest aircraft—team leaders are selected to watch over about twenty companions. The group leaders report to half a dozen supervisors who meet regularly to advise the manager of the entire contingent, which is called a *kloter*.

The members of each *kloter* live in the same province and frequently in the same district or neighborhood. To spot one another quickly in the mass of pilgrims, each group wears distinctive batik clothing in designs that are popular in their region, and they carry matching color-coded luggage. Everyone wears a new photo identity card where it can be seen at all times, and female hajjis wear identity bracelets that look like everyday jewelry.

Indonesians combine this small-group model with an unusually flexible system of air transport. Rather than maintaining an oversized fleet of jumbo jets year-round, during hajj season the state airline leases dozens of planes from foreign airlines, complete with pilots and crews. For about three months, they create a continuous air bridge to Jeddah from special hajj terminals in five regional airports—two in Java and one each in Sumatra, Kalimantan, and Sulawesi. When the last hajjis have returned home, the fleet melts away to be reassembled only after pilgrimage officials finish negotiations with all the other government agencies that help set quotas for the next hajj season.

In financing the hajj, Indonesians have shown far less imagination. Malaysia's technique of using the banking system to create millions of hajj nest eggs is still in its infancy in Indonesia. In Jakarta, public and private banks hang out colorful banners advertising special pilgrimage accounts, calling them *tabung haji* accounts—the same name used in Malaysia. Unlike the Malaysian model, however, Indonesia's version has no "affirmative action" benefits for Muslim entrepreneurs who want to use the accumulated capital to catch up with Chinese and foreign competitors. The new accounts have not yet caught on in Indonesia, and most pilgrims who are not government workers or members of the armed forces still finance their trips by selling off assets. I discussed the *tabung haji* program with managers of the Thamrin branch of the National Bank of Commerce in downtown Jakarta during the 1996 hajj season. They eagerly explained the terms of the account and handed me the application forms. When I asked how much business they were doing, they told me that with an initial deposit of 250,000 rupiah—at that time, about $120—I could be the first subscriber.

The pilgrimage agency is especially bold in interpreting hajj symbolism. Along with the usual package of guidebooks on transportation, prayers, and health tips, each pilgrim receives a tantalizing forty-page booklet, *The Wisdom of the Hajj*. It exhorts pilgrims to look beyond the formal rituals to see "deeper truths" that will change their lives and relationships after returning from the Holy Cities.[9]

The agency "helps pilgrims understand and experience meanings hidden in every act of worship during the hajj." Printed materials are supplemented with slide shows and lectures that touring speakers give prospective hajjis in every province a few weeks before their departure. *The Wisdom of the Hajj* tells pilgrims: "Human beings are symbolic creatures, skilled in using symbols to express basic feelings and values that are often difficult to convey in words." Anticipating the criticism of secularists, the authors juxtapose the *Ka'ba* and the Indonesian flag.

The *Ka'ba* is nothing more than a pile of stones in the shape of a cube. In itself, it possesses no power to cause good or harm. The *Ka'ba* is merely a symbol God created as the center of the hajj in order to signify the pilgrim's complete devotion to God alone. From its constituent materials, the national flag seems only a cheap piece of cloth. But seen as a vessel of spiritual values, the flag is a cherished symbol of national majesty and dignity that cannot be purchased at any price.

Although many interpretations are controversial, officials never suggest their symbolic translations are authoritative or incompatible with others.

Agency handbooks describe the *Ka'ba* as a sanctuary where pilgrims experience the brotherhood and sisterhood of all humanity, including non-Muslims. The *sa'y* illustrates not only Hagar's faith and devotion to her infant but also the incalculable debt that everyone owes to men and women, both young and old, who sacrifice for others. 'Arafat is a "place of liberation," where pilgrims are freed not only from past sins but also from social hierarchy. The stonings at Mina reenact Ibrahim's struggle against the devil and every pilgrim's lifelong battle against temptation and social corruption. A hajj that is acceptable to God leaves pilgrims with spiritual serenity yet also with renewed determination to better themselves and their societies.

Hajj officials are well aware of the broader social and political conditions that shape their work. Many view themselves as part of a state-sponsored campaign of Islamic renewal.

Bambang Pranowo's research in Central Java documents the many agents of Islamization in *abangan* (religiously nonobservant) villages under the New Order. He and his colleagues are conducting similar studies in other provinces with scholars from Australia, the Netherlands, Japan, and the United States.[10]

## Rapid Growth and Regional Differences

After Suharto revamped the Ministry of Religious Affairs, pilgrimage rates began to skyrocket. Nationwide rates more than doubled after 1970 and then redoubled in the 1990s (Table 8.1).

Under Suharto, Indonesia's pilgrimage passed through three phases. During the 1970s, oil and timber booms financed a chain of record-breaking hajjs that set new highs every two or three years. A brief setback followed the recession and deregulation of the early 1980s, when foreign exchange was scarce. Then, around 1986, hajj growth surged more than ever, reaching levels unheard of in any other country. By the mid-1990s, Indonesia was sending even more pilgrims than Iran roused in the most militant years of the Islamic revolution. In a period of increasing privatization, the pilgrimage became a highly

TABLE 8.1 Indonesian pilgrimage rates by region, 1950–1996 (average annual number of pilgrims per million Muslims)

| Region | 1950–1955 | 1956–1960 | 1961–1965 | 1966–1970 | 1971–1975 | 1976–1980 | 1981–1985 | 1986–1990 | 1991–1996 |
|---|---|---|---|---|---|---|---|---|---|
| Northern Sumatra | 91 | 71 | 53 | 85 | 237 | 421 | 33 | 386 | 748 |
| Central Sumatra | 87 | 127 | 136 | 134 | 301 | 438 | 328 | 390 | 699 |
| Southern Sumatra | 86 | 148 | 231 | 172 | 238 | 351 | 155 | 203 | 288 |
| Sumatra | 79 | 115 | 140 | 131 | 256 | 400 | 257 | 309 | 526 |
| | | | | | | | | | |
| Jakarta | 327 | 179 | 145 | 307 | 1,486 | 789 | 741 | 593 | 2,774 |
| West Java | 131 | 147 | 146 | 133 | 394 | 399 | 320 | 344 | 1,027 |
| Central Java | 98 | 68 | 54 | 59 | 97 | 131 | 125 | 163 | 375 |
| Yogyakarta | 38 | 17 | 18 | 25 | 41 | 65 | 94 | 114 | 393 |
| East Java | 104 | 86 | 76 | 105 | 268 | 286 | 281 | 315 | 698 |
| Java | 106 | 100 | 89 | 107 | 317 | 301 | 276 | 298 | 853 |
| | | | | | | | | | |
| Nusa Tenggara | 254 | 262 | 200 | 306 | 446 | 648 | 549 | 576 | 1,021 |
| Kalimantan | 305 | 404 | 374 | 490 | 1,015 | 943 | 733 | 784 | 1,398 |
| Sulawesi | 199 | 180 | 245 | 193 | 282 | 688 | 721 | 814 | 1,505 |
| Maluku-Irian Jaya | 355 | 453 | 566 | 289 | 579 | 741 | 534 | 421 | 829 |
| Outer Islands | 262 | 264 | 283 | 295 | 512 | 757 | 684 | 741 | 1,362 |
| | | | | | | | | | |
| Indonesia | 117 | 129 | 130 | 142 | 344 | 403 | 368 | 406 | 965 |

profitable state enterprise. Hajj revenues equaled income from Indonesia's top export—sales of wood and wood products to Japan.

## Jakarta

The highest hajj rates are in Jakarta, where state workers and military personnel receive extra vacation time and discounted fares to take their families to the Holy Cities. In the Sukarno era, Jakarta residents made the hajj a bit more often than Muslims on Java and Sumatra but less than people on the other islands (Figure 8.2). From 1970 onward, Jakarta was consistently among the top pilgrim sources, and during the 1990s it led the nation.

Jakarta's hajj is also unusual because of its sharp fluctuations. The sensitivity of pilgrimage to short-term changes in political and economic conditions was more evident in Indonesia's capital and commercial center than in the rest of the country. The spurts of hajj activity in Jakarta during the early 1970s were the work of Ali Sadikin, the city's popular governor, who poured windfall oil profits into public housing, roads, and religious activities. Sadikin was one of the best known members of "Petition 50"—a circle of retired military officers and politicians that boldly criticized Suharto's one-man rule.[11] Ali Sadikin's hajj freelancing was a rare exception, and it was the last exception Suharto

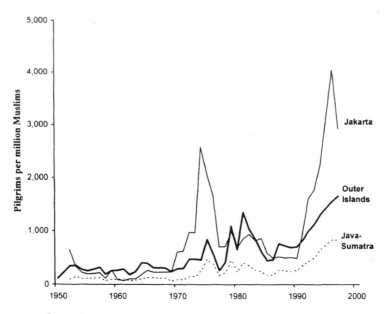

FIGURE 8.2 Pilgrimage rates in Jakarta, Java-Sumatra, and the Outer Islands, 1950–1996

permitted. For the remainder of the New Order, no one but the president and his allies used the hajj for political gain.

Jakarta's hajj dipped with the economic downturn of the early 1980s and plunged after the Tanjung Priok riots of 1984. Tanjung Priok was the high point of Suharto's confrontation with Muslims who resented the antireligious tone of his Pancasila campaign.[12] Angry marchers claimed that soldiers desecrated their mosque while removing wall posters criticizing the government. The army fired on the crowd, killing several protesters. When the organizers were put on trial, a yearlong wave of bombings hit Jakarta and other cities. From 1985 to 1990, Jakarta's pilgrimage fell to its lowest point since the 1960s.

As the violence subsided and Islamic organizations fell in line with the "Pancasila only" policy, the Jakarta hajj heated up again. This time, the president himself lit the fire.

In 1988, Suharto clashed with top army officers objecting to his vice-presidential choice and his family's high-handed business dealings. The most powerful critic was Benny Murdani, a former intelligence chief despised by Muslims as the personification of bias in favor of Christian and Chinese minorities and as the man who ordered the Tanjung Priok shootings.[13]When Suharto clashed with Murdani, the president sought a rapprochement with Islamic leaders.

Jakarta's pilgrimage resumed its growth in 1990—five years after the hajj recovered in the rest of the country. By then, the president was planning his own journey to Mecca. Immediately, Jakarta's hajj bolted into the national leadership, surpassing even the efforts of Ali Sadikin.

## Java

In the rest of Java—especially in West Java—hajj rates also climbed rapidly (Figure A8.1). Pilgrimage there consistently ran ahead of other Javanese regions (excluding Jakarta). But in the 1990s, its hajj shot up to levels normally seen only in the outer islands. West Java's pilgrimage rests on a vigorous economy combining commercialized agriculture with modern industry. Whereas most of Java is still marked by widespread poverty, West Java is notable for growing, but unshared, wealth (Figure 8.3).

Bandung is the heart of a linguistic, musical, and artistic revival among the Sundanese people—a community comprising about a quarter of Java's population that has long resented the political dominance of ethnic Javanese. Bandung has produced some of the country's leading Islamic publishers and missionary groups. Its mosques and markets are brimming with Indonesian translations of works by Muslim writers from all over the world. Only Yogyakarta can boast of a more vigorous cultural life.

East Java's pilgrimage followed close behind West Java's, despite deeper rural poverty. The bastion of the Nahdlatul Ulama, East Java has been the target of multiple Islamization campaigns by local *pesantrens* (religious boarding schools), as well as modernist preachers from outside the province.[14]

The *kiais* of East Java form a loose hierarchy of religious teachers who have consolidated their authority over several generations. Most of the senior *'ulama*

| | | |
|---|---|---|
| 1 Aceh | 9 Jakarta | 18 West Kalimantan |
| 2 North Sumatra | 10 West Java | 19 Central Kalimantan |
| 3 West Sumatra | 11 Central Java | 20 South Kalimantan |
| 4 Riau | 12 Yogyakarta | 21 East Kalimantan |
| 5 Jambi | 13 East Java | 22 North Sulawesi |
| 6 Bengkulu | 14 Bali | 23 Central Sulawesi |
| 7 South Sumatra | 15 West Nusa Tenggara | 24 South Sulawesi |
| 8 Lampung | 16 East Nusa Tenggara | 25 Southeast Sulawesi |
| | 17 East Timur (1975-2002) | 26 Maluku |
| | | 27 Irian Jaya |

FIGURE 8.3 The provinces of Indonesia

descended from a small set of merchant and landowning families. Frequently, they marry off their daughters to their most promising students and then support them in founding new schools that expand the family network.[15] Many 'ulama are also mystical leaders managing a pesantren and a Sufi order at the same time. Although they portray themselves as the custodians of Shafi'i jurisprudence, they also derive their reputation and income from dispensing folk religion.

Modernist Muslims, who often regard any superstition as paganism, denounce the NU for dabbling in dream interpretation and communication with the dead. In defense, kiais argue that Sufism and Javanese arts help them make Islamic teachings more appealing to simple people who need to understand religion in their own terms before they can grasp its deeper meaning.

Partisans of the NU commonly point to the hajj in contrasting their "Indonesian" Islam with the "dogmatism" of the modernists. They argue that their mystical approach encourages Muslims to make the hajj not once but several times, if possible. They believe that as a Muslim advances to higher levels of spiritual insight, the hajj will reveal new truths with each performance. In this view, every hajj is unique and can never be replicated, even by the same pilgrim. According to many NU advocates, the modernists discourage multiple hajjs by portraying them as wasteful. They note that groups like the Muhammadiyah often advise Muslims to make only one hajj and then to contribute to schools and charities at home instead of spending more money in Mecca.

Although the NU argument is plausible, the data do not confirm it, even in Java (Table A8.1). Hajj rates vary not with the relative strength of traditionalist versus modernist Islam but with economic conditions, particularly the severity of rural poverty. East Java, where the NU is strongest, has only an average hajj rate by Javanese measures. In Jakarta, West Java, and Yogyakarta, where modernists have the upper hand, hajj rates are either higher or lower than in East Java, depending on living standards. Economic differences also help explain Javanese partisan attachments. During the closely fought elections of 1955, poverty weakened both major Islamic parties while enhancing the appeal of secular nationalists and, above all, the communists.[16]

The hajj is weakest in Central Java and Yogyakarta, the poorest districts in Java and the heartland of abangan folk culture. Although poverty's depressing effect on pilgrimage is clear, the role of local culture is much harder to assess.

Central Java is filled with local pilgrimage sites, such as the tombs of the wali sanga—the heroic "nine saints" who brought Islam to the island in the fifteenth and sixteenth centuries.[17] Visiting saintly tombs has mixed implications for the hajj. If visitation reinforces beliefs in spirit worship and miracles, a local pilgrimage might be mistaken as a substitute for the hajj, especially by people with no realistic prospect of ever seeing Mecca. On the other hand, the same local pilgrimages can draw superstitious, nonpracticing Muslims into a wide network of Islamic institutions, increasing the likelihood that they or their children will make the hajj when it comes within their reach. Indeed, many who visit the saints are prospective hajjis making brief "preparatory" pilgrimages before traveling to Mecca.[18]

Legends of the nine saints' exploits in converting medieval Javanese kingdoms blend Qur'anic, Sufi, and Hindu themes, giving Islamic preachers an inexhaustible supply of popular parables that entertain as well as instruct. Many Javanese preachers, both modernist and traditionalist, skillfully use such elements of folk culture to spread Islam in what was long presumed to be a hostile environment.

Besides the tombs of the saints, Central Java also contains hundreds of pilgrimage centers that are far less compatible with the hajj. Many are graves of venerated ancestors and aristocrats who claimed divine attributes. Others are natural landmarks such as caves, mountains, and volcanoes said to contain spirits of the founders of nearby villages and towns.

One of the most famous is Gua Semar (Semar Cave) at the reputed geographic center of Java. The cave—with its entrance guarded by a large banyan tree—lies on the edge of a mountain forest that circles a volcanic lake. Before Suharto made the hajj, he often came here to meditate prior to announcing important decisions. During the 1970s and 1980s, Suharto's Muslim critics viewed these pilgrimages as an emblem of his attachment to Javanese spiritualism, confirming their suspicion that he wanted to grant these sects the same legal protection enjoyed by Indonesia's official religions—Islam, Christianity, Hinduism, and Buddhism.

Suharto's well-known mystical background helped to enhance the drama of his journey to Mecca, yielding even greater political dividends than if he had been just a run-of-the-mill Muslim. Not only did he make a grand gesture of conciliation toward Islamic adversaries but also he appeared to abandon spiritualist practices dear to powerful army officers.

Yogyakarta consistently had the lowest hajj rates in all of Indonesia. There is no better example of poverty's power to discourage pilgrimage. For many years, this province occupied the lowest rank on several measures of economic well-being for both urban and rural residents.[19] Yogyakarta is the only Indonesian city where I saw people dying in the streets.

Crushing poverty neutralized distinctive cultural characteristics that might otherwise support a strong hajj. The local sultanate—a generous patron of Islam—survived after independence despite nationalists' hostility to royal prerogatives everywhere else.[20] Popular religion, especially in the city, is influenced by orthodox Sufi teachings that bring adherents nearer to the Shari'ah (Islamic law).

Indonesia's largest Islamic modernist movement, the Muhammadiyah, was born in Yogyakarta and kept its headquarters there long after it spread through the rest of the country.[21] It is particularly ironic that the hajj should be so languid in the cradle of the Muhammadiyah, which has fought to bring

Indonesians closer to Muslims in the Middle East. All of Muhammadiyah's early leaders were hajjis, and most studied in Cairo or the Hejaz. For nearly a century, Muhammadiyah has raised Indonesians on the teachings of Muhammad 'Abduh, the famous Egyptian reformer who urged Muslims to blend Western science with the best in all Islamic schools. In most of Indonesia, a strong Muhammadiyah presence goes hand in hand with a vigorous hajj, but not in Yogyakarta.

### Sumatra

Sumatra is the most striking example of a regional pilgrimage suffering from wrenching political and economic reversals. No other region has experienced more ups and downs in its relations with the central government.

Both before and after independence, it was Sumatra that launched the key challenges to Java's bid for hegemony. Sumatran politicians such as Muhammad Hatta, Indonesia's first vice president, and Muhammad Natsir, the head of Masjumi, were among Sukarno's greatest rivals. Hatta and Natsir had huge followings among Muslims in the outer islands who resented Jakarta's squeezing the resource-rich provinces to prop up an overpopulated Java.[22]

During the 1950s, Sukarno eroded Masjumi's power by embracing the biggest Javanese parties, first the nationalists and then the communists. As Masjumi saw its influence evaporate, it identified with regional rebellions against Jakarta. When Sukarno assumed dictatorial powers under "Guided Democracy," Masjumi's top leaders fled to West Sumatra and joined the short-lived Revolutionary Government of the Republic of Indonesia, proclaimed by mutinous army officers in 1958.[23] Masjumi's involvement in the revolt was disastrous for the party and the Sumatran areas that formed its historic base. After Jakarta crushed the uprising, Sukarno banned Masjumi and appointed Javanese as local commanders and governors.

The later years of Sukarno's regime were a bitter time for Sumatrans, especially the Minangkabau highlands and the central forests, which were treated like conquered territory. Many still describe this as the start of Jakarta's "occupation" and the forced "Javanization" of their homelands.

When Suharto came to power, he skillfully turned Sumatrans' resentment to his advantage. He offered the vanquished island a new deal: give up the struggle against Javanese power and learn to compete in Jakarta with other regions desperately needing economic aid.[24] Buying local support with doles and investment, the New Order transformed Sumatra from the most troublesome region into a model of center-periphery patronage that he replicated across the archipelago.

Suharto built his strategy around two segments of the Sumatran elite. To lead provincial governments, he chose native Sumatrans who had worked in a central ministry and kept one foot in Jakarta. They, in turn, courted Islamic groups that had opposed Sukarno's leftward drift and were willing to back Golkar in return for support of religious education and the hajj.

At the polls, results seemed encouraging for the ruling party from one end of the island to the other. Golkar's vote rose steadily in nearly every Sumatran province, especially in the 1987 and 1992 elections. Most of the increase was at the expense of the official Islamic party, the PPP, which never attracted more than a fraction of Masjumi's followers. Sumatrans supported Golkar more than voters in any other region except Sulawesi. During the 1990s, they moved against a mild nationwide trend favoring the opposition. Although Golkar had peaked in the country as a whole, it was soaring in most of Sumatra.

In return for their support, Sumatrans received only modest benefits from the New Order. Between 1973 and 1990, central and southern Sumatra had the country's slowest increases in per capita income. Nationwide, only nine provinces fell behind in both income and growth; four were in Sumatra.[25]

Many of Sumatra's problems stem from its vulnerability to price shifts for exports of oil and cash crops. Both family farms and estates were hurt by competition from Malaysian rubber and South American coffee. Declining export revenues hit Aceh and North Sumatra as well as the central provinces—West Sumatra, Riau, and Jambi.

Southern Sumatra suffered the added shock of mass immigration. The south was a prime target of the "transmigration" policy that relocated millions of impoverished Javanese in new agricultural settlements. Lampung, Bengkulu, and South Sumatra became home to transplanted peasants who are poorer today than the kin they left behind.

Economic and social disruption left Sumatra with an unusually weak pilgrimage. Comparing interisland hajj rates, Sumatra resembles Java more than any other region. This is not a welcome connection for proud Sumatrans accustomed to looking down on the Javanese, especially in matters of religion. Many Sumatrans still speak as though they are better Muslims than the Javanese. They are keenly aware of Sumatra's historic ties with the Malay and Arab worlds, constantly recalling—and exaggerating—their ancestors' exploits in spreading Islam to other Indonesians.[26]

Despite these well-known stereotypes, however, Sumatra and Java have shared surprisingly similar rates of pilgrimage for many decades. Under Sukarno, Sumatra's hajj rates were a bit higher than Java's, but with Suharto the balance tipped in Java's favor. Sumatra's early lead in hajj activity stemmed from a fairly low rate of rural poverty compared with Java. That advantage disappeared as income rose faster in Java. During the New Order, Sumatra and Java resembled one another more than ever. Today, religious and economic differences on both islands are greater than the differences between them.

On Sumatra, contrasting hajj patterns point to deepening cleavages between provinces. In the 1990s, pilgrimage was positively related to income but negatively related to votes for Golkar (Figure A8.2). Hajj was strongest in the wealthier north, where proposals to share oil revenues with local residents only slightly dampened the appeal of the Islamic opposition. Pilgrimage was weakest in the poorer south, where migrant farmers needing constant state support became one of Golkar's most loyal constituencies. Growing north-south divisions were fueled by new disparities in wealth and influence that aggravated long-standing ethnic and religious tensions.

In many Sumatran provinces, hajj rates are higher or lower than one would expect from the extent of economic development. Throughout the island, local religious and party organizations play an important role in encouraging or dampening pilgrimage.

The hajj is unusually weak in the southernmost provinces. In Lampung and Bengkulu, transmigrants have built little in the way of associational life. They still lack the kinds of religious charities that allow people in more established communities to make the hajj despite modest means.

In South Sumatra—the island's most prosperous area—voluntary groups are strong but politically fragmented. In the cosmopolitan city of Palembang, Christians and Muslims gave strong support to both opposition parties, producing an unusually competitive multiparty system. Unlike most Sumatrans, Palembang's residents channeled their associational resources toward encouraging political pluralism instead of the hajj.

Central Sumatra is the area where Islamic groups and Golkar came together most effectively to promote each other and the pilgrimage at the same time. The connection was particularly clear in Jambi and West Sumatra, where the hajj flourished despite low income. Jambi was from the beginning Golkar's greatest bastion in Sumatra. West Sumatra—a former Masjumi stronghold—flirted with the Islamic opposition until 1987 but then followed Jambi into the government's fold. The defection of West Sumatra's Muslims broke the back of the PPP on the island, leaving it no solid support outside remote and rebellious Aceh.

In contrast, the more fortunate provinces to the north were cushioned by local oil and natural gas industries. This economic advantage permitted Muslims in Riau, North Sumatra, and Aceh to sustain strong pilgrimages without compromising their political independence as much as their southern neighbors.

## The Outer Islands

Sumatra's fate reminded others that they could achieve more by cooperating with Jakarta than by confronting it. Although Suharto kept Sumatra under tight reins, he was more sympathetic to less developed regions.

The more difficulty the army faced in putting down regional revolts under Sukarno, the more likely it was that local elites would share power and wealth in the New Order. In Sulawesi and Kalimantan, former guerrillas who went over to the government's side were rewarded with posts in the provincial administrations and with generous cuts of new investments pouring into local economies.[27] Soaring hajj rates in Sulawesi and Kalimantan reflect the benefits Muslims in both areas derived from greater influence in government and business (Figure A8.3).

The most dramatic improvement was in South Sulawesi. Under Sukarno, its Buginese and Makassarese communities made the hajj more frequently than most Indonesians, but compared with other outer islanders their participation was mediocre. South Sulawesi's rural economy was crippled by Islamic insurgents, and the key port city of Ujung Pandang lost business to smugglers and profiteering commanders in Christian-dominated North Sulawesi.

During the 1958 revolution, the army received decisive support from Muslim forces in South Sulawesi. Despite their ongoing quarrels with Jakarta, dissident southern units helped the government crush the American-supported mutiny in North Sulawesi.[28] South Sulawesi's decision helped to isolate the Sumatran rebels, who had hoped to spark a chain reaction of uprisings across the outer islands. Comrades of Sulawesi's most powerful guerrilla chief, Kahar Muzakkar, accepted amnesties and joined the republican army, ending a decade of armed resistance.[29]

Even before Suharto became president, he negotiated arrangements with local elites that paved the way for Sulawesi's pacification. Jakarta agreed to appoint more native sons to provincial army and government positions. Power shifted from the Christian north to the Muslim south—away from the minorities of Minahasa and Tana Toraja who had helped the Dutch and toward Buginese and Makassarese leaders willing to denounce religious warfare against the nationalist state.[30] The New Order rebuilt the roads and infrastructure the insurgency had devastated and turned Ujung Pandang into the shipping and military hub of eastern Indonesia.

Hajj growth in Kalimantan contrasts with Sulawesi in two important ways. The Kalimantan pilgrimage developed at a slower pace, tapering off as the region lost control of its own timber and oil revenues in the 1970s. Kalimantan's weaker pilgrimage also reflects a far less amicable relationship with the central government. As in South Sulawesi, native elites in East and South Kalimantan gained greater influence in business and politics after helping the army defeat Islamic insurgents. But in Kalimantan the insurgency was less threatening, and the subsequent concessions to local elites were short-lived.[31]

Similar shifts occurred in the regions of eastern Indonesia. Maluku had the highest hajj rates in the country under Sukarno. Before 1965, pilgrimage in Maluku was often twice the level in Nusa Tenggara, the chain of impoverished islands east of Java. But when Maluku's spice trade collapsed, Suharto did little to diversify the local economy. Instead, Jakarta poured resources into Java's neighbors, trying to resuscitate some of Indonesia's most backward societies. The government invested so heavily in tourism, food production, and resettlement that Nusa Tenggara became the most subsidized area of the country.[32] Pilgrimage in the east closely tracked these economic swings. Nusa Teng-gara's hajj pulled ahead of Maluku's after 1980. Meanwhile, Maluku's pilgrim-age—once the nation's strongest—sank even lower than Java's.

## Pilgrims' Social and Economic Backgrounds

Indonesia's hajjis display an unusual national profile and a wealth of regional variations. Pilgrims are evenly distributed in terms of gender and age but not by occupation and education.[33]

Indonesia is one of the few countries where female pilgrims outnumber males year after year. Between 1968 and 1975, women were 44 percent of In-donesia's pilgrims when worldwide only 33 percent of all hajjis were female. By the 1980s, women were a clear majority in Indonesian delegations (Table A8.2).

Indonesian hajjis are also quite young. Only one pilgrim in six is older than sixty, and hajjis in their thirties are nearly as numerous as those in their fifties. Between 1985 and 1989, the average age for all Indonesian hajjis was forty-six. Another sign of relative youth is the small proportion of people who perform multiple hajjs. More than 90 percent were making the pilgrimage for the first time (Table A8.3).

Judging from their educational and occupational profiles, most hajjis be-long to lower middle-class families. More than 60 percent had no more than an elementary education, and less than a quarter had completed secondary school (Table A8.4). Farmers account for 30 percent of all pilgrims, with an equal share describing themselves as housewives. Merchants and civil servants are the next largest categories, followed by a small group of retirees (Table A8.5).

Regional contrasts inside Indonesia are at least as profound as differences between entire nations elsewhere. Java's hajjis include the highest ratio of farmers and one of the lowest proportions of women. Pilgrims from Sumatra, on the other hand, are the oldest and most educated in the country, and they are predominantly female.

Gender disparities are particularly striking in East Java and West Sumatra. Only 44 percent of East Java's pilgrims are female, compared with 61 percent in West Sumatra—an internal gap equivalent to cross-national differences be-tween Lebanon and Yemen or between South Africa and Nigeria.

Backgrounds of Javanese and Sumatran hajjis parallel the contrasting so-cial bases of Islamic movements that have taken root in those regions. Differ-ences between the NU and its modernist rivals do, indeed, encourage distinct hajj profiles—not in terms of the sheer numbers they send to Mecca but in the kind of people they mobilize. The NU, based in rural Java, encourages pilgrimage mainly among young men with no more than an elementary or *pesantren* education. The Muhammadiyah and other reform groups are more popular in urban areas, particularly in Sumatra, where they have invested heavily in modern schools and women's associations. Muhammadiyah's long emphasis on attracting older married couples nurtures a decidedly family-oriented hajj among middle-class Sumatrans, whereas the NU's network focuses on Javanese farmers and their sons.[34]

Nusa Tenggara's pilgrims stand out in many ways. They are some of Indonesia's least educated hajjis. Twenty-seven percent never finished elementary school, and only 13 percent made it through high school. Even more conspicuous are the predominance of merchants and the scarcity of women. Half of all hajjis in Nusa Tenggara who report an occupation identify themselves as traders. Female participation—a mere 35 percent—is at least thirty years behind the rest of the country.

In contrast to the conservative portrait of Nusa Tenggara's pilgrims, Sulawesi and Kalimantan spearheaded demographic trends that caught on in other regions. Sulawesi and Kalimantan boast some of the strongest pilgrimages in the nation, sending the youngest hajjis and the highest percentages of females.

Surprisingly, there is no evidence that these progressive tendencies result from higher levels of education. Hajjis from Kalimantan have the same educational attainment as those from Java, and Sulawesi's pilgrims have only slightly more schooling than Nusa Tenggara's. A more likely explanation is that, in eastern Kalimantan and South Sulawesi, vigorous interisland trade and emigration create greater opportunities for youth and women of all backgrounds, whereas Nusa Tenggara's merchant enclaves preserve patriarchal traditions that are withering elsewhere.[35]

Jakarta's pilgrims are striking, both politically and demographically. No other group of hajjis is so dependent on the state. In all of Indonesia, government employees and their families regularly take up about 20 percent of the hajj quota, and another 10 percent is reserved for the armed forces. In Jakarta, however, more than half of all pilgrims are on the public payroll—nearly double the national average. State employees are particularly likely to make multiple hajjs. Fourteen percent of the government and military quotas go to former hajjis—twice the national rate of repeat pilgrimage. These are the same civil servants and soldiers who were the rank and file of the old ruling party, Golkar. Their pilgrimage became an annual festival—the state on parade—providing a coveted fringe benefit for government workers, a spiritual retreat for party loyalists, and a grand display of official piety.

The Jakarta hajj is a key investment in the political elite's image as God-fearing nationalists who spread Islam through state and society. In contrast to Turkey, where army officers and bureaucrats still bristle when ministers inject their religious beliefs into state business, Indonesian officials look for any opportunity to convince their citizens that they are good Muslims. Since Suharto's pilgrimage, nearly every provincial governor has become a hajji. The few governors who have not already made the pilgrimage before their appointments usually do so within a year or two.

Hoping to allay fears that the army was obsessed with rooting out Islamic extremism even where it never existed, Suharto made a special effort to involve military officers in the hajj. Military families are encouraged to take advantage of special hajj privileges, and retired officers are often chosen to lead groups of civilian pilgrims. In 1996, leadership of the entire Indonesian hajj was entrusted to General Feisal Tanjung, the air force commander and armed forces' chief of staff.

## Pilgrimage and the Realignment of Social and Political Cleavage

Indonesians often describe their country as hopelessly divided by regions, classes, and parties. The hajj is enmeshed in all of these conflicts but not in the way partisans and analysts usually expect. A map of long-term hajj rates for the twenty-seven provinces reveals spatial patterns cutting across all the zones commonly regarded as fixed products of nature and history (Table A8.6 and Figure 8.4).

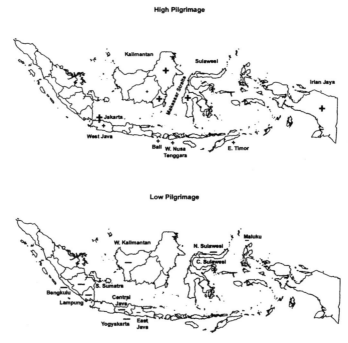

FIGURE 8.4 Centers of high and low pilgrimage in Indonesia, 1974–1996

Pilgrimage does not support the notion that Indonesia is an inherently dual society. Hajj patterns do not mirror the old colonial rift between Java and the outer islands, nor do they project the newer split between a modernizing west and a stagnating east that many economists identified after independence.

In every part of the archipelago, zones of high and low pilgrimage alternate in a checkerboard fashion. The uneven pattern of participation appears in the northern chain of islands from Kalimantan to Irian Jaya, as well as in the southern chain from Sumatra to Timor. The same picture emerges on both sides of the east-west axis formed by the Straits of Makassar. Even provinces on the same island differ radically from their neighbors. All major islands and island groups contain areas with both high and low hajj rates.

The most active pilgrimage zones lie within a triangle near the country's geographic center. Jakarta, the eastern coast of Kalimantan, and the western shore of Sulawesi are the corners of the triangle. Each corner is also linked to nearby provinces that became secondary centers of hajj activity in the New Order.

Pilgrimage spread in three directions—from Jakarta to Bandung and West Java, from coastal Kalimantan to the interior, and from South Sulawesi to Muslim trading diasporas in the southern and eastern islands. The hajj is least popular in the overpopulated agricultural heartlands of Central Java and South Sumatra. Smaller pockets of weak pilgrimage appear in isolated areas of Kalimantan and the commercial backwaters between the Banda and Sulawesi seas.

The distribution of pilgrimage does not suggest a sharp polarity between center and periphery; instead, it points to overlapping networks of communications and trade that link developing economies in diverse cultural zones. The social and economic roots of pilgrimage are crystal clear[36] (Table A8.7). Hajj correlates with general measures of prosperity and urbanization, as well as specific styles of production and consumption.

Pilgrimage is strongest in exporting areas, earners of foreign exchange from manufacturing and forestry products. Although hajj is weaker in predominantly agricultural provinces, there have been striking changes since the mid-1970s. Pilgrimage fell sharply where farmers grow market-sensitive cash crops, and it rose slightly where they rely on state-subsidized rice production.

Hajj is closely tied to many measures of transportation and mass communications. The strongest links are with air travel and maritime trade rather than overland transport. In fact, pilgrimage is negatively correlated with the quality of local roads.

Hajj is particularly popular in economic growth centers that are more closely tied to one another through interisland commerce than to their immediate hinterlands. Pilgrimage's strength in communities that depend on long-distance communication is evident in the high correlations for television viewing, cinema attendance, and telephone usage.

Surprisingly, hajj activity has little connection to central government penetration of the provinces. Pilgrimage is negatively correlated with public school enrollment, as well as with membership in agricultural cooperatives, scout organizations, and family planning groups.

Measures of public health have no consistent link to pilgrimage. Positive connections with hospital beds and protein consumption are offset by negative connections with life expectancy and infant survival. Hajj has no relation at all to important cultural variables such as the relative size of the Muslim and non-Muslim communities or the prevalence of the national language, Bahasa Indonesia.

One of the more intriguing questions about Suharto's extravagant sponsorship of the hajj is whether it earned electoral benefits for the ruling party's candidates.[37] During the 1970s, pilgrimage correlated with support for the PPP and with opposition to Golkar (Table A8.8). By the 1980s, however, hajj no longer seemed related to votes for any political party. Although Golkar still enjoyed no nationwide advantage in provinces with high hajj activity, the government neutralized whatever edge the Islamic opposition enjoyed in those areas. This alone would have been a substantial political return on Suharto's pilgrimage investments.

The political gains look even more impressive if we control for economic factors. Votes for Golkar in 1992—the year immediately after Suharto's trip to Mecca—closely tracked pilgrimage rates. Golkar was even more popular in provinces with high hajj rates than its Islamic opponents had been at their peak in 1977. Suharto not only checked the PPP's inroads among Muslim voters but also lured many of their early supporters into the Golkar camp.[38]

By turning Golkar into the leading "Islamic" party, Suharto put a new twist on the long rivalry between modernist and traditionalist Muslims. The electoral map of the face-off between Golkar and the PPP looked very similar to the configuration of the 1950s, when Masjumi and Nahdlatul Ulama battled for Muslim votes. Golkar picked up most of its support in old Masjumi strongholds, whereas the PPP was rooted in NU bastions. Suharto's religious overtures resonated most in exactly those quarters where he needed to gain favor: descendants of the militant modernists he excluded from politics rather than the pliable traditionalists who accepted his invitation to play the loyal opposition.

## Hajj Memoirs as Political Marketing Tools

Personal accounts of pilgrimage have become a popular form of religious writing in the last two decades. In 1983 the short story writer Danarto published a series of lighthearted articles, "A Man from Java Makes the Hajj."[39] Danarto decides to go to Mecca after returning from Paris and learning he has miraculously fallen into a pile of money. His accidental pilgrimage exposes a far greater miracle—that hajjis from around the world can display so much love amid the filth and belligerence of the "two greedy cities."

Along the way, Danarto lampoons every nationality, including his own. Zealous Iranians force themselves to go without food and sleep for days. Gigantic Yorubas charge like wild elephants scattering pint-sized Asians in all directions. Indians clutching the *Ka'ba* are like bats clinging to a fruit tree. Arabs and Javanese are both "extremist races"—one is too aggressive, the other too passive. "Be a Muslim, but not an Arab," he exhorts. What most impresses Danarto is the determination of all pilgrims to defend their rights and beliefs—a crucial concern of Indonesian intellectuals trying to adapt to pious popular culture without compromising their already precarious liberties.

Suharto's hajj helped this literary genre take off a few years later. When Suharto announced his pilgrimage plans, Indonesians joked that he would be the first reigning Javanese monarch to visit Mecca. After he returned home, his publicists chose an image that was more paternalistic than regal. The Department of Religious Affairs issued a well-illustrated commemorative volume tracing "Father Harto's" daily progress through the Holy Land.[40]

Suharto's personal piety is touted on every page. The cover sports a large color photo of the stern-faced president and first lady in *ihram* garb and clutching pocket-sized prayer books. From beginning to end, Suharto is at prayer in every conceivable location—aboard the presidential airplane, at the Prophet's tomb, kissing the Black Stone, and back in the mosque near his Jakarta residence.

The Suhartos' pilgrimage is emphatically a family affair. The presidential party includes five of the six Suharto children and their spouses. Special attention is given to the eldest daughter, Tutut (Siti Hardijanti Rukmana), and the youngest son, Tommy (Hutomo Mandala Putra)—the children whose business deals brought worldwide disgrace.

The president is careful to share the spotlight with his political protégés. At the audience with Saudi King Fahd, Suharto is accompanied by Munawir Sjadzali, the minister of religious affairs; Mensesneg Murdiono, the president's chief of staff; and General Try Sutrisno, the armed forces' commander, who later ascended to the vice presidency. Suharto also balances the major religious factions, filling his entourage with top figures from Muhammadiyah, Nahdlatul Ulama, and Golkar.

The latest trends in hajj narrative carry neither the satirical bite of Danarto nor the majestic pretense of Suharto. Instead, they reveal the inner lives of the rich and famous through their pilgrimages. Celebrity authors make their experiences accessible to middle-class Indonesians contemplating the hajj and pondering how it might change their lives. Many writers are public figures trying to promote themselves to a pious and prosperous audience that forms a key part of the electorate. Their divergent interpretations of the hajj provide a splendid insight into the competition between aspiring Islamic leaders.

A wide assortment of narratives appears in a collection of interviews, *The Hajj: A Journey of Tears, The Pilgrimage Experiences of Thirty Leaders*.[41] The personalities include nine of Indonesia's most illustrious *'ulama*, several intellectuals and technocrats, a handful of career women, two retired generals, a movie star, a singer, a painter, a poet, and a comedian. The editors invite each to explain the significance of pilgrimage so that "what began as private, individual experiences can spread and become experiences of the larger *umma* along with the symbolic meanings they conceal."

I would like to highlight the remarks of two interviewees at the center of current controversies on Islam and politics, Amien Rais and Nurcholish Madjid. Amien and Nurcholish are friendly rivals who clash intellectually and politically while sharing a great deal personally. Both earned their doctorates at the University of Chicago, Amien in political science and Nurcholish in Islamic studies. Amien and I were classmates during the 1970s, and later, when I was on the faculty, Nurcholish and I shared the rostrum at a divinity school colloquium.

After returning to Indonesia, each breathed new life into religious movements that had been crippled by patriarchy and factional squabbling. As they grew more outspoken, Amien and Nurcholish inevitably became lightning rods in the debate over the role of Islam in the New Order and afterward.

Amien's critics portrayed him as an Islamic militant who exploited communal tensions to advance his political ambitions. Nurcholish was accused of selling out to Suharto and echoing the hypocritical line that religion and politics should be kept apart.

During the crisis that culminated in Suharto's downfall in 1998, Amien and Nurcholish became political icons. Each played a decisive role in pushing the old man off the throne—Amien in the streets and Nurcholish inside the presidential palace.[42] Indonesia's new democracy is brimming with political talent, but it is fair to say that these two leaders are widely regarded as the pride of the Islamic modernists—Amien as their most intellectual politician and Nurcholish as their most political intellectual.

Amien is now the speaker of the People's Consultative Assembly, the expanded session of the national legislature that elects and impeaches the president. After the 1999 elections, he brokered the deal that made Abdurahman Wahid president and Megawati Sukarnoputri vice president. In 2001, Amien presided over Wahid's impeachment, and, when Megawati came to the assembly to take the presidential oath, he walked her down the aisle.

Amien's career took off when he became the head of Muhammadiyah and the assistant director of the Indonesian Association of Muslim Intellectuals (ICMI), where he was considered a protégé of B. J. Habibie. Amien's election to the Muhammadiyah presidency in 1994 marked the rise of a new generation of professionals and civil servants whose modern education distinguished them from the *'ulama* and shopkeepers who had dominated the movement since the early twentieth century.

Even before taking the helm at Muhammadiyah, Amien challenged Indonesia's strongest political taboo by speaking openly about President Suharto's need to plan his own succession. Amien called on the president to go on national television and explain directly to the people how he intended to achieve a peaceful and democratic change of government. He urged Suharto to act promptly before succumbing to illness, corruption, and illusions that he was "like a small God."[43]

When rivals attacked Amien for dragging Muhammadiyah into dangerous waters, he touched off an even greater row by insisting that the group needed to rethink its entire theological and intellectual orientation.[44] Under his prodding, Muhammadiyah shed its long preoccupation with education and social work to promote vigorous debate about democracy, industrialization, and ethnic conflict. Amien's critics feared he was overplaying a weak hand and would provoke the army. On the other hand, skeptics insisted that behind its tougher rhetoric Muhammadiyah was merely cozying up to Suharto and trying to outmaneuver its rivals. In defense, Amien suggested that other Muslim leaders should follow Muhammadiyah's example of wielding power without groveling to the army or swaggering before the masses.

Nurcholish keeps a bit more distance from the daily battles of modernist and traditionalist groups. He has his own think tank in Jakarta instead of working with a single faction. Nonetheless, Nurcholish is a classic product of the *pesantrens*, and he remains close to the Nahdlatul Ulama. He is a cousin of the NU leader Abdurrahman Wahid and the grandson of Hasyim Asyari, the famous *kiai* who headed the NU from its origin in 1926 until his death in 1947. Many of the young *'ulama* who helped elect Abdurrahman Wahid as NU chief in 1984 were associates of Nurcholish who wanted to update the group's teachings while toning down its criticism of the government.[45]

Before becoming an icon, Nurcholish was himself a celebrated iconoclast. In 1970, he called for the renewal and demystification of Indonesian Islam. This was hardly radical by Indonesian standards, but Nurcholish described his program as "secularization"—a term with far more negative connotations in Indonesia than in Western circles, both then and now.[46] He spent the next twenty years assuring irate audiences he was simply urging the greater use of reason, not the demise of Islam.

Nurcholish fleshed out many projects that early modernists popularized but failed to develop, especially reinterpreting religious texts in light of science and philosophy. He certainly helped Islamic modernism receive a fuller airing before NU followers than the modernists themselves could have achieved.

Nurcholish is best known for his staunch opposition to creating an Islamic state and even an Islamic party. He scorns the Masjumi and its would-be successors for turning the ideal of an Islamic state into a sacred cow. He argues that Islam prescribes no specific political institutions and that pretending otherwise corrupts religion and politics at the same time.

Nurcholish urges Muslims to turn away from all types of magic—ideological as well as mystical—and to combine classical Islam with Indonesia's distinctive pluralism and tolerance. Nurcholish's views were extremely congenial to Suharto's Pancasila campaign. Both men argued that Muslims should have no objection to accepting Pancasila as the "sole basis" of the political system because Islam is a religion and Pancasila is a national ideology. One is sacred; the other is profane—end of discussion.

While the Pancasila controversy was still raging, Nurcholish's stock plummeted with Muslim intellectuals the more it rose with the government. But once Suharto won the argument, he encouraged giving Pancasila an Islamic flavor, and Nurcholish's ideas lost the semiofficial aura that had both helped him and embarrassed him.

After Suharto's hajj, Muslim writers began using their new freedom in discussions of the pilgrimage. Personal accounts of the hajj became relatively safe vehicles for shaping public opinion in Suharto's waning years and beyond. Both Amien and Nurcholish wrote colorful descriptions of their pilgrimages that skillfully blended religious and political discourse at a time when the regime was congratulating itself for having severed such links once and for all.

Amien describes four hajjs spanning a period of sixteen years.[47] As he matures and enjoys greater success, he sees pilgrimage taking on greater social and political significance, first in Indonesia and then globally. Each time, he focuses his prayers on more universal questions, highlighting the particular sites and symbols that seem most relevant to the dominant themes of his hajj.

When Amien makes his first pilgrimage, in 1974, he is only thirty years old and has just received his master's degree from Notre Dame University. This hajj is a solitary rite of passage as he works his way back to Indonesia, traveling through Europe, the Middle East, and Pakistan. Amien gives a psychological account of his time in Mecca that emphasizes initial emotions— being overcome with tears when seeing the Ka'ba—as well as subsequent changes in his daily routine, such as developing greater discipline in prayer.

Political commentary is limited to indirect criticism of the New Order's concessions to foreign capital. Amien's return to Jakarta coincides with the Malari incident—the riots and looting that greeted the Japanese prime minister's state visit. He notes that the alarming scope of the violence frightened the government into adopting one of Muhammadiyah's key economic demands—requiring all foreign investors to enter joint ventures with Indonesian partners.

On Amien's second hajj four years later, his wife accompanies him, and attention shifts to family problems. They want her to become pregnant. They both pray at Multazam, the "place of attachment" at the base of the *Ka'ba's* eastern side just between the Black Stone and the ornately decorated door. Pilgrims commonly stop here and embrace the *Ka'ba* physically as a sign of their pact with God. The spot has special significance for women, who often press their bodies against God's house while pleading for children. Amien and his wife find their prayers answered within a month. A friend who is still childless after ten years of marriage has also asked them to pray for her at Multazam. Soon, she, too, becomes pregnant.

Although Amien's second hajj concentrates on intimate life-cycle issues, he was already engrossed in the debate over Islam's connections with practical politics. At the time, he was living in Cairo and interviewing members of the Muslim Brotherhood while preparing a doctoral thesis on the movement's revival during the presidency of Anwar Sadat. Amien sought to explain the brotherhood's ups and downs in Egypt, drawing lessons that later guided his own effort to rejuvenate Muhammadiyah.[48] Nonetheless, he still experienced the hajj as changing his personal life more than the world around him.

Amien's third pilgrimage, in 1987, forces him to reevaluate the hajj's links to political power. At first, he resolves that this hajj will be more spiritual than previous visits, when he was preoccupied with career and family. He decides to block out the jostling and gossip of his fellow pilgrims by reading the Qur'an from cover to cover. But no amount of concentration can suppress his growing annoyance with being stepped on at every turn, with the retired naval officer who scolds him for not praying enough in Medina, and with his own feelings of superiority toward the throngs surrounding him.

Amien's quest for a hajj of detachment and meditation is swept away once and for all by the bloody clash between Iranian demonstrators and Saudi police in the Grand Mosque. This time, his most lasting insight is a painful awareness of the ignorance, weakness, and division of the Islamic world. The hajj strengthens his desire to be a better Muslim, but it pushes him to work for a "united front" to enhance the power of Muslims everywhere.

Amien's fourth hajj, in 1990, is a full-blown political mission. He and four other members of Muhammadiyah's board of directors travel as guests of the Saudi government. All make the pilgrimage with their wives except for one woman who remains at home with an infant child. The Saudis put them up at five-star hotels in Jeddah and Medina. At 'Arafat, they spend the day in a lavish tent equipped with fourteen air conditioners. Covering themselves with blankets to stay warm, they debate whether hajjis who enjoy such comforts can gain the same merit as the millions who are outside roasting in the desert sun.

Now in their mid-forties and the parents of five children, Amien and his wife agree they have more worldly possessions than necessary. They pray not for personal and family matters, but for Muhammadiyah, Indonesia, and the global community of Islam. Amien's wife and a colleague begin composing a notebook of prayers for Muslims around the world, with special attention to

Palestine, Afghanistan, and Kashmir. Amien notes that, as he grows older, the hajj feels like a vitamin renewing his spirit to build a stronger Islamic society in Indonesia and internationally.

Amien concludes by reminding readers that the 'umra is never equal to the hajj, no matter how many times they visit the Holy Cities. He urges Muslims to make the hajj early in life—in their thirties if possible, but certainly before turning fifty. Younger pilgrims, he notes, are more capable of handling the hajj's physical demands, and they are more likely to translate their insights into lasting social change.

Nurcholish disagrees with Amien on nearly every major issue of hajj interpretation.[49] For Nurcholish, pilgrimage has the power to transform the spiritual lives of individuals, but it has no political meaning for the community. Only in the earliest years of Islam was the hajj tied to principles such as humanism, unity, and the rights of women. Nurcholish recognizes that Muhammad's sermon at 'Arafat inspired early Muslims to promote social change, but he thinks it has no practical effect today.

Nurcholish sees little reason to fear Iranian efforts to disrupt or manipulate the hajj. He notes that pilgrims spend most of their time indoors in tents and hotel rooms, where they seldom speak with anyone from another country. Most of the discussion they hear in the Holy Cities is no different from what they listen to every day, and it is as though they traveled thousands of miles to do just what they do at home.

Nurcholish insists that most pilgrims are preoccupied with survival and have no interest in talking politics. Afraid of being swept up in a torrent of strangers, they venture outdoors as little as possible. Even when they must go out to perform required rituals, they cling to their own groups and avoid speaking to other pilgrims.

Nurcholish is one of the few commentators—in Indonesia or elsewhere—who believe the hajj's political significance is weaker today than it was during the Prophet's lifetime. He contends that, in current conditions, multiple hajjs degenerate into mindless rituals, where pilgrims cannot grasp the "true meaning" of their acts. Contradicting Amien Rais, Nurcholish advises Indonesians to make no more than two or three pilgrimages. After that, if they still wish to revisit Mecca, he suggests they make an 'umra instead. Because the 'umra can be performed at any time of year, he argues, it provides a calmer and cleaner setting for worship and reflection than the chaotic hajj.

Nurcholish doubts that multiple hajjs or 'umras are necessary for Indonesians to become better Muslims. He contends that Indonesians are already more attached to Islam than most people think—particularly the dogmatic Muslim reformers and Western academics who mistakenly identify Islam with the Arabic-speaking world. Nurcholish notes that Indonesia has been absorbing Islam's universal civilization for centuries via the Malay language and adapting it to local conditions, just as al-Shafi'i and other jurists did in medieval times. He thinks it is foolish for Indonesians to imitate Arabs or anyone else. Rather, they should continue innovating. To underscore how unsuitable Arab customs are for Indonesians, Nurcholish recalls that, during his first pilgrimage, every one of his uninitiated traveling companions vomited and fell ill the moment they encountered Saudi food and table manners.

Nurcholish sees Indonesia's multicultural society as a wide-open laboratory where Muslims can nurture tolerance toward one another as well as toward non-Muslims. Yet, he believes such an experiment can succeed only if Indonesians realize that Islam teaches flexible principles, not ready-made policies they can market in sound bites and slogans.

## Islamic Pluralism after Suharto

Suharto's attempt to prop up his regime with Islam changed the balance of power between Indonesia's two largest religious movements, Muhammadiyah and Nahdlatul Ulama. When the New Order was consolidating power, "General" Suharto favored religious spokesmen he could control. But the president's strategy shifted once he needed counterweights to the army. "Haji Muhammad" Suharto wanted Muslim politicians who would be useful allies, not mere pawns. Whereas the "old" New Order courted the leaders who seemed most docile, the "new" New Order put a premium on strength and competence.

Suharto's preference for the modernists stemmed from immediate, tactical considerations, as well as fundamental differences in the social roots and leadership styles of the rival movements. Now that Islamic organizations are free to battle openly for power, the same factors that impressed the former dictator give the modernists an advantage they have not enjoyed since the early years of independence.

The Nahdlatul Ulama has become the victim of its own reputation for skilled maneuvering. NU leaders always tried to position themselves as power brokers willing to lend legitimacy to the government of the day in return for preferential treatment over competitors. The NU adapted to colonial rule by the Dutch and Japanese, as well as to the secular dictatorships of Sukarno and Suharto. The recurring pact was endorsement of non-Muslim government in exchange for preeminence in running religious education, the hajj, and Islamic courts. NU leaders presented their movement as an indispensable "anchor" or "bridge" in a fragile society where no government could afford to be entirely secular or entirely Islamic. Willingness to bargain with all sides allowed the NU to outlast more powerful contestants during the Sukarno era and to emerge as the leading Muslim block in the New Order's lopsided three-party system.

But Suharto induced the NU to play an awkward and unfamiliar role that sapped its strength. During the 1970s, the NU tried to be a loyal opposition in a regime that regarded criticism as inherently disloyal. Cooperating with authoritarianism earned them a niche in parliament, but they were ignored on the very issues that cut to the heart of their interests: family law, Javanese cults, and nominations of the party they supposedly directed.

Many times, NU legislators reacted with uncharacteristic defiance. During debates over a new marriage bill, they encouraged crowds of angry students to demonstrate outside the parliament building. When the army pressed for recognition of pre-Islamic mystics, NU deputies walked out of parliament. Suharto met these tactics head-on, putting his handpicked candidates at the helm of the PPP and ordering state agencies to withhold contracts from NU-affiliated businesses.[50]

Collisions with the government aroused so much antagonism between factions in the Nahdlatul Ulama that an upheaval was unavoidable. After the 1982 elections, supporters of Abdurrahman Wahid deposed the parliamentary leaders who had dominated the NU since independence. The Javanese 'ulama and merchants who had suffered most from Suharto's reprisals took back the power they had ceded to professional politicians from the outer islands.

The main targets of the revolt were Idham Chalid and Ali Yafie, party bosses who used their control of patronage to manage the NU's branches from Jakarta. The new leaders vowed to remove the NU from partisanship and "return to the line" of 1926—the limited educational and social missions that had inspired the movement's founders. NU leaders withdrew from the Islamic opposition party, and their followers began to vote for Golkar.

Desperate for government aid to pull the backward rural areas of East and Central Java into the mainstream, the NU gave in to Suharto on one issue after another throughout the 1980s. Unfortunately for the NU, its new leaders tried to fall in step with Suharto precisely when he was changing course and wooing Islamic modernists who urged their followers to become more outspoken and politically engaged. By the time Suharto made his hajj, he was tilting toward modernist organizations and intellectuals that were credible successors of the Masjumi.

Soon after Suharto completed his hajj, he gave his blessing to a series of Islamic modernist demands for changes in cultural and economic policy. The modernist agenda was far more ambitious than anything the NU had proposed during its leadership of the Islamic opposition in the 1970s. When B. J. Habibie agreed to head the Indonesian Association of Muslim Intellectuals (ICMI), modernists gained a valued partner. ICMI's economic nationalism merged Habibie's desire for state-owned heavy industry with Muhammadiyah's call for antimonopoly laws to rein in Chinese and multinational corporations. When Suharto reshuffled his cabinets, he was clearly trying to strike a balance between foreign capital and *pribumi* (native Indonesian) business.[51]

Meanwhile, many in Muhammadiyah demanded a stronger voice for business in their own movement. They urged Muhammadiyah's Economic Committee to become a pressure group for indigenous trade and industry. Some even suggested founding an Islamic development bank and launching a Malaysian-style affirmative action program for Muslim entrepreneurs. Attempts to strengthen the Economic Committee were yet another sign of the *'ulama*'s decline in favor of young professionals and newly rich businessmen.[52]

Muhammadiyah's new leaders must manage growing disputes between factions claiming to represent different social bases. Some argue that merchants and manufacturers have always been the cutting edge of Islamic civilization in Indonesia and that it is perfectly natural for them to assert greater political leadership. Others insist Muhammadiyah must ease the plight of struggling workers and farmers so it does not merely become a spokesman for the privileged. Responding to this dispute, Amien Rais proposed that Muhammadiyah collect a mandatory religious tax (*zakat*) from all members who are "professionals" so the funds could be invested for the benefit of poorer members.[53]

Muhammadiyah is governed by a collective leadership of thirteen directors elected from evenly matched factions based in Yogyakarta and Jakarta. Collegial decision making tries to contain a number of rising tensions—between an aging membership and a youthful population, between entrepreneurship and philanthropy, and between a tradition of voluntary, unpaid leadership and the new cadre of full-time professionals managing a nationwide system of schools, clinics, and charities.

Disagreements over Muhammadiyah's political role divide it more than any other issue. From its inception, the movement has agonized over how to translate popularity and resources into national influence. After ninety years of experience, today's leaders have ample ammunition to argue that their predecessors were either too reckless or too timid in calculating political risk.

The stronger Muhammadiyah becomes, the more difficult it is for its leaders to agree about which is the greater danger: inviting military retaliation that could destroy their hard-won gains or surrendering to secularists who would make it impossible to live as good Muslims. Suharto's search for support among Islamic modernists undoubtedly strengthened the more assertive faction in Muhammadiyah. The current leaders are confident they have found a workable compromise by disavowing an Islamic state while insisting that the armed forces bow to the will of the majority.

The people who run Muhammadiyah today are certain they define the mainstream of modern Indonesia. The generation of educated Muslims that thrived under Suharto also helped depose him, and today they are filled with confidence that they can govern in their own right.

In contrast, the Nahdlatul Ulama is a study in disillusion and alarm. Regardless of whether the NU chose accommodation or opposition, most of its members never shared in the growing prosperity of the Suharto era. No amount of political maneuvering could disguise their weakness and utter dependence on state patronage. Suharto snubbed the NU not because he perceived them as less loyal than the modernists but because he considered them less dangerous and less useful.

Angered by the president's tilt toward the modernists, Abdurrahman Wahid became the first NU leader to complain that the government was giving "too much" power to Muslims. Wahid publicly warned Suharto that he was playing with fire by encouraging Islamic "extremists" who would try to turn Indonesia into the Algeria or Lebanon of Southeast Asia.[54] As Muhammadiyah and ICMI moved closer to Golkar, Wahid tried to draw the Nahdlatul Ulama toward a secularist coalition with Megawati's Democratic Party of Indonesia (PDI), with Christian and Chinese minorities, and even with the army.

Many of Wahid's colleagues feared he had become a lone wolf pulling them into an unwanted brawl with the president. Sensing his isolation, Wahid tried to reassure local leaders that Suharto still endorsed him. Wahid was reelected in 1989 and 1994 only after he guaranteed delegates to the NU's national conventions that he had patched up his quarrels with the president and that the government would follow through with financial aid that it had promised their businesses and communities.[55]

Wahid's difficulties demonstrated that even though reform-minded intellectuals had risen to prominence in the NU, it was nonetheless the provincial *'ulama* who dominated the organization. For every Nurcholish Madjid urging a new theology, there are hundreds of *kiais* upholding Javanese folkways and the authority of the "yellow books"—the old-time glosses on the Qur'an and hadith that are the heart of *pesantren* studies. Unlike the university graduates who use ICMI and Muhammadiyah as political launching pads, the NU's intellectuals often seem like figureheads who are free to enjoy notoriety in Jakarta and abroad as long as they stay clear of the autocratic families running the movement's schools, mosques, and brotherhoods.

The resurgence of *'ulama* influence in the NU also aggravated regional conflicts that Abdurrahman Wahid's predecessors managed with considerable skill. Idham Chalid and Ali Yafie were party kingpins, but they were also prominent natives of Kalimantan and Sulawesi who helped the NU reach beyond its Javanese origins.

From the perspective of the outer islands, the coup that replaced them with Abdurrahman Wahid destroyed the only checks against domination by Java. The NU contracted toward its regional and social roots precisely when the Muhammadiyah was opening branches in every corner of the country and recruiting leaders across the spectrum of modern occupations.

The competition between the Muhammadiyah and the Nahdlatul Ulama is now in its eighth decade. Both groups are older than the Indonesian nation-state, and both helped fashion the constitutional compromise that created it. Most of the time, they have faced one another as evenly matched contenders representing conflicts along several dimensions—theological, socioeconomic, regional, and political.

Today their rivalry is livelier than ever, but it is far from a contest of equals. The modernists have penetrated all major institutions of Indonesian society, and they are enthusiastic practitioners of democracy and capitalism. Meanwhile, NU leaders realize that educationally and economically their members have fallen well behind the rest of the country, and they worry they may never catch up.

The hajj has been a constant source of friction between the Muhammadiyah and the Nahdlatul Ulama and a barometer of their on-again, off-again association. Indeed, the NU was born out of an early dispute over the pilgrimage. Traditionalist *'ulama* created the NU in 1926 because they feared the Muhammadiyah would exert undue influence over the "puritanical" Saudi regime that had just seized control of the Hejaz.[56] The NU's original mission was to ensure that Indonesia sent two separate delegations to the international Islamic conference in Mecca that deliberated the future of the pilgrimage and the Holy Cities. Conservative scholars formed their own group to make sure the Saudis respected the privileges of the Shafi'i community, especially customary visits to Medina and the martyrs' cemeteries they threatened to destroy. These scholars soon became the nucleus of the Nahdlatul Ulama.

Conflicts over the hajj also drove the NU out of the Masjumi coalition in 1952. When Muhammadiyah temporarily took control of the Ministry of Religious Affairs, the NU bolted the alliance and became a partner in nationalist-led governments that guaranteed NU followers the lion's share of the pilgrimage business.

Suharto took the hajj administration away from the NU not simply to quiet complaints about corruption but also to break their hold over state jobs and funds. Nationalizing the hajj was a key step in reasserting presidential control over the religious bureaucracy after years of colonization by NU partisans. When NU politicians presented Golkar with honest opposition, Suharto decided to deprive them of even a symbolic attachment to the hajj. The PPP had selected the *Ka'ba* as its party emblem—a natural choice for the party that voters were supposed to view as the "Islamic" alternative. Concerned over the appeal of such a potent symbol, Suharto forced the PPP to replace the *Ka'ba* with an innocuous five-pointed star.[57]

As Suharto leaned more and more on Islam, he identified the hajj with the state and, most desperately, with himself. Suharto's hijacking of the pilgrimage was a particularly sad tale for NU stalwarts who remembered the days when the hajj was their own family enterprise.

On the other hand, Islamic modernists who moved closer to Suharto showed renewed enthusiasm for the hajj. For modernists, Suharto's pilgrimage policies signified gains on several fronts—the steady Islamization of the government, the growing prosperity of the Muslim middle class, and the heightened prestige of Indonesia in world affairs.

The contrasting pilgrimage memoirs of Nurcholish Madjid and Amien

Rais illustrate how profoundly the New Order recast Indonesia's hajj in the minds of NU and Muhammadiyah sympathizers. Nurcholish expresses a disenchantment common among Muslims who regret the growing manipulation of the hajj by governments and politicians. According to Nurcholish, today's pilgrimage has little connection to Muhammad's vision. In the hands of modern states, the hajj promotes exactly the kind of ethnic and cultural parochialism that Islam deplores; instead of immersing them in a living historical community, it atomizes them and isolates them.

Amien is infinitely optimistic. In the Islamic modernist imagination, Indonesia's burgeoning hajj symbolizes far more than the well-being of their religion; it embodies the dreams of their families, the fruit of their labors, and the latent power of their nation.

# 9

# Nigeria

*"One Nation, under God"*

During the spring of 1999, Nigerians celebrated a rebirth of democracy after fifteen years of military repression and economic disaster. Even before the formal handover ceremonies on May 29, it was clear the new regime was staking its future on forging a common bond out of religion—the very factor many Nigerians see as their weakest link.

As president-elect Olusegun Obasanjo prepared to take office, Nigerian television began punctuating evening programs with a special music video that soon became the unofficial theme song of the democratic transition. Nearly every hour, a full orchestra accompanied the popular vocalist Onyeka Onwenu as she sang a prayer of thanksgiving and a patriotic hymn combined. "One Nation, under God" told disillusioned Nigerians of all faiths that they had survived a long national nightmare because they drew inner strength from a common trust in Providence. While the audience viewed film clips of churches and mosques across the country, Onwenu's refrain reassured them: "We've been through some hard times, but He always showed us the way. Now, our diversity is our strength as we face a brand new day."

At the same time, a young and defiant voice was denying that anything had really changed at all. Nigeria's hottest rap star, Charlie O, called the handover ceremonies a "party for the rich" that ordinary people would have to watch on television because they couldn't afford even a couple of days in Abuja, the pricey new capital city, where their representatives seemed more remote than ever. In fact, Charlie O caustically noted, thousands of Abuja residents were forced to leave town during the festivities because their landlords had promised their apartments to visiting "dignitaries." The incoming president pledged to fight corruption, but the angry rapper warned the new administration that they were taking off on the wrong foot and that he'd be watching to see if they broke their word: "We want power to da people. Are you listenin', Mis-ta Pres-i-dant?"

Although Abuja's futuristic landscape boasts several religious landmarks, they testify more to Charlie O's indictment of enduring inequality than to President Obasanjo's vision of communal harmony. As the mighty and humble traded possession of the capital for the handover weekend, they all passed two houses of worship that symbolize the disparity in power between Muslims and Christians.

Abuja's Central Mosque is a jewel of synthetic architecture that pulls every eye to its golden Arabian dome, its slender Turkish minarets, its sandy Moroccan façade, and its deep blue Persian tiles. This outer opulence yields to the simplicity and solitude of a surprisingly understated interior. The combination is magnetic—summoning worshipers and then banishing every distraction the instant they enter the sanctuary.

Nearby stands the rusting skeleton of an unfinished cathedral, the ecumenical project Nigerian churches launched at the same time Muslims began building the Central Mosque. In the early 1980s, the government of Shehu Shagari gave equal grants of land and money to Christian and Muslim groups so each could create a religious center in downtown Abuja. But Christian leaders delayed construction as they quarreled over the design and use of a multifaith complex. By the time they adopted a plan, spiraling construction costs had exhausted their funds, and they were forced to suspend work indefinitely. Fifteen years later, the cathedral remains a mass of concrete and protruding iron rods, crowned with the hollow frame of a would-be steeple and a slender cross. It is one of Abuja's saddest eyesores and, in the opinion of many church leaders, their most tragic failure.

Christians frequently told me that the dazzling mosque and the empty cathedral are a metaphor of their political ineptitude, compared with the astute Muslims. I heard this self-criticism from countless church officials, politicians, and parishioners determined to turn their divided groups into counterweights against Muslim dominance in government and business.

Although Christian leaders believe they have a long way to go before achieving political parity, they have already ended what they long perceived as a galling example of religious discrimination—state-sponsored pilgrimage for Muslims but not Christians. The same government that funded the construction of the Abuja mosque and cathedral also gave in to Christian demands for public assistance to pilgrims traveling to Canterbury, Lourdes, Rome, and Jerusalem. Gradually, Christians persuaded the government to create a full-fledged national pilgrimage board providing the same services Muslims had enjoyed since the 1970s.

Today, the Muslim and Christian pilgrims' boards share the same headquarters in an unadorned apartment building in the shadow of the Abuja Sheraton. The director of Muslim pilgrimage is located on the second floor, and his Christian counterpart's office is just one floor up. Christian pilgrimage is still small compared with the hajj—only about 3,000 persons annually versus an average of 20,000 Muslims. Yet for the first time Christians can rightly claim that momentum is on their side. In less than twenty years, Christian pilgrimage has grown from a tangle of sects headed in different directions at different times to a full-service package tour centered on Jerusalem and sanctioned by the Nigerian and Israeli governments. During the same period, Nigeria's hajj shrank to a fraction of the 100,000 people that traveled to Mecca each year in the late 1970s, when they regularly formed one of the largest contingents in the world.

The contraction of the hajj is the result not merely of a deteriorating economy but also of deliberate efforts by several governments to slash religious travel among Muslims while encouraging it for Christians. The goal was to quiet Christian resentment over the admitted favoritism that Nigeria's rulers have shown toward Islam since colonial times. Muslim politicians also hoped that Christians would abandon their strict interpretations of secularism if they benefited from the same sort of aid the state provided to Islam. From this perspective, even Muslims stood to gain if they let Christians "catch up" in the sensitive arena of pilgrims' affairs. Before long, however, this balancing act sparked a daily duel between rival pilgrimage movements—a duel that parallels the struggle for power and souls across the country.

Muslim and Christian leaders are extraordinarily candid in linking pilgrimage to religious conversion and political ambition. Prominently displayed in the offices of many hajj officials, I saw quotations from speeches of Ahmadu Bello, the spiritual and political leader of northern Nigeria whose assassination by southern army officers in 1966 helped to ignite the civil war. The young hajj director in Abuja—a native of Kano with a political science doctorate from UCLA—chose a famous passage in which Bello told young Muslims not to think he was indispensable to Islam's advance. Their own generation, he said, was destined to complete his campaign for "One North and One People"—a northern region united by Islam and holding the balance of power in the country. In Kano, hajj officials selected a more exuberant passage in which Bello looked forward to the day when all Nigerians would be Muslims. He proclaimed Islam "the best religion" because it encourages the honesty and hard work needed to make Nigeria a strong nation. Finally, he added, "Politics and religion are inextricably linked and I am proud to practice both simultaneously."

Christian leaders are equally blunt about the role of pilgrimage in joining faith and power. Unlike Muslim officials, they tell their story with maps as well as rhetoric. The Anglican archbishop of Abuja was pivotal in persuading the government to create a Christian Pilgrims' Board. Although he personally feels that pilgrimage is unimportant in Christianity, he pushed for government sponsorship because his colleagues and parishioners insisted it was a vital step toward equality with Muslims. The archbishop noted that this sentiment was especially strong among Christian minorities in the northern states, where Muslim hostility has bred a more militant group of church leaders.

Twice during our conversation he walked to a large wall map filled with colored pins and thumbtacks to emphasize how quickly the Anglican communion was penetrating the culturally mixed Middle Belt and the northern Muslim heartland. He reminded me that a Christian clergyman had just been elected governor of Benue, that a Christian lay leader won the governor's race in Plateau, and that another Christian was deputy governor of Kaduna. Then he showed me, one by one, the new churches and dioceses springing up in Sokoto, Katsina, Kano, Bauchi, and Borno. "Where is the 'Islamic North' now?" he asked. "It's nothing but a myth."

A few days later, the director of Christian pilgrimage used his own wall map to trace the ebbs and flows of religious conversion. When I asked him to describe the evolution of Christian pilgrimage, he started by discussing the creation of hajj boards as an outgrowth of Ahmadu Bello's missionary activities in the Middle Belt. At first, I thought he'd mistakenly assumed that I was asking about Muslim pilgrimage because we were introduced by one of his colleagues in the Hajj Division. Soon, however, I realized that in his mind all these events formed a single process—a long tug-of-war between Islam and Christianity that encompassed every region and every aspect of public life.

The director of Christian pilgrimage was careful to point out that many animists who converted to Islam in Bello's day did so under duress. After the civil war, he noted, Christian missionaries regained the initiative and brought thousands of nominal Muslims into new churches. Raising his arm to the top of the map and sweeping downward, he simulated the quick Muslim thrust into the animist strongholds of central Nigeria. Then, lifting just his hand slowly upward, he traced the steady Christian countermovement into the north.

In his view, pilgrimage—both Muslim and Christian—was a weapon in this struggle. Muslim pilgrims' boards were a legacy of Islamization campaigns in the 1960s and 1970s. State support for multiple Christian pilgrimages signaled that Muslims were losing momentum in the 1980s. And head-to-head competition between pilgrimages to Mecca and Jerusalem since the 1990s showed that Christians had finally learned to work together in securing equal rights.

"The Hajj Is Not for Everyone"

Hajj management in Nigeria has more than its share of idiosyncrasies. One of my most surprising discoveries was that Nigerian hajj officials have no desire to send large numbers of people to Mecca. They are far more likely to act as gatekeepers who weed out anyone they deem unfit for pilgrimage and anyone who might damage Nigeria's reputation abroad. I know of no other country that devotes so much effort to screening hajj applicants or where selection is so tainted by favoritism.

Even the pilgrimage reformers who instituted the screening measures in the 1980s now believe they helped destroy the hajj under the dictatorships of Ibrahim Babangida and Sani Abacha. Religious scholars and civil servants hoped that a system of mandatory tests and interviews would discourage the illegal migration and petty trading that have plagued Nigeria's pilgrimage while opening more slots for first-time applicants who were more deserving. Gradually, however, they realized they had given subsequent dictators just the tools they needed to slash the hajj in the name of austerity and pack it with cronies.

Official discouragement of the hajj has a long history in Nigeria. In precolonial times, the sultanates of Borno and Kanem sponsored large-scale pilgrimages. But their Fulani and Hausa neighbors to the west restricted travel to prevent conquered communities from fleeing by using the hajj as a cover for mass migration.[1] The British were suspicious of any international contact that might expose Nigerian Muslims to the religious fanaticism that challenged them in the Sudan. Fearful that returning pilgrims would breed imitators of the Mahdi, colonial administrators kept a tight lid on the hajj by issuing detailed medical and financial regulations similar to measures adopted by the rulers of independent Nigeria.[2]

Even Ahmadu Bello argued that state sponsorship of the hajj was largely a means for the federal government to control embarrassing behavior by Nigerians abroad. At first, Bello wanted to dampen conflicts over the millions of "permanent pilgrims" that comprised a Hausa-speaking diaspora along the land routes to Saudi Arabia between Chad and Ethiopia.[3] As Bello traveled more frequently to Mecca, he also realized that all Nigerians were being stigmatized as beggars and troublemakers because of rampant crime and indigence among unsupervised pilgrims. John Paden recounts Bello's horror and humiliation upon seeing a group of burly Nigerians physically attack the stone pillars at Mina, believing they were wrestling with Satan himself instead of an effigy.[4] Such incidents convinced Bello and his followers that the new pilgrim boards would have to examine applicants carefully so they wouldn't disgrace the entire country.

The heart of the screening process is the notion of "qualification"—istita'a in Arabic. Normally, this refers to the minimal requirements for pilgrimage that Muslim jurists accepted for centuries with little dispute. All major legal schools agree that all people can make the hajj who are Muslim, who have reached early adolescence, and who have accumulated enough savings so their absence won't create hardship for their families. Hajj officials in Nigeria have lengthened this list many times, giving themselves plenty of leeway for subjective interpretation and discriminatory enforcement.

The most elaborate screening system is in Kaduna, where hajj directors claim to conduct face-to-face interviews lasting between ten and thirty minutes with every candidate in the city. Applicants are evaluated by a committee including pilgrimage officers, regular police, security police, physicians, religious leaders, and members of community groups representing businesspeople, journalists, women, and pensioners. The committee gives each candidate a score ranging between one and ten on two factors: "religious knowledge" and "personal character." The religious knowledge section is an oral exam that quizzes interviewees on basic points of ritual such as ablution, prayer, and the opening verse of the Qur'an. Each year about 10 percent of the applicants fail the test. They must then undergo private religious instruction at their own expense and return for another interview at a later date—usually the following year.

The personal character section investigates possible criminal charges, unpaid debts, and medical problems. The committee also probes for signs the applicant might "abscond" in Saudi Arabia—overstay the hajj visa and not return to Nigeria. Members of the Ahmadiya sect—considered heretical in both Nigeria and Saudi Arabia—are denied permission to make the pilgrimage. Interviewers ask explicit questions about links to blacklisted groups, but they do not exclude members of the Anwar Movement, a domesticated offshoot of the Ahmadis that recognizes the finality of Muhammad's prophecy.

Those who pass both parts of the interview must also sign a two-page pledge of good conduct. This is a formal promise to avoid a laundry list of bad deeds such as engaging in political demonstrations, smuggling, drug running, loitering, begging, and sleeping in public places. Part of the covenant is a guarantee to refrain from illegal trade and from bringing foreign goods into Nigeria.[5] When I saw this item, I read it aloud to a group of officials in the Kaduna hajj office. But instead of stopping at the end of the sentence, I continued as though still following the text: "except for Chinese carpets." Instantly, the room shook with laughter, as everyone looked at the wide-eyed chairman of the screening committee, who minutes earlier had shown me two exquisite Chinese carpets that he'd brought back from his latest trip to Mecca. They were still wrapped in burlap, standing in a corner of his office—the very room he used to interview prospective pilgrims.

"No, no," he protested. "It says *illegal* trade. These are okay. I didn't exceed my customs exemption. It's perfectly legal. We *all* do it."

Indeed, they do. The streets of Kaduna are lined with fine carpets from all over the world neatly displayed in the open air at makeshift mini-marts between busy bus stops and taxi stands. The hawkers tell you everything is Saudi Arabian until you ask directly about the country of origin. Then they proudly explain that the carpets are made in every country between Istanbul and Beijing, but that Nigerian pilgrims scoop them up in Mecca and turn them into quick cash back home.

The screening process in Kaduna is mild compared with tougher measures advocated in other hajj offices. At the headquarters in Abuja, the deputy director went to the heart of the matter. "The hajj is not for everyone," he declared. "We must be careful about the people we send, and if they use the hajj for illegal purposes, they should be punished." Then he showed me a letter of commendation he'd received from the Office of the President for initiating a special court system called "hajj tribunals." The idea of speedy justice for perpetrators of pilgrimage fraud might seem attractive in principle, but by this time Nigerians had had their fill of extraconstitutional courts answerable to no one but the military. My friend assured me that the new tribunals were operating smoothly in Kano, where they were needed most desperately. But he readily acknowledged his creation was unlikely to survive the transition to democracy because, as he put it, "There will be too much concern with 'the rule of law.'"

Christian pilgrimage managers lost no time in erecting screening procedures that are even more restrictive than the Muslim system. The leading Catholic member of the screening committee for Christian pilgrims is a frail and sweet-tempered monsignor who lives next to the cardinal's residence in the plush Asokoro district of the capital city. He explained that, for Christians, pilgrimage selection was complicated by the direct involvement of the Israeli government. So many Nigerian pilgrims took up illegal residence in Israel that authorities in Jerusalem now insist on interviewing in person every prospective visitor from Nigeria.

Each year, Israelis send consular officers to Lagos, Abuja, and Port Harcourt, where they meet pilgrim candidates from surrounding states. Interviews are granted to only those candidates who have already been cleared by local pilgrimage boards that resemble the Kaduna hajj panel in their vetting practices. Jerusalem also refuses to grant pilgrimage visas to Nigerians below the age of forty-five, claiming the risk of overstays is simply too high for young people with few job prospects at home.

## Free Markets and Free Riders

Pilgrimage officials in Nigeria also surprised me with constant references to economics. In Malaysia and Indonesia, hajj leaders talk a great deal about making money and investing it but not about using economic policy to influence pilgrim behavior. From Malaysian leaders, I heard about managing port-folios, but in Nigeria discussions centered on managing people and providing them efficient incentives.

Economics training is widespread among Nigerian civil servants, and some informants might have resorted to jargon because they knew I was an attorney and social scientist. Yet in Kano, hajj officials spent so much time criticizing their agency for oscillating between market strategies and direct regulation that I dug more deeply into their educational backgrounds. The director had a master's degree in economics, and his deputy kept a "day job" as a high school economics teacher.

An economics degree is by no means a requirement for this discourse. It was the "father" of the hajj tribunals in Abuja—a lifelong student of Islamic philosophy—who produced the most sophisticated market analysis of the Ni-gerian pilgrimage. As part of an ongoing debate among top hajj managers over future reforms, he prepared a remarkable report, complete with dollar esti-mates of market segments, profiles of typical "consumers" from different social groups, and plans for dividing market share with private business.

Much of the current discussion among hajj officials concerns "interna-tional pilgrims"—a euphemism for the thousands of Nigerians who bypass government boards in favor of travel agents who procure visas and foreign exchange informally and usually illegally. My friend's marketing study re-minded his colleagues that no Nigerian government ever acquired a monopoly over the hajj business. He tried to persuade them to use market incentives to coax lost profits back to the public treasury instead of wasting resources on a total travel ban no one could enforce.

Even modest privatization policies are a hard sell among Nigeria's hajj bureaucrats. They have long portrayed international pilgrims as thieves and prostitutes or as a bunch of "free riders" who get to Mecca on the cheap and then sneak into official hajj camps without paying a penny. Unauthorized pil-grims are described as being in league with crooked tour operators who squeeze their pigeons dry before dumping them in Saudi Arabia without funds or return tickets.

Reformers like the deputy director argue that the illegal hajj traffic is much larger than the government admits—at least 6,000 people per year—and that it persists because official boards alienated both the upper and lower ends of the pilgrim market. Hajj officials estimate that the largest group of interna-tional pilgrims—about half of all illegal travelers—are low or average income earners who simply seek the cheapest means to fulfill their religious obliga-tions. These people were hit the hardest by repeated increases in the hajj tariff that austerity governments imposed to conserve foreign exchange. Instead of openly slashing the hajj quota, military rulers pushed up the cost of pilgrimage services so only a tiny fraction of the population could afford them. This drastically reduced the size of the Nigerian hajj while increasing demand for no-frills alternatives among people unwilling to postpone travel indefinitely.

Market forces proved such an efficient means of reducing the number of pilgrims that Nigerian officials lost interest in the rancorous international debate over hajj quotas. While countries like Turkey, Malaysia, and Iran were nagging the Saudis to raise their quotas, Nigerians silently accepted one reduction after another. Abuja made no objection when the Saudis pegged the Nigerian quota to the low estimates of the 1991 census or when they decided to cut even that amount in half by excluding the non-Muslim population from the count. Hajj managers reasoned that, given their devastated economy, all the plausible quotas were beyond their reach anyway, and it made no difference whether Nigeria's unused allowance was large or small.

An unintended consequence of the government's decision to provide fewer services at higher cost was a reprivatization of about a quarter of the business that hajj boards had taken away from freewheeling travel agents three decades before. The retired general who presided as the "sole administrator" of the Office of Pilgrim Affairs after 1996 is an avid defender of the state's crumbling monopoly over the hajj. He wanted to drive the private operators from the field once and for all by enforcing the letter of the law. But many of his colleagues in Abuja and in the state offices believe the agency is better off making its peace with private interests before the hajj slips even further out of the government's hands.

A sizable faction in the hajj bureaucracy favors turning private travel agents into partners in an expanded business that is regulated but not dominated by the state. Reformers would allow private operators to focus on niche markets dissatisfied with existing services, as long as the agents agree to follow government guidelines for selecting and supervising pilgrims. One version of this plan would require pilgrims to pay all fees directly to the hajj boards, which would subtract a commission and release remaining funds to businesses that put up performance bonds. In return, travel agents would share the state's onerous policing duties. They would sit alongside security officials during the initial screenings and assume vicarious liability for any criminal wrongdoing by "their" hajjis.

Pilgrimage bureaucrats are considering privatization because many of Nigeria's most influential Muslim leaders are demanding that the government get out of the hajj business altogether. The strongest attacks on hajj boards are coming from the very circles that created them—the emirs, 'ulama, and diplomats who told Ahmadu Bello that only the state could manage a religious enterprise with such far-reaching political implications.

The most prominent critic was the late Ibrahim Dasuki, an old Bello confidant and diplomat who was Nigeria's first hajj liaison in Saudi Arabia and a founder of the National Pilgrims' Board. In 1988, Babangida installed Dasuki as the sultan of Sokoto—the ceremonial leader of Nigeria's Muslims—even though a rival candidate enjoyed popular support. Before long, the generals learned that Dasuki was more independent than they realized. In one of their most celebrated run-ins, Dasuki complained that the hajj had suffered years of mismanagement under the military and should be turned over to the Supreme Council of Islamic Affairs, a private body of royal patrons and religious leaders. In 1996, President Sani Abacha sacked the outspoken sultan and placed him in detention pending trial on charges of bank fraud.

That same year, Saudi Arabia imposed a total ban on Nigerian pilgrims because of reports they were carrying infectious meningitis.[6] Even today, Nigerian hajj officials insist the ban was a deliberate attempt to humiliate Abacha for deposing Dasuki. They argue that the meningitis scare was no reason to close the Holy Cities to Nigerians worldwide, especially those living in unaffected regions such as Europe and the United States. One of Dasuki's friends—a professor of Islamic studies and a former hajj director—claims King Fahd was furious with Abacha for refusing to see the personal emissary he sent to mediate between the government and the deposed sultan. In Abuja, hajj officials go further, suggesting the Saudis were retaliating on behalf of the United States for Abacha's earlier jailing of Mushid Abiola, winner of the nullified presidential elections in 1993.

Nigerian-Saudi relations are still tainted by lingering bitterness over the 1996 confrontation. Abacha tried to squelch any criticism of hajj management by Dasuki and Saudi sympathizers. He dissolved the flexible state boards representing community groups and replaced them with "sole administrators" who take orders only from Abuja.

To head up the streamlined administration, Abacha chose General Ahmad Daku, a well-connected artillery commander from Katsina state who had served Babangida as the military governor of Sokoto and Kano. Thus, the same soldier who put down the weeklong riots that greeted Dasuki's ascension to the sultanate in 1988 took the helm at the embattled pilgrimage agency when Dasuki was banished eight years later.[7]

As pilgrimage director, Daku turned the tables on critics in Saudi Arabia by charging that Saudis were furnishing Nigerian hajjis substandard services at inflated prices. When Saudis complain that Nigeria never pays its bills on time, he tells them Nigeria cannot afford "sinecure payments" for unused accommodations they are forced to book months before anyone knows how many pilgrims will register.

Daku cannot antagonize the Saudis too much because he needs them to regain control over his own pilgrims. Unless Saudi Arabia is willing to turn away Nigerians who are not approved by the hajj boards, Abuja has no hope of capturing the lucrative underground traffic. Normally, the Saudis were unwilling to go that far. Nigerians could always obtain hajj visas through personal connections, and everyone knew that Saudi police looked the other way when foreigners took up residence after performing the hajj. However, by 1999, a tight oil market drove Saudi authorities to step up expulsions of illegal aliens, and they welcomed Nigeria's offer to attack the problem at its source. That year's hajj was the first in which Saudi Arabia agreed to admit Nigerians only if they registered with state boards.

## "Babangida Is the Devil"

Nigerians constantly impressed me by blaming Ibrahim Babangida for corrupting the hajj and everything else in the country. Babangida's regime (1985–1993) was Nigeria's longest period of military rule, and it subjected millions of people to wrenching austerity. Yet his infamy carries an added charge—an amazingly negative cult of personality many claim he encourages to keep everyone guessing what he might do next.

I never had to ask anyone his opinion of Ibrahim Babangida. I always heard it without prompting, as though it provided essential context, giving meaning to everything else. The most common description—the one I heard in such disparate cities as Kano, Ilorin, and Lagos—was "Babangida is the devil." A governor who regularly clashed with Babangida explained that the general was never offended by the phrase but preferred to call himself "an evil genius." Both terms caught on, and I heard them from people of all backgrounds.

The road that circles the "Three Arms Zone" of Abuja—the site of the National Assembly, the presidential residence, and the Supreme Court—is named Ibrahim Babangida Drive, and many in the capital still speak as though he surrounds the government in person as well as in spirit. After the death of his brutal successor, Sani Abacha, Babangida was widely credited with brokering the selection of Olusegun Obasanjo as a compromise presidential candidate who could placate all of the major factions—the impatient Yoruba opposition, the frightened northern establishment, and the disgraced military.

Hajj offices across the country are filled with civil servants and ex-soldiers who were Babangida protégés. After Obasanjo took power, he sacked hajj directors in the bigger states, but holdovers from the military era remain well ensconced in the Abuja headquarters.

When Dasuki's friends say Babangida "destroyed the hajj," they have several things in mind. First, there was the collapse in numbers. Under Babangida, Nigeria never sent more than 30,000 pilgrims to Mecca, and the average was closer to 20,000. This was far short of the oil-boom years, when Nigeria regularly topped the 100,000 mark, and it was the smallest pilgrimage since independence. Only non-Muslim colonialists more effectively discouraged Nigerians from performing the hajj. In addition, there was the abuse of new screening measures that were supposed to reduce profiteering and serial pilgrimage. Elaborate screening seemed to be a cruel joke when economic misery put foreign travel out of reach for all but the most privileged. As the pain of "structural adjustment" tore unevenly through a society already split by immense inequality, political connections became more indispensable than ever to winning a place on the shrunken hajj rolls.

Under Babangida, Nigeria's hajj became a bastion of the strong. Babangida's enemies usually dwell on his habit of packing top-level hajj delegations with cronies and relatives, but the regressive impact of his polices on the social composition of the hajj is evident across the board. In contrast to the 1970s, when Nigerian hajjis represented a cross-section of society, pilgrimage under Babangida favored northerners over southerners, men over women, and the elderly over the young.

It is as though independent Nigeria had two separate hajjs—one before Babangida and another afterward. From 1960 onward, Nigeria's hajj expanded and contracted like an accordion (Figure 9.1). Pilgrimage opened to Muslims from all regions and social backgrounds. Except for a brief interruption during the civil war, expansion continued until the end of the oil boom in the early 1980s.

The contraction was already under way before military rule hardened under Babangida. But he quickened the pace, squeezing the life out of a pilgrimage that languishes even today.

The hajj recovered some vitality when Babangida resigned amid the uproar over Mushid Abiola's nullified election. From 1993 through 1995, Nigeria sent between 30,000 and 56,000 people to Mecca each year. The spurt was both

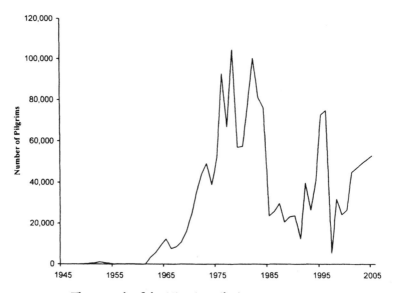

FIGURE 9.1 The growth of the Nigerian pilgrimage, 1947–2004

reassuring and alarming to pilgrim managers. It showed that the military still believed the hajj was worth resuscitating when they needed popular support to weather a political crisis. Yet hajj boards realized the surge reflected the growth of illegal pilgrims and Nigerians living abroad. Whether the hajj was expanding or contracting, one of every four pilgrims never signed up for the state-run program. When hajj operations fell apart again after the meningitis scare of 1996, the pilgrims' boards pleaded for Saudi cooperation in rebuilding their vanishing monopoly.

In the eyes of many former hajj managers, Babangida's most unforgivable sin was putting Islamic and Christian pilgrimage on the same level. The men who created Nigeria's hajj boards are former diplomats, politicians, and religious scholars who were followers of Ahmadu Bello. Today, many are still running universities, government agencies, and businesses all over Nigeria. Each has personal criticisms of the soldiers and police who replaced them as hajj directors, but they all condemn the "concessions" Babangida made to Christians on pilgrimage.

Describing the elevation of Christian pilgrimage, they sound like a generation forced to watch the desecration of its collective legacy: "Pilgrimage is not a religious obligation for Christians as it is for Muslims." "Nigerian Christians have no tradition of pilgrimage. For them, it is pure politics." "Christians merely use pilgrimage to imitate Muslims. After they return, many adopt the title 'J.P.' (Jerusalem Pilgrim) and some go around calling themselves 'Alhaj.'"

For Christians battling religious discrimination, the pilgrimage was just the tip of the iceberg. The Christian Association of Nigeria (CAN) skewered Babangida for secretly turning Nigeria into an Islamic state. At a time when independent parties and associations were nonexistent, CAN snowballed into a mini-opposition movement channeling free-floating dissent into religious protest.[8]

Creating parity between the Jerusalem and Mecca pilgrimages helped contain this opposition. It also spurred Christian and Muslim leaders to trade places in their long-standing debate over whether Nigeria's secular constitution allows the state to sponsor any pilgrimage. As churches became politically assertive, they backed away from demanding that the state should stay out of religion altogether. Mainline churches were desperate for official status to fend off the wave of Pentecostal and charismatic preachers depleting their flocks and revenues. Instead of pressing the usual line of strict secularism, church leaders urged the government to strengthen moderates against fundamentalists who were threatening both Christianity and Islam.[9]

Muslim leaders moved in the opposite direction. Disillusioned with soldiers and technocrats, they embraced the idea of privatizing the hajj. Instead of viewing the private sector as inherently corrupt, they saw it as the most promising way to rescue the hajj administration they created from its authoritarian "hijackers." Emirs and 'ulama echo Ibrahim Dasuki's demand that the government hand over hajj management to the Supreme Islamic Council, but they cannot agree on a common plan of action. Several council members favor partial privatization; others want the council to run the hajj directly, but they want pilgrims' boards to remain public bodies so they can exercise police powers and live off the federal budget.

Most hajj managers care little whether the boards are run by the government, the council, or both. Their plea is for relief from the endless cycle of reorganizations that lets each government sweep away the rules and records of its predecessors. Everywhere in Nigeria, pilgrimage officials complain about the chronic lack of continuity in policy and personnel that erases all institutional memory.

The assistant director of the Kano office showed me a well-documented research paper he had presented to a scholarly conference on the history of the Nigerian hajj. He decided to do the project because no one in the hajj administration could explain how or why their organization had been turned inside out so many times in just four decades of postcolonial government. No other hajj official at the federal or state level had his grasp of the matter or even his curiosity about it.

Many Nigerians see no anomaly in Babangida and Abacha's favoring Christian pilgrimage over the hajj. Several people reminded me that Nigeria's hajj frequently fared better under Christian rulers than under Muslim-led governments. Hence, there should be no surprise when the tables turn. Politicians of both religions know they can win support from members of other faiths by paying their pilgrimage expenses with public funds.

Even before independence, it was a Christian-Rosicrucian and not a Muslim who established the first government-sponsored hajj program. Obafemi Awolowo, governor of the Western Region, created hajj boards to serve his religiously mixed Yoruba constituency years before Ahmadu Bello followed suit in the Northern Region.[10] Awolowo's support of Islam earned him a wide following among Muslim voters. In his unsuccessful presidential campaigns of 1979 and 1983, he drew large crowds in northern cities including Sokoto, forcing Shehu Shagari's supporters to redouble their efforts to win what were supposedly their safest districts.[11]

Yakubu Gowon, the president who turned local hajj boards into a nationwide system, was also a Christian. Gowon was the general who guided Nigeria through the years of civil war and reconstruction. His father was a well-known Anglican evangelist. Gowon's background made it important to reassure Muslim elites he bore no hostility to Islam, especially after he carved up the Northern Region into six separate states to help centralize power in the federal government. Gowon subsidized the hajj and took Nigeria into the Organization of the Islamic Conference. He also nationalized the century-old system of mission schools and hospitals that shaped a large part of Nigeria's military and political leadership. According to many church leaders, Gowon was so solicitous of Muslim fears that he unwittingly confirmed Christians' feelings that the state viewed them as second-class citizens.[12]

Christian leaders note that discriminatory policies they fought during the 1980s and 1990s originated in the Gowon era. Despite their loathing for Babangida and Abacha, militant clergy acknowledge they received better hearings from Muslim strongmen than from Gowon because Muslims were eager to prove they were no longer beholden to northern kingmakers.

Although Gowon and Babangida are demonized by coreligionists who see them as too sympathetic to other faiths, their pilgrimage policies exemplified a desire to build coalitions across Nigeria's gaping ethnic and regional divides. Christian politicians got a head start in the politics of interfaith pilgrimage, but their Muslim counterparts quickly caught on to the value of reciprocity.

## Ethnic and Regional Biases of Military Rule

Military governments squeezed the geographic core of pilgrimage to a mere handful of favored states. Between 1977 and 1982, the Nigerian delegation averaged about 61,000 people per year. Fifteen years later, it was less than 21,000[13] (Table A9.1). Under Babangida's predecessors, Nigeria's per capita hajj rates were about 35 percent higher than the world average. Under his successor, Nigerian rates were less than half the international norm.

These contractions hit every state, but their impact was very unequal. The biggest losers were commercial centers like Lagos and Kano that were vulnerable to disruptions in foreign trade and finance. Agricultural areas fared better, particularly in the far north and east, where small farmers were less dependent on cash economies.

Nigerians in and out of government told me that although economic troubles decimated the hajj, they actually improved the quality of the experience by refocusing attention on its religious purpose after years of tasteless commercialization. They reasoned that those who go to Mecca in hard times are likely to be pious peasants who saved all their lives to make a single journey rather than frivolous city folk setting off on a shopping spree.

However, economics told only part of the story. Politics and ethnicity were even more important in shifting the geographic basis of pilgrimage. The states where the hajj suffered the least were in the northwestern and central regions, especially Niger, Kaduna, and Sokoto. These were precisely the states where Babangida and his coterie had their deepest roots. Changes in the relative strength of the hajj reflected a general shift of power from Kano, the most industrialized and cosmopolitan city in the north, to Sokoto, bastion of the Fulani aristocracy that traces its lines to the nineteenth-century caliphate.

Many of the northern soldiers and civil servants who orchestrated that power shift came from villages and towns in neighboring states that profited from the diversion of public investment from Kano to the countryside. Besides Sokoto, the greatest beneficiaries were Niger, Babangida's home, and Kaduna, the old British garrison town that blossomed into the military and political center of northern Nigeria.

In contrast, hajj rates fell dramatically in the south. Muslims form a tiny minority in southeastern states. Many are migrants from the north—traders and religious teachers who had an astonishing propensity for pilgrimage before military rule. After the economic downturn, they could no longer make the hajj at phenomenal rates, but they remained well above the national average.

The region hardest hit was Yorubaland, the heart of agitation for democracy and the most implacable opponent of the north's hegemonic pretensions. In the relative freedom and prosperity of the Obasanjo and Shagari eras, Lagos and Kwara connected Yorubaland to a broad band of hajj activity stretching from the Atlantic Ocean in the southwest to Borno in the northeast (Figure 9.2). Fifteen years later, Yoruba states formed a solid block with the lowest hajj rates in the nation.

From 1977 to 1982, pilgrimage cut across all boundaries, regional and

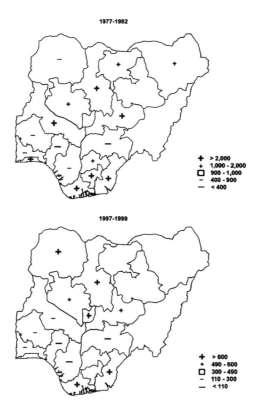

FIGURE 9.2 Hajj rates in the states of Nigeria

ethnic. High hajj rates appeared nearly everywhere along the two transnational railways linking Lagos and Port Harcourt with Kaduna and then continuing northward to Kano and Borno. After a decade and a half of military rule, Nigeria was a far more divided country. The fault line began just south of the new capital city, separating the Hausa northwest from the Yoruba southwest. It traced not the northward path of the colonial engineers who united the country but the southward course of the River Niger, demarcating ancient cultural and political zones that continue to view one another with deep hostility.

Military rule had a dramatic impact on every correlate of hajj activity, whether economic, cultural, or political[14] (Table A9.2). In the fifteen states where Muslims are more than 5 percent of the population, the hajj became disconnected from all measures of social and economic development. At the same time, the role of ethnicity and politics increased enormously.

Between 1977 and 1982, hajj participation reflected only modest differences between Yoruba and Hausa-Fulani communities. By 1999, ethnic disparities were glaring. Hajj activity developed strong and opposing connections with the two groups as it receded from religiously mixed Yoruba areas to Muslim-dominated Hausa states.

All these cleavages—regional, ethnic, and religious—became highly politicized. During the multiparty contests of 1979 and 1983, hajj participation had no strong relation to voter support for either Shagari, the northern Muslim, or Awolowo, the Yoruba Christian. Both politicians were avid coalition builders who constantly reached beyond their core constituencies in national campaigns.

In contrast, during the 1990s, regional voting closely paralleled inequalities in hajj activity. In 1993, Abiola did best in states where military regimes suppressed the hajj, and he did worst where they propped it up. In 1999, support for Obasanjo showed the reverse pattern. In the polarized atmosphere of the 1990s, neither Abiola nor Obasanjo could overcome the perception that they represented a specific region. In both cases, the winning candidate's religion seemed irrelevant to voters who believed that regional and ethnic interests were paramount. Northerners labeled the Yoruba Abiola "the southern candidate," even though he was a Muslim. Southerners were even more convinced that ex-general Obasanjo was "the northern candidate," even though he is both Yoruba and Christian. Hence, there was the double irony of a Muslim candidate who lost in strong hajj areas in 1993 and a Christian who won them six years later.

Similar trends appear even if we exclude Yorubaland and focus on the ten states that comprised the former Northern Region before the civil war. Here, too, hajj participation lost its earlier connections to economic development and to ethnic and religious diversity. Pilgrimage became closely identified with the northernmost states, where Islam has the longest history, rather than the Middle Belt, where tribal minorities preserve traditional religions. In Middle Belt states, hajj activity follows the path of religious conversions. The hajj is stronger west of Abuja, where Islam enjoys the advantage—especially in Niger—and it is weaker east of Abuja, where Christianity has greater success—particularly in Benue.

The main exception is Plateau, whose capital city, Jos, is a hotbed of missionary activity for evenly matched Christian and Muslim groups struggling to gain the upper hand in a region where half the population holds to traditional beliefs. In Plateau, sectarian tensions helped elevate hajj rates for twenty years, despite the economic and political shocks that decimated pilgrimage elsewhere. When Christian pilgrimage caught on during the 1990s, it took off in Plateau, making that state a leader in travel to Jerusalem, as well as to Mecca.[15]

In the former Northern Region, the hajj reflects political divisions as well as ethnic and sectarian differences. Voting patterns show a pluralistic system where numerous power centers compete for regional dominance. Shagari's strong ties to Sokoto always cost him votes in Kano, Kaduna, and Borno—high hajj states where independent voters preferred homegrown splinter parties.

Fragmentation in the Muslim north increased the bargaining power of Middle Belt politicians, no matter what their religions, who could tip the balance in Shagari's favor. His pivotal support in the Middle Belt came from two non-Hausa states, Niger and Benue—one Muslim and the other Christian.

In the old Northern Region, hajj participation actually had a strong negative correlation with Shagari's vote and a slight positive correlation with Awolowo's. The only time party votes in the north overlapped with hajj activity was in 1993, when Abiola carried the urbanized states where pilgrimage plummeted and lost the more rural states where the military kept it alive.

The ascendance of Sokoto and its Middle Belt allies at the expense of their neighbors shows that military rule was by no means a simple case of the north oppressing the south. Power, prosperity, and pilgrimage also shifted away from northern states that were not on good terms with Babangida and his successors. The hajj data reveal striking examples of regional discrimination in both parts of the country (Figure 9.3).

Kaduna and Lagos were vibrant pilgrimage centers during the Shagari era, but they moved in opposite directions under military government. There is no better example of north-south bias than the contrasting fortunes of Kaduna, the thriving power base of the north, and Lagos, the sinking commercial capital of the south.

Nonetheless, even in the north, there are many states where hajj activity oscillated between extreme highs and lows because their political alliances changed drastically under democracy and dictatorship. The most obvious case is the well-known rivalry between Sokoto and Kano.[16] Yet Kano's fall was modest compared with the fate of Kwara, the aspiring bridge between north and

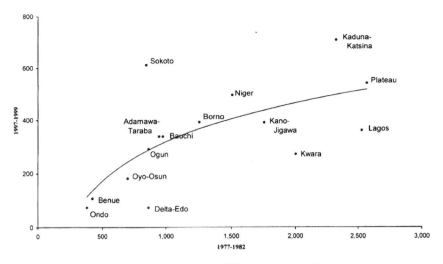

FIGURE 9.3 Hajj rates in the states of Nigeria, 1977–1982 and 1997–1999

south that had the great misfortune of being the neighbor and rival of Niger State—Babangida's home.

## Kwara versus "the Power State"

Niger and Kwara face one another across the long upper branch of the River Niger (Figure 9.4). Historically, both served as gateways for traders and armies moving north and south and as tributary states of neighboring kingdoms that constantly pressed upon their borders. Each state has a distinct approach to deriving political advantage from its strategic location. Niger seeks stable alliances with its former overlords in the north, whereas Kwara prides itself on preserving greater freedom of maneuver.

Niger is firmly tied to the Muslim north by generations of vassalage to the Fulani jihadists and their heirs. It is the center of the Nupe, a small, insular community focused on survival rather than expansion. Kwara, the northern-most part of Yorubaland, was an early relay point for Islam's long march from the Sahel to the Atlantic. Its leaders still identify, culturally and politically, with both the Islamic north and the Yoruba south.[17]

In practice, Kwara's ambition and flexibility often work against it. Kwara's predicament is that, to position itself as a bridge, it cannot identify too closely with either north or south, yet its very effort to carve out a dual status antagonizes both sides. Much of the problem stems from a perception that Kwara's leaders constantly trade on their region's faded reputation as an Islamic for-

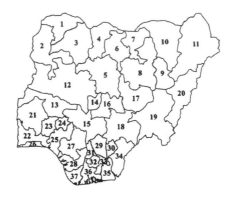

| NORTH | MIDDLE BELT | SOUTHWEST | SOUTHEAST |
|---|---|---|---|
| 1 Sokoto | 12 Niger | 21 Oyo | 29 Enugu* |
| 2 Kebbi* | 13 Kwara | 22 Ogun | 30 Ebonyi** |
| 3 Zamfara** | 14 Abuja | 23 Osun* | 31 Anambra |
| 4 Katsina* | 15 Kogi* | 24 Ekiti** | 32 Imo |
| 5 Kaduna | 16 Nasarawa** | 25 Ondo | 33 Abia* |
| 6 Kano | 17 Plateau | 26 Lagos | 34 Cross River |
| 7 Jiawa* | 18 Benue | 27 Edo* | 35 Akwa-Ibom** |
| 8 Bauchi | 19 Taraba* | 28 Delta | 36 Rivers |
| 9 Gombe** | 20 Adamawa | | 37 Bayelsa** |
| 10 Yobe* | | | |
| 11 Borno | | | |

\* Created in 1991
\*\* Created in 1996

FIGURE 9.4 The states of Nigeria

tress. Ilorin, the state capital, was the first Yoruba power to embrace Islam as a universal faith, while most of the south still viewed it as the cult of tribal foes. In larger cities such as Kano and Lagos, people are well aware of Ilorin's pioneering work in spreading Islam, but they are not convinced it merits any deference to Kwara's modern rulers, especially in political questions.

Nigeria has always had multiple centers of Islamic learning, where preachers had to decide when to bend to local customs and when to break them. By such standards, Ilorin hardly seems unique. Kwara's politicians are apt to get themselves into hot water when they boast that their community has created a model synthesis of Islam and indigenous culture that somehow eluded the rest of Nigeria. Such pretensions usually backfire, reinforcing popular suspicions that northern Yorubas are neither fish nor fowl, "too pagan" for the north and "too fanatic" for the south.

Like Niger, Kwara was also the home of a despised military strongman—Tunde Idiagbon, the number two figure in the Buhari regime that overthrew Shagari's civilian government in 1983. When Babangida seized power, one of his first acts was to purge Idiagbon and his allies from the army. Once he was defanged, Idiagbon took a high-profile post in the state industrial enterprises, where he became known as "the Man of Steel," a bitter honorific, given his subsequent powerlessness.

After Babangida sacked Idiagbon, Kwara's leaders complained they were shut out of the top levels of government. That discriminatory legacy of military rule is unmistakable to anyone visiting Niger and Kwara in succession. Niger's roads are the best in the country, and modern agribusiness is thriving. By comparison, Kwara belongs to another era. Driving across Kwara takes twice as long as traveling through Niger, even though the distance is only half as great. Kwara's economic woes come into view the instant one crosses the river at Jebba, the junction where modern railroads first met up with the ancient maritime route to Mali and West Africa.

Today, Jebba's piers are empty. Looking upstream or downstream, there is not a ship or barge in sight—only colossal islands of silt blocking passage in all directions. Land transport is not much better. The highway between Ilorin and Ibadan is a death trap littered with charred skeletons of vans and trucks squeezing traffic into single file along most of the tree-lined route.

Soon after Buhari and Idiagbon were deposed, Babangida ensured that Niger—and not Kwara—would reap the benefits of his rule. He canceled plans to turn the battered Ilorin-Ibadan road into a modern divided highway. When Kwara's governor pleaded with him to dredge the River Niger to reopen it to navigation, he dispatched the needed engineers and equipment to the oil-rich delta region instead. When Kwara's leaders thought they were going to get a new airport to replace Lagos as the hub for cargo flights, Babangida upgraded facilities in Lagos.

The greatest blow to Kwara's economy was the collapse of its dreams to control western Nigeria's most precious natural resources, water and electricity. Just east of the Benin frontier, the upper Niger forms the Kainji Reservoir, a lake that winds across the borders of three states. The reservoir is part of a powerful development authority that oversees reclamation and electrification throughout central and northern Nigeria. The federal government originally located the organization's headquarters in Kwara, but Babangida had it moved to Niger.

Even after losing the project headquarters, Kwara still retained a major hydroelectric station just inside its borders at the town of Baro. Because the plant was already finished, the generals could not snatch the plum from Baro. Instead, they grabbed the town and plant together by redrawing the state boundaries and annexing both to Niger.

At about the same time, Abuja approved a new system of vehicle registration that allowed each state to display an appropriate motto on its license plates. In Babangida's homeland, the authorities chose "Niger: The Power State," an apt description of their grip on vital resources and of the clout they used to attain it.

Finding themselves shut out of the federal government, Kwara's leaders feared the generals were also encouraging religious extremists to undercut them at home. Ilorin has long been plagued by Christian-Muslim tension, as well as intra-Muslim strife. A paternalistic emirate poses as the guardian of communal harmony, but it has always fostered a feudalistic order, with its clients at the top and Christians at the bottom. As Kwara lost ground to other states, its elite faced growing opposition from both evangelical Christians and Islamic radicals denouncing the status quo.

In more prosperous times, Kwara's notables could rely on the hajj to bolster religious and social hierarchy. Each year, politicians and businesspeople picked up the tab for hundreds of pilgrims who could not have gone any other way. Some years, the governor alone sponsored thirty hajjis. A Muslim entrepreneur who had seen many of these ostentatious acts of charity tried to give me an idea of their political effects. "Imagine," he said, "there are people who save all their lives to make the hajj and, then, some politician tells them to keep their money and go to Mecca at government expense. That's power."

When Kwara's fortunes plummeted, Ilorin's rulers could no longer use the hajj to rally support. With the state's economy in a tailspin and Abuja in hostile hands, they had neither the financial nor political resources to sustain a lavish pilgrimage. A sagging hajj prodded the oligarchy to find other ways of using religion for political gain.

One group backed the emir's effort to resuscitate feudal privilege by attacking the Christians, while another faction tried to prepare Muslims for a more competitive future by reforming Islamic education. As this contradiction became apparent, it drove a wedge between the royal family and the professional class that had served them in the past.

The Emir of Ilorin began deflecting popular frustrations toward the local Christian minority. He cast himself as the protector of a besieged Islamic community whose magnanimity was exploited by aggressive Christian missionaries taking instructions from Abuja and the United States. By expressing political and economic grievances in religious terms, the emir's followers turned Kwara into one of Nigeria's most dangerous flash points for sectarian conflict. Their cynical "post-hajj" strategy spurred Muslim hatred of Christians and portrayed the ruling elite as the hapless target of fanatics in both faiths.

Alhaji Sani A. Lawal, former governor of Kwara who is the emir's chief counsel, traced the problem to Babangida's dependence on the Christian technocrats who shaped his austerity programs and sold them to international financial circles. According to Lawal, Babangida accepted too many of the churches' demands, including stepped-up freedom for missionary work, because several of his top advisors were Christians and because he knew his regime was losing Muslim support.

The step-up in church activity was especially provocative in Ilorin, where Muslims were accustomed to living with a Christian minority that was supposed to be seen but not heard. As economic opportunities narrowed, Muslims resented seeing top slots in the universities and civil service go to Christian candidates whose better English skills signaled their attachment to Western schools.

The collapse of old social barriers made Ilorin Muslims more determined than ever to bolster the residential segregation underpinning their historic dominance. The emir complained that the spread of chapels and meeting halls violated the customary ban on church construction inside the old city center. Muslim residents claimed that Christians not only flouted the ban but also made a point of holding noisy choir services when everyone else was trying to sleep. The emir's protests attracted little attention outside Ilorin until he threatened to enforce the ancient "law" by bulldozing unauthorized chapels in the restricted neighborhoods.[18]

The emir's attempt to resurrect his authority triggered a flurry of lawsuits challenging the emirate system as a whole. At the height of the debate, Lawal defended the emir, but on political rather than legal grounds. In his opinion, the emir was performing a valiant service by expressing local discontent at a time when no one else was willing to stand up to military oppression. "We feel invaded," he told me. "Our people are very diverse ethnically, and Islam is the only thing holding them together. If they feel their religion is under attack, there can be war."

This is not the warning of an Islamic militant. It comes from a British-trained lawyer whose bookshelves are crammed with memoirs of Great Power icons such as Henry Kissinger and Anthony Eden, as well as Moshe Dayan and Golda Meir. Indeed, we met through a Christian friend, a bank manager whose wife was an associate in Mrs. Lawal's law office.

Unlike the emir, the ex-governor believes the greatest danger to Ilorin's Muslims is their own isolation. Instead of criticizing Christian advances, Lawal tells conservative Muslims that their children's progress will be impossible without reforms in religious education. He focuses on creating schools that combine Islamic studies with science and business courses. He is especially keen to use publications of liberal Muslim writers, but he insists they be in English and from Western countries. In his state, he explains, the prestige of English is so great that religious arguments in any other language carry little weight among the youth, even if they already know Arabic. To his distress, much of what reaches Kwara in both languages are Libyan diatribes that portray graduates of Nigeria's modern schools as victims of colonialist brainwashing.

Compared to Lagos and Jos—where rival Islamic movements pitch a variety of special schools to mobility-conscious Muslims in religiously mixed environments—educational reform in Ilorin has barely begun. In most of Nigeria, I discovered people were eager to adapt innovations in religious education from other nations, including Turkey, Pakistan, and Indonesia. Although I found similar interest in Ilorin, I was surprised that leaders there were just starting to pay attention to a host of new schools that have already taken root in their own country.

Ilorin's prominent families still send their sons to Saudi Arabia for religious studies, only to discover that their diplomas have little value to Nigerian employers. Their plight creates an urgent desire for private schools that can provide them with suitable teaching positions while giving younger Muslims the skills they need in the business world. The market for modern Islamic education is flourishing in Nigeria, and thousands of entrepreneurs are stimulating the demand as well as satisfying it.

Kwara is a latecomer to this movement because local *'ulama* still see the new schools as offshoots of groups they consider either too heterodox, like the Ahmadiya, or too orthodox, like the fundamentalist critics of the Sufi orders. Yet the prestige of the *'ulama* is at least as precarious as the emir's. Long accustomed to thinking of themselves as esteemed religious teachers, Kwara's elite now see their people looking elsewhere for new ideas, especially to Nigeria's preeminent centers of wealth and power.

## Kaduna: "The Mafia," the Emirs, and the Tribes

The most dramatic example of regional bias under military rule is the contrast between the persistent strength of the hajj in Kaduna and its sharp decline in Lagos. Kaduna is a major pilgrimage center, no matter who controls the federal government. Compared with the country as a whole, Kaduna's hajj benefited more from times of prosperity and democracy, and it suffered less during years of depression and dictatorship. Kaduna is the only state where hajj activity remained well above the national average throughout the last three decades. In contrast, the hajj in Lagos is particularly volatile. No region suffered more than Lagos from the change in regimes. In democratic Nigeria, Lagos Muslims were national leaders in hajj participation, but when the political tables turned, they sank just as quickly as the less developed parts of the south. Between 1982 and 1999, Nigeria's hajj rate fell to a third of its former level, but in Lagos, the rate plummeted to a seventh of the earlier mark. Lagos was still the major pilgrimage center in the south, but its commanding lead over the other Yoruba states vanished.

Kaduna enjoys a combination of political, economic, and cultural advantages that give it the country's most resilient pilgrimage. Kaduna has been the political heart of the north since colonial times, and nowadays many argue it plays a similar role for all Nigeria. Developed by the British as a strategic garrison town that was the base for conquering the emirates, under Ahmadu Bello it became the capital of the northern region and the training ground for the political and military elite who ruled Nigeria after independence. The north's powerful political parties have been headquartered in Kaduna, and the army's top officers rotate through the senior staff college located there. Nigerians commonly refer to Kaduna's overlapping party, business, and military circles as "the Kaduna Mafia"—a legendary cabal that journalists and academics have dissected countless times since the civil war.[19] Popular fascination with the Mafia stems from a widespread belief that Kaduna, rather than Lagos or Abuja, is the true meeting ground for Nigeria's kingmakers.

Its pivotal role was most obvious during the notorious coup of Gideon Okar that nearly toppled Babangida in 1990. The mutiny of southern officers carried the day in Lagos and Abuja, but not in Kaduna, which held the largest troop concentrations. While the coup was still in progress, its leaders announced they intended to expel the northernmost—and overwhelmingly Muslim—states from the country. At that point, Kaduna commanders threw their support to the government, and the mutiny collapsed.

For Kaduna's hajj managers, the state's reputation as a political powerhouse is a mixed blessing. They are delighted to have the patronage of illustrious neighbors with matchless connections in business and government, but they find it difficult to deal with hundreds of powerful petitioners who never take no for an answer. As one Kaduna director put it, "How do you tell a retired colonel he and his wife can't make the hajj this year because Abuja changed the deadline for applications?"

Reflecting its privileged constituency, the hajj agency in Kaduna enjoys greater autonomy from the national headquarters than the pilgrims' boards in other regions. Local sponsors fund many services other states cannot afford. Kaduna pilgrims carry an array of photographs, identification bracelets, and medical certificates to keep track of people and baggage along the route. The pilgrims' board distributes several free publications, including three separate hajj guides in English and Hausa, as well as a special version in traditional Hausa that uses modified Arabic script. The logo on the cover pages sums up the board's scrupulous attention to service: a picture of the *Ka'ba* encircled by the slogan "A Smooth Hajj Is Our Goal."

By issuing its own guidebook, the Kaduna board is showing its impatience with the federal government's foot-dragging on an important policy. Nigeria is the only country I visited where the central hajj agency does not issue every pilgrim an official handbook describing the key hajj rituals and interpreting their meanings. Pilgrimage managers in Abuja believe an official manual is necessary, but they cannot agree on what it should say. I once showed the national hajj director a few popular guides I had found in neighborhood markets and bookshops. He insisted that such glosses were filled with misinformation, yet he had nothing to offer in their place. Later, his deputy showed me a manuscript of a hajj manual the agency was evaluating for possible adoption. It was the unsolicited work of a young writer with no reputation as a religious authority and no backing in the government. With half its chapters strewn across some well-worn office furniture, the would-be manual seemed destined to remain a manuscript for years to come.

The members of the Kaduna board take the initiative when Abuja procrastinates, and they have no qualms about pointing out their bosses' shortcomings. In Kano and Lagos, hajj directors sprinkled criticisms of the national office amid constant references to their friendships with people working there. The Kaduna managers blasted Abuja head-on. They complained that headquarters was making policy unilaterally instead of bringing the state directors together in annual meetings and listening to their recommendations. Most of all, they resented Abuja's indifference to personal contact with pilgrims. "Headquarters doesn't register a single pilgrim," the assistant director said. "They just issue orders and ask us to send reports and audits once a year."

Besides its political advantages, Kaduna's hajj is buoyed by a diversified economy. Its bedrock is a modern service sector with scores of government and military installations that generate steady incomes for a quarter of the workforce. Entire neighborhoods are reserved as residential districts for civil servants and security forces. Kaduna is northern Nigeria's largest industrial center after Kano, and it also serves as a major transportation center. It is the site of one of the few oil refineries in Nigeria that works as many days as it shuts down.

Kaduna is the one city in Nigeria where ordinary people can enjoy the comforts of middle-class life. It lacks both the whimsical opulence of Abuja and the gaping class divisions of Lagos. Neighborhoods at both ends of the social spectrum are filled with shopping malls, schools, libraries, churches, and mosques. As in Kano, streets are filled with children. However, in Kaduna, most are students wearing red or blue school uniforms over crisp white shirts and blouses, while in Kano they are street kids hawking five-naira bags of juice and water at every intersection.

Outside the capital city, Kaduna's population is ethnically and religiously diverse but highly stratified and segregated. Muslims predominate in the north and Christians in the south. In central districts, the major faiths are more evenly balanced, with Muslims forming a slight majority in the capital and in the state as a whole.

Throughout Kaduna, religion is a powerful marker of ethnicity and status. Muslims are overwhelmingly Hausa or Gwari, whereas Christians are scattered over fifty tribes. Muslims monopolized traditional government, and most indigenous Christians are descendants of their former subjects and slaves.[20]

In this part of central Nigeria, religious conversion and intermarriage are generally condemned as acts of disloyalty toward one's ethnic group. When I asked pilgrimage managers why there was so much tension between Muslims and Christians in Kaduna, they concurred that the root problems were ethnic and political rather than religious. The hajj director summarized the prevailing mentality succinctly: "We are not like the Yoruba, where no one cares what religion their relatives belong to. If our people change religions, their families reject them whether they are Christian or Muslim."

The relative parity in size of the religious communities is no guide to their political strength, past or present. Most of the state falls within the former territory of the Emirate of Zaria, the southernmost Hausa kingdom that was the gateway for Muslim conquests and slave raiding in the pagan Middle Belt. Many tribes resisted incorporation into the emirate by accepting vassalage or resettling in isolated forestlands. South of Zaria, the emirate's effective control weakened with distance from the palace. Royal power had to be content with a fluid system of fealty, where the sultan often purchased compliance from his own governors, as well as local chieftains and tribal councils.[21] This was a form of "indirect rule" that seemed too unwieldy to the British, but their replacement proved far less stable. In trying to impose a more orderly chain of command, colonial administrators greatly expanded the sometimes nominal authority of Muslim rulers over southern tribes that remained overwhelmingly non-Muslim.

At the same time, the British deliberately upset the religious status quo in Kaduna, contradicting their pledge to uphold it in the northern region as a whole.[22] The British distinguished between "Muslim areas" and "pagan areas." The pagan areas were transitional zones like southern Kaduna, where rulers were Muslims but the population was not. During World War I, Christian missionaries were allowed to enter the pagan areas, and by the 1930s they were virtually exempted from restrictions that shielded Islam in the rest of the north.

After World War II, Christianity became a rallying point for protest against continued Muslim rule in Kaduna's southern districts. The most popular mission schools were in towns like Kagoro, where local tribes still had the right to elect their own chieftains. Christian students from other parts of Kaduna attended these schools, returning home to spread similar aspirations for autonomy. Soon, a Christian-led separatist movement began to demand a new state for territory south of the capital city.[23]

Southern Kaduna has good reason to claim that its pleas for autonomy have been pushed aside to satisfy other communities with greater influence. In 1987, the northernmost districts of Kaduna were allowed to form the new state of Katsina, removing nearly half the old state's population and the majority of its agriculture. In contrast to southern Kaduna, Katsina's religious and historical distinctiveness was an asset instead of a liability. Its population is almost exclusively Muslim, and graduates of Katsina College—one of the oldest Western schools in northern Nigeria—have filled top posts in the army and government since the days of Ahmadu Bello.

A lucrative benefit Katsina derived from statehood was the opportunity to develop its own hajj business. Katsina has had a strong pilgrimage for decades because of long-standing ties with the Middle East and West Africa. A large colony of Katsina natives has lived in Saudi Arabia for several generations. Their children have become Saudi citizens and operate as middlemen in Nigeria's trade with the Gulf countries.[24]

Katsina profits from a steady flow of Hausa-speaking pilgrims from neighboring Niger. Many citizens of Niger prefer to begin their hajj from Kano because it is closer to their homes than Niamey, their own capital. Most of these people pass through Katsina, where they purchase counterfeit passports and register as Nigerian pilgrims.[25]

Exploiting these opportunities was easier once Katsina controlled its own administration, especially when President Abacha appointed a former general from Katsina as national pilgrimage director. In today's hajj organization, Katsina comprises an entire "region"—the only one of eight hajj regions devoting its full staff and budget to a single state.

In the competition for statehood, Kaduna's Christians were also passed over in favor of a nearby group of Muslims that enjoyed none of Katsina's advantages. Southern Kaduna even lost the name its leaders chose for their proposed state, Nasarawa. The state of Nasarawa came into existence in 1996 not in southern Kaduna but in the western part of Plateau, its immediate neighbor. The new state did, indeed, address the grievances of a religious minority complaining of discrimination, but they were Muslims who resented growing Christian influence in Jos.[26]

Frustrated in their quest for recognition, the Christians of southern Kaduna have resumed their protests against the customary rights of Muslim notables to appoint district government heads. In Kafanchan, the southernmost city in Kaduna, these quarrels touched off several bloody clashes, and Muslims retaliated by attacking churches and Christian students all across the state.

Kaduna's pilgrimage embodies all the major social rifts that typify the central savanna. Pilgrimage rates in local governments reflect divisions between north and south, city and countryside, and upper class and working class[27] (Table A9.3 and Figure 9.5).

The highest rates are in the city of Kaduna, where participation is four times greater than in the rest of the state. Residents of the wealthiest neighborhood, Kawo, make the pilgrimage four times more often than Muslims in the poorest district, Makera.

Sharp urban-rural contrasts prevail in every part of the state. Regardless of whether pilgrimage is strong or weak in a particular region, hajj rates are two or three times higher in urban centers than in the countryside. The city of Zaria leads all northern districts with a hajj rate slightly higher than trends in working-class quarters of the state capital. In the less urbanized northeast, pilgrimage is concentrated in Anchau and Lere, market towns near the busy highway linking Jos and Kano. Northern Kaduna's lowest hajj rates appear in the most rural areas—the isolated Hausa villages of Igabi and Ikara, as well as

FIGURE 9.5 Pilgrimage rates in the local governments of Kaduna State, 1999

the northwestern district of Birnin Gwari dominated by non-Hausa tribes that are more recent converts to Islam.

Pilgrimage is even weaker in the urban south than in the rural north. In southern Kaduna, the hajj is most popular among Muslim minorities living in commercial and administrative centers such as Kujama, Kachia, and Kafan-chan. These are former garrison towns the Zaria Emirate developed to subdue southern tribes in the nineteenth century. They are still surrounded by non-Muslim hinterlands, and the hajj weakens quickly with distance from district headquarters. In the southernmost districts of Jema'a, where the missions have their strongest roots and separatist sentiment runs deepest, the hajj barely exists.

The social background of Kaduna's pilgrims varies widely from one district to another, especially in terms of gender and age (Figure 9.6). Economic and political factors determine the overall size of the hajj, but ethnicity and edu-cation are most important for female participation.[28]

Women hajjis are far more prominent in the city of Kaduna than anywhere else in the state. Nearly equal numbers of women and men make the hajj in almost every district. The sole exception is a small group of mostly male civil servants and soldiers who are permitted to use official hajj allowances for them-selves but generally not for relatives.

Female participation is strong in both middle-class and working-class neighborhoods. Lower income residents go to Mecca less often than their wealthier neighbors, but when poor families save enough to afford the trip, they give women the same opportunities that affluent women enjoy.

Outside the capital city, Kaduna's hajjis are overwhelmingly male. Yet male dominance varies considerably, rising in the north and falling in the south.

FIGURE 9.6 Percent of female pilgrims in the local governments of
Kaduna State, 1999

The largest differences in female participation appear between ethnic
groups. The most striking contrast is between non-Hausa communities—the
Gwari in the northwest versus the southern tribes of Jema'a and Kagarko.
Among the Gwari, only one pilgrim in nine is a woman, but in the south,
female hajjis are about 40 percent of the total.

Gwari adopted Islam more widely than the southern tribes but also preserved a patriarchal family structure. Southern Muslims are few in number,
but many are from families where at least one parent had a Christian or animist
upbringing that allows women wider freedom outside the home.

Predominantly Hausa areas fall between these extremes. Outside the capital city, Hausa women usually are about 30 percent of the pilgrims. However,
there is a great deal of variation among Hausa communities. Women hajjis
are most common in the Zaria suburb of Sabon Gari. Like many *sabon garis*
("new cities") throughout Hausaland, this one is a magnet for migrants from
diverse ethnic and religious backgrounds who were unwelcome in conservative
Muslim quarters inside the old city walls.

Demographic trends in Zaria and Sabon Gari adhere closely to this historical pattern even today. Net migration to Zaria is negligible, whereas Sabon
Gari's migration rate is the highest in the state after the capital city.[29] Different
types of urbanization in the two towns produce striking disparities in their
pilgrimages. Hajjis are more numerous in Zaria, where Muslims live in relative
isolation, but female and male pilgrims are more evenly balanced in Sabon
Gari, where social pluralism exposes Muslims to flexible gender roles.

Hausa women are least likely to participate in the pilgrimage in districts
near the borders with Katsina and Kano: Giwa, Kudan, Soba, and Kubau. After
Birnin Gwari, this region has the state's lowest level of female pilgrimage.

These towns and villages have more in common with the rural core of Hausaland to the north than with communities south of Zaria, where Hausa-speaking Muslims coexist with many ethnic and religious groups.

A prime example is the tiny district of Kudan. A conservative Hausa community where female pilgrimage is extremely rare, Kudan was the site of the longest border dispute between the governments of Katsina and Kaduna. The quarrel over Kudan was more than a battle over territory. It was also a contest between politicians in Katsina and Kaduna promoting different conceptions of Hausa identity—one stressing ethnocentrism and the other assimilation.

In Katsina's relatively homogeneous society, Hausa identity emphasizes ethnic and genealogical origins that preserve distance between tribes and classes. However, in the more diverse environment of Kaduna, the Hausa are seen as a cosmopolitan community welcoming anyone who adopts their religion, language, and customs.[30] In view of the enduring gender gap in the pilgrimages of Kudan and its neighbors, it is hardly surprising that Katsina politicians representing hierarchical tendencies in Hausa society believe their constituency also embraces parts of northern Kaduna.

The average age of pilgrims in Kaduna is only thirty-nine for men and thirty-six for women. Age differences between males and females are seldom greater than five years on average, but the pattern of male seniority is remarkably consistent from one end of the state to the other. Areas with the highest female participation are also areas where women perform the hajj earliest in life.

Women hajjis are younger and more numerous where female enrollment in primary and secondary school is above average. The connection between female pilgrimage and female education is most obvious in the city of Kaduna, but it is uniform across the state.[31]

The combination of education and ethnicity provides a powerful explanation of female hajj participation in Kaduna. Modern education entered the region's ethnic communities at different rates, narrowing the gender gap in some cases and magnifying it in others.

In many rural areas, missionaries provided better educational and medical services than the government. Most of these schools and clinics are open to people of all religious and ethnic backgrounds. They are particularly attractive to Muslims living outside Hausa core areas, where families are accustomed to overlooking sectarian differences to satisfy basic needs.

In southern Kaduna, where mission schools are often the only alternative, Muslims face fewer pressures against educating daughters than they would in Hausa-dominated districts. Once they are exposed to a wide range of people and ideas, Muslim girls are better prepared for a host of other broadening experiences, including the hajj.

The growth of mission schools has not produced a similar result in Birnin Gwari, where Muslim women confront tighter social restrictions than among the Hausa. In Gwari communities, Muslim parents accepted mission teachers selectively, sending them their sons more often than their daughters. With regard to both education and hajj, the gender gap is largest among Gwari, narrower for Hausa, and smallest for the Muslim minorities of the south.

## Lagos: Family, Migration, and Community

Lagos is the mirror image of Kaduna in politics, economics, and culture. Whereas Kaduna is the placid bastion of the northern elite, Lagos is the tumultuous rallying point of the southern opposition.

In every presidential election since 1977, Lagos voters have supported the southern candidate by a margin of at least 80 percent. In 1999, the losing candidate, Olu Falae, carried 88 percent of the Lagos vote—his biggest majority in the country. The decision to uproot the nation's capital and transplant it in the Abuja wilderness was a candid admission of the profound hostility that surrounded the federal government in black Africa's greatest metropolis. Northern Nigerians became convinced Lagos was ungovernable and that it threatened to make a hostage of any government that did not identify with the south, especially with the increasingly alienated Yoruba.

Although Lagos remained Nigeria's commercial capital whether the economy was expanding or contracting, the city's very preeminence became a source of weakness. As the focal point for industry and foreign trade, it is the city least able to tolerate severe disruptions in the flow of money and goods from abroad. The ravages of structural adjustment hit Lagos hardest, particularly in slums and working-class suburbs on the mainland. By the 1990s, these outlying districts comprised nearly 80 percent of the population of Greater Lagos—compared with 40 percent in 1963 and 20 percent in 1952.[32]

In the state of Lagos as a whole, hajj participation is just as lopsided as the distribution of wealth[33] (Table A9.4 and Figure 9.7). Tiny Lagos Island has a pilgrimage three times as strong as any other area—a natural reflection of the insane concentration of commerce and services in a central business district that is in permanent paralysis from nearly daily floods, fires, and riots.

FIGURE 9.7 Pilgrimage rates in the local governments of Lagos State, 1999

Traveling outward from Lagos Island, the intensity of pilgrimage closely tracks the quality of residential housing. Hajj rates fall sharply in the working-class districts closest to the city and then rise in outlying suburbs, where land use and occupations are more diversified. On the state's semirural periphery, hajj rates fall to their lowest levels in the poor maritime communities hugging the Atlantic coastline and the marshlands of Lagos Lagoon.

In addition to its economic preeminence, Lagos Island possesses religious and political strengths that promote a vigorous pilgrimage.[34] During most of the colonial period, the Muslim natives of Lagos Island watched passively as land and power fell into the hands of Europeans and Westernized African immigrants. When residents finally launched a political movement to salvage their corner of the island, Islam was decisive in forging a communal identity and a network of neighborhood associations. Mosques and charitable groups provided forums for the coalition of chieftains, market women, and middle-class politicians that dominated local government after independence.

Muslim communities of Lagos Island are well organized, pluralistic, and competitive. Rival factions have fought to control major mosques ever since the nineteenth century. Losers often set up their own congregations, guaranteeing multiple sources of innovation and dissent.

The earliest conflicts pitted conservative northern scholars linked to Ilorin against Yoruba proponents of popular Islam. Many northerners were Hausa and Nupe teachers who opposed the "mixing" of conventional Islam with folk religion. However, they had no more success in resisting Yoruba syncretism than their counterparts in Hausaland who battled Sufi eclecticism.

The strongest threat to conservative 'ulama came from the modernist Ahmadiya movement that appealed to the wealthiest and most educated Muslims on Lagos Island. Ahmadis took the lead in translating the Qur'an into English and harmonizing its teachings with science and philosophy. They launched the first private schools to combine religious and secular subjects—an experiment that quickly spread to dozens of Yoruba towns up to Ilorin.[35]

As Ahmadis' heterodox views attracted growing hostility, they feared the government would nationalize their profitable school network. The desire to protect the Ahmadiya's educational achievements was one of the main reasons the movement split into two groups during the 1980s. A weaker faction wanted to maintain ties with the original order in India, whereas a larger "Nigerian" tendency ended its quarrel with mainstream Islam by acknowledging the finality of Muhammad's prophecy. The new group, Anwar al-Din, eventually won control of the schools and still runs them as an independent system.[9.36]An important by-product of competition between Islamic tendencies on Lagos Island is that Ahmadis' educational innovations inspired similar efforts by other groups. Today, the island is brimming with private schools offering modern Islamic education to girls and boys from all social classes.

Hajj rates are also high in Eti-Osa and Ikeja, where Muslims are not as well organized but where they enjoy higher living standards. Eti-Osa includes Victoria Island and Ikoyi—the city's most exclusive neighborhoods. Thirty years ago, Ikeja was a remote suburb whose modern economy was little more than the state government. Today, it is the focal point of urban planning in Greater Lagos—surrounded by a frantic airport, a ring of industrial parks, and endless strip malls. Development strategy concentrated investment in Ikeja, neglecting deepening squalor in suburbs closer to the city. As in Eti-Osa, pilgrimage rates in Ikeja are twice as high as in the rest of the state.

The hajj is weakest in districts at the bottom of the economic ladder. The lowest rates are in peripheral areas that were detached from Ogun State when Lagos became the federal capital. Pilgrimage activity is particularly low in the southwestern district of Badagry and the northeastern region of Epe, which include isolated villages that still depend on fishing for their livelihood. The only other area with such a low level of hajj is the corridor of suburban slums running through Ojo, Mushin, and Shomolu.

A handful of districts with moderate pilgrimage rates are between the extremes of rich and poor, center and periphery. Three of them—Agege, Iko-rodu, and Ibeju-Lekki—are farming communities, where suburban sprawl is less disruptive than in the neighborhoods nearer the city.

Pilgrimage is also fairly strong in Lagos Mainland, a district that includes the older working-class neighborhoods of Surulere, Yaba, and Ebute Metta. As its name suggests, Lagos Mainland is not a suburb but the westernmost part of the city. It contains more than 70 percent of the city's population and serves as the transport hub for the entire metropolis—the point where major highways and rail routes converge to link Lagos Island with the rest of the country.

What most distinguishes Lagos Mainland is its high level of female pilgrimage. Sixty percent of its hajjis are females, a level rivaled only by Lagos Island, where Muslim women have dominated the popular markets for generations. Lagos Mainland is not a regional leader in pilgrimage, but it demonstrates an intriguing trend that typifies the state as a whole—a weakening hajj that still provides a central role for women.

In Lagos, as in Kaduna, culture is more important than politics or economics in explaining female participation. However, in Nigeria, there are so many plausible explanations tied to culture that it is difficult to weigh their relative importance. In comparing female pilgrimage in Lagos and Kaduna, three aspects of culture stand out: family structure, migration, and neighborhood organization. Each factor encourages female participation, but their contributions vary, depending on the groups we compare.

Family structure is more relevant among the Yoruba than among the Hausa and Gwari. In Lagos, where Yoruba women enjoy greater freedom, there is no gender gap in hajj activity, but in Kaduna, more patriarchal Hausa and Gwari communities promote wide disparities in favor of males.

Within Lagos itself, variations in female participation parallel intraethnic distinctions between Yoruba groups tracing their origins to different parts of Yorubaland. Female pilgrimage is higher for migrants than for nonmigrants, and among migrants it varies according to state of origin.

When we focus on the six mainland districts, female hajj rates reflect differences in the communities that migrants established after coming to the city. Even among Yorubas, female pilgrimage is stronger in older, better organized neighborhoods than in chaotic, crime-ridden areas where voluntary associations and local governments are still rudimentary at best.

The most persuasive cultural argument depends on the specific populations in question. Family structure is useful in comparing the Yoruba with other ethnic groups, but migration and local origin distinguish Yoruba subgroups living side by side in Lagos. Concerning Yoruba migrants, neighborhood organization supersedes both family structure and local origin. In organization building, the migrants themselves still fall short of the only indigenous group that resisted their onslaught—the tight-knit Muslim community of Lagos Island.

Many Yoruba argue that the prominence of female hajjis in Lagos reflects the higher status of Yoruba women in urban households compared with their Hausa counterparts. When I asked hajj managers in Lagos—both female and male—why their state sent more women than men to Mecca, they replied that Yoruba men take great pride in sending their mothers on the pilgrimage.

According to the director of the Lagos Pilgrims' Board, if a woman is advanced in years and her sons have only modest means, they usually delay their own pilgrimages so she can go first. "In Yoruba families," he explained, "it is primarily the mother that teaches religion to the children, especially the boys. That is why Yoruba sons are very close to their mothers and why sons try so hard to fulfill their mothers' dreams of making the hajj."

At first, I assumed the director was overgeneralizing. His explanation sounded like the ethnic self-promotion one hears everywhere in Nigeria, and I was skeptical that it would stand up to closer scrutiny. That was before I looked closely at the demographic characteristics of Lagos pilgrims and compared them with hajjis from Kaduna.

Yorubas send a higher percentage of women on the hajj than Hausa. Yorubas—both males and females—also make their pilgrimages later in life than the Hausa. Interethnic age differences are about four years for men (43 for the Yoruba versus 39 for the Hausa) and eight years for women (44 for the Yoruba versus 36 for the Hausa).

Among Yoruba hajjis, females are slightly older than males, whereas among the Hausa, males are much older than females. In Lagos, women hajjis are about one year older than men, and in many districts the difference is five to eight years. In Kaduna, male pilgrims are older—about three years on average—and the pattern holds in every district (Figure 9.8).

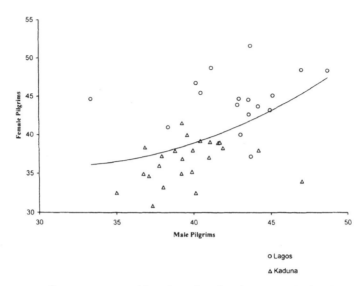

FIGURE 9.8 Average ages of female and male pilgrims in the local governments of Lagos and Kaduna states, 1999

The Lagos hajj director's explanation fits the data, lending credibility to stereotypes Yoruba and Hausa Muslims promote about one another's pilgrimage customs. Each group asserts that the other fails to show adequate respect for the hajj.

In northern Nigeria, many people told me Yoruba spend more money on weddings, carnivals, and funerals than on religious pursuits.[37] In this view, Yoruba put the hajj on the back burner because of social pressures to invest in other rites that enhance family status and communal solidarity. Even the Yoruba of Ilorin criticized their southern kin for accepting debt as a way of life to partake in ostentatious gift giving, whether they could afford it or not.

In southern Nigeria, people complain the Hausa debase the hajj by turning it into a family vacation and shopping spree. Critics of the Hausa claim they go on pilgrimage too early and too often, diluting its spiritual value and making it a measure of their position in this world instead of the next.

Nonetheless, the Lagos director's emphasis on ethnic contrasts cannot explain variations of hajj activity in his own state, where Yoruba are the vast majority in every district (Figure 9.9). Participation of Yoruba women in pilgrimage, trade, and education is most obvious on Lagos Island, where market women were indispensable in mobilizing small property owners for political action.[38] Their commercial contacts extend to neighborhoods on the mainland, where working women from other parts of Yorubaland follow their example in dominating small-scale trade.

FIGURE 9.9 Percent of female pilgrims in the local governments of Lagos State, 1999

Although female pilgrimage is strongest in the city, the mainland suburbs are not far behind. All the mainland districts have high female hajj rates despite the huge social distance separating middle-class Ikeja and Agege from the slums of Shomolu, Mushin, and Ojo. Except for Lagos Island, what most distinguishes the neighborhoods with high rates of female pilgrimage is that they are overwhelmingly migrants from other states.

Migration rates in all six mainland districts are astronomical. The proportion of primary school students whose families moved to Lagos from other states ranges from 86 percent in Shomolu to 93 percent in Lagos Mainland. More than half the mainland migrants came from just three southwestern states—Ogun (24%), Oyo (17%), and Ondo (12%).[39]

In Greater Lagos, the emancipating effects of urban migration greatly magnify whatever advantages Yoruba women derive from egalitarian family structures. Away from the constraints of village and small-town life, migrant women exploit a broader range of opportunities in employment, education, and travel. These new opportunities make it easier for women to participate in the hajj. And the hajj, in turn, helps migrant women and their families advance in a cosmopolitan society that places a premium on the trappings of piety and wealth.

The propensity of migrant women to make the hajj depends on where their families lived before coming to the city. Migrants from all the Yoruba states settled everywhere in the mainland, but there are many cases of targeted migration where families from the same state cluster together. Natives of Ogun gravitate to the government centers of Ikeja and Agege, migrants from Oyo settle in the commercial zones of Lagos Mainland, and peasants from Ondo flock to the slums of Shomolu.

Female pilgrimage increases with the degree of urbanization in states where the migrants originated. Women hajjis are most numerous where there are concentrations of migrants from Oyo—the most urban state in Yorubaland—and they are fewest where there are big migrations from Ondo—the most rural state in the southwest.

On the mainland itself, education and neighborhood organization are critical. Within these six districts, the strongest correlates of women's pilgrimage are female secondary school enrollment, membership in cooperative societies, and local government expenditures.

Mainland women are most likely to make the hajj where well-developed neighborhood institutions provide a sense of community, not where living standards are the highest. Areas like Surulere, just within the city limits, have a distinct advantage over more prosperous suburbs around Ikeja, where the growth of schools and community organizations lags behind the influx of new residents.

## Christian Pilgrimage: The Old Jerusalem and the New Jerusalem

Nigeria is one of the few countries in the world where the state sponsors two large-scale pilgrimages, one for Muslims and another for Christians. Government and church leaders share several motives for endowing Christian pilgrimage with equal status alongside the hajj.

On many occasions, Nigerians feared they might be headed for a second and bloodier civil war, with battle lines drawn by religion rather than ethnicity. Sectarian violence made Nigeria's rulers eager to co-opt as many religious moderates as possible. Establishing a "Christian hajj" helped the regime mend fences with critics in the clergy while isolating radical groups recruiting in the churches and mosques.

For Nigeria's oldest Christian denominations, winning a state-sponsored pilgrimage was a double victory. Mainline churches extracted important concessions from the government, boosting their authority when millions of parishioners were defecting to a new breed of charismatic Christianity that offers instant miracles and living prophets.

In the 1980s, Nigerian Muslims watched a long line of messiahs and rebels lead thousands of people to their deaths, and there was fear that similar agonies were brewing for Christians. The decision to provide state backing for pilgrimage to Jerusalem was a mutual effort by government and religious leaders to stop a hemorrhage in Nigerian Christianity that was threatening both church and state.

From the beginning, the Christian Association of Nigeria (CAN) was conceived as an antidote to charismatic Christianity. The military and the mainline churches sought to exclude the newer Protestant movements, even though they were crashing the association's meetings to demand admission. When the new churches did gain acceptance, they had to accept a quota system giving them only 20 percent of the voting power compared with 40 percent for Catholics and 40 percent for Anglicans, Methodists, Baptists, Presbyterians, and evangelicals.[40]

Charismatic churches flourished by offering ordinary Christians what they no longer found in the old-time religion—relief from the daily anguish of a society that had lost hope, as well as freedom. The new churches are filled with miracles. For millions of Nigerians, they provide divinely inspired crisis intervention that touches every aspect of personal and family life. Their preachers promise compelling benefits—not "grace" and "salvation" in the next life but "revelation" and "breakthrough" now. Many new churches blend spiritual healing with the lure of wealth and success: "Those who seek God will also find riches and power."

A state-sponsored pilgrimage to Jerusalem gave Christians yet another arena for conflict. The proliferation of sects ensured constant friction over who would control the pilgrimage and who could mobilize the greatest numbers. Church leaders even disagree about the meaning of pilgrimage and its practical benefits.

The quarrel over Christian pilgrimage is more political than doctrinal. Nigerian clergymen support or criticize pilgrimage according to their perception of how it affects their churches' power relative to rival denominations and Islam. The current system of Christian pilgrimage is the product of so many compromises that no group is truly attached to it.

Catholics are the most willing to argue that pilgrimage is sanctioned by tradition and scripture, but they see Jerusalem as just one of several sacred destinations, along with Rome, Lourdes, and Fatima. Anglican clergy were indifferent to the pilgrimage campaign until they felt pressure from parishioners who valued it as a political weapon. Then they became its vanguard.

The most skeptical were newer Protestant churches. When the government began supporting Christian pilgrimage, it channeled assistance through CAN instead of state pilgrims' boards. Because CAN was controlled by their competitors, the new denominations viewed the pilgrimage program as yet another attempt to deny them recognition and resources. Their suspicion ebbed somewhat in the mid-1990s, when the government took pilgrimage management away from the mainline churches and gave it to the civil service.

Although many charismatic churches recruit pilgrims, they still express ambivalence about the value of pilgrimage. One of the strongest attacks I heard came from a television evangelist who took up the issue during his weekly broadcast, The Moment of Truth. According to this born-again Yoruba, "Pilgrims to Jerusalem do not realize that there is a New Jerusalem—the Church—which is not limited to a specific place or time."

To him, the New Jerusalem is a metaphor for the lessons of the Gospel—lessons Christians must understand in terms of their own times and conditions. "Saint Peter had no special opinion on democracy, communism, or abortion," he noted. "Pilgrims will find no truths about these matters in the old Jerusalem or in any other journey to the past."

Disputes over pilgrimage extend well beyond the clergy. I was amazed to discover how easily the issue sparked fights among ordinary citizens, especially those looking for an excuse to settle old scores. In Abuja, I met a group of Christians who nearly came to blows when one claimed the only Jerusalem pilgrims he knew were frauds.

The instigator was a charismatic deacon from Borno that I bumped into at the business center of the Abuja Sheraton. With a dozen guests and employees following our conversation, he said, "I have seen many Christian pilgrims in Borno, but all are fakes—absconders from the south, every one of them."

He claimed southerners register for the pilgrimage in Borno because they can make bookings there more quickly than in states where Christians are more numerous. He explained that once they leave the country, they abandon their groups and settle illegally in Israel or Europe. Just a year earlier, he said, police at the Rome airport detained all the Nigerians on his flight because a handful of pilgrims had fled into the city.

"The police surrounded us with dogs and held us at gunpoint while they searched for fugitives." Then, raising his voice so everyone would be sure to hear, he advised me, "Don't bother going to southern Nigeria. The people there are nothing but a pack of lazy liars. They have ruined this country."

At that point, four men—all southern Christians—started a shouting match with the deacon: "We fought the war to keep this nation together and then you northerners brought it to its knees." "Did those oil fields belong to your fathers or ours?" "Why do your people hold all the top posts and contracts when we have the degrees and qualifications?"

All this fury was heaped on a fellow Christian, not a Muslim or Hausa. This was a north-south quarrel par excellence—a battle over power and wealth where native sons cast aside religion and ethnicity to focus on higher stakes. Suddenly, Nigeria was no longer a complex society with multiple identities and crisscrossing loyalties. The intricacies of sect and tribe might perplex census takers and anthropologists, but what ignited these foes was the raw contempt of top dog and underdog.

Controversy has not stopped the Jerusalem pilgrimage from spreading to every part of the country. Pilgrimage rates for Christians are only a seventh as great as for Muslims, but Christian participation is more dispersed geographically than participation in the hajj[41] (Table A9.5 and Figure 9.10). While the core of hajj activity contracted to a handful of states, the Jerusalem pilgrimage spread everywhere between Lagos and Bauchi.

Today's map of Christian pilgrimage looks remarkably like the nationwide coverage of the hajj in the early 1980s—before military rulers limited Muslim pilgrimage to their favored constituencies in the north. In time, the very breadth of the Jerusalem pilgrimage could become a unifying factor. The same pilgrimage that spawned so much controversy among Nigerian Christians

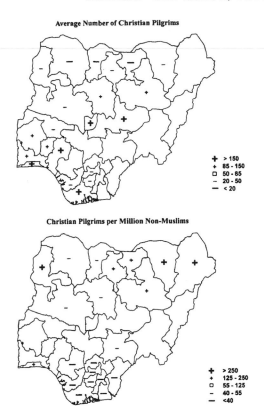

**Average Number of Christian Pilgrims**

| | |
|---|---|
| + | > 150 |
| + | 85 - 150 |
| □ | 50 - 85 |
| − | 20 - 50 |
| — | < 20 |

**Christian Pilgrims per Million Non-Muslims**

| | |
|---|---|
| + | > 250 |
| + | 125 - 250 |
| □ | 55 - 125 |
| − | 40 - 55 |
| — | <40 |

FIGURE 9.10 Christian pilgrimage in the states of Nigeria, 1995–1998

might one day help moderate regional and sectarian tensions that have divided them for generations.

The core areas of pilgrimage to Jerusalem are regions where neither Christianity nor Islam dominates. Two-thirds of the Christian pilgrims live in Yorubaland and the Middle Belt, where Christians and Muslims of all shades live side by side. These are the most religiously diverse regions and also the states where Christian and Muslim pilgrimages are most interconnected and competitive (Figure A9.1).

Pilgrimage to Jerusalem lags behind pilgrimage to Mecca nearly everywhere in Nigeria, but in Yorubaland and the Middle Belt the gap is closing. These are key battlegrounds where Christian and Muslim preachers clash head to head and Abuja most obviously subsidizes dueling pilgrimages. The fiercest rivalry is in Abuja and Plateau, near the geographic heart of the country. The federal capital and the city of Jos are mixed societies where pilgrimage aids the mobilization and countermobilization of antagonistic religions.

In Abuja, religious tensions are so high that residents find hidden religious meaning even in the city's layout and architecture. A Christian businessman told me he had never approved of the new National Assembly building because he was convinced its splendid green dome was intended to resemble a mosque. If the legislature meets in a site that looks like a mosque, he reasoned, they might be tempted to pass laws that look like the Shari'ah.

Similarly, when a Muslim civil servant helped me find an obscure address, his navigation tip included a political bite. He explained it was easy to get around Abuja because the city was planned along two axes that intersect near the government complex. "Just remember," he said, "Abuja was built in Christian territory, so naturally they made it in the shape of a cross."

In Jos, the symbolism of religious rivalry is more rooted in daily routine. The municipal marketplace is the center of the region's economy and a model of commercial order. At midday, business comes to a standstill for prayers at the nearby mosque and dozens of Bible reading sessions that assemble inside the market. As Muslims close their shops and march outside, they exchange few words with Christian groups they pass. Noontime prayer in Jos is an impressive display of fellowship and solidarity—but only among members of the same faith.

Nigeria may seem extreme in promoting pilgrimage policies that exacerbate ethnic and regional divisions, but it is by no means unique. In every country we have examined in depth, politicians regularly treat the hajj as a means for rewarding supporters and excluding opponents. Perhaps the greatest paradox of the modern hajj is that it effectively dissolves distinctions between Muslims from different countries while hardening them at home. In the final chapter, we will see that pilgrimage managers usually pursue the hajj's universalistic ideals with greater success in international relations than in the domestic arena.

# 10

# The West Is Not Alone

*The Hajj in World Politics and Law*

The hajj has transformed international relations as much as domestic politics. Across the Islamic world, governments have learned that unilateral action is not enough. Even the most resourceful hajj administrations are bound to fail without imaginative international cooperation.

The problems are too urgent and overwhelming to leave to a single country, even one as wealthy and powerful as Saudi Arabia. The need for a global pilgrimage policy and a permanent international authority to implement it is a driving force behind the Organization of the Islamic Conference (OIC). Debates over hajj policy frame the struggle for power in international Islamic organizations and affect relations between Muslim states and their world diplomacy.

## Islamic Multilateralism: Blending Power, Law, and Religion

The international relations of the hajj are a fascinating interplay of power, law, and religion. Managing the world's greatest pilgrimage requires juggling a host of competing interests and values. Every Muslim is a stakeholder, including those who never become pilgrims and generations not yet born.

Saudi Arabia clings to sovereignty over the Holy Cities, drawing lifeblood from its unique role as protector and embodiment of Islam's spiritual core. Muslims everywhere expect rulers to guarantee their freedom to visit God's house and to fulfill their religious duties according to the Prophet's model and their ancestors' customs. They rely on fourteen centuries of state practice and religious teaching to determine whether any restriction is a reasonable regulation or an unwarranted obstruction of efforts to obey God's commands.

Nowadays every pilgrim sees and feels the threat overcrowding creates to human life and the sacred environment. Rapidly, if belatedly, Muslims recognize the urgency of safeguarding the hajj and the Holy Cities as part of the common heritage of humanity.

The new hajj regime is a skillful compromise between conflicting approaches of sovereignty, free access, and common heritage preservation.[1] Saudi Arabia retains formal jurisdiction, but the OIC makes policy and oversees implementation. Pilgrims enjoy freedom of travel, but they must take turns according to a quota that binds all countries while allowing equitable fine-tuning for special needs. Collective management is strong enough to affirm the interests of the environment and future generations but far from Iranian demands for an Islamic trusteeship that would end Saudi control altogether.

The OIC was the architect of the compromise. It provided a forum where negotiators could link hajj reforms to bargaining over many issues. Contenders were willing to accept trade-offs on pilgrimage policy because they expected concessions in equally important areas with no direct connection to the hajj.

A critical issue coinciding with debates over hajj reform was the balance of power in the OIC itself. The OIC began as a creature of Saudi Arabia and its wealthy neighbors, but by the 1980s many states demanded collective leadership.[2] Saudis could not ignore these demands. They were under constant assault from Khomeini and opponents in both Shi'ite and Sunni camps. Everyone saw Saudi plans to restrict access to the Holy Cities as a slap against Iran.[3] Asian and African states were willing to adopt a hajj regime that parried Iran's effort to put the Holy Cities under OIC control. In return, non-Arab states gained greater influence at every level of the OIC and more financial aid from Gulf countries.

Three distinct blocs emerged—Arab, Asian, and African—signaling a shift toward power sharing between rival factions. The OIC divides offices and prestige among the blocs with a sliding scale of representation that varies from one field to another.

Overrepresentation of Arab interests is greatest at the top, in summit meetings where heads of state of all members gather every three years. Six of ten summits convened in Arab countries, always in monarchies: Morocco (three times), Saudi Arabia, Kuwait, and Qatar. Asia hosted three summits—in Pakistan, Iran, and Malaysia—and Africa hosted only one, in Senegal.[4] Annual gatherings of foreign ministers rotate more evenly. Half of the twenty-eight meetings were in the Arab world, nine in Asia, and five in Africa. Non-Arab states exert their greatest influence through the Secretary Generalship, the director of the OIC's Jeddah headquarters and its specialized agencies in a dozen countries. Two Africans controlled the secretariat for thirteen years—one year less than the combined terms of four Arab managers—and two Asians led it for eight years.

Factionalism weakens the Saudis' grip, but it gives them countless opportunities to play on rivalries between the regions and within them. Saudi Arabia does not need to dominate the OIC; it can build defensive alliances with states everywhere that feel vulnerable to neighbors aspiring to be regional superpowers. A good index of Saudi diplomacy is the informal pecking order of OIC members: early joiners versus latecomers; agenda setters versus passive participants. Malaysia, not Indonesia, is the star member in Southeast Asia. Pakistan overshadows Turkey and Iran. Senegal and the poorer states of the Sahel outshine Nigeria. In the Arab bloc, Morocco and the Gulf monarchies are more prominent than Egypt, Algeria, Iraq, and Yemen.

Representation clearly favors Arabs and Africans over Asians. Two-thirds of the world's Muslims live in Asia, compared to about a fifth in Arab countries and a tenth in Africa. Yet the OIC selects only 25 percent of its leaders and 30 percent of its venues from Asia. Shares of the Arab and African blocs are double or triple their shares of total Muslim population.

Interbloc competition reflects political and economic differences between regions. The wealthiest Arab states seek support from the poorest African members to neutralize large and rapidly developing Asian countries. Asian states complain that the OIC spends too much time recycling Arab quarrels instead of building economic and diplomatic coalitions that can bargain with the rest of the world. Rivalries between the Arab old guard and disgruntled Asians give added weight to Africans, who account for a third of the members but only a small fraction of the world's Muslims.

In June 2000, the OIC clashed over selecting a new secretary general. This dispute illustrated these alignments with unusual clarity. By agreement, leadership of the secretariat rotates among the three regions. The outgoing incumbent was an Arab—Azeddin Laraki from Morocco—and the Asians, noting they were next in line, nominated two candidates to succeed him: a Turkish front-runner and an alternate from Bangladesh. After four days of deadlock, foreign ministers meeting in Kuala Lumpur unexpectedly appointed yet another Moroccan, Abdelouahed Belkeziz.[5] Turkey's bid would have succeeded had it not coincided with its military-backed government's crackdown on Islamist parties. For cautious diplomats with no desire to antagonize Turkish secularists, Morocco was a safe harbor—a swing state, Arab but not Middle Eastern, and closely tied to West Africa's popular Sufi movements. Asians agreed to wait an extra turn and instead were content with Malaysia's success in pushing trade and financial reform to the top of the OIC agenda.

In contrast to these formulas of proportional representation, the hajj regime adopted a fresh and bold egalitarianism. By capping overseas pilgrims at about one million and pegging national quotas to population size, the OIC ended forever, in a single stroke, the long predominance of Arab pilgrims. The main beneficiaries of the hajj quotas were large Asian and African states demanding a greater role in OIC policy-making bodies. A vigorous hajj is a hallmark of power and prosperity for every nation. Claiming an equal place in Islam's greatest assembly is a powerful statement of ascendance in the Muslim world and beyond. Even countries that suffered from the quotas accepted them as part of a more equitable power-sharing arrangement that will strengthen them in the long term. Turkey, Malaysia, and Iran objected to the quotas at first and demanded exemptions or delays in implementation. In return for acquiescence, all attained a greater voice in OIC affairs, and Iran's new president, Ayatollah Khatami, hosted the Islamic Summit Conference in 1997.

Western governments are just beginning to come to grips with these changes. During American and British interventions in Afghanistan and Iraq, Washington and London tried to appeal directly to Muslim public opinion by publishing essays in international Arabic newspapers and appearing on Arabic television.[6] Yet this could be no more than a small step in reaching the vast audiences they needed to convince. Most voices denouncing the United States and the United Kingdom spoke neither Arabic nor English. They spoke the leading languages of today's hajj and its new majority—Urdu, Pashto, Turkish, Farsi, Indonesian, Malay, Hausa, Afrikaans, and Wolof. These voices were loudest exactly where hajj participation is the strongest, decade after decade—in Karachi, Jakarta, Kuala Lumpur, Istanbul, Kano, and Dakar.

## The Hajj as Customary International Law

Like any effort to adapt international law to new problems, hajj management depends on the balance of power between sovereign nations with the most at stake. The hajj regime is similar to transnational bargaining processes that grapple with contentious issues such as human rights, trade, and arms control. In each case, states create an impressive body of international law and then argue incessantly about its meaning and scope.

Some new law takes the familiar shape of treaties based on explicit consent. Yet much is customary international law rooted in the changing practices of states and subjective understandings of what is legally required and what is merely common usage.[7] Global hajj management is a classic example of a regime based on evolving and hotly disputed customary international law.

As an example of international law, hajj management closely parallels maritime law. Like the law of the sea, the hajj is a field where customary rules that governed for centuries broke down rapidly and where the formation of new rules exposed sharp disagreement over the role of international law.[8] Just as the maritime powers of the West used their navies to enforce a universal code for the high seas, the great land empires of the Islamic world used their armies to provide safe passage for Muslims visiting the Holy Cities. In each instance, a few hegemonic powers laid down the law, but trade and travel everywhere benefited.

Long-honored understandings about freedom of access crumbled as nations asserted conflicting claims to the same resources. A larger number of states had to negotiate sweeping changes in the maritime and hajj regimes, trying to balance a wider range of interests. After years of tough bargaining, the UN and the OIC reconciled seemingly incompatible principles of universal access and exclusive jurisdiction. They even embraced goals of conservation and equity that traditional regimes ignored.

Compared with the systems they replaced, the new maritime and hajj regimes took root with remarkable speed and effectiveness. A handful of dissenters tried to obstruct them, with the United States refusing to sign the law of the sea treaty and Iran denouncing the pilgrimage accord. Yet, when the overwhelming majority of nations adapted to the new rules, they acquired the force of customary international law. Confronted with global consensus, the holdouts fell into line.

Parallels in the maritime and hajj reforms show that customary international law presents the same problems and opportunities for all states and policy fields. When state practice is uniform and stable, governments readily acknowledge customary international law as universally binding. When practice is changing and inconsistent, it is hard to summon convincing evidence that any rules exist. When old customary international law breaks down, disputes are inevitable because deviant behavior might be a violation of still valid law or an innovation ready to ripen into a new rule.

All states must be sensitive to change in customary international law because it is truly universal, binding on every nation whether or not it formally endorses the new norm. Customary international law is the most glaring exception to the general rule that sovereign states obey only rules of their own making. Consent is still required in theory but rarely in practice. States interpret silence as tacit acceptance, creating a legal obligation to conform to a practice once the international community recognizes that it has crystallized into a rule.[9] In principle, objectors have the right to opt out of a new rule, but only if they express opposition quickly, publicly, and persistently. Even then, continued objection carries prohibitive costs, and nearly all states yield to a true international consensus.[10] This was the fate of the United States when it opposed changes in the law of the sea and of Iran's bloody campaign against pilgrimage quotas.

Iran and the United States are splendid examples of states that used vestiges of the "persistent objector" exception with different degrees of success. Defiant leaders—Ayatollah Khomeini and Ronald Reagan—rejected new international regimes that acquired nearly universal acceptance. Later governments capitulated, realizing there was no hope of influencing the new arrangements if they shut themselves out of the process. Iranians emerged from their bitter quarrel in the OIC with concessions that made them look like "efficient objectors." Americans received so little from their campaign against the UN Convention on the Law of the Sea that they were more like "pointless objectors."

Iran disrupted the hajj with demonstrations and boycotts, but, after Khomeini passed away, they struck a special deal for their pilgrims and led the very international organization they condemned. The U.S. Navy shifted from policing the dead three-mile rule for territorial waters to pleading for ratification of the Law of the Sea Convention and its twelve-mile limit.[11] Admirals grasped a reality that eluded politicians—the world's greatest maritime power can win support for rules it needs only if it complies with rules it dislikes.

Customary international law can support or threaten the balance of power, depending on which states control the initiative in the lawmaking process. Modern international organizations shifted the initiative from a handful of great powers acting unilaterally to multistate assemblies whose members all enjoy equal voting power. Customary international law formerly allowed the strong to create rules for the weak; now it enables the many to legislate for the mighty.[12]

The hajj is an international regime based on customary international law, but it is far more. The hajj is the clearest embodiment of a worldwide religion subordinating interests of nation-states to the duty of all Muslims to comply with God's commands. The hajj depends on rules made by nation-states acting through international organizations. Nonetheless, all these supposedly sovereign actors recognize many limits on their power: They are accountable to a transcendent authority, custodians of a cosmopolitan civilization far older than their fledgling nations, and responsible for articulating religious ideals that speak to all humanity.

The hajj brings Muslim nations together with wide-ranging and unintended consequences. King Faysal used the hajj to launch the OIC as the preeminent international body of the Islamic world. By the 1980s, the hajj and the OIC were deliberately transforming one another. Diplomats reformed the hajj and OIC together, striking a more equal balance between their countries and creating a new voice in world affairs.

Countries that learned to cooperate in managing the hajj learned to cooperate in other fields. Guided by a combination of faith and interest, they produced an international regime and an international organization that fit into the United Nations system without simply mimicking Western models.

## Twin Revolutions: World Politics and International Law

The intersection of religion with power and law thrusts the hajj to the vanguard of new thinking about global order. After decades of estrangement, international relations and international law are rediscovering one another and their common links to religion.[13] As barriers between disciplines crumble, Westerners are beginning to appreciate interactions between political, legal, and spiritual issues that Muslims take for granted.[14]

Theorists of world politics are increasingly critical of the "realist" assumption that politics among nations is a state of anarchy where the only restraint on power is countervailing power. Regime theory stresses the rise of permanent international institutions with broad rule-making authority.[15] A thickening web of cooperation creates "governance without government"—states avoid global government yet voluntarily surrender portions of sovereignty to supranational bodies to cope with complex problems that overwhelm solitary actors.[16]

Students of international cooperation believe mutual reliance becomes habit forming as it nurtures trust and paves the way for more ambitious experiments. People with common interests can also forge common values and identities. A world of nations is not natural, merely a product of limited imagination. Once we grasp that political life is of our own making, we can remake it in ways we barely fathom.[17]

When "realism" was in its heyday, sovereignty was indivisible; international law was toothless morality; world opinion was idealistic metaphor.[18] Now we are flooded with accounts of the waning nation-state overshadowed by a cast of transnational actors every government must placate but none can control. The once majestic category of sovereign states has spawned degenerate offspring: "failed states," "quasi states," and "rogue states." The future belongs to assertive "transnational civil society"—multinational corporations, nongovernmental organizations, and social movements—as well as underground networks trafficking in drugs, terror, and human beings.[19]

The deepest revolution is the new regard for individual citizens and humanity as a whole—the flesh-and-blood personalities whose rights and interests all but vanished in the fixation on nation-states. Nations are no longer the sole subjects of international law. Individuals can obtain judicial relief against sovereign states—including their own—for human rights abuses and civil wrongs. Instead of viewing nations as supreme givens, we see them from the perspective of the people who sustain them and the planet that transcends them.

Today's thinkers are more optimistic about overcoming obstacles to collective action. The proliferation of regimes and organizations heralds "international society." Many argue we should turn the realist axiom on its head: Anarchy is the exception, and cooperation is the rule.[20] For some younger theorists, even regime theory is too cautious in envisioning alternative worlds. "Constructivist" writers see the nation-state as just another imagined community alongside universal attachments to transcontinental religions and civilizations and to humanity in general. If world politics is a historical construct, there is nothing stopping us from reconstructing it.[21]

The pull of universalism is stronger than ever, forcing us to wonder if international society foreshadows a truly global community—a world connected by common sentiment and morality, not just by compatible interests. Describing such a community as "global" means its ethics would be a universal creation of all cultures and civilizations, not a Western hand-me-down.[22]

It is hard to imagine a global ethic without also thinking about a higher law, and that inevitably points to the collective teachings of world religions. As international relations shifts our sight from anarchy to community, it resumes its interrupted conversations with international law and the humanities.[23]

Meanwhile, international law is in the midst of its own revolution. International lawyers see law from two angles. Most law is a human creation bound to particular societies and eras. This is the law of sovereign legislators—supreme authorities with power to enforce their will and no earthly soul above them. Lawyers also speak of a universal law originating in a higher source—God, or nature, or an irreducible core of the human condition. This is the law giving every person an innate sense of justice and of right and wrong. Its principles are evident—even self-evident—to all rational minds. It governs everyone everywhere, including sovereign states and their leaders.[24]

Neither view ever displaces the other. Most international lawyers fashion eclectic arguments that appeal to both, ignoring the inevitable inconsistencies. They typically begin with a "positivist" assertion that states are obligated to obey laws because the laws are of their own making; nations freely choose to be bound, and they can break their word only if they are prepared to see everyone else follow suit. The same lawyers then add a "naturalist" argument that states are obliged to obey many laws whether they choose to or not, especially laws grounded in accepted morality or the common practice of civilized peoples. Because jurists are ever mindful that sovereign powers are reluctant to bow to either line of reasoning, they rely on both in hopes that two theories of obligation might persuade where one would fail.

Post-Enlightenment lawyers were reluctant to recognize religious sources of law. They argued that religious beliefs are unverifiable and easily manipulated by unscrupulous politicians eager to justify coercion. Many believed international law took root in Europe precisely because secular rulers saw it as an antidote to disastrous religious wars. The supposed lesson is that sovereigns will bow only to a law that bows to them first by relying on state consent. A universal law derived from divine inspiration or natural reason is worse than a hopeless dream; it is a mortal threat to peace and freedom.

When the world wars of the twentieth century proved that nationalism could be as murderous as religion, nonconsensual approaches to international law made a stunning comeback. Contemporary lawyers doubt that consent is an adequate basis for rule making, and many claim it is unnecessary. Today's jurists regularly blend consensual and nonconsensual sources. Some might justify universal obligations by invoking the "conscience of civilized nations" rather than natural law or Holy Scripture, but the results are much the same.

## The Renaissance of Nonconsensual International Law

International law is increasingly eager to finesse the requirement of consent or dispense with it altogether.[25] Three sources of law are vital to that effort: peremptory norms, general principles of international law, and customary international law.

Peremptory norms are universal rules binding everyone and enforceable everywhere. Nineteenth-century jurists recognized such rules, categorically outlawing piracy and slavery. The Nuremberg and Tokyo tribunals opened the door wider by affirming unconditional individual responsibility for crimes against peace, war crimes, and crimes against humanity. The human rights movement added universal prohibitions on genocide, murder, torture, prolonged arbitrary detention, and racial discrimination.[26]

More and more, international law is not the law of nations but the law of humankind. Jurists the world over are fascinated by the prospect of a universal law derived from principles shared by nearly all cultures. The search for overlapping values spurred a boom in comparative legal studies, moving beyond well-known connections between common law and civil law systems to explore cross-fertilization between Western and non-Western legal traditions.[27]

A century ago, Westerners saw international law as a product of Europe. They grudgingly conceded that the family of civilized nations could include a handful of Asian states but only if the "newcomers" embraced sweeping reforms dictated by the Great Powers. The world's oldest civilizations seemed destined to become wards of the youngest.[28]

Today, international law strives to be a global standard, reflecting contributions of all civilizations while being the property of none. No field exemplifies the new mentality better than human rights law. Early human rights advocates assumed they were championing Western principles against legacies of despotism and patriarchy in Asia and Africa. They asked, "How compatible are indigenous cultures with international law?" This usually meant "How *incompatible* are *their* values of Islam, Confucianism, Hinduism, and animism with *our* values of rationalism and liberalism?"[29]

Now, Westerners ask how well their own societies measure up. Across Europe and North America, applying human rights law at home sparks bitter struggles in the courts and political process.[30] Battles are particularly fierce in the United States and Great Britain, forcing citizens to consider whether they need international law as much as it needs them. Countries that regard themselves as the cradle of civil liberty are falling short in protecting religious and racial minorities, asylum seekers, torture victims, juveniles, the mentally handicapped, and defendants subject to the death penalty.

The new universalism of international law has shaken Great Britain more than any other country. In little more than a century, the world's greatest exporter of legal thinking has become an importer, facing multiple pressures from the European Union (EU) and its former colonies. While the EU urges Britain to accept uniform codes, all of Europe faces millions of well-organized immigrants from Asia and Africa calling for the opposite—laws addressing the special needs of non-Western minorities.[31]

The new prominence of Asian and African peoples in Western societies triggered a spirited debate over legal pluralism as an alternative to assimilation and homogenization. Immigrants are asking democracies to guarantee their rights to dress, marry, and worship according to customs Westerners neither understand nor condone.[32] In many cities, Muslims, Hindus, and Sikhs rely on a parallel set of informal courts applying hybrid rules to families that live and work in several countries simultaneously. Western judges and politicians have barely discovered these practices and must decide whether to legitimate or suppress them.[33]

Cultural diversity is forcing Westerners to make difficult judgments about whether they can protect freedom of belief without safeguarding the right to practice those beliefs in daily life. European human rights bodies tackled these problems head-on—disputes over schoolgirls wearing headscarves, traditional marriages flouting formalities, and employees taking time off for Friday noon prayers.[34] Most decisions strengthened accusations of religious discrimination. Commissioners and judges overwhelmingly supported defendant governments over complaining immigrants while interpreting religious and legal traditions admittedly beyond their competence.[35]

The EU states are reluctant to recognize customs of nonwhite immigrants because they already have their hands full persuading their own citizens to embrace a European identity and legal system. Worse yet, they fear concessions to non-Westerners will enrage indigenous ethnic groups fighting for autonomy or independence.

Asians and Africans are more comfortable with legal pluralism and less preoccupied with whether laws are uniform or coherent. Most adapted long ago to multilayered systems blending laws from many cultures—including transplants from Western jurisdictions.[36] Non-Westerners' tolerance of—even preference for—eclectic laws explains the rising interest in mixed legal systems and legal pluralism. Social scientists and students of comparative law are discovering that most legal systems are hybrids where multiple worldviews coexist.[37] Every culture contains inherent tensions it manages, with changing exceptions and ambiguities just as important as the rules themselves.

Legal systems display a logic that is more political than formal—like a toughly negotiated trade agreement rather than a mathematical proof. Legal pluralists believe such political logic helps balance differences in identities and values—differences all societies should preserve no matter how great the lure of regional integration and globalization.[38] After generations of absorbing Western cultures, voluntarily and involuntarily, non-Westerners are reshaping the laws of the former tutors and their basic understanding of law itself.

Non-Westerners have an even deeper impact on customary international law, the most controversial source of nonconsensual norms. Asia and Africa use their strength in the United Nations to transform the law and the process creating it. For the Third World, this corrects a historical injustice. Before World War II, they saw international law as a child of imperialism—rules made by strong and wealthy states that new nations had to accept as the price of admission to the international community.

Great powers adapted to the new majority, confident their military and economic might would compensate for diluted influence in diplomacy and law. Yet in the field of customary international law, dominant states felt change was too rapid and too radical. The United States, France, and Russia claimed Third World countries corrupted customary international law by insisting that newly proclaimed norms were universally binding, even if powerful states rejected them.[39] When Third World jurists say announcing new norms is simply the "progressive development of international law," opponents ridicule them as manufacturing "instant custom."[40]

Critics charged that norms no longer emerge from a steady accretion of consensus but from ad hoc "conference diplomacy," where assemblies issue sweeping proclamations in one field after another as though they were global legislatures.[41] Substituting words for conduct destroys the only objective standard international lawyers have for identifying custom—the real behavior of sovereign states. Pronouncing phony custom will merely cause states to lose respect for all international law and wonder if there is any reason to be conscientious world citizens.

Revolutions in international relations and international law have passed beyond the point where complaints about "instant custom" could resuscitate dying orthodoxy. The twin upheavals rekindled ancient dreams of creating a global community with universal norms, and such norms are arising with a speed that seemed inconceivable when realism and positivism held sway.

When, during the 1960s, I was an undergraduate in the classroom of the great realist thinker Hans Morgenthau, we heard nothing to prepare us for the world we see today. Not one of us dreamed that the family of a Paraguayan torture victim could win a judgment in a U.S. court against the police chief who led his interrogation, that moral outrage and economic sanctions could destroy apartheid, or that a head of state could be brought to trial for slaughtering his own people. It was common knowledge that the classic doctrines of sovereignty, immunity, and jurisdiction provided airtight defenses against such fantasies.

Nor did Morgenthau think it necessary to utter a word concerning religion, except to recall Stalin's query about how many divisions the pope commands. Today, religion is again at center stage. Our fate hinges not just on balancing power but on harmonizing civilizations, and the civilizations embracing most of humanity identify more than ever with cosmopolitan religions boasting sophisticated traditions of law. Conversations between world civilizations are also explorations of core values and legal systems that reveal similar ideals and discontents in traditions we often presume are irreconcilable.

## Rule-Skepticism in Islam and the West: Custom as a Source of Law and a Source of Dissension

As international law grows independent of any particular culture, its very universality engenders resistance. The vision of global community appeals to those believing all civilizations have something to teach one another but not to those convinced that their own values and institutions are superior. Every society contains powerful groups in both camps, and their internal combat can be as intense as any dispute between cultures. Cosmopolitans claim that an emerging system of international law and morality belongs to everyone. Traditionalists respond that global standards are so vague and artificial they belong to no one and, worse yet, they threaten indigenous values and pave the way for foreign control.

Incorporating international norms in domestic law is particularly difficult in countries accustomed to leading a major civilization. In the East as well as the West, proud and accomplished people are always tempted to assume that if any set of values will become a standard for the world, it is their own. Observers of religious revivals around the world depict them in these terms—as defensive reactions to a homogenizing globalization and as extremist assertions of superiority.

Yet great civilizations do not endure unless they constantly absorb and synthesize contributions from many cultures. Tolerance and flexibility are essential characteristics of the very heritages hard-line traditionalists are so determined to insulate. Cosmopolitans see no reason to surrender tradition to traditionalists. Those who participate in shaping international norms and spreading them at home usually find no difficulty in summoning support from their own religious legacies.

Disputes over international law go well beyond specific rules, sparking deeper conflict over rules about how to incorporate international norms in domestic law. These are disagreements concerning the basic norm that governs rule making itself—what the British legal philosopher H. L. A. Hart termed the "rule of recognition."[42] The so-called rule of recognition is really an amalgam of many rules regulating sources of law, methods of interpretation, and distributions of constitutional authority. The degree of consensus over these rules is a key measure of the strength of any legal system, national or international, but new global norms can threaten that consensus on all levels. Internalizing international law can be just as difficult as creating it.

Many rules about sources of international law are still evolving and controversial. Even when proponents of a new norm prevail in multistate forums, they often fight the same battle all over again in their own countries, and the domestic battle can be more divisive than the international debate. Adopting a sensitive global norm in national law often adds fuel to cultural and constitutional quarrels smoldering and close to ignition. What part of international law is already domestic law? Are nations more entitled to scrutinize global norms touching core values such as contraception and capital punishment, or do they have the same obligation to comply in all fields? Who has the authority to make these decisions?

Internationally and domestically, debates over new rules tend to escalate into broader debates about rules of recognition. Today's global lawmaking process is more politicized and contentious than ever before because it encompasses an unprecedented number of actors, issues, and forums. It cuts across all the conventional boundaries between domestic and international, public and private, legal and moral—boundaries that not long ago strictly limited who could decide what questions in which assemblies.[43]

Global lawmaking is also never ending. Contestants are engaged in long-term struggles that address many audiences at the same time. No defeat is permanent, and no victory is complete. Losers can always find another arena for appeal—a different court, a new election, a wider media campaign. Winners can always strive for deeper commitment to emerging norms—from grudging acceptance to routine compliance to widespread socialization. True internalization passes through all these stages, so an advocate's work is never finished.

Intensely politicized global lawmaking comes at a high price. It sows uncertainty as to whether there exists any settled core of law. This is the malaise Hart dubs "rule-skepticism."[44] Hart acknowledges that all rules are indeterminate, leaving an area of ambiguity where creative interpretation is inevitable and desirable. He was one of the first positivist writers to embrace doubt as inherent to the very concept of law. Indeterminacy gives all law an "open texture" that allows jurists the discretion to make new rules even while claiming merely to apply existing ones.

His harshest criticism targets "formalists" who exaggerate law's clarity and coherence and pretend rules speak for themselves.[45] Yet, Hart argues, rule-skepticism errs in the opposite direction—exaggerating uncertainty at the margins of the law and failing to see that it remains "determinate enough at the center." Hart opines that, in many societies, jurists oscillate between the two fallacies, portraying rules as ironclad at one time and virtually nonexistent at another.[46]

Hart is particularly disdainful of those who claim international law is not "real law" because there is no sovereign power to enforce it. He concedes that international law is relatively primitive, but he insists it is nonetheless binding law that people feel obliged to honor because of conscience and pervasive social pressure—not simply because of the threat of force.[47]

Skepticism also has benefits, and Hart underestimates its value for societies that need to reassess fundamental principles. His major example of a country where disputes over the rule of recognition threatened constitutional order is South Africa—a regime that suffered from too little skepticism rather than too much, and where constitutional crisis could not have come soon enough.[48]

Today, a more politicized process of global lawmaking breeds rule-skepticism in many Western and Islamic countries that doubt their ability to shape international norms they are willing to apply at home. International law is no longer a European creation, and it is unlikely that any culture will dominate it in the future. The United States and the Muslim world will undoubtedly have pivotal roles in developing global norms, but there is no American or Islamic version of international law waiting to take command.

Americans and Muslims wanting to influence international law have to reclaim aspects of their own traditions that favor tolerance and cooperation against fantasies of superiority and hegemony. If even the most powerful civilizations realize they cannot control global lawmaking, they might choose to stress the compatibility of their heritages instead of their differences. In that case, rule-skepticism would prove far more beneficial than Hart ever imagined.

Islamic and Western jurists share a talent for creating new law by reinterpreting tradition instead of contradicting it. Many features of the common law are similar to Islamic practice, and both heritages bear a family resemblance to Roman law. All are classic examples of "lawyers' law," created by centuries of professional judges and counselors-at-law that deftly drew new rules out of old ones through case-by-case application of open-ended principles to changing conditions.[49] Their dominant technique is to apply a supposedly self-limiting style of analogical reasoning to produce similar decisions from similar facts, broadening or narrowing a rule at the margins to suit shifting needs of equity and public interest. Each tradition produced vast, pluralistic bodies of law that stubbornly resisted codification and uniformity, leaving wide leeway for minority views and lasting variation between regions, specializations, and competing schools.

Common law and Islamic jurists are renowned for understating their discretion and disavowing any explicit legislative role. They are masters at conserving their independence by deferring to arms and might and by claiming to fill in gaps where the primary lawgiver is silent or unclear. That independence, in turn, allows them to constantly transform law through a combination of interpretive skills and equitable powers. By selectively mining reservoirs of divergent authority, common lawyers and Islamic jurists counterbalance many biases they perceive in their societies and legal traditions.[50]

International law forces jurists in all countries to reexamine their deepest differences and decide whether indigenous principles are compatible with global norms. Such debates raise core questions about what is essential to a legal tradition and how it should evolve.

In the United States and the Islamic world, international law is sparking a reassessment of long-standing prejudices under attack from many directions. Muslims are challenging an ancient bias against man-made law based on independent reason, and Americans are questioning a modern bias against the ideal of a higher law transcending human will. Reformers in both traditions are striving for a more even balance of reason and inspiration—a more reasoned inspiration to give Muslims greater freedom of thought and a more inspired reason to give Americans greater idealism.

In both cases, much of the debate revolves around contested notions of custom. Arguments over customary international law have a knack for aggravating festering conflicts about interpreting tradition—the intentions of the Founding Fathers, the meanings of the Prophet's example, the fidelity or indifference of later generations to the enlightenment of the original sources.

Common law and Islamic jurists mythologize custom to disguise their power in creating it. Instead of portraying customary law as the law of the courts, they describe it as the practice of time immemorial, the sacred path of the Book and the ancestors, the living will of the people, or the universal rule of the realm. Such mythology becomes increasingly transparent as the rise of international law pushes custom making into the political arena. When civilizations have to decide what they can contribute to the global community and what they can learn from it, their people ask more candidly than ever what their traditions truly represent and what they want them to become.

## Islamic Pluralism and International Law: Rebuilding the Global Ka'ba

Muslims are struggling with the same dilemmas as Westerners in reconciling inherently pluralistic traditions with emerging global norms. Most of the time, they must do so without the advantages of democracy and free expression.

People dominated by generals, princes, and mullahs cannot enjoy the open exchange of ideas vital to adapting a living religion to changing times.

The connection between Islam and freedom may be uncertain in Western minds, but Muslims cast their votes for democracy in country after country whenever they have the chance. While Westerners still ask, "How compatible is Islam with democracy?" Muslims around the world are asking, "Is true Islam possible without democracy?"

Across the Muslim world, millions are coping with authoritarian rulers that tighten their grip as their societies change faster than ever. The more desperate regimes become, the more they lean on Islam to prop themselves up—and the more skilled their critics become at knocking them over. Every attempt to make Islam more rigid seems only to make it more fluid.

Both formalism and rule-skepticism are thriving in contemporary Islam. The twin vices Hart saw as alternating dangers in most traditions are spreading simultaneously in this one. Governments and official 'ulama can insist that rules are frozen and self-explanatory, but they cannot prevent critics from advancing contrary readings of the same multilayered sources, especially since they have been reinterpreted countless times in the past. Official moves toward formalism merely strengthen the resolve of reformers and dissidents to escape the dead hand of traditionalism and the fist of authoritarianism.

The crux of the debate between Muslim formalists and skeptics is the classic disagreement over whether to focus on rules or on principles. Islam is compliance with the will of God as revealed in the Qur'an. However, does this mean obeying specific rules that are forever fixed or heeding general principles that require new rules for changing conditions? The Qur'an is inspired and universal, but what about the thousands of fallible human inferences that created the Shari'ah, Islamic law?

Humanity's fingerprints are everywhere in Islamic law. The deepest impressions came from minds that were the most illustrious of their day—but they were merely scholars, not prophets. They took guidance from the exemplary behavior of Muhammad and the earliest Muslims—but they, too, were humans capable of error. If human reason was indispensable to understanding God's will in the past, why should its role be any weaker today, when our knowledge in all fields is so much greater than before?

The common thread in reformist Islam is thinking of religion as a flexible set of universal principles instead of a fixed code of rules.[51] Modernists view Islam's principles as inspired, but they see most rules as man-made and needing constant improvement. Although they argue from various viewpoints, many are skilled in relying on traditional sources and interpretive techniques to reach quite untraditional conclusions.

The hajj is central to modernist Islam. The irrepressible communitas of pilgrimage encourages precisely the renewal and reassessment they consider essential to Islam in general. The hajj is a constant reminder that Muslims' reach always exceeds their grasp: Islamic ideals of cooperation, equality, and tolerance are alive in their hearts, even when stifled in society and daily life.

Modernists urge pilgrims to take advantage of their unique opportunities for reflection and hope they will return with open-minded views of their home-lands and their place in the world. Reformers believe if the hajj accomplishes this much, it will invigorate religious imagination, no matter how oppressive the governments that organize the pilgrims or how old-fashioned the 'ulama that guide them.

Contemporary debates over Islam and international law proceed within remarkably consistent contours. Since the establishment of the United Nations and the end of colonialism, Muslim writers have struggled with the core ques-tion of whether to fashion a single international law inspired by all civilizations or an Islamic international law with a distinctive personality.

Those who speculate about following a separate path also debate how their Islamic visions would relate to United Nations efforts. Would Islamic inter-national law interact with other projects and share their aspirations? Would it go its own way with little regard for alternatives it could not direct? Could Islamic international law itself become the universal order, absorbing or re-placing competing visions?

With the rise of the Organization of the Islamic Conference, the center of gravity shifted decisively toward a unitary approach to international law encom-passing all civilizations regardless of religion. The rhetoric of a separate path still reverberates, but the OIC rejects the idea of a distinctively Islamic inter-national law. The OIC considers itself an integral part of the United Nations system—like any other regional organization, but one stressing shared values and identity more than proximity or special policy domains. The OIC aims to be an interest group in the existing international system; it has no illusions of becoming the international system, and it discourages Muslims from harbor-ing such illusions.

One litmus test of the OIC's commitment to the status quo is its refusal to establish a separate international court, lest it appear to challenge the au-thority of the International Court of Justice (ICJ).[52] The OIC Secretariat received several requests to adjudicate boundary disputes between member states, in-cluding powerful Gulf kingdoms with rival claims to mineral-rich desert zones. Nonetheless, it consistently urges parties to follow the rest of the international community in submitting to ICJ jurisdiction.[53] This gives clear notice to Mus-lims and non-Muslims alike that the OIC will permit no forum shopping, particularly in winning international recognition for secure borders.

Before the creation of the OIC and afterward, leading voices in these de-bates spoke within a stable range. On one side, apologists claim existing in-ternational law is already Islamic in spirit because the Qur'an foreshadowed its basic principles and Muslims have nurtured them for centuries.[54] At the opposite end of the spectrum, Islamic radicals repudiate international law as a tool of Western domination that impious elites foist on Muslims instead of strengthening their own unique heritage.[55]

Both extremes—apologists and radicals—assume that a straight line connects the Qur'an and the Prophet with their visions of world order. They jump to conclusions about specific rules and institutions, and they justify them with cryptic quotations from scripture and prophetic sayings. Most dispense with the hard work of argument—providing evidence, interpretation, and persuasion that might sway audiences not already convinced.

These extremist approaches persist on the margins, but they have lost ground to voices calling for an international law that reflects compromises between all civilizations. The take-it-all and leave-it-all attitudes to existing international law continue the struggle, but with diminishing effect on policy and public opinion. Today, the most influential voices belong to two groups of writers I would describe as liberals and reformers.

Both groups express plausible arguments about the ways Muslims can contribute to international law and share its benefits. Neither assumes Islam and international law are inherently compatible or incompatible. They see multiple points of overlap and divergence creating the same challenge for Muslims as for everyone else—negotiating global norms and institutions that all civilizations can support but none can dominate.

The thrust of the liberal argument is that Islam has always played an important role in shaping international law—particularly in laying its modern foundations before and after the European Renaissance—and that Islamic influences will grow still stronger in the future.[56] Above all, liberals are consummate bridge builders. Many are diplomats, judges, and academics with long experience in international organizations and tribunals. Frequently educated in Western as well as Islamic law, they embody the constant blending of neighboring civilizations.

Liberals see Islam in perfect synchrony with the critical rethinking of international law and international relations that is sweeping Western countries, especially the pervasive discontent with realism and positivism. They see these changes as evidence that Westerners are awakening after a long intoxication with nationalism and ethnocentrism to reclaim the universal and humanist ideals that distinguished Western civilization before the rise of colonialism and world war. Liberal Muslims are eager to reinforce these trends, reminding counterparts in the West that Islam has championed similar ideals all along. They believe that, together, liberals of the Muslim world and the West are the most progressive influence on the global imagination—natural partners in any effort to make international law more effective, inclusive, and just.

Reformist writers share much of the liberal viewpoint, but they are far more critical of the current condition of Islam.[57] They believe Muslims have a great deal of work to do at home before trying to change the rest of the world. Reformers argue that Islamic ideals have become too ambiguous and too far removed from Muslim practice to guide human progress. Before anything else, Muslims must change their own thinking and behavior; they need to create an Islam that is more humane and scientific. Instead of rewriting international law, Muslims should start obeying it so their lives as well as their rhetoric can inspire others.[58]

Consistent with this predilection to look within, reformers give greater weight to local problems than to global visions. They criticize the OIC as an ineffective regional organization and call on its leaders to become more assertive in mediating conflicts between Muslim states and lobbying in the United Nations. They want Muslim jurists and intellectuals to interpret legal and religious sources with boldness and originality, drawing on their superior knowledge of modern science to challenge the waning authority of the *'ulama*.[59]

Most controversially, reformers also want Muslims to admit that parts of their tradition flatly contradict international law so they can get down to the difficult task of changing those views and practices. They want Muslims to abandon attitudes condoning the use of force in several areas: portraying jihad as military struggle instead of spiritual striving, permitting the death penalty for apostates despite the Qur'anic prohibition of compulsion in matters of faith, and attacking noncombatant civilians rather than heeding Muhammad's instructions on the conduct of war.[60]

Liberals and reformists look to religion as a way of putting more ethics into law and more law into politics. Their ambitions are quite similar to those of Western writers leading the twin revolutions in international relations and international law.[61] Like many in the West, they are convinced that a global community depends on more than converging interests and countervailing power; it must rest on universal values rooted in the legal and religious traditions of all major civilizations.

Liberals and reformists are equally eager for Muslims to lead in fashioning global values, but they focus on different goals. Liberals stress Islam's abiding links to other civilizations—especially the West—while reformists highlight the inherent pluralism of Islam itself. Liberals want to ensure an Islamic imprint on the customary law of nations, and reformists want Muslims to embrace a view of inherited custom open to the totality of their own civilization, not just an archaic portion of it.

Liberals speak primarily to international organizations, conferences, and tribunals where all cultures are shaping the law of tomorrow. Reformists remind Muslims everywhere that their heritage has always produced and absorbed new knowledge in philosophy, science, and mysticism, as well as in commerce, statecraft, and the creative arts. All these channels make the teachings of the Qur'an and Muhammad's early followers accessible to everyone, Muslims and non-Muslims alike. Reformists insist that the legal scholars of the past added to those teachings—even while claiming to add nothing at all—but that no one can exhaust their implications or freeze their meanings.

In the Islamic world as in the West, internationalists see human relations as fallible products of our beliefs and actions—not eternal verities imposed by God and nature. Having imagined our communities as nations and states, we are free to reimagine them as a single universe. Having constructed our social institutions, we must be prepared to reconstruct them to match our changing ideals and identities.

Western and Islamic internationalists also share a false sense of self-sufficiency undercutting their efforts to shape a global ethic. Their internationalism can be astonishingly myopic. Just as Westerners find it hard to shed ethnocentrism, Muslims suffer from monotheistic bias. Although Judeo-Christian civilization and Islamic civilization seem obsessed with one another—oscillating between mutual attraction and repulsion—both give short shrift to the rest of humanity.

Even if the extended family of Judeo-Christian-Islamic civilization eventually pulls itself together, they still have to acknowledge and negotiate their kinship with multitudes of "others"—the Hindus and Sikhs, the Buddhists and Confucians, the polytheists, animists, and nontheists accounting for most of the world's population. All the great religions have unfulfilled promises of universalism. Their leaders will have plenty of opportunities to show us they can sort out their own conflicts as they claim to create a more humane conscience for us all.

Creating a global community seems less daunting after making a pilgrimage, especially one that stirs us—physically and spiritually—in a single pot with all humanity. Wherever such pilgrimages take us—to Mecca or Jerusalem, to the rivers of India or the mountains of China, to Graceland or the Lincoln Memorial—they point to a similar conclusion. Everyone is a guest of God, and, however we imagine his earthly home, we are constantly building it according to a design that changes as we change ourselves.

# Appendix

## FIGURES

TABLE A4.1 Pilgrimage growth and changing means of transportation, 1946–1987

| Years | Average number of pilgrims | Average rate of increase (percent) | Percent arriving by air | Percent arriving by land | Percent arriving by sea |
|---|---|---|---|---|---|
| 1946–1950 | 79,773 | 113.6 | 7.2 | 9.7 | 83.1 |
| 1951–1955 | 159,195 | 99.5 | 14.7 | 18.1 | 67.2 |
| 1956–1960 | 221,207 | 39.0 | 17.3 | 27.4 | 55.2 |
| 1961–1965 | 250,263 | 13.1 | 26.9 | 28.2 | 44.9 |
| 1966–1970 | 341,986 | 37.6 | 34.6 | 37.1 | 28.3 |
| 1971–1974 | 616,465 | 80.3 | 51.6 | 27.7 | 20.3 |
| 1975–1979 | 809,138 | 31.2 | 58.1 | 32.2 | 9.7 |
| 1980–1984 | 894,109 | 10.5 | 73.1 | 20.7 | 6.2 |
| 1985–1987 | 889,622 | 0.5 | 74.8 | 20.3 | 4.9 |

TABLE A4.2 Leading sources of pilgrims, 1947–1987 (annual average number of pilgrims)

| 1947–1950 | | 1951–1955 | | 1956–1960 | |
|---|---|---|---|---|---|
| 1. India & Pakistan | 26,765 | 1. Egypt | 28,382 | 1. N. Yemen | 44,968 |
| 2. Egypt | 18,568 | 2. Pakistan | 23,943 | 2. Egypt | 33,175 |
| 3. Indonesia | 9,289 | 3. N Yemen | 23,297 | 3. W. Africa | 18,127 |
| 4. Turkey | 5,154 | 4. India | 10,938 | 4. India | 17,109 |
| 5. Iran | 5,022 | 5. W. Africa | 9,939 | 5. Pakistan | 16,651 |
| 6. W. Africa | 4,245 | 6. Indonesia | 7,634 | 6. Iran | 13,498 |
| 7. Malaysia | 3,612 | 7. Sudan | 7,431 | 7. Indonesia | 10,755 |
| 8. Sudan | 2,946 | 8. N. Africa | 6,812 | 8. Gulf States | 10,238 |
| 9. N. Yemen | 2,858 | 9. Syria | 5,486 | 9. S. Yemen | 8,284 |
| 10. N. Africa | 2,406 | 10. Iran | 5,071 | 10. Syria | 7,911 |
| 11. Philippines | 1,739 | 11. Malaysia | 4,359 | 11. Sudan | 5,831 |
| 12. Syria | 1,513 | 12. Turkey | 3,885 | 12. Palestine | 5,389 |
| 13. S. Yemen | 1,158 | 13. Iraq | 3,116 | 13. Malaysia | 4,498 |
| 14. USSR | 859 | 14. Thailand | 3,034 | 14. Iraq | 4,077 |
| 15. Lebanon | 676 | 15. Palestine | 3,007 | 15. Jordan | 3,479 |
| 16. Iraq | 672 | 16. S. Yemen | 2,739 | 16. Afghanistan | 2,385 |

(continued on next page)

| 1947–1950 | | 1951–1955 | | 1956–1960 | |
|---|---|---|---|---|---|
| 17. Senegal | 420 | 17. Gulf States | 2,384 | 17. Morocco | 2,202 |
| 18. Afghanistan | 298 | 18. Jordan | 2,298 | 18. Libya | 1,995 |
| 19. S. Africa | 296 | 19. Afghanistan | 1,371 | 19. Thailand | 1,778 |
| 20. China | 160 | 20. Lebanon | 1,354 | 20. Senegal | 1,761 |

| 1961–1965 | | 1966–1970 | | 1971–1974 | |
|---|---|---|---|---|---|
| 1. Pakistan | 22,149 | 1. Turkey | 42,985 | 1. Pakistan | 56,958 |
| 2. India | 19,476 | 2. N. Yemen | 33,737 | 2. Iran | 49,702 |
| 3. Egypt | 17,774 | 3. Pakistan | 22,727 | 3. N. Yemen | 49,239 |
| 4. Turkey | 16,355 | 4. Iran | 22,389 | 4. Nigeria | 43,772 |
| 5. Iran | 16,192 | 5. Iraq | 19,480 | 5. Turkey | 41,346 |
| 6. N. Yemen | 14,351 | 6. Syria | 17,405 | 6. Egypt | 41,267 |
| 7. Syria | 12,303 | 7. Sudan | 17,360 | 7. Indonesia | 33,917 |
| 8. Indonesia | 12,010 | 8. India | 15,981 | 8. Iraq | 31,268 |
| 9. Iraq | 10,890 | 9. Indonesia | 15,333 | 9. Sudan | 29,736 |
| 10. Sudan | 10,624 | 10. Libya | 14,734 | 10. Syria | 28,638 |
| 11. Nigeria | 9,089 | 11. Nigeria | 13,462 | 11. Libya | 22,778 |
| 12. Libya | 6,722 | 12. Egypt | 11,984 | 12. Algeria | 22,133 |
| 13. Jordan | 6,530 | 13. Morocco | 9,621 | 13. India | 18,637 |
| 14. Malaysia | 5,540 | 14. Algeria | 7,661 | 14. Morocco | 18,017 |
| 15. Algeria | 5,157 | 15. Kuwait | 6,948 | 15. Jordan | 16,981 |
| 16. Palestine | 4,744 | 16. Malaysia | 6,907 | 16. Malaysia | 11,951 |
| 17. Morocco | 4,576 | 17. Jordan | 6,763 | 17. Afghanistan | 10,874 |
| 18. Kuwait | 3,729 | 18. Afghanistan | 6,528 | 18. Tunisia | 8,157 |
| 19. Afghanistan | 2,968 | 19. S. Yemen | 5,080 | 19. Kuwait | 7,264 |
| 20. Niger | 2,859 | 20. Lebanon | 4,441 | 20. Lebanon | 6,942 |

| 1975–1979 | | 1980–1984 | | 1985–1987 | |
|---|---|---|---|---|---|
| 1. N. Yemen | 93,610 | 1. Egypt | 100,534 | 1. Iran | 153,924 |
| 2. Turkey | 82,010 | 2. Iran | 86,687 | 2. Egypt | 108,898 |
| 3. Nigeria | 75,631 | 3. Pakistan | 79,481 | 3. Pakistan | 91,069 |
| 4. Pakistan | 57,631 | 4. N. Yemen | 72,726 | 4. Turkey | 64,343 |
| 5. Iran | 54,306 | 5. Nigeria | 71,856 | 5. Indonesia | 52,885 |
| 6. Iraq | 53,026 | 6. Indonesia | 59,411 | 6. N. Yemen | 48,683 |
| 7. Indonesia | 46,639 | 7. Turkey | 38,557 | 7. India | 37,963 |
| 8. Egypt | 40,070 | 8. Algeria | 33,541 | 8. Algeria | 28,553 |
| 9. Algeria | 40,021 | 9. Iraq | 33,346 | 9. Sudan | 27,613 |
| 10. Syria | 39,718 | 10. Syria | 33,118 | 10. Iraq | 25,976 |
| 11. Libya | 31,961 | 11. Sudan | 32,519 | 11. Nigeria | 25,527 |
| 12. Sudan | 27,084 | 12. India | 27,568 | 12. Malaysia | 25,312 |
| 13. Jordan | 23,743 | 13. Libya | 27,047 | 13. Morocco | 25,060 |
| 14. Morocco | 21,035 | 14. Malaysia | 22,518 | 14. Libya | 18,938 |
| 15. India | 20,516 | 15. Jordan | 22,352 | 15. Jordan | 17,815 |
| 16. Tunisia | 8,031 | 16. Morocco | 21,849 | 16. Bangladesh | 15,444 |
| 17. Malaysia | 7,931 | 17. Bangladesh | 16,098 | 17. Syria | 13,973 |
| 18. S. Yemen | 7,664 | 18. Tunisia | 9,900 | 18. Oman | 11,960 |
| 19. Somalia | 6,752 | 19. S. Yemen | 9,706 | 19. Tunisia | 8,814 |
| 20. Afghanistan | 5,986 | 20. Oman | 8,709 | 20. Kuwait | 7,719 |

| | | | | | | | | |
|---|---|---|---|---|---|---|---|---|
| 1. Iran | 57,076 | 8. Iraq | 29,213 | 15. Jordan | 15,546 |
| 2. N. Yemen | 52,299 | 9. Syria | 24,922 | 16. Malaysia | 12,506 |
| 3. Pakistan | 51,723 | 10. Sudan | 23,909 | 17. Bangladesh | 7,083 |
| 4. Egypt | 49,458 | 11. Algeria | 22,436 | 18. Kuwait | 6,314 |
| 5. Turkey | 46,403 | 12. India | 22,313 | 19. Afghanistan | 6,127 |
| 6. Nigeria | 40,915 | 13. Libya | 20,464 | 20. S. Yemen | 6,088 |
| 7. Indonesia | 35,543 | 14. Morocco | 16,095 | | |

TABLE A4.3 Pilgrimage rates by country, 1947–1987 (annual pilgrims per million Muslims)

| Arabian Peninsula | 1961–1987 | 1947–1950 | 1951–1955 | 1956–1960 | 1961–1965 | 1966–1970 | 1971–1974 | 1975–1979 | 1980–1984 | 1985–1987 |
|---|---|---|---|---|---|---|---|---|---|---|
| Kuwait | 9,916 | 150 | 5,700 | 18,568 | 15,541 | 15,026 | 10,484 | 6,100 | 5,592 | 4,644 |
| Bahrain | 11,713 | 590 | 5,254 | 16,401 | 18,848 | 11,968 | 10,359 | 8,473 | 9,111 | 11,395 |
| Qatar | 17,386 | 625 | 10,411 | 19,775 | 28,923 | 24,542 | 15,088 | 11,325 | 11,846 | 9,405 |
| UAE | 12,986 | — | 3,223 | 11,137 | 18,941 | 9,117 | 9,600 | 14,452 | 13,484 | 11,886 |
| Oman | 5,250 | — | 442 | 1,350 | 2,428 | 3,116 | 4,270 | 4,456 | 8,994 | 10,229 |
| S. Yemen | 4,075 | 1,645 | 3,260 | 8,540 | 3,059 | 4,061 | 3,888 | 4,876 | 4,978 | 3,271 |
| N. Yemen | 10,624 | 866 | 6,656 | 11,604 | 5,390 | 6,815 | 12,142 | 17,901 | 12,628 | 7,700 |

| Fertile Crescent | | | | | | | | | | |
|---|---|---|---|---|---|---|---|---|---|---|
| Jordan | 9,445 | 123 | 4,178 | 5,384 | 6,906 | 5,269 | 11,171 | 12,719 | 10,959 | 7,495 |
| Syria | 4,275 | 587 | 1,985 | 2,372 | 3,294 | 3,909 | 5,260 | 6,137 | 4,373 | 1,616 |
| Lebanon | 3,960 | 1,275 | 2,342 | 2,367 | 3,327 | 3,620 | 5,305 | 3,193 | 5,012 | 2,865 |
| Iraq | 2,992 | 150 | 657 | 664 | 1,743 | 2,813 | 3,486 | 5,017 | 2,623 | 1,785 |
| Palestine | 3,945 | 667 | 4,519 | 7,750 | 8,169 | 1,029 | 1,801 | 3,812 | 6,746 | 3,584 |

| Red Sea | | | | | | | | | | |
|---|---|---|---|---|---|---|---|---|---|---|
| Egypt | 1,414 | 1,052 | 1,475 | 1,540 | 746 | 440 | 1,360 | 1,189 | 2,612 | 2,621 |
| Sudan | 2,028 | 531 | 1,180 | 792 | 1,262 | 1,780 | 2,631 | 2,171 | 2,417 | 1,831 |
| Djibouti | 2,278 | — | — | — | — | — | — | 2,737 | 2,223 | 1,587 |
| Somalia | 989 | — | — | 200 | 482 | 592 | 692 | 2,181 | 1,112 | 799 |

| North Africa | | | | | | | | | | |
|---|---|---|---|---|---|---|---|---|---|---|
| Libya | 9,788 | — | — | 2,100 | 6,741 | 10,719 | 11,668 | 13,421 | 9,067 | 5,332 |
| Algeria | 1,412 | — | — | 69 | 537 | 693 | 1,592 | 2,459 | 1,815 | 1,355 |
| Tunisia | 1,099 | — | — | 230 | 271 | 278 | 1,729 | 1,555 | 1,564 | 1,264 |
| Morocco | 982 | — | — | 273 | 470 | 768 | 1,221 | 1,279 | 1,100 | 1,107 |
| Mauritania | 704 | 8 | 43 | 774 | 642 | 448 | 77 | 850 | 777 | 748 |

(continued on next page)

TABLE A4.3 (continued)

| West Asia | 1961–1987 | 1947–1950 | 1951–1955 | 1956–1960 | 1961–1965 | 1966–1970 | 1971–1974 | 1975–1979 | 1980–1984 | 1985–1987 |
|---|---|---|---|---|---|---|---|---|---|---|
| Turkey | 1,250 | 273 | 184 | 43 | 606 | 1,450 | 1,210 | 2,090 | 876 | 1,346 |
| Iran | 1,720 | 301 | 290 | 727 | 820 | 975 | 1,698 | 1,660 | 2,306 | 3,617 |
| Afghanistan | 395 | 37 | 156 | 256 | 218 | 438 | 642 | 430 | 321 | 274 |

**South Asia**

| | | | | | | | | | | |
|---|---|---|---|---|---|---|---|---|---|---|
| Pakistan | 698 | — | 351 | 22 | 271 | 245 | 956 | 842 | 992 | 1,006 |
| Bangladesh | 139 | — | — | — | — | — | 84 | 84 | 218 | 192 |
| India | 369 | 270 | 306 | 441 | 457 | 330 | 314 | 310 | 377 | 462 |
| Sri Lanka | 499 | 53 | 177 | 207 | 313 | 703 | 83 | 412 | 643 | 1,068 |
| Maldive Is. | 565 | — | — | — | — | — | — | 259 | 510 | 1,564 |

**Southeast Asia**

| | | | | | | | | | | |
|---|---|---|---|---|---|---|---|---|---|---|
| Malaysia | 2,428 | 1,505 | 1,666 | 1,460 | 1,822 | 1,952 | 2,614 | 1,511 | 3,529 | 3,619 |
| Thailand | 1,571 | — | 4,029 | 2,150 | 2,025 | 2,199 | 2,152 | 406 | 1,345 | 1,118 |
| Singapore | 3,635 | — | — | — | — | 957 | 2,312 | 3,158 | 6,381 | 6,519 |
| Brunei | 5,063 | — | — | — | — | 1,000 | 2,000 | 2,098 | 7,738 | 15,756 |
| Philippines | 759 | 1,783 | 1,175 | 1,140 | 446 | 1,896 | 218 | 472 | 897 | 539 |
| Indonesia | 300 | 146 | 110 | 142 | 144 | 163 | 318 | 381 | 451 | 367 |
| Burma | 65 | — | 53 | 182 | 63 | — | — | 7 | 95 | 112 |
| Cambodia | 100 | — | — | — | — | — | 25 | 141 | 188 | 12 |

**West Africa**

| | | | | | | | | | | |
|---|---|---|---|---|---|---|---|---|---|---|
| Nigeria | 1,306 | 247 | 500 | 787 | 326 | 498 | 1,691 | 2,450 | 1,982 | 616 |
| Chad | 1,140 | — | — | — | 576 | 1,466 | 1,738 | 1,179 | 965 | 768 |
| Niger | 594 | — | — | — | 361 | 735 | 1,081 | 583 | 439 | 215 |
| Mali | 444 | — | — | — | 400 | 342 | 420 | 609 | 511 | 343 |
| Senegal | 839 | 285 | 605 | 954 | 989 | 771 | 855 | 980 | 825 | 468 |
| Gambia | 1,007 | — | — | — | — | — | — | 1,025 | 975 | 1,032 |
| Guinea | 761 | — | — | — | 558 | 891 | 895 | 527 | 1,085 | 511 |
| Burk. Faso | 953 | — | — | — | 506 | 711 | 884 | 1,481 | 1,407 | 581 |
| Ivory Coast | 627 | — | — | — | 371 | 573 | 894 | 773 | 663 | 399 |
| Ghana | 507 | — | — | — | 228 | 240 | 578 | 1,150 | 427 | 364 |
| Togo | 621 | — | — | — | 195 | 377 | 624 | 1,120 | 833 | 554 |
| Benin | 854 | — | — | — | 299 | 686 | 1,009 | 935 | 1,442 | 683 |
| Cameroon | 767 | — | — | — | 425 | 885 | 1,155 | 690 | 790 | 589 |
| Central Afr. | 1,034 | — | — | — | — | 850 | 1,019 | 1,485 | 1,006 | 662 |
| G. Bissau | 343 | — | — | — | — | — | — | 310 | 310 | 453 |
| Liberia | 216 | — | — | — | 129 | 257 | 222 | 282 | 203 | 200 |
| S. Leone | 282 | — | — | — | 127 | 305 | 469 | 278 | 328 | 118 |

| East Africa | 1961–1987 | 1947–1950 | 1951–1955 | 1956–1960 | 1961–1965 | 1966–1970 | 1971–1974 | 1975–1979 | 1980–1984 | 1985–1987 |
|---|---|---|---|---|---|---|---|---|---|---|
| Ethiopia | 198 | 16 | 80 | 71 | 200 | 313 | 279 | 109 | 164 | 70 |
| Uganda | 1,565 | — | — | — | 671 | 849 | 2,831 | 4,066 | 208 | 237 |
| Kenya | 540 | — | — | — | 80 | 503 | 646 | 548 | 835 | 687 |
| Tanzania | 165 | — | — | 30 | 35 | 199 | 204 | 205 | 192 | 146 |
| Zambia | 628 | — | — | — | — | 845 | 883 | 578 | 325 | 434 |
| Rwanda | 29 | — | — | — | — | — | — | 18 | 36 | 37 |
| Burundi | 111 | — | — | — | — | — | — | 79 | 170 | 66 |
| Zaire | 133 | — | — | — | 77 | 60 | 55 | 424 | 116 | 26 |
| Malawi | 16 | — | — | — | — | — | — | 15 | 17 | 16 |
| Mozambique | 35 | — | — | — | — | — | — | 83 | 6 | 3 |
| Madagascar | 55 | — | — | — | 15 | 104 | 65 | 26 | 65 | 51 |
| Zimbabwe | 136 | — | — | — | — | — | — | 111 | 78 | 277 |
| South Afr. | 3,983 | 670 | 502 | 478 | 1,397 | 4,506 | 7,514 | 2,865 | 3,491 | 4,224 |
| Comoros Is. | 650 | — | — | — | — | — | — | 440 | 904 | 578 |
| Mauritius | 1,224 | — | — | — | 273 | 419 | 1,463 | 1,754 | 1,733 | 2,024 |

| Europe | | | | | | | | | | |
|---|---|---|---|---|---|---|---|---|---|---|
| UK | 1,790 | — | — | — | 121 | 833 | 1,385 | 1,706 | 3,292 | 4,482 |
| France | 199 | — | — | — | 11 | 168 | 232 | 285 | 261 | 262 |
| Germany | 12 | — | — | — | 1 | 1 | 1 | 5 | 31 | 46 |
| Switzerland | 50 | — | — | — | — | — | — | 54 | 15 | 101 |
| Netherlands | 300 | — | — | — | — | — | — | 179 | 277 | 540 |
| Belgium | 52 | — | — | — | — | — | — | 50 | 50 | 60 |
| Denmark | 170 | — | — | — | — | — | — | 100 | 117 | 375 |
| Sweden | 299 | — | — | — | — | — | — | 128 | 205 | 743 |
| Spain | 126 | — | — | — | — | 320 | 48 | 72 | 23 |
| Portugal | 343 | — | — | — | — | 482 | 775 | 170 | 91 | 138 |
| Greece | 1,082 | — | — | 174 | 96 | 964 | 1,609 | 1,591 | 1,342 | 767 |
| Cyprus | 71 | — | — | — | — | — | — | 17 | 164 | 8 |
| Yugoslavia | 269 | — | — | 15 | 44 | 359 | 454 | 260 | 262 | 212 |

| Americas and Australia | | | | | | | | | | |
|---|---|---|---|---|---|---|---|---|---|---|
| Trinidad | 1,118 | — | — | — | — | — | — | 584 | 1,156 | 1,945 |
| Surinam | 173 | — | — | — | — | — | — | — | — | 752 |
| Guyana | 52 | — | — | — | — | — | — | — | — | 225 |
| USA | 73 | — | — | — | 6 | 15 | 31 | 72 | 150 | 222 |
| Canada | 110 | — | — | — | 3 | 3 | 40 | 75 | 214 | 471 |
| Australia | 377 | — | — | — | 14 | 40 | 96 | 164 | 598 | 2,006 |

TABLE A4.4 Regional distribution of the world's Muslims and pilgrims, 1947–1987

| Region | Percent Muslims | 1947–1950 | 1951–1955 | 1956–1960 | 1961–1965 | 1966–1970 | 1971–1974 | 1975–1979 | 1980–1984 | 1985–1987 |
|---|---|---|---|---|---|---|---|---|---|---|
| Arabian Peninsula | 1.4 | 4.6 | 17.8 | 28.6 | 11.5 | 15.4 | 11.2 | 14.5 | 12.1 | 9.8 |
| Fertile Crescent | 3.3 | 3.3 | 9.5 | 10.1 | 16.4 | 14.4 | 13.8 | 15.3 | 11.3 | 7.3 |
| Red Sea | 7.3 | 24.1 | 22.4 | 17.8 | 13.0 | 9.1 | 11.8 | 9.2 | 15.5 | 15.9 |
| North Africa | 6.4 | 2.7 | 4.3 | 2.7 | 7.7 | 9.9 | 11.7 | 12.6 | 10.5 | 9.3 |
| Arab world total | 18.4 | 34.8 | 54.0 | 59.6 | 48.6 | 48.8 | 49.2 | 51.2 | 49.4 | 42.3 |
| | | | | | | | | | | |
| West Asia | 12.1 | 12.7 | 6.6 | 7.7 | 14.8 | 21.2 | 16.2 | 17.5 | 14.6 | 25.1 |
| South Asia | 30.9 | 30.0 | 21.9 | 15.3 | 18.6 | 11.6 | 13.1 | 10.4 | 13.9 | 16.4 |
| Southeast Asia | 17.5 | 16.6 | 10.2 | 8.4 | 9.0 | 8.4 | 8.1 | 7.1 | 10.2 | 4.6 |
| West Africa | 8.8 | 5.2 | 6.9 | 9.0 | 7.8 | 7.8 | 10.2 | 12.0 | 10.6 | 4.6 |
| East Africa | 3.0 | 0.6 | 0.5 | 0.4 | 0.9 | 1.5 | 1.4 | 0.9 | 0.7 | 0.7 |
| Europe | 0.6 | — | — | — | 0.2 | 0.3 | 0.4 | 0.3 | 0.4 | 0.5 |
| Americas and Australia | 0.5 | — | — | — | — | — | — | — | 0.1 | 0.2 |
| Socialist bloc | 8.1 | — | — | — | 0.1 | 0.4 | 0.3 | 0.1 | 0.1 | 0.1 |

TABLE A4.5 Economic, geographic, and religious predictors of pilgrimage rates, 1961–1987 (multiple regression)

**Total Sample**

| Years | $N$ | Per capita Income | Distance from Mecca | Percent Muslim | $p.1$ | $p.2$ | $p.3$ | $R$ | $R^2$ |
|---|---|---|---|---|---|---|---|---|---|
| 1961–1987 | 92 | .483 | −.292 | .397 | .000 | .000 | .000 | .719 | .501 |
| | | | | | | | | | |
| 1961–1965 | 57 | .569 | −.391 | .182 | .000 | .003 | .135 | .693 | .451 |
| 1966–1970 | 62 | .567 | −.433 | .216 | .000 | .000 | .051 | .717 | .490 |
| 1971–1974 | 65 | .467 | −.467 | .279 | .000 | .000 | .010 | .713 | .484 |
| 1975–1979 | 85 | .286 | −.281 | .387 | .002 | .006 | .000 | .619 | .361 |
| 1980–1984 | 90 | .361 | −.161 | .426 | .000 | .090 | .000 | .624 | .368 |
| 1985–1987 | 92 | .419 | −.051 | .405 | .000 | .605 | .000 | .582 | .316 |

**Asia and Africa**

| Years | $N$ | Per capita Income | Distance from Mecca | Percent Muslim | $p.1$ | $p.2$ | $p.3$ | $R$ | $R^2$ |
|---|---|---|---|---|---|---|---|---|---|
| 1961–1987 | 69 | .621 | −.256 | .157 | .000 | .003 | .065 | .801 | .624 |
| | | | | | | | | | |
| 1961–1965 | 53 | .552 | −.210 | .160 | .000 | .083 | .183 | .703 | .464 |
| 1966–1970 | 55 | .610 | −.205 | .133 | .000 | .060 | .218 | .756 | .546 |
| 1971–1974 | 57 | .483 | −.283 | .182 | .000 | .012 | .099 | .733 | .511 |
| 1975–1979 | 69 | .318 | −.310 | .235 | .003 | .005 | .033 | .636 | .377 |
| 1980–1984 | 69 | .461 | −.170 | .237 | .000 | .105 | .029 | .647 | .392 |
| 1985–1987 | 69 | .600 | .065 | .197 | .000 | .520 | .062 | .670 | .423 |

| Years | N | Per capita Income | Distance from Mecca | Percent Muslim | p.1 | p.2 | p.3 | R | R² |
|---|---|---|---|---|---|---|---|---|---|
| 1961–1987 | 62 | .666 | −.276 | .134 | .000 | .004 | .161 | .746 | .533 |
| | | | | | | | | | |
| 1961–1965 | 47 | .411 | −.241 | .161 | .002 | .085 | .246 | .568 | .276 |
| 1966–1970 | 48 | .550 | −.132 | .051 | .000 | .317 | .698 | .596 | .311 |
| 1971–1974 | 50 | .489 | −.218 | .158 | .000 | .085 | .211 | .633 | .362 |
| 1975–1979 | 62 | .510 | −.328 | .172 | .000 | .003 | .113 | .664 | .412 |
| 1980–1984 | 62 | .748 | −.187 | .129 | .000 | .038 | .149 | .781 | .590 |
| 1985–1987 | 62 | .876 | .045 | .051 | .000 | .490 | .441 | .885 | .772 |

TABLE A5.1 Female pilgrims from Pakistan by region, 1974–1988 (percent)

| Region | 1974–1977 | 1985–1988 |
|---|---|---|
| Punjab | 43.1 | 46.4 |
| Sindh | 39.5 | 43.4 |
| Frontier | 22.6 | 28.3 |
| Baluchistan | 12.5 | 17.7 |
| Tribal Areas | 6.4 | 19.6 |
| Pakistan total | 36.6 | 41.2 |

TABLE A5.2 Age distribution of Pakistani pilgrims by gender and region, 1985–1988 (percent)

| | Male | | | Female | | | Total | | |
|---|---|---|---|---|---|---|---|---|---|
| | 18–35 | 36–60 | >60 | 18–35 | 36–60 | >60 | 18–35 | 36–60 | >60 |
| Punjab | 12.3 | 52.8 | 34.9 | 11.2 | 65.6 | 23.1 | 11.8 | 58.8 | 29.5 |
| Sindh | 21.5 | 58.1 | 20.4 | 22.7 | 63.0 | 14.3 | 22.0 | 60.2 | 17.7 |
| Frontier | 14.8 | 61.3 | 23.9 | 11.3 | 72.2 | 16.4 | 13.8 | 64.4 | 21.8 |
| Baluchistan | 16.4 | 67.3 | 16.3 | 10.4 | 72.7 | 16.9 | 15.3 | 68.2 | 16.4 |
| Tribal Areas | 19.2 | 69.3 | 11.4 | 6.8 | 82.4 | 10.9 | 16.8 | 71.9 | 11.3 |
| Pakistan | 14.8 | 56.7 | 28.5 | 13.2 | 66.2 | 20.5 | 14.2 | 60.7 | 25.3 |

TABLE A5.3 Pilgrimage, development, and party vote by region in Pakistan

|  | Punjab | Urban Sindh | Rural Sindh | Frontier | Baluchistan | Pakistan |
|---|---|---|---|---|---|---|
| Population (%) | 56.6 | 9.8 | 12.8 | 15.7 | 5.1 | 100.0 |
| Pilgrims (%) | 58.5 | 14.4 | 4.3 | 17.8 | 5.0 | 100.0 |
| Pilgrims (per million) | 645 | 895 | 256 | 727 | 696 | 641 |
| Agricultural workers (%) | 49.1 | 17.1 | 72.6 | 62.1 | 71.4 | 52.1 |
| Industrial workers (%) | 11.8 | 16.3 | 3.0 | 3.0 | 1.4 | 9.2 |
| Vehicles (per million) | 10,026 | 48,919 | 7,003 | 12,997 | 16,445 | 13,875 |
| Televisions (per million) | 18,744 | 60,399 | 6,511 | 4,393 | — | 17,857 |
| Literacy (%) | 27.4 | 46.2 | 25.1 | 16.7 | 10.3 | 26.2 |
| Qur'anic Literacy (%) | 40.6 | 47.0 | 29.6 | 41.0 | 22.3 | 38.4 |
| Muslim League vote, 1993 (%) | 45.3 | 34.9 | 28.3 | 27.5 | 7.5 | 39.9 |
| People's Party vote, 1993 (%) | 38.8 | 43.6 | 56.4 | 15.8 | 18.7 | 37.9 |

TABLE A5.4 Major correlates of pilgrimage in Pakistan, 1974–1990 (Pearson's $r$, $N = 50$)

|  | 1974–1977 | 1978–1983 | 1984–1988 | 1989–1990 | 1974–1990 |
|---|---|---|---|---|---|
| Service workers | .479 | .691 | .810 | .836 | .758 |
| Industrial workers | −.068 | .108 | .381 | .443 | .201 |
| Agricultural workers | −.358 | −.584 | −.768 | −.809 | −.668 |
| Tractors | .217 | .359 | .516 | .529 | .428 |
| Tube wells | .547 | .509 | .298 | .309 | .482 |
| Qur'anic literacy | .112 | .434 | .701 | .710 | .509 |
| High school enrollment | .208 | .298 | .521 | .653 | .422 |
| Literacy | .016 | .224 | .531 | .598 | .336 |
| Televisions | .376 | .217 | .303 | .484 | .327 |
| Urbanization | .228 | .280 | .449 | .524 | .380 |
| Hospital beds | .476 | .581 | .592 | .626 | .620 |
| Vehicles | .423 | .509 | .575 | .606 | .571 |
| Pashto | .414 | .473 | .334 | .194 | .423 |
| Punjabi | −.141 | .051 | .312 | .383 | .129 |
| Urdu | .131 | .077 | .177 | .244 | .155 |
| Siraiki | −.067 | .027 | .011 | .030 | −.002 |
| Baluchi-Brahvi | −.020 | −.211 | −.352 | −.338 | −.241 |
| Sindhi | −.275 | −.479 | −.513 | −.503 | −.484 |

TABLE A5.5 Pilgrimage and party vote in Pakistan, 1970–1993 (Pearson's $r$, $N = 50$)

| | Pakistan People's Party | Pakistan Muslim League | Jamiat Ulama-i-Islam | Jamiat Ulama-i-Pakistan | Pakistan Islamic Front | Other parties |
|---|---|---|---|---|---|---|
| 1970 | −.317 | −.171 | .368 | −.147. | (c) | .142 |
| 1988 | −.276 | .345 | .213 | .146 | (c) | −.177 |
| 1990 | −.124 | .279 | .193 | (b) | (c) | −.220 (d) |
| 1993 | −.138 | .292 (a) | .142 | (b) | .039 | −.158 (d) |

(a) Nawaz Sharif faction.
(b) Joined multiparty coalitions in 1990 and 1993.
(c) Jamaat-i-Islami party that previously joined coalitions led by the Pakistan Muslim League.
(d) Primarily Pakhtun and Baluchi ethnic parties.

TABLE A5.6 The relative influence of development, ethnicity, and party vote in predicting Pakistani pilgrimage rates (multiple regression, $N = 50$)

| | 1988 Elections | | 1990 Elections | | 1993 Elections | |
|---|---|---|---|---|---|---|
| | beta | p. | beta | p. | beta | p. |
| Urbanization | .302 | .010 | .286 | .021 | .365 | .002 |
| Punjabi-Pashto-Urdu | .394 | .001 | .425 | .001 | .453 | .000 |
| PPP vote | −.357 | .002 | −.228 | .056 | −.320 | .005 |
| | | | | | | |
| $R$ | .679 | | .623 | | .721 | |
| $R$ squared | .461 | | .388 | | .520 | |

Regression of urbanization; households speaking Punjabi, Pashto, or Urdu; and vote for the Pakistan People's Party on average pilgrimage rates 1974–1990.

TABLE A5.7 Hajj rates in Pakistani districts, 1974–1990 (average annual number of pilgrims per million Muslims)

| District/REGION | 1974–1977 | 1978–1983 | 1984–1988 | 1989–1990 | 1974–1990 |
|---|---|---|---|---|---|
| Attock | 477 | 850 | 945 | 843 | 789 |
| Rawalpindi | 731 | 996 | 1,269 | 1,360 | 1,057 |
| Jhelum | 406 | 816 | 1,447 | 1,671 | 1,006 |
| Gujrat | 371 | 640 | 926 | 911 | 693 |
| Gujranwala | 681 | 737 | 768 | 840 | 745 |
| Sialkot | 363 | 549 | 836 | 857 | 626 |
| Sheikhupura | 309 | 322 | 432 | 529 | 375 |
| Lahore | 832 | 844 | 1,049 | 1,276 | 952 |
| Sargodha | 552 | 474 | 665 | 734 | 579 |
| Jhang | 294 | 277 | 305 | 422 | 306 |
| Faisalabad | 539 | 497 | 666 | 809 | 593 |
| Sahiwal | 452 | 341 | 452 | 507 | 419 |
| Multan | 603 | 489 | 783 | 845 | 644 |
| Bahawalnagar | 614 | 504 | 486 | 591 | 535 |
| Bahawalpur | 777 | 905 | 817 | 978 | 858 |
| Mianwali | 365 | 425 | 444 | 583 | 435 |

(continued on next page)

| District/REGION | 1974–1977 | 1978–1983 | 1984–1988 | 1989–1990 | 1974–1990 |
|---|---|---|---|---|---|
| Muzaffargarh | 318 | 314 | 385 | 530 | 361 |
| Dera Ghazi Khan | 349 | 366 | 424 | 332 | 375 |
| Rahimyar Khan | 351 | 392 | 399 | 479 | 395 |
| PUNJAB | 527 | 586 | 736 | 835 | 645 |
| Jacobabad | 403 | 153 | 66 | 69 | 176 |
| Sukkur | 369 | 267 | 258 | 314 | 294 |
| Larkana | 302 | 166 | 168 | 114 | 192 |
| Dadu | 267 | 191 | 202 | 117 | 203 |
| Thatta | 279 | 121 | 112 | 220 | 167 |
| Nawabshah | 377 | 219 | 173 | 161 | 236 |
| Khairpur | 557 | 360 | 172 | 120 | 323 |
| Sanghar | 351 | 197 | 151 | 168 | 216 |
| Tharpakar | 612 | 167 | 108 | 150 | 252 |
| Hyderabad | 456 | 290 | 376 | 529 | 382 |
| Karachi | 1,154 | 1,004 | 1,235 | 1,384 | 1,152 |
| SINDH | 576 | 454 | 545 | 663 | 534 |
| Chitral | 324 | 299 | 307 | 537 | 335 |
| Dir | 234 | 543 | 583 | 366 | 461 |
| Swat | 665 | 813 | 681 | 547 | 708 |
| Hazara | 269 | 459 | 452 | 362 | 401 |
| Malakand | 441 | 577 | 512 | 434 | 509 |
| Mardan | 480 | 528 | 630 | 531 | 547 |
| Peshawar | 862 | 873 | 911 | 845 | 878 |
| Kohat | 1,188 | 1,645 | 1,651 | 1,281 | 1,496 |
| Bannu | 835 | 854 | 1,009 | 915 | 902 |
| Dera Ismail Khan | 1,049 | 1,402 | 1,172 | 1,173 | 1,224 |
| FRONTIER | 593 | 767 | 800 | 696 | 727 |
| Zhob | 2.320 | 1,271 | 477 | 480 | 1,191 |
| Quetta | 2,245 | 1,786 | 1,816 | 2,147 | 1,945 |
| Chagai | 2,050 | 1,419 | 572 | 715 | 1,235 |
| Loralai | 1,047 | 537 | 364 | 472 | 598 |
| Sibi | 278 | 179 | 166 | 253 | 207 |
| Kacchi | 140 | 78 | 53 | 25 | 79 |
| Kalat | 398 | 262 | 128 | 104 | 236 |
| Lasbela | 88 | 61 | 62 | 93 | 72 |
| Makran | 198 | 130 | 134 | 89 | 143 |
| Kharan | 694 | 235 | 111 | 143 | 296 |
| BALUCHISTAN | 914 | 651 | 558 | 737 | 696 |
| Mohmand | 212 | 328 | 477 | 182 | 328 |
| Bajaur | 206 | 537 | 414 | 488 | 417 |
| Khyber | 686 | 952 | 1,553 | 1,129 | 1,087 |
| Kurram | 899 | 1,286 | 1,576 | 851 | 1,229 |
| North Waziristan | 841 | 1,676 | 2,112 | 2,079 | 1,655 |
| South Waziristan | 167 | 226 | 579 | 451 | 342 |
| TRIBAL AREAS | 356 | 585 | 869 | 705 | 629 |
| PAKISTAN | 563 | 592 | 706 | 780 | 641 |

TABLE A6.1 Female pilgrims in
Malaysia, 1968–1995 (percent of
total pilgrims)

| Years | Percent |
|---|---|
| 1968–1975 | 53.3 |
| 1979–1980 | 54.8 |
| 1981–1985 | 55.3 |
| 1986–1990 | 55.5 |
| 1991–1995 | 55.6 |
| 1979–1995 | 55.4 |

TABLE A6.2 Malaysian pilgrims by age groups, 1987–1995 (percent of total pilgrims)

| Age | 1987–1990 | 1991–1992 | 1993–1995 | 1987–1995 |
|---|---|---|---|---|
| 90+ | 0.1 | 0.0 | 0.5 | 0.2 |
| 80–89 | 0.7 | 0.5 | 0.7 | 0.6 |
| 70–79 | 6.2 | 6.1 | 6.4 | 6.0 |
| 60–69 | 22.2 | 23.7 | 21.0 | 22.0 |
| 50–59 | 35.2 | 36.6 | 37.6 | 34.8 |
| 40–49 | 20.3 | 19.1 | 21.2 | 19.5 |
| 30–39 | 11.2 | 10.6 | 10.2 | 10.3 |
| 20–29 | 2.9 | 2.5 | 1.8 | 2.4 |
| 10–19 | 0.8 | 0.5 | 0.6 | 0.6 |
| <10 | 0.3 | 0.2 | 0.2 | 0.2 |

TABLE A6.3 Occupations of Malaysian pilgrims, 1979–1995 (percent of total pilgrims)

| | 1979–1980 | 1981–1985 | 1986–1990 | 1991–1995 | 1979–1995 |
|---|---|---|---|---|---|
| Housewife | 31.6 | 37.6 | 40.0 | 30.4 | 35.6 |
| Self-employed | 5.1 | 14.1 | 11.2 | 16.9 | 13.6 |
| Civil servant | 12.9 | 13.5 | 13.9 | 11.8 | 13.0 |
| Farmer | 16.7 | 16.1 | 10.1 | 7.5 | 11.2 |
| Pensioner | 5.9 | 5.9 | 8.4 | 9.7 | 8.0 |
| Trader | 4.9 | 4.7 | 4.4 | 4.1 | 4.4 |
| Private sector | 4.7 | 0.8 | 2.2 | 3.0 | 2.3 |
| Teacher | 0.0 | 0.1 | 2.5 | 3.8 | 2.2 |
| Student | 9.5 | 0.7 | 0.9 | 3.2 | 2.1 |
| Worker | 2.5 | 1.5 | 1.5 | 2.2 | 1.8 |
| Child | 0.4 | 0.4 | 1.4 | 0.1 | 0.6 |
| Fisherman | 0.2 | 0.3 | 0.3 | 0.6 | 0.4 |
| Other | 1.3 | 0.7 | 1.5 | 1.3 | 1.2 |
| Unknown | 4.0 | 3.5 | 1.7 | 5.3 | 3.6 |

TABLE A6.4 Pilgrimage and socioeconomic characteristics in Malaysia, 1969–1995 (Pearson's r, N = 13)

| | 1969–1970 | 1971–1975 | 1976–1980 | 1981–1985 | 1986–1990 | 1991–1995 | 1969–1995 |
|---|---|---|---|---|---|---|---|
| Muslims | .488 | .222 | .375 | .456 | −.039 | −.406 | .123 |
| Buddhists | −.323 | .016 | .212 | −.051 | .519 | .803 | .379 |
| Confucians | −.412 | −.259 | −.173 | −.359 | .163 | .552 | .007 |
| Hindus | −.214 | .087 | .218 | .001 | .504 | .697 | .381 |
| Christians | −.259 | −.253 | −.655 | −.479 | −.492 | −.365 | −.536 |
| Tribals | −.191 | −.267 | −.484 | −.320 | −.330 | −.194 | −.368 |
| | | | | | | | |
| Malays | .520 | .303 | .599 | .634 | .254 | −.063 | .407 |
| Chinese | −.430 | −.104 | −.030 | −.248 | .325 | .688 | .171 |
| Indians | −.228 | .135 | .249 | .001 | .489 | .684 | .383 |
| Others | −.388 | −.259 | −.454 | −.540 | −.425 | −.336 | −.514 |
| | | | | | | | |
| Rural water | −.298 | .007 | .372 | .157 | .732 | .868 | .546 |
| Urban water | −.824 | −.572 | −.343 | −.420 | .166 | .482 | −.131 |
| Average age | −.409 | .003 | .159 | −.105 | .482 | .759 | .325 |
| Age dependency | .511 | .014 | .001 | .274 | −.265 | −.605 | −.133 |
| | | | | | | | |
| Literacy | −.209 | .110 | .542 | .250 | .644 | .751 | .553 |
| Primary edu. | −.189 | −.563 | −.103 | −.062 | .274 | .301 | .034 |
| Secondary edu. | .114 | .327 | .581 | .290 | .626 | .771 | .614 |
| Higher edu. | −.045 | .605 | .537 | .218 | .183 | .185 | .331 |
| No school | .171 | −.124 | −.568 | −.281 | −.664 | −.767 | −.583 |
| | | | | | | | |
| Urbanization | −.235 | .308 | .244 | −.016 | .137 | .395 | .210 |
| GDP per cap. | −.495 | .111 | .103 | −.169 | .125 | .362 | .101 |
| Manufacturing | −.294 | .371 | .222 | −.104 | .183 | .463 | .201 |
| | | | | | | | |
| GDP agric.* | .222 | −.231 | −.136 | .086 | −.061 | −.307 | −.128 |
| GDP industry* | −.539 | −.110 | −.263 | −.468 | −.265 | .055 | −.330 |
| GDP services* | .188 | .413 | .423 | .307 | .323 | .366 | .473 |

*Excluding Sabah and Sarawak.


TABLE A6.5 Pilgrimage and party vote in Malaysia, 1969–1999 (Pearson's r, N = 13)

| Election | Barisan Nasional | Parti Islam SeMalaysia | Democratic Action Party | Parti Melayu Semangat '46 | Parti Keadilan |
|---|---|---|---|---|---|
| 1959* | −.502** | .741** | — | — | — |
| 1964* | −.513** | .707** | −.177** | — | — |
| 1969 | −.149 | .620 | −.297** | — | — |
| 1974 | .180 | *** | −.228** | — | — |
| 1978 | −.245 | .473 | .071** | — | — |
| 1982 | −.130 | .552 | −.140 | — | — |
| 1986 | −.092 | −.001 | .434 | — | — |

| Election | Barisan Nasional | Parti Islam SeMalaysia | Democratic Action Party | Parti Melayu Semangat '46 | Parti Keadilan |
|---|---|---|---|---|---|
| 1990 | .598 | −.441 | .521 | .289 | — |
| 1995 | .654 | −.276 | .577 | −.354 | — |
| 1999 | .268 | −.390 | .629 | — | .383 |

*Voting in 1959 and 1964 was correlated with the 1969–1970 pilgrimages.
**Excluding Sabah and Sarawak.
***PAS was part of the Barisan Nasional in the 1974 elections.

TABLE A6.6 Party vote in the 1999 elections and hajj participation, 1969–1995 (Pearson's $r$, $N = 13$)

| Barisan Nasional | Barisan Alternatif | UMNO | Parti Islam SeMalaysia | Democratic Action Party | Parti Keadilan |
|---|---|---|---|---|---|
| −.285 | .590 | .045 | .206 | .371 | .221 |

TABLE A7.1 The shrinking gender gap in religious education in Turkey, 1973–1995

| Year | Junior high schools (percent female) | | Senior high schools (percent female) | | İmam-Hatip/general (percent) | |
|---|---|---|---|---|---|---|
| | İmam-Hatip | General | İmam-Hatip | General | Junior high | Senior high |
| 1973 | 2.4 | 28.4 | 1.4 | 31.7 | 1.8 | 6.6 |
| 1980 | 12.0 | 33.4 | 9.3 | 35.7 | 11.3 | 8.9 |
| 1986 | 15.4 | 35.2 | 15.4 | 43.0 | 8.5 | 13.0 |
| 1990 | 28.6 | 36.8 | 23.7 | 42.9 | 9.9 | 12.5 |
| 1995 | 41.0 | 38.4 | 38.2 | 42.3 | 13.4 | 15.7 |

TABLE A7.2 Turkish pilgrimage rates by province, 1979–1993

| Province/REGION | 1979–1984 | 1985–1989 | 1990–1993 | 1979–1993 |
|---|---|---|---|---|
| Edirne | 232 | 578 | 319 | 371 |
| Kırklareli | 343 | 720 | 397 | 483 |
| Tekirdağ | 400 | 1,139 | 684 | 722 |
| İstanbul | 701 | 1,363 | 731 | 930 |
| THRACE | 635 | 1,245 | 697 | 855 |
| | | | | |
| Çanakkale | 744 | 1,440 | 547 | 923 |
| Balıkesir | 804 | 1,748 | 544 | 1,049 |
| Manisa | 656 | 1,384 | 253 | 791 |
| İzmir | 345 | 681 | 373 | 464 |
| Aydın | 392 | 690 | 342 | 478 |
| Muğla | 184 | 410 | 310 | 293 |
| AEGEAN | 497 | 998 | 379 | 633 |

(continued on next page)

TABLE A7.2 (continued)

| Province/REGION | 1979–1984 | 1985–1989 | 1990–1993 | 1979–1993 |
|---|---|---|---|---|
| Bursa | 1,252 | 2,477 | 1,118 | 1,625 |
| Bilecik | 1,150 | 1,720 | 597 | 1,193 |
| Eskişehir | 1,197 | 1,586 | 599 | 1,167 |
| Kütahya | 2,138 | 2,414 | 1,064 | 1,944 |
| Afyon | 1,083 | 1,609 | 743 | 1,168 |
| Uşak | 829 | 1,855 | 841 | 1,174 |
| Denizli | 699 | 1,348 | 711 | 919 |
| Burdur | 698 | 1,384 | 957 | 996 |
| Isparta | 821 | 1,630 | 983 | 1,134 |
| WESTERN | 1,155 | 1,883 | 895 | 1,328 |
| | | | | |
| Ankara | 838 | 1,480 | 1,022 | 1,101 |
| Çankırı | 603 | 1,110 | 935 | 861 |
| Çorum | 733 | 1,407 | 805 | 977 |
| Amasya | 629 | 1,201 | 841 | 876 |
| Tokat | 568 | 1,186 | 794 | 834 |
| Yozgat | 778 | 1,895 | 869 | 1,175 |
| Sivas | 480 | 984 | 690 | 704 |
| Kayseri | 1,167 | 2,390 | 1,066 | 1,548 |
| Nevşehir | 1,232 | 3,022 | 1,401 | 1,874 |
| Kırsehir | 890 | 1,822 | 940 | 1,214 |
| Niğde | 696 | 1,540 | 1,044 | 1,070 |
| Konya | 1,324 | 2,453 | 930 | 1,595 |
| CENTRAL | 881 | 1,773 | 984 | 1,206 |
| | | | | |
| Kocaeli | 896 | 1,438 | 262 | 908 |
| Sakarya | 1,203 | 2,520 | 493 | 1,453 |
| Bolu | 958 | 2,001 | 744 | 1,249 |
| Zonguldak | 525 | 740 | 529 | 598 |
| Kastamonu | 481 | 992 | 742 | 721 |
| Sinop | 320 | 639 | 344 | 433 |
| Samsun | 580 | 1,354 | 833 | 905 |
| Ordu | 306 | 530 | 425 | 412 |
| Giresun | 353 | 803 | 566 | 560 |
| Gümüşhane | 771 | 1,274 | 791 | 944 |
| Trabzon | 861 | 1,778 | 785 | 1,146 |
| Rize | 659 | 1,522 | 962 | 1,027 |
| Artvin | 219 | 446 | 319 | 321 |
| BLACK SEA | 642 | 1,286 | 597 | 845 |
| | | | | |
| Antalya | 333 | 831 | 580 | 565 |
| İçel | 354 | 640 | 412 | 465 |
| Adana | 275 | 620 | 445 | 435 |
| Hatay | 231 | 687 | 308 | 404 |
| MEDITERRANEAN | 294 | 674 | 437 | 459 |
| | | | | |
| Kars | 168 | 410 | 281 | 279 |
| Ağrı | 110 | 329 | 194 | 205 |
| Erzurum | 474 | 961 | 615 | 674 |

| Province/REGION | 1979–1984 | 1985–1989 | 1990–1993 | 1979–1993 |
|---|---|---|---|---|
| Erzincan | 669 | 1,144 | 734 | 845 |
| Tunceli | 4 | 47 | 41 | 28 |
| Bingöl | 214 | 639 | 360 | 395 |
| Muş | 131 | 261 | 120 | 171 |
| NORTH EAST | 287 | 633 | 383 | 428 |
| | | | | |
| Malatya | 344 | 728 | 481 | 506 |
| Elazığ | 401 | 818 | 700 | 620 |
| Maraş | 407 | 886 | 316 | 542 |
| Gaziantep | 517 | 1,180 | 390 | 704 |
| Adıyaman | 158 | 509 | 311 | 316 |
| Urfa | 484 | 1,087 | 197 | 608 |
| Diyarbakır | 336 | 786 | 343 | 488 |
| Mardin | 438 | 688 | 129 | 439 |
| Siirt | 217 | 535 | 671 | 440 |
| Bitlis | 182 | 326 | 126 | 215 |
| Van | 176 | 671 | 294 | 372 |
| Hakkâri | 239 | 435 | 228 | 301 |
| SOUTH EAST | 360 | 808 | 350 | 507 |

TABLE A7.3 The social and economic correlates of pilgrimage in Turkey, 1979–1993 (Pearson's r, N = 67)

| | Total pilgrims | Male pilgrims | Female pilgrims | Percent female |
|---|---|---|---|---|
| Urban income | .467 | .397 | .502 | .622 |
| Rural income | .404 | .294 | .485 | .688 |
| | | | | |
| Literacy | .481 | .400 | .526 | .634 |
| Junior high school students | .280 | .183 | .358 | .561 |
| Newspapers | .116 | .035 | .190 | .395 |
| | | | | |
| Vehicles | .394 | .280 | .481 | .644 |
| Telephones | .472 | .388 | .522 | .627 |
| Hospital beds | .316 | .307 | .301 | .288 |
| Electricity consumption | .322 | .246 | .375 | .580 |
| | | | | |
| Industrial workers | .350 | .276 | .398 | .482 |
| Service workers | .147 | .062 | .224 | .419 |
| Agricultural workers | −.248 | −.161 | −.318 | −.481 |
| | | | | |
| Landowners | −.104 | .027 | −.229 | −.537 |
| Landowners and renters | .119 | −.008 | .239 | .529 |
| Land renters | −.064 | −.170 | .049 | .346 |
| | | | | |
| Turkish | .496 | .454 | .501 | .558 |
| Kurdish | −.489 | −.442 | −.499 | −.592 |
| Arabic | −.219 | −.233 | −.187 | −.014 |
| Slavic languages | −.031 | −.070 | .011 | .201 |

(continued on next page)

| | Total pilgrims | Male pilgrims | Female pilgrims | Percent female |
|---|---|---|---|---|
| Urban mosques | .552 | .508 | .554 | .388 |
| Rural mosques | .133 | .279 | −.027 | −.331 |
| Qur'an course students | .681 | .667 | .643 | .418 |
| İmam-Hatip students | .415 | .479 | .317 | .068 |
| Islamic associations | .588 | .581 | .550 | .338 |

TABLE A7.4 Pilgrimage and party vote in Turkey, 1979–1993 (Pearson's *r*, *N* = 67)

| Party | Total pilgrims | Male pilgrims | Female pilgrims | Percent female |
|---|---|---|---|---|
| Democratic Party (DP) 1950 | .282 | .221 | .320 | .424 |
| Justice Party (AP) 1969 | .512 | .433 | .554 | .565 |
| Motherland Party (ANAP) 1983 | .633 | .606 | .612 | .463 |
| Rightist parties 1995 | .445 | .517 | .336 | .098 |
| National Action Party (MHP) 1995 | .285 | .263 | .286 | .264 |
| Welfare Party (RP) 1995 | .181 | .276 | .071 | −.235 |
| Motherland Party (ANAP) 1995 | .156 | .280 | .018 | −.121 |
| True Path Party (DYP) 1995 | .078 | −.044 | .197 | .412 |
| Leftist parties 1995 | .048 | −.069 | .163 | .478 |
| Democratic Left Party (DSP) 1995 | .125 | .027 | .215 | .428 |
| Republican Peoples Party (CHP) 1995 | −.091 | −.176 | .003 | .327 |
| [Kurdish] People's Democratic Party (HADEP) 1995 | −.419 | −.384 | −.423 | −.484 |

TABLE A7.5 The combined effects of politics, culture, and economics on Turkey's pilgrimage, 1979–1993 (multiple regression, *N* = 67)

| | Beta | Probability |
|---|---|---|
| Qur'an course students | .408 | .000 |
| Urban mosques | .372 | .000 |
| RPP vote, 1995 | −.215 | .027 |
| Turkish | .194 | .140 |
| Rural income | .144 | .152 |

*R* = .812, *R* squared = .659.

TABLE A8.1 Pilgrimage, income, and party vote in Java

| | Pilgrimage rates | | GDP per capita · (dollars) | | Party vote, 1955 (percent) | | | |
|---|---|---|---|---|---|---|---|---|
| | 1950–1970 | 1974–1996 | 1971 | 1990 · | Masjumi | NU | PNI | PKI |
| Jakarta | 242 | 1,415 | 248 | 1,668 | 26.0 | 15.7 | 19.6 | 12.0 |
| West Java | 145 | 571 | 88 | 445 | 26.4 | 9.6 | 22.1 | 10.8 |
| East Java | 98 | 408 | 89 | 516 | 11.2 | 34.1 | 22.8 | 23.2 |
| Central Java | 67 | 198 | 74 | 388 | 9.3 | 20.3 | 34.1 | 25.3 |
| Yogyakarta | 24 | 167 | 76 | 373 | 17.6 | 13.0 | 27.2 | 31.1 |

TABLE A8.2 Female pilgrims and repeating pilgrims in Indonesia, 1985–1989 (percent)

| Region | Female | Made at least one previous pilgrimage |
|---|---|---|
| Sumatra | 56.6 | 6.4 |
| Java | 49.5 | 5.9 |
| Nusa Tenggara | 35.0 | 3.0 |
| Kalimantan | 56.0 | 6.9 |
| Sulawesi | 63.8 | 2.7 |
| Maluku-Irian Jaya | 51.0 | 1.9 |
| Government-military | 52.0 | 14.4 |
| Indonesia | 52.3 | 5.5 |

TABLE A8.3 Ages of Indonesian pilgrims, 1985–1989 (percent)

| Region | <29 | 30–39 | 40–49 | 50–59 | 60+ |
|---|---|---|---|---|---|
| Sumatra | 3.1 | 13.9 | 26.8 | 30.9 | 25.3 |
| Java | 7.5 | 21.0 | 27.9 | 26.7 | 16.9 |
| Nusa Tenggara | 5.3 | 31.7 | 31.0 | 20.9 | 11.1 |
| Kalimantan | 13.9 | 30.5 | 27.1 | 17.9 | 10.6 |
| Sulawesi | 14.6 | 30.0 | 28.6 | 18.4 | 8.4 |
| Maluku-Irian Jaya | 14.0 | 27.4 | 23.7 | 19.9 | 15.0 |
| Government-military | 6.3 | 14.3 | 26.5 | 29.7 | 23.2 |
| Indonesia | 8.2 | 21.9 | 27.8 | 25.5 | 16.6 |

TABLE A8.4 Educational backgrounds of Indonesian pilgrims, 1985–1989 (percent)

| Region | Less than elementary | Elementary | Junior high | Senior high | University |
|---|---|---|---|---|---|
| Sumatra | 13.6 | 42.0 | 17.7 | 20.4 | 6.3 |
| Java | 17.1 | 48.2 | 13.4 | 15.5 | 5.8 |
| Nusa Tenggara | 27.2 | 46.0 | 13.3 | 9.3 | 4.2 |
| Kalimantan | 13.3 | 52.7 | 14.0 | 16.2 | 3.8 |
| Sulawesi | 22.0 | 48.2 | 13.7 | 12.1 | 4.0 |
| Maluku-Irian Jaya | 24.9 | 51.7 | 11.3 | 8.8 | 3.3 |
| Government-Military | 7.3 | 29.9 | 25.3 | 26.9 | 10.6 |
| Indonesia | 16.1 | 45.9 | 15.3 | 16.8 | 5.9 |

TABLE A8.5 Occupational backgrounds of Indonesian pilgrims, 1985–1989 (percent)

| Region | Farmer | Merchant | Civil servant | Pensioner | Housewife |
|---|---|---|---|---|---|
| Sumatra | 27.3 | 21.0 | 12.2 | 5.4 | 34.1 |
| Java | 38.5 | 21.5 | 10.7 | 4.1 | 25.2 |
| Nusa Tenggara | 11.4 | 50.2 | 8.4 | 2.0 | 28.0 |
| Kalimantan | 18.3 | 24.4 | 12.8 | 3.9 | 40.6 |
| Sulawesi | 23.1 | 23.7 | 13.4 | 2.5 | 37.3 |
| Maluku-Irian Jaya | 25.8 | 30.0 | 7.2 | 1.8 | 35.2 |
| Government-military | 12.7 | 16.4 | 17.2 | 10.0 | 43.7 |
| Indonesia | 30.5 | 21.7 | 12.0 | 4.6 | 31.2 |

TABLE A8.6 Indonesian pilgrimage rates by province, 1974–1996 (average annual number of pilgrims per million Muslims)

| Region | 1974–1979 | 1980–1989 | 1990–1996 | 1974–1996 |
|---|---|---|---|---|
| Aceh | 389 | 445 | 732 | 512 |
| North Sumatra | 370 | 383 | 643 | 455 |
| West Sumatra | 318 | 378 | 631 | 434 |
| Riau | 380 | 400 | 814 | 515 |
| Jambi | 825 | 497 | 567 | 613 |
| South Sumatra | 425 | 319 | 363 | 363 |
| Bengkulu | 267 | 246 | 307 | 270 |
| Lampung | 290 | 112 | 184 | 185 |
| SUMATRA | 352 | 326 | 513 | 388 |
| Jakarta | 1,495 | 710 | 2,489 | 1,458 |
| West Java | 521 | 336 | 987 | 580 |
| Central Java | 136 | 144 | 373 | 208 |
| Yogyakarta | 59 | 101 | 386 | 172 |

| Region | 1974–1979 | 1980–1989 | 1990–1996 | 1974–1996 |
|---|---|---|---|---|
| East Java | 313 | 308 | 680 | 418 |
| JAVA | 363 | 284 | 806 | 459 |
| | | | | |
| Bali | 384 | 585 | 1,634 | 832 |
| W. Nusa Tenggara | 662 | 592 | 1,027 | 739 |
| E. Nusa Tenggara | 281 | 477 | 717 | 490 |
| East Timor | — | 609 | 964 | — |
| NUSA TENGGARA | 586 | 561 | 995 | 694 |
| | | | | |
| West Kalimantan | 370 | 266 | 426 | 342 |
| Central Kalimantan | 619 | 669 | 1,163 | 798 |
| South Kalimantan | 1,325 | 1,161 | 1,767 | 1,386 |
| East Kalimantan | 1,426 | 1,299 | 1,961 | 1,529 |
| KALIMANTAN | 902 | 837 | 1,328 | 999 |
| | | | | |
| North Sulawesi | 116 | 120 | 229 | 151 |
| Central Sulawesi | 442 | 391 | 577 | 460 |
| South Sulawesi | 609 | 1,132 | 2,048 | 1,246 |
| Southeast Sulawesi | 180 | 336 | 779 | 420 |
| SULAWESI | 459 | 808 | 1,428 | 887 |
| | | | | |
| Maluku | 699 | 445 | 448 | 520 |
| Irian Jaya | 711 | 1,291 | 1,891 | 1,297 |
| EASTERN INDONESIA | 618 | 570 | 743 | 640 |
| | | | | |
| INDONESIA | 413 | 396 | 901 | 548 |

TABLE A8.7 The strongest correlates of hajj participation in Indonesia, 1974–1996 (Pearson's *r*)

| | All Indonesia (27 provinces) | | | | Minus Jakarta, East Timor, and Irian Jaya (24 provinces) | | | |
|---|---|---|---|---|---|---|---|---|
| | 1974–1979 | 1980–1989 | 1990–1996 | 1974–1996 | 1974–1979 | 1980–1989 | 1990–1996 | 1974–1996 |
| GDP per capita | .703 | .420 | .631 | .636 | .609 | .547 | .486 | .568 |
| Urbanization | .704 | .314 | .563 | .559 | .602 | .495 | .325 | .481 |
| | | | | | | | | |
| Air passengers | .771 | .573 | .726 | .736 | .657 | .656 | .589 | .667 |
| Port revenues | .527 | .478 | .398 | .489 | .557 | .511 | .416 | .513 |
| Buses and trucks | .540 | .343 | .540 | .524 | .283 | .344 | .303 | .331 |
| | | | | | | | | |
| Non-energy exports | .578 | .556 | .338 | .503 | .662 | .510 | .315 | .498 |
| Cash crops | −.417 | −.538 | −.675 | −.617 | −.316 | −.493 | −.628 | −.533 |
| Forestry, fish, & livestock | .650 | .580 | .470 | .596 | .694 | .668 | .517 | .650 |

(continued on next page)

| | All Indonesia (27 provinces) | | | | Minus Jakarta, East Timor, and Irian Jaya (24 provinces) | | | |
|---|---|---|---|---|---|---|---|---|
| | 1974–1979 | 1980–1989 | 1990–1996 | 1974–1996 | 1974–1979 | 1980–1989 | 1990–1996 | 1974–1996 |
| Agric. workers | −.614 | −.260 | −.596 | −.545 | −.419 | −.425 | −.524 | −.491 |
| Service workers | .656 | .252 | .586 | .546 | .514 | .471 | .525 | .534 |
| TV viewers | .656 | .263 | .563 | .523 | .502 | .393 | .311 | .414 |
| Cinema viewers | .726 | .375 | .536 | .568 | .605 | .478 | .349 | .486 |
| Telephones | .604 | .231 | .584 | .512 | .448 | .460 | .454 | .482 |

TABLE A8.8 Pilgrimage and party vote in Indonesia, 1971–1999

| | (Pearson's r) All Indonesia (27 provinces) | | | Minus Jakarta, East Timor, and Irian Jaya (24 Provinces) | | |
|---|---|---|---|---|---|---|
| | Golkar | PPP | PDI | Golkar | PPP | PDI |
| 1971 | −.226 | .302 | −.023 | −.059 | .195 | −.155 |
| 1977 | −.354 | .354 | −.065 | −.193 | .331 | −.343 |
| 1982 | .160 | −.083 | −.237 | .087 | .038 | −.334 |
| 1987 | .076 | .016 | −.074 | .017 | .149 | −.146 |
| 1992 | −.103 | .083 | .149 | .023 | .024 | −.021 |
| 1999 | .022 | .025 | .096 | .158 | .002 | .019 |

Using hajj rates for corresponding five-year periods.

(Multiple Regression)

| | (27 Provinces) | | (24 Provinces) | |
|---|---|---|---|---|
| | beta | p | beta | p |
| Air passengers | .620 | .000 | .570 | .000 |
| Cash crops | −.500 | .001 | −.502 | .002 |
| Golkar 1992 | .401 | .008 | .393 | .018 |
| PPP 1977 | .232 | .083 | .295 | .052 |
| Multiple R | .873 | | .835 | |
| Multiple R squared | .762 | | .698 | |

Using average hajj rates for 1974–1996.

TABLE A9.1 Hajj rates in the states of Nigeria, 1977–1982 and 1997–1999

| State/REGION | Average number of hajjis per year | | Hajjis per million Muslims | | Percent Muslim |
|---|---|---|---|---|---|
| | 1977–1982 | 1997–1999 | 1977–1982 | 1997–1999 | 1980 |
| Sokoto-Kebbi | 5,423 | 3,796 | 843 | 611 | 95 |
| Kaduna-Katsina | 10,658 | 4,077 | 2,324 | 707 | 75 |
| Kano-Jigawa | 14,211 | 3,187 | 1,753 | 390 | 94 |
| Borno-Yobe | 5,236 | 1,434 | 1,259 | 392 | 93 |
| Bauchi | 2,936 | 1,218 | 975 | 337 | 83 |
| NORTH | 38,464 | 13,712 | 1,463 | 500 | 89 |
| | | | | | |
| Niger | 2,256 | 1,007 | 1,507 | 495 | 84 |
| Kwara | 3,366 | 463 | 2,001 | 272 | 65 |
| Plateau | 2,945 | 680 | 2,565 | 540 | 38 |
| Adamawa-Taraba | 2,057 | 683 | 945 | 337 | 56 |
| Benue | 748 | 202 | 421 | 108 | 49 |
| Abuja | — | 1,239 | — | 606 | 54 |
| MIDDLE BELT | 11,372 | 4,273 | 1,390 | 480 | 56 |
| | | | | | |
| Oyo-Osun | 3,365 | 632 | 699 | 182 | 62 |
| Ondo-Ekiti | 524 | 96 | 378 | 75 | 34 |
| Ogun | 1,365 | 421 | 861 | 291 | 62 |
| Lagos | 3,719 | 1,195 | 2,527 | 360 | 58 |
| Bendel | 917 | 102 | 862 | 74 | 29 |
| SOUTHWEST | 9,890 | 2,444 | 958 | 224 | 50 |
| | | | | | |
| Anambra-Enugu | 196 | 69 | 1,221 | 386 | 3 |
| Imo-Abia | 578 | 33 | 5,257 | 341 | 2 |
| Cross River-Akwa Ibom | 273 | 65 | 2,628 | 750 | 2 |
| Rivers | 193 | 141 | 3,866 | 1,624 | 2 |
| SOUTHEAST | 1,240 | 308 | 2,906 | 686 | 2 |
| | | | | | |
| Nigeria | 60,966 | 20,737 | 1,345 | 435 | 54 |

TABLE A9.2 Correlates of hajj participation in Nigeria, 1977–1982 and 1997–1999

| | North, Middle Belt, and West (N = 15) | | North & Middle Belt (N = 10) | |
|---|---|---|---|---|
| | 1977–1982 | 1997–1999 | 1977–1982 | 1997–1999 |
| Agricultural workers | −.464 | −.180 | −.435 | −.279 |
| Manufac. workers | .622 | .383 | .775 | .476 |
| Service workers | −.081 | .029 | −.514 | .163 |
| Construction workers | .449 | .012 | .502 | .687 |
| Civil servants | .603 | .033 | .629 | −.011 |
| | | | | |
| Development index | .318 | −.256 | .295 | −.199 |
| Urbanization | −.462 | −.697 | −.220 | −.519 |
| Farm size | −.015 | .609 | −.344 | .426 |

(continued on next page)

| | North, Middle Belt, and West (N = 15) | | North & Middle Belt (N = 10) | |
|---|---|---|---|---|
| | 1977–1982 | 1997–1999 | 1977–1982 | 1997–1999 |
| Potable water | .522 | .088 | .618 | .671 |
| Hospital size | .280 | −.300 | .702 | .160 |
| Pharmacies | .443 | −.042 | .744 | .104 |
| Newspapers | .374 | −.197 | .198 | −.257 |
| Fuel consumption | .448 | −.021 | .614 | .287 |
| Roads | −.016 | −.382 | .408 | −.143 |
| Govt. budget | .440 | .002 | .238 | −.159 |
| Primary students | −.054 | −.627 | −.070 | −.657 |
| Secondary students | −.138 | −.589 | .325 | −.213 |
| University students | −.429 | −.639 | −.176 | −.586 |
| Polytechnic students | .265 | .099 | .715 | .531 |
| Qur'an school studs. | — | — | .517 | .721 |
| Islamic sec. students | — | — | .103 | .564 |
| Hausa-Fulani | .205 | .677 | .067 | .573 |
| Yoruba | −.147 | −.453 | .274 | −.296 |
| Muslim 1980 | .169 | .579 | −.184 | .297 |
| Muslim 1952 | — | — | .072 | .510 |
| Christian 1952 | — | — | .468 | −.221 |
| Traditional 1952 | — | — | −.159 | −.530 |
| Shagari 1979 | −.074 | — | −.508 | — |
| Awolowo 1979 | −.217 | — | .210 | — |
| Shagari 1983 | −.107 | — | −.404 | — |
| Awolowo 1983 | −.154 | — | .122 | — |
| Abiola 1993 | — | −596 | — | −.454 |
| Obasanjo 1999 | — | .333 | — | .015 |

TABLE A9.3 The hajj in the local governments of Kaduna State, 1999

| Local government/ REGION | Hajjis per million population | Percent female hajjis | Average age, males | Average age, females | Average age, total |
|---|---|---|---|---|---|
| BIRNIN GWARI | 313 | 11.36 | 41.90 | 38.20 | 41.47 |
| Zaria | 909 | 33.33 | 37.95 | 37.75 | 37.72 |
| Sabon Gari | 465 | 43.43 | 37.09 | 34.67 | 36.04 |
| Makarfi | } 397 | 36.51 | 36.74 | 34.96 | 36.09 |
| Kudan (Hunkuyi) | | 8.33 | 39.60 | 40.00 | 39.62 |
| Giwa | 552 | 26.60 | 39.26 | 41.56 | 39.87 |
| Igabi | 278 | 30.12 | 36.84 | 38.36 | 37.30 |

| Local government/ REGION | Hajjis per million population | Percent female hajjis | Average age, males | Average age, females | Average age, total |
|---|---|---|---|---|---|
| Soba | 400 | 24.00 | 40.46 | 39.22 | 40.16 |
| ZARIA | 506 | 31.88 | 38.17 | 37.30 | 37.90 |
| | | | | | |
| Ikara | 284 | 39.22 | 39.97 | 38.00 | 39.20 |
| Kubau (Anchau) | 516 | 23.53 | 41.60 | 38.95 | 40.98 |
| IKARA | 395 | 29.41 | 41.07 | 38.47 | 40.31 |
| | | | | | |
| Kaduna North (Doka) | 775 | 51.02 | 38.81 | 37.91 | 38.35 |
| Kaduna South (Makera) | 679 | 39.13 | 38.04 | 33.25 | 36.16 |
| HQ 1 (Tudun Wada) | 1,634 | 53.98 | 39.28 | 36.91 | 38.00 |
| HQ 2 (Kawo) | 2,887 | 46.60 | 39.91 | 35.22 | 37.72 |
| HQ 3 (Gabasawa) | 906 | 18.18 | 41.09 | 39.08 | 40.73 |
| KADUNA CITY | 1,576 | 47.46 | 39.51 | 36.22 | 37.95 |
| | | | | | |
| Lere | 570 | 30.95 | 41.01 | 37.08 | 39.79 |
| Kauru | 172 | 31.81 | 37.33 | 30.86 | 35.27 |
| LERE | 424 | 31.08 | 40.47 | 36.13 | 39.12 |
| | | | | | |
| Chikun (Kujama) | 187 | 32.26 | 40.14 | 32.50 | 37.68 |
| Kajuru | 75 | 30.00 | 41.71 | 39.00 | 40.90 |
| Kachia | 158 | 30.00 | 37.78 | 36.00 | 37.25 |
| Kagarko | 44 | 50.00 | 35.00 | 32.50 | 33.75 |
| Zangon Kataf (Zonkwa) | 94 | 28.57 | 44.20 | 38.00 | 42.43 |
| KACHIA | 119 | 31.64 | 40.30 | 35.00 | 38.62 |
| | | | | | |
| Jema'a (Kafanchan) | 69 | 40.00 | 39.22 | 35.50 | 37.56 |
| Sanga (Gwantu) | 23 | 33.33 | 47.00 | 34.00 | 42.67 |
| Jaba (Kwoi) | 15 | — | — | — | — |
| Kaura (Kagoro) | 0 | — | — | — | — |
| JEMA'A | 47 | 42.10 | 40.64 | 34.87 | 38.21 |
| | | | | | |
| TOTAL STATE | 563 | 38.93 | 39.34 | 36.55 | 38.25 |
| Excluding Kaduna City | 342 | 30.77 | 39.22 | 37.04 | 38.54 |

TABLE A9.4 The hajj in the local governments of Lagos State, 1999

| Local government/ REGION | Hajjis per million population | Percent female hajjis | Average age, males | Average age, females | Average age, total |
|---|---|---|---|---|---|
| Lagos Island | 1,004 | 58.18 | 44.18 | 43.73 | 43.86 |
| Eti-Osa | } 339 | 35.55 | 48.71 | 48.41 | 48.57 |
| Apapa | | 38.46 | 45.14 | 45.16 | 45.15 |
| Lagos Mainland | } 133 | 75.00 | — | — | — |
| Surulere | | 56.52 | 40.19 | 46.78 | 43.67 |
| LAGOS CITY | 281 | 55.16 | 44.97 | 44.48 | 44.70 |

(continued on next page)

| Local government/ REGION | Hajjis per million population | Percent female hajjis | Average age, males | Average age, females | Average age, total |
|---|---|---|---|---|---|
| Ikeja | }283 | 53.57 | 43.04 | 48.50 | 47.53 |
| Alimosho | | 49.48 | 43.58 | 42.66 | 43.14 |
| Agege | }157 | 51.32 | 43.71 | 37.19 | 40.66 |
| Ifako-Ijaye | | 46.15 | 47.00 | 48.50 | 47.53 |
| Shomolu | }115 | 54.90 | 40.19 | 46.78 | 43.67 |
| Kasofe | | 35.13 | 42.84 | 43.92 | 43.26 |
| Mushin | }112 | 46.03 | 41.18 | 48.74 | 44.59 |
| Oshodi-Isolo | | 50.00 | 42.95 | 44.73 | 43.69 |
| IKEJA | 158 | 49.58 | 42.91 | 43.08 | 43.00 |
| IKORODU | 160 | 48.27 | 43.70 | 51.64 | 47.86 |
| Epe | 120 | 50.00 | 40.50 | 45.50 | 43.50 |
| Ibeju-Lekki | 161 | 25.00 | — | — | — |
| EPE | 129 | 43.75 | 40.50 | 45.50 | 43.50 |
| Badagry | 25 | 33.33 | 49.66 | — | 49.66 |
| Ojo | | 55.55 | 33.33 | 44.66 | 39.00 |
| Amuwo-Odofin | } 85 | 39.58 | 44.96 | 43.25 | 44.27 |
| Ajeromi-Ilfeladun | | 40.00 | 38.37 | 41.00 | 39.60 |
| BADAGRY | 79 | 42.70 | 42.04 | 43.16 | 42.17 |
| TOTAL STATE | 168 | 50.73 | 43.26 | 44.11 | 43.67 |
| Excluding Lagos Island | 143 | 49.18 | 43.23 | 44.15 | 43.66 |

TABLE A9.5 Nigerian pilgrims to Jerusalem (1995–1998) and Mecca (1997–1999) by state

| State/REGION | Average number of pilgrims to Jerusalem | Average number of pilgrims to Mecca | Jerusalem pilgrims per million non-Muslims | Mecca pilgrims per million Muslims |
|---|---|---|---|---|
| Sokoto-Zamfara | 12 | 2,698 | 55 | 635 |
| Kebbi | 28 | 1,098 | 273 | 559 |
| Kaduna | 94 | 2,312 | 54 | 1,049 |
| Katsina | 12 | 1,764 | 54 | 500 |
| Kano | 44 | 2,588 | 126 | 474 |
| Jigawa | 19 | 599 | 167 | 217 |
| Borno | 73 | 893 | 410 | 379 |
| Yobe | 35 | 541 | 360 | 415 |
| Bauchi-Gombe | 99 | 1,218 | 134 | 337 |
| NORTH | 416 | 13,712 | 110 | 500 |

| State/REGION | Average number of pilgrims to Jerusalem | Average number of pilgrims to Mecca | Jerusalem pilgrims per million non-Muslims | Mecca pilgrims per million Muslims |
|---|---|---|---|---|
| Niger | 21 | 1,007 | 54 | 495 |
| Kwara | 48 | 377 | 89 | 375 |
| Kogi | 64 | 171 | 66 | 145 |
| Plateau-Nassarawa | 165 | 680 | 80 | 540 |
| Adamawa | 73 | 417 | 79 | 354 |
| Taraba | 59 | 266 | 89 | 314 |
| Benue | 74 | 116 | 53 | 86 |
| Abuja | 153 | 1,239 | 91 | 606 |
| MIDDLE BELT | 657 | 4,273 | 90 | 480 |
| | | | | |
| Oyo | 96 | 428 | 73 | 200 |
| Osun | 89 | 203 | 103 | 157 |
| Ondo-Ekiti | 172 | 96 | 69 | 75 |
| Ogun | 88 | 421 | 99 | 291 |
| Lagos | 374 | 1,195 | 155 | 360 |
| Delta | 45 | 30 | 24 | 40 |
| Edo | 52 | 71 | 34 | 113 |
| SOUTHWEST | 916 | 2,444 | 81 | 224 |
| | | | | |
| Anambra-Ebonyi | 47 | 25 | 17 | 298 |
| Enugu | 75 | 44 | 24 | 468 |
| Imo | 44 | 6 | 18 | 127 |
| Abia | 51 | 27 | 22 | 570 |
| Cross River | 65 | 38 | 35 | 1,003 |
| Akwa Ibom | 79 | 27 | 33 | 553 |
| Rivers-Bayelsa | 107 | 141 | 25 | 1,624 |
| SOUTHEAST | 468 | 308 | 25 | 686 |
| | | | | |
| NIGERIA | 2,457 | 20,737 | 59 | 435 |

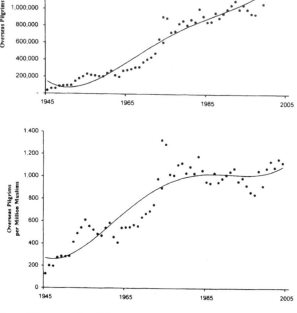

FIGURE A4.1 The growth of the overseas pilgrimage to Mecca, 1945–2003

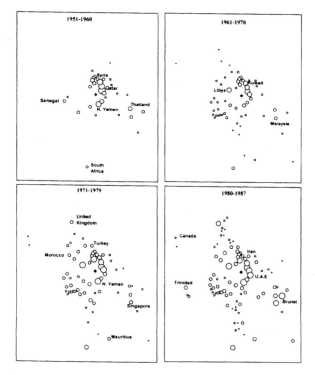

FIGURE A4.2 The global expansion of the hajj, 1951–1987 (pilgrims per million Muslims)

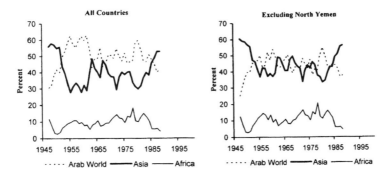

FIGURE A4.3 The regional distribution of pilgrims

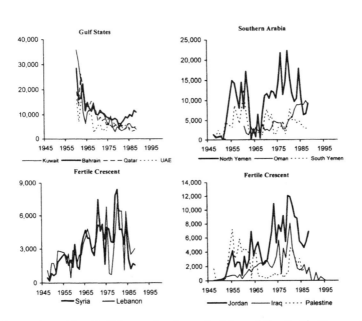

FIGURE A4.4 The Gulf States, Southern Arabia, and the Fertile Crescent

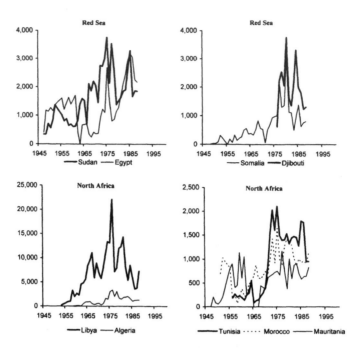

FIGURE A4.5 The Red Sea and North Africa

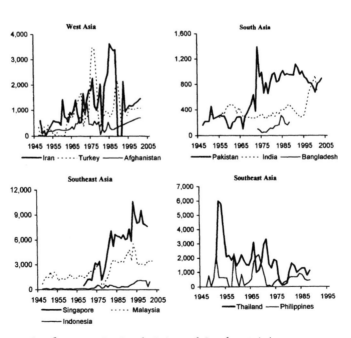

FIGURE A4.6 West Asia, South Asia, and Southeast Asia

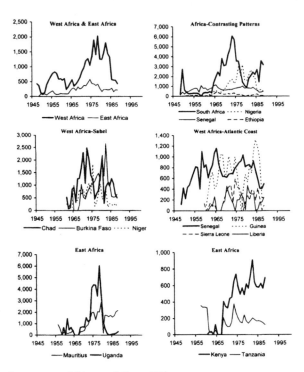

FIGURE A4.7 West Africa and East Africa

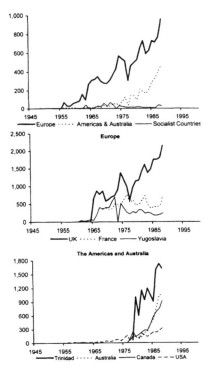

FIGURE A4.8 Europe, the Americas and Australia, and the socialist countries

303

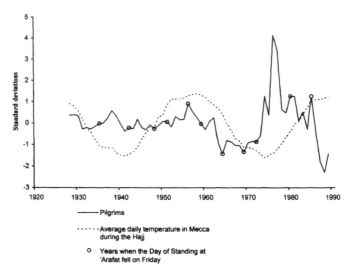

FIGURE A4.9 Climatic and astronomical correlates of the hajj, 1928–1987

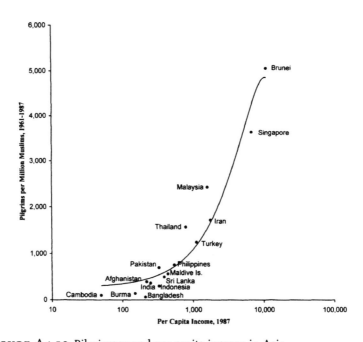

FIGURE A4.10 Pilgrimage and per capita income in Asia

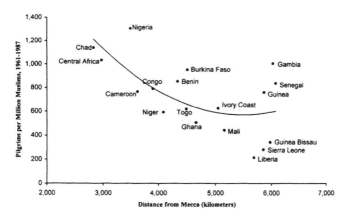

FIGURE A4.11 Pilgrimage and distance from Mecca in West Africa

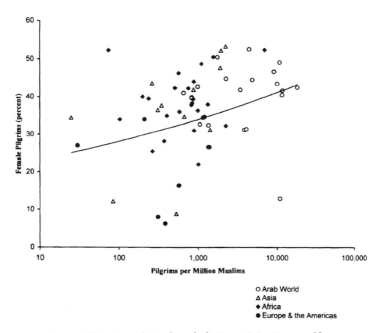

FIGURE A4.12 Global trends in female hajj participation, 1968–1975

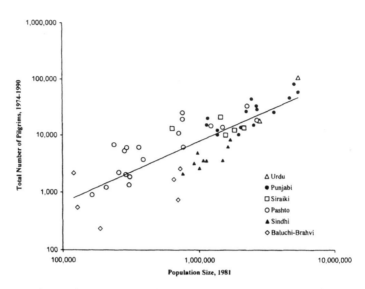

FIGURE A5.1 Pilgrimage and ethnicity in Pakistan (origins of Pakistani pilgrims according to the dominant languages spoken in their home districts)

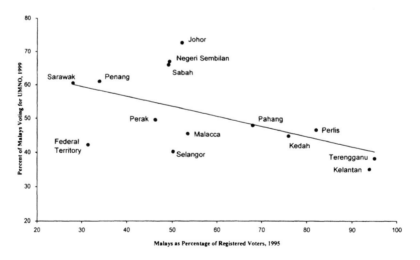

FIGURE A6.1 UMNO's share of the Malay vote and Malay share of the voting population, 1999

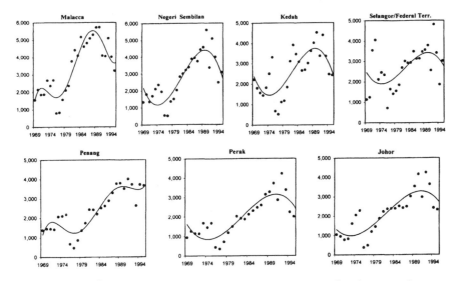

FIGURE A6.2 Pilgrimage rates in the West Coast States of Malaysia, 1969–1995

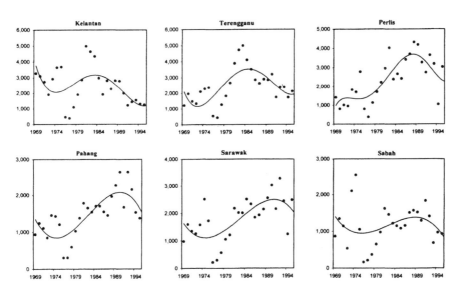

FIGURE A6.3 Pilgrimage rates in the Northern and Eastern states of Malaysia, 1969–1995

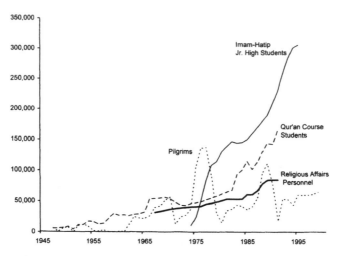

FIGURE A7.1 The growth of state-supported religious activities in Turkey, 1947–1996

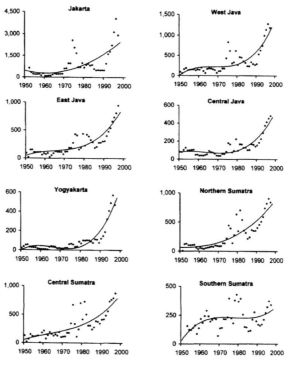

FIGURE A8.1 Pilgrimage rates in Java and Sumatra, 1950–1996

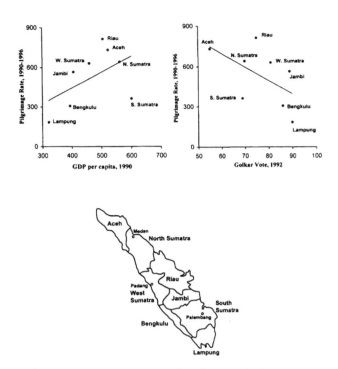

FIGURE A8.2 Pilgrimage, income, and Golkar vote in Sumatra

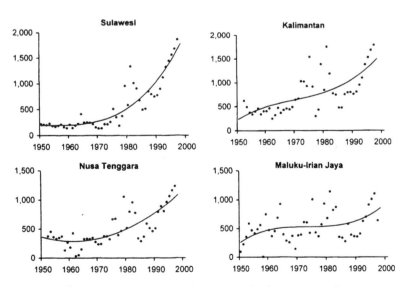

FIGURE A8.3 Pilgrimage rates in the Outer Islands, 1950–1996

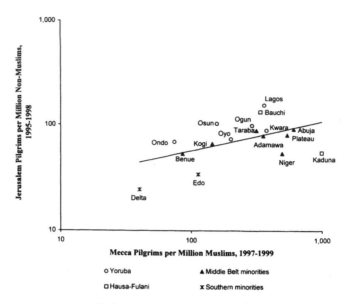

FIGURE A9.1 Rates of pilgrimage to Jerusalem and Mecca in the religiously mixed states of Nigeria, 1995–1999 (states where Muslims comprise between 10 and 90 percent of the population)

# Notes

CHAPTER 1

1. One of the best discussions of hajj rituals in English is Ahmad Kamal, *The Sacred Journey* (New York: Duell, Sloan and Pearce, 1961).

2. Alaa Shahine, "14 Pilgrims Trampled at Hajj Ritual," Associated Press, February 11, 2003.

3. Data on Saudi Arabia's hajj activities is from the Ministry of Planning, the Ministry of Pilgrimage, the Ministry of Health, and the Saudi Press Agency. Extensive news coverage of preparations for the hajj can be found in *Dawn* (Pakistan), *Islamic Voice* (India), *Vanguard* (Nigeria), *The Cape Times* (South Africa), *Republika* (Indonesia), *The Star* (Malaysia), *The Straits Times* (Singapore), *Zaman* (Turkey), *The Tehran Times*, *The North Africa Journal* (Algeria), *Gulf News* (Dubai), and *The Guardian* (UK).

4. The hajj quota was officially adopted by the seventh conference of the Islamic Foreign Ministers held in Amman in 1987.

5. Saudi Press Agency, August 27, 1998, and March 20, 2000. Internal pilgrims fell from about one million in 1996 to 440,000 in 2001.

6. Clarke Brooke, "Sacred Slaughter: The Sacrificing of Animals at the Hajj and Id al-Adha," *The Journal of Cultural Geography* 7 (1987): 67–88.

7. "Saudi Clergy to Make Hajj Safer," Associated Press, April 13, 1998 (reporting a new *fatwa* allowing the stoning of the devil to begin at dawn instead of after midday).

8. Youssef M. Ibrahim, "Saudi Arabia Beheads 16 Kuwaitis Linked to Pro-Iranian Terrorism," *New York Times*, September 23, 1989, p. 1.

CHAPTER 2

1. Annemarie Schimmel, *The Triumphant Sun: A Study of the Works of Jalaloddin Rumi* (London: East-West, 1988), 329–31, 382–87.

2. Ibid., 386.

3. Ibid., 325–31.

4. Annemarie Schimmel, "Iqbal in the Context of Indo-Muslim Mystical Reform Movements," in *Islam in Asia*, vol. 1, ed. Yohanan Friedmann (Jerusalem: Magnes Press, 1984), 213, 221–22.

5. Muhammad Iqbal, *Secrets of Collective Life*, trans. A. R. Tariq (Lahore: Islamic Book Service, 1977), particularly chapter 19, "The Collective Life of a Nation Requires a Visible Centre and the Centre of the Muslim Nation is the *Ka'ba*."

6. Annemarie Schimmel, *Gabriel's Wing: A Study into the Religious Ideas of Sir Muhammad Iqbal* (Leiden: E. J. Brill, 1963), 42, 127, 195–96.

7. Iqbal, *Secrets of Collective Life*, 8–9, 26, 74, 116, 135, 146, 162, 170–71, 224–25; Muhammad Iqbal, *The Secrets of the Self*, trans. Reynold A. Nicholson (London: Macmillan, 1920), 9, 29–30, 85, 143; and V. G. Kiernan, *Poems from Iqbal* (Bombay: Kutub, 1947), 30–34.

8. Kiernan, *Poems*, 112, 142, 205–10, 296–97.

9. From E. M. Forster, *Two Cheers for Democracy* (New York: Harcourt, Brace, 1951), 290. "The Complaint" is the lament of a faithful Muslim imploring God to explain why he has caused Muslims so much hardship while showering benefits on non-Muslims, especially in the West. D. J. Mathews, *Iqbal: A Selection of the Urdu Verse* (New Delhi: Heritage, 1993), 30–41.

10. Matthews, 185, 309–12.

11. Ibid., 162–63, 229–32.

12. Ibid., 218–27, 257–63.

13. Muhammad Iqbal, *The Reconstruction of Religious Thought in Islam* (Lahore: Ashraf, 1962), chapter 6.

14. On the connections Shari'ati saw between the hajj and Islam in general, see Steven R. Benson, "Islam and Social Change in the Writings of 'Ali Sharia'ti: His Hajj as a Mystical Handbook for Revolutionaries," *The Muslim World* 81 (1991): 9–26. On the influence of Shari'ati's views in current debates over the clergy, see Valla Vakili, "Abdolkarim Soroush and Critical Discourse in Iran," in *Makers of Contemporary Islam*, ed. John L. Esposito and John O. Voll (New York: Oxford University Press, 2001), 150–237.

15. 'Ali Shari'ati, *Hajj*, trans. Somayah and Yaser (Bedford, OH: Free Islamic Literatures, 1977), vii–viii, 112–13, 134, 150–51.

16. Ibid., ix–x, 24–25, 39–45.

17. Ibid., 88–98.

18. Ibid., 39–45.

19. Ibid., 21–22, 51–52.

20. Ibid., 99–107, 122–29, 142–43.

21. Ibid., 103–6.

22. Ibid., 108–10.

23. Ibid., 111.

24. Ibid., p. 84.

25. Ibid., 115, 118.

26. Ibid., 1–4, 78–80.

27. Ibid., 21–22, 83, 120. Annemarie Schimmel, *Deciphering the Signs of God: A*

*Phenomenological Approach to Islam* (Albany: State University of New York Press, 1994).

28. Shari'ati, *Hajj*, 22.

29. Ibid., 154.

30. Mohammed Arkoun, *Lectures du Coran* (Paris: Maisonneuve et Larose, 1982), 159–61, 164–67.

31. Ibid., 166–70.

32. Ibid., 173.

33. Ibid., 165.

34. Ibid., 166–67, 172–73.

35. Ibid., 159, 170.

36. Ibid., 174–75.

37. Ibid., 175.

38. Arkoun, *Lectures*, 168; Abu Hamid al-Ghazali, *Imam Gazzali's Ihya Ulum-id-Din*, trans. Fazlul Karim (Lahore: Sind Sagar Academy, 1978), chapter 7; and Gustave E. Von Grunebaum, *Muhammadan Festivals* (New York: Henry Schuman, 1951), chapter 2.

39. Henry Corbin, *Temple and Contemplation* (London: KPI, 1986), chapter 4.

40. Arkoun, *Lectures*, 175.

CHAPTER 3

1. Victor Turner and Edith Turner, *Image and Pilgrimage in Christian Culture: Anthropological Perspectives* (New York: Columbia University Press, 1978), 93–95, 174.

2. Ibid., 32.

3. Toufic Fahd, "Le pèlerinage à la Mekke," in *Les pèlerinages de l'antiquité biblique et classique à l'occident médiéval*, ed. Freddy Raphael (Paris: Librairie Orientalist Paul Geuthner, 1973), 71–83.

4. Gerard Siebert, "Réflexions sur la notion de Pèlerinage dans la Grèce antique," in Raphael, *Les pèlerinages*, 31–53.

5. Maurice Roche, *Mega-Events and Modernity: Olympics and Expos in the Growth of Global Culture* (London: Routledge, 2000).

6. Karl Mannheim, *Ideology and Utopia: An Introduction to the Sociology of Knowledge* (New York: Harcourt, Brace and World, 1963).

7. Jean-Jacques Waardenburg, *L'Islam dans le miroir de l'occident* (Paris: Mouton, 1969), 18–27.

8. G. W. J. Drewes, "Snouck Hurgronje and the Study of Islam," *Bejdragen tot de taal-, land- en volkenkunde van Neêrlandsch Indië* 113 (1957): 1–15.

9. C. Snouck Hurgronje, "Le pèlerinage à la Mekke," in *Selected Works of C. Snouck Hurgronje*, ed. G. H. Bousquet and J. Schacht (Leiden: E. J. Brill, 1957), 173, 207.

10. C. Snouck Hurgronje, *Mohammedanism: Lectures on Its Origin, Its Religious and Political Growth, and Its Present State* (New York: G. P. Putman's, 1916), 58–59.

11. Johannes Pedersen, *The Scientific Work of Snouck Hurgronje* (Leiden: E. J. Brill, 1957), 1–31.

12. D. Van Der Meulen, *Don't You Hear the Thunder: A Dutchman's Life Story* (Leiden: E. J. Brill, 1981), chapter 3.

13. Harry J. Benda, "Christiaan Snouck Hurgronje and the Foundations of Dutch Islamic Policy in Indonesia," *Journal of Modern History* 30 (1958): 338–47.

14. C. Snouck Hurgronje, "The Holy War 'Made in Germany,'" in *Verspreide Geschriften van C. Snouck Hurgronje* (Bonn and Leipzig: K. Schroeder, 1923–27), 3:282–84.

15. C. Snouck Hurgronje, "Notes sur le mouvement du pèlerinage de la Mecque aux indes néerlandaises," *Revue du Monde Musulman* 10 (October 1911): 397–413; Jacob Vredenbregt, "The Haddj: Some of Its Features and Functions in Indonesia," *Bejdragen tot de taal-, land- en volkenkunde van Neêrlandsch Indië* 118 (1962): 91–154.

16. C. Snouck Hurgronje, *Mekka in the Latter Part of the 19th Century*, trans. J. H. Monahan (Leiden: E. J. Brill, 1970), 290–91.

17. C. Snouck Hurgronje, "Le gouvernement colonial néerlandais et le système islamique," 14 *Revue du Monde Musulman* (1911): 482–83.

18. C. Snouck Hurgronje, "The Holy War," 284.

19. William Ochsenwald, *Religion, Society, and the State in Arabia: The Hijaz under Ottoman Control, 1840–1908* (Columbus: Ohio State University Press, 1984).

20. Jacques Jomier, *Le Mahmal et la caravane égyptienne des pèlerins de la Mekke (XIIIe–XXe siècles)* (Cairo: L'Insitut Français d'Archéologie Orientale, 1953).

21. Hussein Shehadeh, "The Kiswah of the Kaabah," *The Middle East* 192 (October 1990): 43–44.

22. Fahd, "Le pèlerinage," 87–90.

23. Jomier, *Le Mahmal*, 67–68.

24. One of the strongest criticisms of Saudi Arabia's hajj management points to the destruction of the architectural and natural environment accompanying the government's massive reconstruction of the historic center of Mecca. A leading environmentalist is Sami Angawi, an architect who founded the Hajj Research Center in 1975 and resigned in 1988. Elaine Scioline, "Saudi Struggles to Save Historic Sites," *New York Times*, February 18, 2002.

CHAPTER 4

1. Christopher Harrison, *France and Islam in West Africa, 1860–1960* (Cambridge: Cambridge University Press, 1988); William R. Roff, "Sanitation and Security: The Imperial Powers and the Nineteenth Century Hajj," *Arabian Studies* 6 (1982): 143–60.

2. Enumerations of pilgrims are from statistical yearbooks of Saudi Arabia and the official periodical of the Saudi Ministry of Hajj and Pious Endowments, which has been published under various titles since 1947. Al-Mamlaka al-'Arabiya al-Sa'udiya, Wizara al-Maliya wa al-Iqtisad al-Watani, Maslaha al-Ihsa'at al-'Amma, *Al-Kitab al-Ihsa'i al-Sanawi* [Statistical Yearbook] (Riyadh: Wizara al-Maliya wa al-Iqtisad al-Watani, various years).

Estimates for the period before World War II are from Mary Byrne McDonnell, "The Conduct of Hajj from Malaysia and Its Socio-Economic Impact on Malay Society: A Descriptive and Analytical Study, 1860–1981" (PhD diss., Columbia University, 1986), 626–28, 631–32.

Data on the size of Muslim populations is from Raymond Delval, ed., *A Map of* the Muslims in the World, Explanatory Summary with Statistic Tables (Leiden: E. J. Brill, 1984); Richard V. Weekes, ed., Muslim Peoples: A World Ethnographic Survey (Westport, CT: Greenwood, 1978).

3. Time magazine selected King Faysal as its "man of the year" for 1974. "Faisal and Oil: Driving toward a New World Order," Time, January 6, 1975.

4. Cumhuriyet (Istanbul), June 21, 1990.

5. "Iran Moves to Tone Down Hajj Demonstrations," Associated Press, March 4, 1998.

6. Kina Kamran, "Khatami's Landmark Visit to Saudi Arabia Reinforces Him at Home," Iran Press Service, May 15, 1999. Iran offers to pay for reconstruction of the al-Baqi' cemetery across from the Prophet's Mosque in Medina so Shi'ite pilgrims can resume visitations there, but Saudi Arabia rejects the proposal. "Muslim Ummah Must Preserve the Spirit of Hajj," Kayhan International (Tehran), February 18, 2002.

7. Sa'odah Elias and Wani Muthiah, "Pilgrims Warned against Getting Haj Visas from Other Countries," The Star (Kuala Lumpur), February 19, 2002.

8. In May 2002, India's parliament overhauled the national hajj system after an acrimonious two-year debate that pitted Congress Party deputies against the Bhartiya Janata Party government and Muslim politicians from many states. Concerning the government's commitment to state-sponsored hajj, see Prime Minister Shri Atal Bihari Vajpayee's address to the All-India Haj Conference. "Full Care of Haj Pilgrims' Needs Will Be Taken," Press Information Bureau, Government of India, August 1999.

9. Jordan's program of religious tourism includes rides on a refurbished version of the Hejaz Railway, accompanied by a theme park and museum targeted to hajjis from Syria, Turkey, and Central Asia. Jordanians remind pilgrims the railway belongs to all Muslims because it was built with mass donations to the Ottoman Sultan before Jordan existed. "Jordan Sees Pilgrimage Railway as Engine for Tourism Growth," Utusan Malaysia, February 1, 1998.

10. Iraq and Iran made their own bilateral agreements on pilgrimage to Kerbala and Najaf. "Iraqi-Iranian Agreements on Pilgrimage Visits," Arabic News, November 15, 1999; "Saddam Allows Iranians to Visit Shiite Shrines," Arabic News, August 19, 1997. Kurds in Iraq and Iran organized a joint hajj caravan from both countries to promote Kurdish causes among pilgrims from other countries. R. M. Ahmad, "Hajj Pilgrimage Joint Committee Meets in Arbil," Kurdish Media News, December 26, 2001.

11. The Islamic Council of Singapore (Majlis Ugama Islam Singapura) has a Web site (http://www.muis.gov.sg/english/Home.aspx?pMenu=1) in English and Malay offering online application forms. It advises prospective pilgrims to register at least two years in advance because of the long waiting list.

12. Brunei's hajj declined recently from more than 3,000 to about 1,000. Brunei pilgrims complain that private airlines sell tickets at bargain prices and then hit them with exorbitant charges for excess baggage when they return home with large purchases from Saudi Arabia. Azrol Azmi and A. M. Zukarnaen, "Royal Brunei Airline to Handle Haj Cargo," Borneo Bulletin, January 2, 2002. The Web site of Brunei's Hajj Bureau is located at http://www.urusan-haji.gov.bn.

13. Surin Pitsuwan, Islam and Malay Nationalism: A Case Study of the Malay-Muslims of Southern Thailand (Bangkok: Thai Khadi Research Institute, Thammasat

University, 1985); Raymond Scupin, "The Social Significance of the Hajj for Thai Muslims," *Muslim World* 72 (1982): 25–33.

14. Khadim Mbacké, "Le pèlerinage à La Mecque: le cas du Sénégal de 1886 à 1986" (PhD diss., Université Cheikh Anta Diop de Dakar, 1991).

15. I. D. Du Plessis, *The Cape Malays* (Cape Town: Maskew Miller, 1944); Abdulkader Tayob, *Islam in South Africa: Mosques, Imams, and Sermons* (Gainesville: University Press of Florida, 1999).

16. After the fall of apartheid, South Africa's Muslims lobbied the African National Congress to set up a permanent Hajj and Umrah Council in 1995. The council sends about 8,000 people on hajj and another 14,000 on 'umra, but economic and organizational problems make planning difficult. Yunus Kemp, "Rand Takes Its Toll on Hajj Pilgrims," *Cape Argus* (Cape Town), February 18, 2002; "Curb Dramatic Increase in Haj Operators Says SAHUC," *al-Qalam* (Durban), May 2001. For the annual report of the South African Hajj and Umrah Council, see http://www.sahuc.org.za/.

17. J. Spencer Trimingham, *The Influence of Islam upon Africa* (London: Longman, 1980). Concerning the Tanzania Hajj Trust, see Jacqueline Mujuni, "Pilgrims Leave for Hajj," *The Express* (Tanzania), February 14, 2002.

18. "Foreign Secretary Launches British Hajj Delegation to Mecca," *Foreign and Commonwealth Office News*, July 2, 2002. The government describes the United Kingdom as "the first historically Christian country to organize such a delegation."

19. Steven L. Burg, *The Political Integration of Yugoslavia's Muslims: Determinants of Success and Failure* (Pittsburgh: Russian and East European Studies Program, University of Pittsburgh, 1983).

20. Natalie Schuck, "France Muslims Agree on Formal Council," Associated Press, December 20, 2002; Elaine Ganley, "Muslims in France Worship Underground," Associated Press, December 19, 2002.

21. Between 8,000 and 11,000 people make the hajj each year from the United States. Ezzedine Said, "U.S. Muslims Seek Spiritual Comfort in Pilgrimage, *Middle East Times* (Cairo), February 16, 2002.

22. "Russia Reaches Accord on This Year's Hajj," *Radio Free Europe/Radio Liberty Newsletter*, October 31, 2001 (noting that Russia would send only 6,000 pilgrims, even though it had been allotted 20,000 places).

23. "Uzbek Police Warn Pilgrims to Toe Line on Saudi Hajj," *B.B.C. News Online*, February 5, 2002 (reporting that police spies accompanied a group of 3,900 pilgrims from Uzbekistan to ensure that they did not contact Uzbek defectors in Mecca).

24. The state-sponsored Chinese Islamic Association still sends only about 2,000 hajjis annually and no more than 200 to 300 from Xinjian and Ningxia provinces, where the Muslims are most numerous. "Muslims in Ningxia Leave for Mecca," *People's Daily*, February 9, 2001. On Muslims in the city of Xi'an, see Maris Boyd Gillette, *Between Mecca and Beijing: Modernization and Consumption among Urban Chinese Muslims* (Stanford, CA: Stanford University Press, 2000).

25. Islamic and Western calendars were coordinated according to Henri Georges Cattenoz, *Tables de concordance des ères hégirienne et grégorienne, 1884–2000/1301–1421* (Rabat, Morocco: Éditions techniques nord-africaines, 1974).

26. United Nations, Statistical Division, *Statistical Yearbook* (New York: United Nations Statistical Division, various years).

27. Statistics on Turkey's pilgrimage are from the Hajj Office of the Directorate of Religious Affairs.

28. In September and October 2000, Kuala Lumpur hosted the first major international conference on hajj management, with fifty-two countries in attendance. The delegates agreed to hold follow-up conferences in six regions. In May 2002, Nigeria hosted a five-day training program in Abuja for hajj managers from fourteen countries in West and Central Africa. Musa Aliyu, "Training the Trainers for Hitch-Free Hajj," *Daily Trust* (Abuja), May 15, 2002.

CHAPTER 5

1. Syed Mujawar Hussain Shah, *Religion and Politics in Pakistan, 1972–88* (Islamabad: National Institute of Pakistan Studies, Quaid-i-Azam University, 1996), 179, 182–86.

2. Shahid Javed Burki, *Pakistan under Bhutto, 1971–1977* (New York: St. Martin's Press, 1980), 195–202.

3. Hastings Donnan, "Symbol and Status: The Significance of the Hajj in Pakistan," *The Muslim World* 79 (July–October 1989): 205–16.

4. Gallup Pakistan, *Pakistan at the Polls, 1990* (Islamabad: Pakistan Institute of Public Opinion, 1991), 37–70.

5. Jamal Malik, *Colonization of Islam: Dissolution of Traditional Institutions in Pakistan* (New Delhi: Manohar, 1996); Musa Khan Jalazai, ed., *Sectarianism and Politico-Religious Terrorism in Pakistan* (Lahore: Tarteeb Books, 1993).

6. Leonard Binder, *Religion and Politics in Pakistan* (Berkeley: University of California Press, 1961), 3–108.

7. Katherine Ewing, "The Politics of Sufism: Redefining the Saints of Pakistan," *Journal of Asian Studies* 42 (February 1983): 251–53, 266–67.

8. Malik, *Colonization*, 85–119.

9. Annual enumerations of pilgrims are from Government of Pakistan, Ministry of Religious Affairs and Minorities Affairs, *Haj Year Book* (Islamabad: Ministry of Religious Affairs and Minorities Affairs, various years between 1974 and 1991).

10. Regional breakdowns of pilgrims by gender are available in Ministry of Religious Affairs and Minorities Affairs, *Haj Year Book*, 1974–77 and 1985–88.

11. S. Akbar Zaidi, ed., *Regional Imbalances and the National Question in Pakistan* (Lahore: Vanguard, 1992); Theodore P. Wright Jr., "Center-Periphery Relations and Ethnic Conflict in Pakistan: Sindhis, Muhajirs, and Punjabis," *Comparative Politics* 23 (April 1991): 299–312.

12. District-level enumerations of pilgrims are from Government of Pakistan, Ministry of Religious Affairs and Minorities Affairs, Hajj Bureau, "Yearly Listings of Pilgrims by District, 1974–1990," Islamabad, 1990.

13. Charles W. Stahl and Farooqi Azam, "Counting Pakistanis in the Middle East: Problems and Policy Implications," *Asian and Pacific Population Forum* 4 (Summer 1990): 1–10, 24–28.

14. Malik Muhammad Saeed Dehwar, *Contemporary History of Balochistan* (Quetta, Pakistan: Third World Publications, 1994), 384–416, 432–36; Janmahmad,

*Essays on Baloch National Struggle in Pakistan* (Quetta, Pakistan: Gosh-e-Adab, 1989), 285–95.

15. Ishtiaq Ahmed, *State, Nation, and Ethnicity in Contemporary South Asia* (London: Pinter, 1998), 196–216.

16. Attar Chand, *Pakistan: Party Politics, Pressure Groups, and Minorities* (New Delhi: Commonwealth Publishers, 1991), 40–53.

17. Barbara Crossette, "Dream of Homeland Revived on Pakistan's Wild Frontier," *New York Times*, December 3, 1990.

18. Data on population, socioeconomic characteristics, and literacy is from Government of Pakistan, Population Census Organization, Statistics Division, *Population Census of Pakistan, 1998* (Islamabad: Population Census Organisation, 1999); Population Census Organization, *1981 District Census Report*, 70 volumes (Islamabad: Population Census Organisation, 1983).

19. Government of Pakistan, Federal Bureau of Statistics, Statistics Division, *Fifty Years of Pakistan in Statistics* (Karachi: Manager of Publications, 1998).

20. Syed Karim Haider, *Pakistan's General Elections, 1997* (Lahore: Pakistan Study Centre, University of the Punjab, 1999), 95–148; Navid Zafar and Ishtiaq Hussain, *Election 93: Facts, Figures, Feats* (Islamabad: Modern Book Depot, 1994), 47–291; and Iftikar Ahmad, *Pakistan General Elections: 1970* (Lahore: South Asian Institute, Punjab University, 1976).

21. Ministry of Religious Affairs and Minorities Affairs, Hajj Bureau, "Yearly Listings of Pilgrims by District, 1974–1990," Islamabad, 1990.

22. Aftab had his own quarrels with party leaders close to Benazir and now heads a separate faction of the PPP, serving as Musharraf's minister of energy. Mohammed Riaz, "The Sherpaos: Meteoric Rise in Politics," *Dawn*, March 23, 2001.

23. Iqbal Akhund, *Trial and Error: The Advent and Eclipse of Benazir Bhutto* (Karachi: Oxford University Press, 2000), 295, 297.

24. Malik, *Colonization of Islam*, 235–39, 321.

25. Akbar S. Ahmed, *Religion and Politics in Muslim Society: Resistance and Control in Pakistan* (New York: Routledge, 1991), 5–10, 92–97, 104.

26. Akbar S. Ahmed, *Social and Economic Change in the Tribal Areas, 1972–1976* (Karachi: Oxford University Press, 1977), 107–15, 160–68.

27. Ahsan Wagha, *The Siraiki Language: Its Growth and Development* (Islamabad: Dderawar, 1990), 1–2, 64, 134–36.

28. C. Shackle, "Siraiki: A Language Movement in Pakistan," *Modern Asian Studies* 11 (1977): 383–87, 398.

29. Riaz Hassan, "Religion, Society, and the State in Pakistan: Pirs and Politics," *Asian Survey* 27 (May 1987): 555.

30. M. Hanif Raza, *Multan: Past and Present* (Islamabad: Colorpix, 1988).

31. Ewing, "The Politics of Sufism," 261–64; Hassan, "Religion, Society, and the State," 562–65.

32. Hassan, "Religion, Society, and the State," 556.

33. Jalazai, *Sectarianism*, 276–86; Malik, *Colonization of Islam*, 303.

34. "Shiite Muslim Killed in Pakistan," Associated Press, November 28, 1998 (reporting 422 religiously motivated murders in Punjab during 1998).

35. Malik, *Colonization of Islam*, 247–49.

36. Akbar S. Ahmed, "Death in Islam: The Hawkes Bay Case," *Man* 21 (1986): 120–34.

37. Maleeha Lodhi, "Pakistan's Shia Movement: An Interview with Arif Hussaini," *Third World Quarterly* 10 (1988): 806–17.

38. Before his election to parliament, retired general Majeed Malik had been an appointed member of Zia's Consultative Assembly. "Shoora Mandi," *The Herald*, November–December, 1990, 33.

39. Molly Moore, "The Battle of the Bhuttos Threatens to Split Ruling Party in Pakistan," *Washington Post*, February 1, 1994.

40. Khawar Mumtaz, "Identity Politics and Women: 'Fundamentalism' and Women in Pakistan," in *Identity Politics and Women: Cultural Reassertions and Feminisms in International Perspective*, ed. Valentine M. Moghadam (Boulder, CO: Westview, 1994), 228–42.

41. Christina Lamb, "Pakistani Women Fight Growing Scandal of Wife Burnings," *Sunday Telegraph* (London), March 13, 2000.

42. Shahla Haeri, "The Politics of Dishonor: Rape and Power in Pakistan," in *Faith and Freedom: Women's Human Rights in the Muslim World*, ed. Mahnaz Afkhami (Syracuse, NY: Syracuse University Press, 1995), 161–74; Simorgh Collective and S. Hussein, *Rape in Pakistan* (Lahore: Simorgh Women's Resource and Publications Centre, 1990).

43. Ministry of Religious Affairs, "Salient Features of Hajj Policy and Arrangements for Hajj," March 17, 2000: http://www.mra.gov.pk/policy_2003.htm.

CHAPTER 6

1. Jabatan Perdana Menteri Malaysia, *Sejarah Perkembangan Tabung Haji Malaysia Tiga Puluh Tahun* [Office of the Prime Minister of Malaysia, The Thirty-Year History of the Development of the Tabung Haji of Malaysia] (Kuala Lumpur: Lembaga Urusan dan Tabung Haji, 1993), 70–74, 83–85.

2. Lembaga Tabung Haji, "Lembaga Tabung Haji: Your Investment Partner," Kuala Lumpur, Investment Department, Lembaga Tabung Haji, 1995, 8, 14–18.

3. "Siasat Langkah Tabung Haji" [Investigating the Activities of Tabung Haji], *Harakah*, September 11, 1998.

4. The scandal broke just when Tabung Haji was trying to persuade managers of the national pension system to allow workers to use early withdrawals from their retirement funds to pay for pilgrimage expenses. The pension fund rejected the idea, and parliament considered reorganizing Tabung Haji to separate investment and pilgrimage functions. "Hamid Othman Tetap Kemuka Syor Kepada Kumpulan Wang Simpanan Perkerja" [Hamid Othman Decides to Make a Proposal to the Employees' Provident Fund], *Utusan Malaysia*, May 15, 2002.

5. Lee Yuk Peng and Sim Leoi Leoi, "Six Tabung Haji Managers Given Show-Cause Letters," *The Star*, March 22, 2002.

6. Lembaga Tabung Haji, *Perangkaan Jemaah Haji Sehingga Musim Haji 1415H* [Statistics of the Hajj Congregations through the Hajj Season of 1415H/1995AD] (Kuala Lumpur: Lembaga Tabung Haji, 1995), 1–3.

7. Saudi Arabia has lost patience with Malaysian violators, deporting about 400

for overstaying their '*umra* visas in 2002 instead of the usual 10 or 20 and requiring the Malaysian government to pick up the tab. "He's No Terrorist: Man with 104 Passports 'Just a Travel Agent,'" *The Straits Times*, February 20, 2002.

8. Jabatan Perdana Menteri Malaysia, *Sejarah*, 136–38.

9. Zainuddin Maidin, *The Other Side of Mahathir* (Kuala Lumpur: Utusan, 1995), 250–52.

10. Lembaga Tabung Haji, *Perangkaan Jemaah Haji*, 5–7, 13–14.

11. Khoo Boo Teik, *Paradoxes of Mahathirism: An Intellectual Biography of Mahathir Mohamad* (Kuala Lumpur: Oxford University Press, 1995).

12. Joel S. Kahn, "Class, Culture, and Malaysian Modernity," in *Social Change in Southeast Asia*, ed. Johannes Dragsbaek Schmidt, Jacques Hers, and Niels Forld (London: Longman, 1998), 81–97.

13. Nayan Chanda, "Politically Incorrect: An Interview with Lee Kuan Yew," *Far Eastern Economic Review*, September 24, 1998.

14. Gordon P. Means, *Malaysian Politics: The Second Generation* (New York: Oxford University Press, 1991), 2–16, 123–30; Diane K. Mauzy, "Decline of 'The Malay Way,'" 28 *Asian Survey* (February 1988): 213–22.

15. Harold Crouch, *Government and Society in Malaysia* (Ithaca, NY: Cornell University Press, 1996), 86, 117–18, 121, 214–15.

16. Peter Searle, *The Riddle of Malaysian Capitalism: Rent-Seekers or Real Capitalists?* (Honolulu: Allen and Unwin and University of Hawaii Press, 1999), 103–53; Edmund Terence Gomez and K. S. Jomo, *Malaysia's Political Economy: Politics, Patronage and Profits* (Cambridge: Cambridge University Press, 1997).

17. Justin Fox, "The Great Emerging Markets Rip-Off," *Fortune*, May 11, 1998.

18. Ahmad Lutfi Othman, *Selepas Mahathir, UMNO for Sale!* [After Mahathir, UMNO for Sale!] (Batu Caves, Selangor: Visi Madani, 1996).

19. Yusof Ismail and Khayati Ibrahim, eds., *Politik Melayu Dan Demokrasi* [Malay Politics and Democracy] (Kuala Lumpur: A. S. Noordeen, 1996).

20. Crouch, *Government and Society*, 86–87, 101, 118, 215.

21. John Hilley, *Malaysia: Mahathirism, Hegemony, and the New Oppostion* (London: Zed, 2001), 19–46.

22. Jomo Kwame Sundaram and Ahmed Shabery Cheek, "The Politics of Malaysia's Islamic Resurgence," *Third World Quarterly* 10 (April 1988): 843–68.

23. Alvin Ung, "Malaysia Warns of Western Takeovers," Associated Press, June 19, 1998.

24. "S and P Downgrades Five Malaysian Banks; Outlook Negative," Associated Press, September 25, 1998.

25. S. Jayasankaran, "Protégé to Pariah: How Anwar Ibrahim Lost Favour with His Former Mentor," *Far Eastern Economic Review*, September 17, 1998; Salim Osman, "The Final Rupture," *The Straits Times*, September 3, 1998.

26. Ranjan Roy, "Malaysian Officials Pressure Press," Associated Press, July 22, 1998.

27. Alvin Ung, "Sex, Lies, and Video in Anwar Trial," Associated Press, December 16, 1998.

28. "Malaysia PM's Son Claims Defamation," Associated Press, October 2, 1999.

29. Alvin Ung, "Fired Malaysia Official Campaigns," Associated Press, September 12, 1998.

30. "Events Leading to Anwar's Arrest," Associated Press, September 20, 1998.

31. Simon Elegant, Murray Hiebert, and S. Jayasankaran, "First Lady of Reform," *Far Eastern Economic Review*, October 1, 1998.

32. Alvin Ung, "Malaysian Cites Scheme versus Anwar," Associated Press, November 5, 1998.

33. Christopher Torchia, "Malaysia Unrest Echoes Indonesia," Associated Press, September 20, 1998.

34. Mahathir complained bitterly that his enemies abused the Internet to spread rumors about his hajj—that he had died in Mecca, that he failed to complete the obligatory rituals, and that he wanted to repent for the lies he concocted about Anwar. "Dr. M Raps Groups for Spreading Lies on the Net," *The Business Times* (Singapore), April 28, 1999; Joceline Tan, "Politics Not Far Behind Even on Pilgrimage," *Singapore Straits Times*, February 26, 2001.

35. The Star, *Tenth Malaysia General Election, 1999* (Kuala Lumpur: Star Publications, 1999).

36. Simon Cameron-Moore, "No One Shaking Mahathir's Tree after Daim's Fall," Associated Press, June 24, 2001.

37. Shanti Nair, *Islam in Malaysian Foreign Policy* (London: Routledge, 1997), 68–69, 143–46, 199, 248.

38. "Malaysia to Host First Hajj Conference outside the Arab World," *Utusan Malaysia*, August 13, 2000.

39. Sean Yoong, "Malaysian Leader Wants Modern Weapons," Associated Press, July 19, 2002.

40. Sean Yoong, "Mahathir to Lead Malaysia until 2003," Associated Press, June 25, 2002.

41. "Malaysia's First Islamic Radio to Air in July," Associated Press, June 22, 2001; Jocelyn Gecker, "Muslims Get Cards to Prove Marriage," Associated Press, January 2, 1999.

42. "Malaysia Seeks Views from Cairo on Islamic State," Associated Press, October 24, 2001.

43. Simon Cameron-Moore, "Mahathir Draws Muslim Rival into Islamic State Row," Associated Press, October 4, 2001.

44. "Malaysian Opposition at Odds over Islamic State," Associated Press, July 2, 2001.

45. Lembaga Tabung Haji, *Perangkaan Jemaah Haji*, 1–3, 5–6.

46. Harold Brookfield, ed., *Transformation with Industrialization in Peninsular Malaysia* (Kuala Lumpur: Oxford University Press, 1994), 122–68.

47. Lembaga Tabung Haji, *Perangkaan Jemaah Haji*, 5–6.

48. Statewide data are from *Information Malaysia* (Kuala Lumpur: Berita Publishing, various years); Malaysia Jabatan Perangkaan, *Buku Tahunan Perangkaan Malaysia, Yearbook of Statistics, Malaysia* (Kuala Lumpur: Jabatan Perangkaan, various years).

49. Statewide election returns are from New Straits Times, Research and Information Services, *Elections in Malaysia: A Handbook of Facts and Figures on the Elec-*

*tions, 1955–1995* (Kuala Lumpur: New Straits Times Press, 1999); The Star, *Tenth Malaysia General Election, 1999* (Kuala Lumpur: Star Publications, 1999).

50. Bahagian Bimbingan Haji, Jabatan Haji, Lembaga Urusan Dan Tabung Haji, *Poster Ibadat Haji* [Section of Pilgrimage Instruction, Office of Pilgrimage, Tabung Haji, An Illustrated Guide to Performing the Hajj] (Kuala Lumpur: Tabung Haji, 1995).

51. Colin Barlow, ed., *Modern Malaysia in the Global Economy: Political and Social Change into the 21st Century* (Cheltenham, UK: Edward Elgar, 2001), 74–93.

CHAPTER 7

1. Turks are particularly interested in the growing political and legal controversies over religious freedom in the United States. "Dinsel Haklar ve Devlet" [Religious Freedoms and the State], *Zaman*, April 21, 1998.

2. İştar Tarhanlı, *Müsülman Toplum, "Laik" Devlet: Türkiye'de Diyanet İşleri Başkanlığı* [Muslim Society, "Secular" State: The Directorate of Religious Affairs in Turkey] (İstanbul: Afa Yayıncılık, 1993), 84–86.

3. In 1979, the directorate implemented centralized hajj management. In 1983, it began regulating *'umra* travel. And in 1988, it started to supervise private travel agents offering hajj packages.

4. In 1977, the directorate began financing hajj services through the Turkish Religious Trust (Türkiye Diyanet Vakfı), and, since 1992, *'umra* travel has been run by a mixed commission of state and private sector managers.

5. *Cumhuriyet*, July 28–29, 1988.

6. *Cumhuriyet*, June 21, 1990.

7. *Cumhuriyet*, June 14–19, 1990.

8. Adıl Tütüncü, "Sincan'da Atatürk Tartışması" [The Ataturk Debate in Sincan], *Milliyet*, October 12, 1998.

9. "Türbanda Gövde Gösterisi" [A Show of Strength in the Turban], *Milliyet*, October 12, 1998; "Türban Eylemindeki Dekan' [The Dean in the Turban Demonstrations], *Sabah*, October 12, 1998; and "Türban Kışkırtması" [The Turban Provocation], *Hürriyet*, October 12, 1998.

10. "Eylemde Latife Hanım Fotoğrafı" [Latife Hanim's Photograph in the Demonstration], *Milliyet*, October 12, 1998.

11. Annual enumerations of pilgrims are from the Hajj Bureau of the Directorate of Religious Affairs.

12. Alan Rush, ed., *Records of the Hajj: A Documentary History of the Pilgrimage to Mecca* (Slough: Archive Editions, 1993), 8: 100–103, 295–96, 348–49.

13. Ibid., 155–58, 331–32, 352–54.

14. Ibid., 215–17, 355–56, 437–38.

15. Tarhanlı, *Müsülman Toplum*, 50–51.

16. Ruşen Çakır, *Ayet ve Slogan: Türkiye'de İslami Oluşumlar* [Verse and Slogan: Islamic Developments in Turkey] (İstanbul: Metis Yayınları, 1990), 218.

17. Türkiye Cumhuriyeti Başbakanlık, Diyanet İşleri Başkanlığı, *İstatistiklerle Diyanet İşleri Başkanlığı* [The Directorate of Religious Affairs in Statistics] (Ankara: Diyanet İşleri Başkanlığı, 1990).

18. "Erbakan'dan 'Siyasi' Hac" ["Political" Hajj by Erbakan], *Akşam*, April 8, 1998.

19. Provincial level data on pilgrimage participation are available from 1979 onward.

20. Michael E. Meeker, "The Black Sea Turks: Some Aspects of Their Ethnic and Cultural Background," *International Journal of Middle East Studies* 2 (1971): 318–45.

21. Bernard Lewis, *The Emergence of Modern Turkey* (London: Oxford University Press, 1961), 241–42, 247–50.

22. İsmail Beşikçi, *Tunceli Kanunu (1935) ve Dersim Jenosidi* [The Tunceli Law of 1935 and the Dersim Genocide] (İstanbul: Belge Yayınları, 1990), 65–70; Michael H. Gunter, *The Kurds and the Future of Turkey* (New York: St. Martin's Press, 1997).

23. Mustafa Kara, *Bursa'da Tarikatlar ve Tekkeler* [Sufi Orders and Convents in Bursa] (Bursa: Uludağ Yayınları, 1990), 31, 143–45, 177–78.

24. İsmail Hakkı Uzunçarşılıoğlu, *Bizans ve Selçukiylerle Germiyan ve Osman Oğulları Zamanında Kütahya Şehri* [The City of Kütahya in the Times of the Byzantines, Seljuks, and Ottomans] (İstanbul: Devlet Matbaasi, 1932), 208–75.

25. "Tarikatçılar Meclis'te: TBMM'ye 100'den Fazla Tarikat-Cemaat Üyesi Milletvekili Girdi" [Members of Sufi Orders in Parliament: More Than 100 Members of Mystical Orders and Associations Enter the Grand National Assembly as Deputies], *Cumhuriyet*, January 6, 1996.

26. Sherif Mardin, *Religion and Social Change in Modern Turkey: The Case of Bediuzzaman Said Nursi* (Albany: State University of New York Press, 1989).

27. Çakır, *Ayet ve Slogan*, 89–98; Gencay Şaylan, *İslamiyet ve Siyaset: Türkiye Örneği* [Islam and Politics: The Example of Turkey] (Ankara: V Yayınları, 1987), 76.

28. *Cumhuriyet*, January 6, 1996.

29. Çakır, *Ayet ve Slogan*, 131; Şaylan, *İslamiyet ve Siyaset*, 101.

30. Mrs. Çiller increasingly reached out to religious voters as she faced accusations of financial wrongdoing. Stephen Kinzer, "Turkey's Ex-Premier Ciller in Comeback as Power Broker," *New York Times*, January 15, 1999.

31. Türkiye Cumhuriyeti Başbakanlık, Diyanet İşleri Başkanlığı, *İstatistiklerle Diyanet İşleri Başkanlığı* [The Directorate of Religious Affairs in Statistics] (Ankara: Diyanet İşleri Başkanlığı, 1990); Yusuf Ziya Özcan, "Ülkemizdeki Cami Sayıları Üzerine Sayısal Bir İnceleme" [A Quantitative Study of Mosques in Turkey], *İslami Araştırmalar (Journal of Islamic Research)* 4 (January 1990): 5–20.

32. For biographies of all of the heads of the Directorate of Religious Affairs since 1924, see the directorate's monthly magazine, *Diyanet*, March 1999. Lütfi Doğan, *Toplumun Temelini Sarsan Belli Başlı Problemler* [The Major Problems Shaking the Basis of Society] (Ankara: Diyanet İşleri Başkanlığı Yayınları, 1988). The conservative Lütfi Doğan (1968–72) from the Black Sea should not be confused with his successor at the directorate (1972–76), Dr. Lütfi Doğan, who is a more progressive theologian and who in 1977 was elected as a deputy of the Republican People's Party from Malatya.

33. Data on mosques, Qur'an courses, and İmam-Hatip schools are taken from Diyanet İşleri Başkanlığı, *İstatistiklerle Diyanet İşleri Başkanlığı* [The Directorate of Religious Affairs in Statistics]. Data on population, language, education, and socioeconomic characteristics are from Türkiye Cumhuriyeti Başbakanlık, Devlet İstatistik En-

stitüsü, *Genel Nüfus Sayımı, Nüfusun Sosyal ve Ekonomik Nitelikleri* [General Population Census, Social and Economic Characteristics of the Population] (Ankara: Devlet İstatistik Enstitüsü, 1992–1994); and Devlet İstatistik Enstitüsü, *Milli Eğitim İstatistikleri* [National Education Statistics] (Ankara: Devlet İstatistik Enstitüsü, various years).

34. Türkiye Cumhuriyeti Başbakanlık, Devlet İstatistik Enstitüsü, *Milletvekili Genel Seçimi Sonuçları* [Results of the Parliamentary General Elections] (Ankara: Devlet İstatistik Enstitüsü, various years).

35. Committee on Foreign Relations, United States Senate, *East or West? Turkey Checks Its Compass* (Washington, DC: U.S. Government Printing Office, 1995); Graham E. Fuller, *From Eastern Europe to Western China: The Growing Role of Turkey in the World and Its Implications for Western Interests* (Santa Monica, CA: RAND, 1993).

36. Şaylan, *İslamiyet ve Siyaset*, 61–69.

37. İsmail Soysal, "İslam Konferansı ve Türkiye, 1969–1984" [The Islamic Conference and Turkey, 1969–1984], *Dışpolitika* 11 (June 1984): 5–30.

38. Nicholas S. Ludington, *Turkish Islam and the Secular State* (Washington, DC: American Institute for Islamic Affairs, The American University, 1984), 3.

39. Gareth M. Winrow, "Turkey and the Newly Independent States of Central Asia and the Transcaucasus," *Middle East Review of International Affairs* 1 (July 1997): http://meria.idc.ac.il/journal/1997/issue2/jvln2a5.html.

40. David B. Ottoway and Dan Morgan, "In Drawing a Route, Bad Blood Flows," *Washington Post*, October 5, 1998.

41. Mehmet Ali Birand, "Erbakan Tehlikeli Sulara Girdi" [Erbakan Has Entered Dangerous Waters], *Sabah*, August 12, 1996.

42. Mehmet Soysal, "Turkish Generals Rain on Erbakan's Day of Glory at D-8 Summit," *Mulimedia*, July 1, 1997.

43. "Komutan Duyarlılığı" [The Commander's Sensitivity], *Milliyet*, June 1, 1998.

44. Nilüfer Göle, ed., *İslamın Yeni Kamusal Yüzleri* [Islam's New Public Faces] (İstanbul: Metis Yayınları, 2000).

45. Şaylan, *İslamiyet ve Siyaset*, 71–104, 147–59.

46. Çakır, *Ayet ve Slogan*, 251–74, 282–85, 296–98.

47. Nilüfer Göle, *Modern Mahrem: Medeniyet ve Örtünme* [The Modern Segregation of Women: Civilization and Covering]) (İstanbul: Metis Yayınları, 1992), 77–128, 136–40.

48. Tarhanlı, *Müsülman Toplum*, 15–37, 61–63, 66–70, 142–44, 182–86.

49. "Umrecilerin Problemleri" [Problems of the 'Umra Pilgrims], *Zaman*, April 9, 1998.

CHAPTER 8

1. Douglas E. Ramage, *Politics in Indonesia: Democracy, Islam, and the Ideology of Tolerance* (London: Routledge, 1995), 10–44.

2. Nasrullah Ali-Fauzi, ed., *ICMI Antara Status Quo dan Demokratisasi* [ICMI: Between the Status Quo and Democratization] (Bandung: Mizan, 1995).

3. Deliar Noer, *Administration of Islam in Indonesia* (Ithaca, NY: Cornell University Southeast Asia Program, 1978), 53–58.

4. Greg Fealy, "'Rowing in a Typhoon,' Nahdlatul Ulama and the Decline of Par-

liamentary Democracy," in *Democracy in Indonesia, 1950s 1990s*, ed. David Bourchier and John Legge (Clayton, Victoria: Monash University Press, 1994), 88–97.

5. Daniel S. Lev, *Islamic Courts in Indonesia: A Study in the Political Bases of Legal Institutions* (Berkley: University of California Press, 1972), 45–46, 52–53, 58–61.

6. A. Gaffar Karim, *Metamorfosis: NU Dan Politisasi Islam Indonesia* [Metamorphasis: The NU and the Politicization of Indonesian Islam] (Yogyakarta: LKIS, 1995), 56–76.

7. Ichlasul Amàl, *Regional and Central Government in Indonesian Politics: West Sumatra and South Sulawesi, 1949–1979* (Yogyakarta: Gadjah Mada University Press, 1992), 134.

8. "Depag Harus Mawas Diri dalam Pelaksanaan Haji" [The Department of Religion Needs to Do Some Soul-Searching in Managing the Hajj], *Kompas*, March 28, 1996.

9. Departemen Agama Republika Indonesia, *Hikmah Ibadah Haji* [The Wisdom of the Hajj] (Jakarta: Direktorat Jendral Bimbingan Masyarakat Islam dan Urusan Haji, 1996).

10. Bambang Pranowo, "Islam and Party Politics in Rural Java," *Studia Islamika* 2 (1994): 1–19.

11. Michael R. J. Vatikiotis, *Indonesian Politics under Suharto: The Rise and Fall of the New Order* (New York: Routledge, 1998), 140–41.

12. Peter Burns, "The Post Priok Trials: Religious Principles and Legal Issues," *Indonesia* 47 (April 1989): 61–88.

13. Adam Schwarz, *A Nation in Waiting: Indonesia in the 1990s* (Boulder, CO: Westview, 1994), 217, 226, 273, 283–85.

14. Robert W. Hefner, "Islamizing Java? Religion and Politics in Rural East Java," *Journal of Asian Studies* 46 (August 1987): 533–54.

15. Martin van Bruinessen, *NU: Tradisi, Relasi-relasi Kuasa, Pencarian Wacana Baru* [The NU: Tradition, Power Relations, and the Search for a New Discourse], trans. Farid Wajidi (Yogyakarta: LKIS/Pustaka Pelajar Yogyakarta, 1994), 285–300.

16. Herbert Feith, *The Indonesian Elections of 1955* (Ithaca, NY: Southeast Asia Program, Cornell University, 1957), 78–79.

17. James J. Fox, "Ziarah Visits to the Tombs of the Wali, The Founders of Islam on Java," in *Islam in the Indonesian Social Context*, ed. M. C. Ricklefs (Clayton, Victoria: Monash University Press, 1991), 19–31.

18. Mark Woodward, *Islam in Java: Normative Piety and Mysticism in the Sultanate of Yogyakarta* (Tucson: University of Arizona Press, 1989), 236–38.

19. Hal Hill, ed., *Unity and Diversity* (New York: Cambridge University Press, 2000), 283–306.

20. Woodward, *Islam in Java*, 3, 7–8, 144–58, 200–201, 205, 213–14.

21. Mitsuo Nakamura, *The Crescent Arises over the Banyan Tree: A Study of the Muhammadiyah Movement in a Central Javanese Town* (Yogyakarta: Gadjah Mada University Press, 1983).

22. Barbara S. Harvey, *Permesta: Half a Rebellion* (Ithaca, NY: Cornell Modern Indonesia Project, 1977), 13–15.

23. Deliar Noer, "Masjumi: Its Organization, Ideology, and Political Role in Indonesia" (master's thesis, Cornell University, 1960).

24. Amal, *Regional and Central Government*, 111–18, 138–62.

25. Hal Hill, *The Indonesian Economy*, 230–33, 237–38.

26. Taufiq Abduallah, "Islam and the Transformation of Tradition in Indonesia: A Comparative Perspective," *Itinerario* 13 (1989): 17–36.

27. Amal, *Regional and Central Government*, 162–86.

28. Harvey, *Permesta*, chapter 5.

29. B. J. Boland, *The Struggle of Islam in Modern Indonesia* (The Hague: Martinus Nijhoff, 1982), 62–68.

30. Amal, *Regional and Central Government*, 123, 162–63, 176–77, 191, 194.

31. Burhan Magenda, *East Kalimantan: The Decline of a Commercial Aristocracy* (Ithaca, NY: Cornell Modern Indonesia Project, 1991), 73–75.

32. Hal Hill, ed., *Unity and Diversity*, 179–206.

33. Demographic data on Indonesian pilgrims is collected by the director of hajj management (Departemen Agama, Direktur Penyelenggaraan Urusan Haji) and published irregularly in the official statistical yearbooks, Biro Pusat Statistik, *Statistik Indonesia, Statistical Yearbook of Indonesia* (Jakarta: Biro Pusat Statistik).

34. Nakamura, *The Crescent Arises over the Banyan Tree*, 119–20.

35. Christine Drake, *National Integration in Indonesia: Patterns and Policies* (Honolulu: University of Hawaii Press, 1989), 16–55.

36. Provincial breakdowns of data on hajj participation, population, and socioeconomic characteristics are available in Biro Pusat Statistik, *Statistik Indonesia, Statistical Yearbook of Indonesia* (Jakarta: Biro Pusat Statistik), published annually.

37. M. Sudibjo, ed., *Pemilihan Umum 1992: Suatu Evaluasi* [The General Election of 1992: An Evaluation] (Jakarta: Center for Strategic and International Studies, 1995), 59–60, 63, 167–69.

38. Because the 1992 elections coincided with the hajj season, more than 95,000 pilgrims cast special ballots while in Saudi Arabia. The official tally was 70.1 percent for Golkar, 27.6 percent for the PPP, and only 2.3 percent for the PDI. Darul Aqsha, Dick van der Meij, and Johan Hendrik Meuleman, *Islam in Indonesia: A Survey of Events and Developments from 1988 to March 1993* (Jakarta: Indonesia-Netherlands Cooperation in Islamic Studies, 1995), 118.

39. Danarto, *A Javanese Pilgrim in Mecca (Orang Jawa Naik Haji)*, trans. Harry Aveling (Clayton, Victoria: Monash University Press: 1989).

40. Toko Gunung Agung, ed., *Perjalanan Ibadah Haji Pak Harto* [The Pilgrimage Journey of Father Harto] (Jakarta: Departemen Agama Republika Indonesia, 1994).

41. Mustofa W. Hasyim and Ahmad Munif, eds., *Haji: Sebuah Perjalanan Air Mata (Pengalaman Beribadah Haji 30 Tokoh)* [The Hajj: A Journey of Tears (The Experiences of Hajj Worship of Thirty Leaders)] (Yogjakarta: Bentang, 1993).

42. Vatikiotis, *Indonesian Politics under Suharto*, 229–30.

43. "M. Amien Rais: 'Muhammadiyah Tidak Akan Pernah Menjilat' " [M. Amien Rais: "Muhammadiyah Will Never Be Bootlickers"], *Forum Keadilan*, July 17, 1995, 39.

44. Kuntowijoyo et al., *Intellektualism Muhammadiyah: Menyongsong Era Baru* [Muhammadiyah's Intellectualism: Welcoming a New Era] (Bandung: Mizan, 1995).

45. Karim, *Metamorfosis*, 22, 40, 97, 185.

46. Greg Barton, "Neo-Modernism: A Vital Synthesis," *Studia Islamika* 2 (April–June 1995): 1–75.

47. M. Amien Rais, "Saya Minta Keturunan, Dikabulkan Allah" [I Asked to Become a Father, God Answered My Prayer], in *Haji: Sebuah Perjalanan Air Mata*, pp. 30–37.

48. Mohammad Amien Rais, "The Muslim Brotherhood in Egypt: Its Rise, Demise, and Resurgence" (PhD diss., University of Chicago, 1981).

49. Nurcholish Madjid, "Haji Itu Transformasi Hidup" [This Hajj Is a Transformation of Life], in *Haji: Sebuah Perjalanan Air Mata*, pp. 153–61.

50. Andrée Feillard, "Les oulémas indonésiens auhourd'hui: de l'opposition à une nouvelle légitimité," *Archipel* 46 (1993): 89–110.

51. François Raillon, "How to Become a National Entrepreneur: The Rise of Indonesian Capitalists," *Archipel* 41 (1991): 89–116.

52. A debate over Muhammadiyah's social bases appeared in Kuntowijoyo et al., *Intellektualism Muhammadiyah*, especially the essays by Lukman Harun and H. Hajriyanto Y. Thohari, 94–103.

53. "Gerakan Pembaruan, tanpa Pembaruan" [A Reform Movement without a Reform], *Forum Keadilan*, July 17, 1995, 15–16.

54. Ramage, *Politics in Indonesia*, 66–69, 72, 195–96.

55. Martin Van Bruinessen, "The 28th Congress of the Nahdlatul Ulama: Power Struggle and Social Concerns," *Archipel* 41 (1991): 185–200.

56. Deliar Noer, *The Muslim Modernist Movement In Indonesia, 1900–1942* (London: Oxford University Press, 1973), 223–25, 228, 299.

57. Schwarz, *A Nation in Waiting*, 172

CHAPTER 9

1. Bawuro M. Barkindo, "The Royal Pilgrimage Tradition of the Saifawa of Kanem and Borno," in *People and Empires in African History: Essays in Memory of Michael Crowder*, ed. J. F. Ade Ajayi and J.D.Y. Peel (London: Longman, 1992), 1–20.

2. Roman Loimeier, "Das 'Nigerian Pilgrimage Scheme': Zum Versuch, den Hagg in Nigeria zu organisieren," *African Spectrum* 23 (1988): 201–14.

3. C. Bawa Yamba, *Permanent Pilgrims: The Role of Pilgrimage in the Lives of West African Muslims in Sudan* (London: Edinburgh University Press, 1995); J. S. Birks, *Across the Savannas to Mecca: The Overland Pilgrimage Route from West Africa* (London: Frank Cass, 1978); John A. Works Jr., *Pilgrims in a Strange Land: Hausa Communities in Chad* (New York: Columbia University Press, 1976); and 'Umar al-Naqar, *The Pilgrimage Tradition in West Africa* (Khartoum: Khartoum University Press, 1972).

4. John N. Paden, *Ahmadu Bello: Sardauna of Sokoto* (London: Hodder and Stoughton, 1986), 532–33.

5. O. E. Tangban, "The Hajj and the Nigerian Economy, 1960–1981," *Journal of Religion in Africa* 21 (1991): 241–55.

6. C. L. Ejembi, E. P. Renne, and H. A. Adamu, "The Politics of the 1996 Cerebrospinal Meningitis Epidemic in Nigeria," *Africa* 68 (1998): 118–34.

7. Iheanyi M. Enwerem, *A Dangerous Awakening: The Politicization of Religion in Nigeria* (Ibadan, Nigeria: Insitut français de recherche en Afrique, 1995), 145.

8. Bauna Peter Tanko, *The Christian Association of Nigeria and the Challenge of the Ecumenical Imperative* (Jos, Nigeria: Bab Anieh, 1991), 117–45.

9. Toyin Falola, "Christian Radicalism in Nigerian Politics," in Paul A. Beckett and Crawford Young, eds., *Dilemmas of Democracy in Nigeria* (Rochester, NY: University of Rochester Press, 1997), 265–82.

10. Pat Williams and Toyin Falola, *Religious Impact on the Nation State: The Nigerian Predicament* (Aldershot, UK: Avebury, 1995), 25.

11. Paden, *Ahmadu Bello*, 714.

12. E. P. T. Crampton, *Christianity in Northern Nigeria* (London: Geoffrey Chapman, 1979), 93–94; Enwerem, *A Dangerous Awakening*, 65–67, 194.

13. Office of the President, Office of Pilgrim Affairs, "Record of Performance of Hajj since Inception of Nigerian Pilgrims Board from 1975 to 1999," Abuja, 1999; Office of Pilgrim Affairs, "Yearly Listings of Muslim Pilgrims by State, 1997–1999," Abuja, 1999; and Hajj Research Team, Institute of Administration, Ahmadu Bello University, *Hajj Research Project, Nigeria*, Prepared for Hajj Research Centre, Ummal Qura University, Mekkah, Kingdom of Saudi Arabia (Zaria: Ahmadu Bello University, 1984).

14. Federation of Nigeria, Federal Office of Statistics, *Socioeconomic Profile of Nigeria, 1996* (Lagos: Federal Office of Statistics, 1996); Federal Office of Statistics, *Social Statistics in Nigeria* (Lagos: Federal Office of Statistics, various years). Election results are taken from Independent National Electoral Commission, *Presidential Election Results, 1999* (Abuja, Nigeria: INEC, 1999); Kolawole Balogun, *Nigeria, June 12 Election* (Osogbo, Nigeria: Africanus, 1993), 14–15; and Toyin Falola and Julius Ihonvbere, *The Rise and Fall of Nigeria's Second Republic: 1979–84* (London: Zed, 1985), 220.

15. Muhammad Sani Umar, "Changing Islamic Identity in Nigeria from the 1960s to the 1980s: From Sufism to Anti-Sufism," in *Muslim Identity and Social Change in Sub-Saharan Africa*, ed. Louis Brenner (London: Christopher Hurst, 1993), 154–78.

16. Bawuro M. Barkindo, ed., *Kano and Some of Her Neighbors* (Kano, Nigeria: Bayero University Press, 1989); John N. Paden, *Religion and Political Culture in Kano* (Berkeley: University of California Press, 1973).

17. Mahdi Adamu, *The Hausa Factor in West African History* (Zaria, Nigeria: Oxford University Press, 1978), 123–34.

18. Demola Akinyemi, "Ilorin: Endless Agitation to Dislodge Fulani," *Vanguard*, July 22, 2001; Stefan Reichmuth, "The Modernization of Islamic Education: Islamic Learning and Its Interaction with 'Western' Education in Ilorin, Nigeria," in *Muslim Identity and Social Change in Sub-Saharan Africa*, ed. Louis Brenner (Bloomington: Indiana University Press, 1993), 179–97.

19. Bala J. Takaya and Sonni Swanle Tyoden, eds., *The Kaduna Mafia: A Study of the Rise, Development, and Consolidation of a Nigerian Power Elite* (Jos, Nigeria: Jos University Press, 1987); Henry Ugbolue and Bashir Kalejaiye, "The Godfathers," *Tempo* (Lagos), March 4, 2000.

20. Ibrahim James, *Studies in the History, Politics, and Cultures of Southern Kaduna Peoples Groups* (Jos, Nigeria: Ladsomas, 1997), 1–28, 196–289; Jibrin Ibrahim, "The Politics of Religion in Nigeria: The Parameters of the 1987 Crisis in Kaduna State," *Review of African Political Economy* 45 (1989): 65–82.

21. M. G. Smith, *Government in Zazzau, 1800–1950* (London: Oxford University Press, 1960), 77–80, 100, 104, 108, 115, 246–47, 259–60; Yusufu Turaki, *The British Colonial Legacy in Northern Nigeria* (Jos, Nigeria: Challenge, 1993).

22. Crampton, *Christianity in Northern Nigeria*, 45–48, 52–54.

23. James, *Studies*, 35, 90, 141, 283.

24. Adamu, *The Hausa Factor*, 12–14, 92.

25. William F. S. Miles, *Hausaland Divided: Colonialism and Independence in Nigeria and Niger* (Ithaca, NY: Cornell University Press, 1994), 257–58; Emmanuel Grégoire, "Islam and the Identity of Merchants in Maradi (Niger)," in *Muslim Identity and Social Change in Sub-Saharan Africa*, ed. Louis Brenner (London: Christopher Hurst, 1993), 106–15.

26. Sen Luka Gwom, *Plateau State Political and Administrative Systems* (Jos, Nigeria: Fab Education, 1993); Elizabeth Isichei, *Studies in the History of Plateau State, Nigeria* (London: Macmillan, 1982), 254–81.

27. Kaduna State Muslim Pilgrims Welfare Board, *Comprehensive List of Pilgrims for the 1999 Hajj Operation* (Kaduna, Nigeria: Kaduna State Muslim Pilgrims Welfare Board, 1999).

28. Barbara Cooper, "The Strength in the Song: Muslim Personhood, Audible Capital, and Hausa Women's Performance of the Hajj," *Social Text* 60 (1999): 87–109; Susan O'Brien, "Pilgrimage, Power, and Identity: The Role of the Hajj in the Lives of Nigerian Hausa Bori Adepts," *Africa Today* 46 (Summer 1999): 11–40.

29. Federation of Nigeria, Federal Office of Statistics, *Major Social Indicators by Local Government Areas, Nigeria, 1993/94* (Lagos: Federal Office of Statistics, 1997); Kaduna State of Nigeria, *Kaduna State in Perspective* (Kaduna, Nigeria: Kaduna State Printing Office, 1990).

30. Adamu, *The Hausa Factor*, 1–16.

31. Catherine Coles and Beverly Mack, eds., *Hausa Women in the Twentieth Century* (Madison: University of Wisconsin Press, 1991), 9–12, 32–33, 44–45, 115, 187–88; Barbara J. Callaway, *Muslim Hausa Women in Nigeria: Tradition and Change* (Syracuse, NY: Syracuse University Press, 1987), 159–85.

32. Robert W. Taylor, ed., *Urban Development in Nigeria* (Aldershot, UK: Avebury, 1993), 130–44; Babatunde A. Williams and Annmarie Hauck Walsh, *Urban Government for Metropolitan Lagos* (New York: Praeger, 1968), ii, 3–12.

33. Lagos State Muslim Pilgrims Welfare Board, "Listing of Pilgrims for the 1999 Hajj Operation," Ikeja, 1999.

34. Pauline H. Baker, *Urbanization and Political Change: The Politics of Lagos, 1917–1967* (Berkeley: University of California Press, 1974); Sandra T. Barnes, *Patrons and Power: Creating a Political Community in Metropolitan Lagos* (Bloomington: Indiana University Press, 1986).

35. Peter B. Clarke and Ian Linden, *Islam in Modern Nigeria* (Munich: Grünewald-Kaiser, 1984), 49–50.

36. Ismail A. B. Balogun, *Islam versus Ahmadiyya in Nigeria* (Lahore, Pakistan: Muhammad Ashraf, 1977).

37. Toyin Falola and Akanmu Adebayo, *Culture, Politics, and Money among the Yoruba* (New Brunswick, NJ: Transaction, 2000), 51–72, 329–34.

38. Ayesha M. Imam, "Politics, Islam, and Women in Kano, Northern Nigeria," in *Identity Politics and Women: Cultural Reassertions and Feminisms in International Perspective*, ed. Valentine M. Moghadam (Boulder, CO: Westview, 1994), 123–44; Amina Mama, *Changes of State: Gender Politics and Transition in Nigeria* (Cape Town, South Africa: University of Cape Town Press, 2000); and Nina Mba, "Kaba and

Khaki: Women and the Militarised State in Nigeria," in *Women and the State in Africa*, ed. Jane L. Parpart and Kathleen A. Staudt (Boulder, CO: Lynne Rienner, 1989), 69–90.

39. Federation of Nigeria, Federal Office of Statistics, *Major Social Indicators by Local Government Areas, Nigeria, 1993/94* (Lagos: Federal Office of Statistics, 1997).

40. Enwerem, *A Dangerous Awakening*, 78–81, 96–97, 138–39.

41. Office of the President, Office of Pilgrim Affairs, "Yearly Listings of Christian Pilgrims by State, 1995–1998," Abuja, Nigeria, 1999; Office of Pilgrim Affairs, "Yearly Listings of Muslim Pilgrims by State, 1997–1999," Abuja, Nigeria, 1999.

CHAPTER 10

1. Mark W. Zacher, "Multilateral Organizations and the Institution of Multilateralism: The Development of Regimes for Nonterrestrial Spaces," in *Multilateralism Matters*, ed. John Gerard Ruggie (New York: Columbia University Press, 1993), 399–439.

2. Abdullah al-Ahsan, *The Organization of the Islamic Conference: An Introduction to an Islamic Political Institution* (Herndon, VA: International Institute of Islamic Thought, 1988).

3. Martin Kramer, "Tragedy in Mecca," *Orbis* 32 (Spring 1988): 231–47.

4. A complete listing of OIC meetings and documents is available at the website of its Permanent Mission to the United Nations: http://www.oic-un.org..

5. Ranjan Roy, "Morocco Still OIC Secretary General," Associated Press, June 29, 2000.

6. Tony Blair, "Khilafna Laysa Ma' al-Islam Bal Ma' al-Irhab wa Muw'ayidihi" [Our Conflict Is Not with Islam but with Terror and Its Supporters], *al-Hayat*, October 11, 2001.

7. Karol Wolfke, *Custom in Present International Law* (Dordrecht: Martinus Nijhoff, 1993).

8. Mark W. Janis, *An Introduction to International Law* (Boston: Little, Brown, 1993), 203–15.

9. Karol Wolfke, "Some Persistent Controversies regarding Customary International Law," *Netherlands Yearbook of International Law* 24 (1993): 2–16.

10. David A. Colson, "How Persistent Must the Persistent Objector Be?" *Washington Law Review* 61 (1986): 957–70.

11. Jonathan I. Charney, "The Persistent Objector Rule and the Development of Customary International Law," *British Yearbook of International Law* 56 (1985): 1–24.

12. Martti Koskenniemi, "The Normative Force of Habit: International Custom and Social Theory," *Finnish Yearbook of International Law* 1 (1991): 77–153.

13. Michael Byers, ed., *The Role of Law in International Politics: Essays in International Relations and International Law* (Oxford: Oxford University Press, 2000).

14. Mark W. Janis and Carolyn Evans, eds., *Religion and International Law* (The Hague: Martinus Nijhoff, 1999).

15. Andreas Hasenclever, Peter Mayer, and Volker Rittberger, *Theories of International Regimes* (Cambridge: Cambridge University Press, 1997).

16. Oran R. Young, *Governance in World Affairs* (Ithaca, NY: Cornell University Press, 1999).

17. Mathias Albert, Lothar Brock, and Klaus Dieter Wolf, eds., *Civilizing World Politics: Society and Community beyond the State* (Lanham, MD: Rowman and Littlefield, 2001).

18. Hans J. Morgenthau, *Politics among Nations: The Struggle for Power and Peace* (New York: Knopf, 1985).

19. Robert O'Brien, Anne Marie Goetz, Jan Aart Scholte, and Marc Williams, *Contesting Global Governance: Multilateral Economic Institutions and Global Social Movements* (Cambridge: Cambridge University Press, 2000).

20. Andrew Hurrell, "International Society and the Study of Regimes: A Reflective Approach," in *Regime Theory and International Relations*, ed. Volker Rittberger (New York: Oxford, 1993), 49–72.

21. Iver B. Neumann and Ole Waever, eds., *The Future of International Relations: Masters in the Making* (New York: Routledge, 1997).

22. Akira Iriye, *Cultural Internationalism and World Order* (Baltimore: Johns Hopkins University Press, 1997).

23. Cornelius F. Murphy Jr., *Theories of World Governance: A Study in the History of Ideas* (Washington, DC: Catholic University of America Press, 1999).

24. Leo Strauss, *Natural Right and History* (Chicago: University of Chicago Press, 1953).

25. Jonathan I. Charney, "Universal International Law," 87 *American Journal of International Law* (1993): 529–51.

26. American Law Institute, *Restatement of the Law (Third), the Foreign Relations Law of the United States* (St. Paul, MN: ALI Press, 1987), sec. 702.

27. Ian Edge, ed., *Comparative Law in Global Perspective* (Ardsley, NY: Transnational, 2000).

28. Iriye, *Cultural Internationalism*, chapter 1.

29. John Strawson, "A Western Question to the Middle East: 'Is There a Human Rights Discourse in Islam?'" *Arab Studies Quarterly* 19 (Winter 1997): 31–58.

30. Harold Hongju Koh, "Bringing International Law Home," *Houston Law Review* 35 (1998): 623–81.

31. Welhengama Gnanapala and Richard Jones, *Ethnic Minorities in English Law* (Stoke on Trent, UK: Trentham, 2000).

32. Diana L. Eck, *A New Religious America: How A "Christian Country" Has Become the World's Most Religiously Diverse Nation* (New York: Harper, 2001).

33. Robert Bistolfi and François Zabbal, eds., *Islams d'Europe: Intégration ou insertion communautaire?* (Paris: Edition de l'Aube, 1995).

34. Carolyn Evans, "Religious Freedom in European Human Rights Law: The Search for a Guiding Conception," in Janis and Evans, *Religion and International Law*, 385–400.

35. Prakash Shah, "Ethnic Minorities and the European Convention of Human Rights: A View from the UK," in Edge, *Comparative Law*, 387–410.

36. Werner Menski, "From Imperial Domination to Bhaji on the Beach: Fifty Years of South Asian Laws at SOAS," in Edge, *Comparative Law*, 131–34, 142–44.

37. Esin Örücü, Elspeth Attwool, and Sean Coyle, *Studies in Legal Systems: Mixed and Mixing* (The Hague: Kluwer, 1996).

38. Masaji Chiba, *Legal Pluralism: Toward a General Theory through Japanese Legal Culture* (Tokyo: Tokai University Press, 1989).

39. Prosper Weil, "Towards Relative Normativity in International Law?" *American Journal of International Law* 77 (1983): 413–42.

40. W. Michael Reisman, "The Cult of Custom in the Late Twentieth Century," *California Western International Law Journal* 17 (1987): 133–45.

41. Weil, "Towards Relative Normativity," 422–23.

42. H. L. A. Hart, *The Concept of Law* (London: Oxford University Press, 1961), 97–107.

43. Harold Hongju Koh, "Transnational Legal Process," *Nebraska Law Review* 75 (1996): 181–207.

44. Hart, *The Concept of Law*, 132–37.

45. Ibid., 120–32, 144.

46. Ibid., 141, 143, 150.

47. Ibid., 208–31.

48. Ibid., 118–19, 149–50.

49. Noel J. Coulson, *Conflicts and Tensions in Islamic Jurisprudence* (Chicago: University of Chicago Press, 1969).

50. Muhammad Khalid Masud, Brinkley Messick, and David S. Powers, eds., *Islamic Legal Interpretation: Muftis and Their Fatwas* (Cambridge: Harvard University Press, 1996).

51. Fazlur Rahman, *Islam and Modernity: Transformation of an Intellectual Tradition* (Chicago: University of Chicago Press, 1982); Leonard Binder, *Islamic Liberalism: A Critique of Development Ideologies* (Chicago: University of Chicago Press, 1988).

52. Al-Ahsan, *The Organization of the Islamic Conference*, 28.

53. OIC Press Release, "Following the [ICJ] Ruling on the Border Dispute: The OIC Secretary General Congratulates the Sisterly States of Qatar and Bahrain," March 24, 2001.

54. An excellent example of the apologist approach juxtaposes Qur'anic verses and portions of contemporary multilateral conventions, including the United Nations Charter, in order to illustrate their supposed interconnections. Mohammad Talaat Al Ghunaimi, *The Muslim Conception of International Law and the Western Approach* (The Hague: Martinus Nijhoff, 1968), 198.

55. Sarvenaz Bahar, "Khomeinism, The Islamic Republic of Iran, and International Law: The Relevance of Islamic Political Ideology," *Harvard International Law Journal* 33 (1992): 145–90.

56. Mohammed Bedjaoui, "The Gulf War of 1980–1988 and the Islamic Conception of International Law," in *The Gulf War of 1980–1988*, ed. Ige F. Dekker and Harry H. G. Post (Dordrecht: Martinus Nijhoff, 1992), 277–99; M. Cherif Bassiouni, ed., *The Islamic Criminal Justice System* (New York: Oceana, 1982); and Gamal M. Badr, "A Survey of Islamic International Law," in Janis and Evans, *Religion and International Law*, 95–101.

57. Abdul Hamid A. Abu Sulayman, *Towards an Islamic Theory of International Relations: New Directions for Methodology and Thought* (Herndon, VA: International Institute of Islamic Thought, 1993); Abdullahi Ahmad An-Na'im, *Toward an Islamic Reformation: Civil Liberties, Human Rights, and International Law* (Syracuse, NY: Syracuse University Press, 1990); Mohammed Arkoun, "The Concept of 'Islamic Reformation,'" in *Islamic Law Reform and Human Rights: Challenges and Rejoinders*, ed. Tore Lindholm and Kari Vogt (Oslo: Nordic Human Rights Publications, 1993), 11–24; and

Sheikh Rached Al-Ghannouchi, "The Islamists and Human Rights," in *Islam and Justice: Debating the Future of Human Rights in the Middle East and North Africa*, ed. Lawyers Committee for Human Rights (New York: Lawyers Committee for Human Rights, 1997), 165–70.

58. An-Na'im, *Toward an Islamic Reformation*, 151, 153, 155, 159.

59. Abu Sulayman, *Towards an Islamic Theory*, 68–69, 142, 145; An-Na'im, *Toward an Islamic Reformation*, 158–59.

60. Abu Sulayman, *Towards an Islamic Theory*, 109–14; An-Na'im, *Toward an Islamic Reformation*, 149, 156–57.

61. David Westbrook, "Islamic International Law and Public International Law: Separate Expressions of World Order," *Virginia Journal of International Law* 33 (1993): 819, 883–84.

# Glossary

*'Alim* (singular form of *'ulama*). A religious scholar.

*'Arafat.* The wide plain about twelve miles east of Mecca, where all pilgrims assemble on the ninth day of Dhu al-Hijjah. The ritual high point of the hajj, where pilgrims are most certain their prayers will reach God directly.

*Ayat.* A verse of the Qur'an. A "mirror" or a symbol. A sign of God.

**Black Stone.** A small stone "from heaven" (perhaps a meteorite) mounted in the southeastern corner of the *Ka'ba*. While performing the *tawaf,* most pilgrims salute it from a distance, but many try to touch or kiss it when the crowd permits. Some traditions describe the stone as an oracle that can settle disagreements and foretell the future; some claim the stone was originally white until it absorbed the sins of the world. Others believe that on Judgment Day the stone will testify before God about all of humanity's bad deeds.

**Communitas.** Victor Turner's term for the irrepressible humanistic and egalitarian feelings he postulated as coexisting in creative tension with hierarchical institutions stressing authority and the division of labor. Turner believed that pilgrimage promotes communitas more than any other type of ritual and that the hajj encourages it more than any other pilgrimage.

**Customary international law.** A well-recognized but increasingly controversial source of international law, derived from prevailing state practice and from evolving perceptions of what the community of nations accepts as binding obligation. International lawyers are divided over the importance of state consent (explicit as well as tacit) in creating customary international law. Nonetheless, they generally agree that when customary international law exists, it supersedes conflicting sources of law, including treaties. Some states can claim a right to exempt themselves from customary international law, but only if they demonstrate they were early and "persistent objectors" to the disputed rule instead of passive observers who slept on their rights or who changed their minds at the eleventh hour.

**Day of Standing.** The tenth day of Dhu al-Hijjah, when all pilgrims gather at the plain of 'Arafat to meditate from morning until sunset.

**Dhu al-Hijjah.** The twelfth month of the Islamic lunar calendar. The month designated for performing the hajj.

**Farewell Hajj.** Muhammad's final hajj just a few months before his death. The occasion of his famous sermon at 'Arafat when he revealed the last verses of the Qur'an, thereby "completing" the religion of Islam.

**Gabriel** (Jibril, in Arabic). The messenger angel that revealed God's word to Muhammad.

**Hagar.** Ibrahim's concubine and the mother of his son, Isma'il.

*Haram.* "Sanctuary." The name of the Grand Mosque in Mecca (al-Masjid al-Haram). In the Arabic "dual" form (*al-Haramayn*), the common title for the two holy cities of Mecca and Medina.

*Hoca.* A religious teacher in Turkey.

**Iblis. Satan.** The jealous angel that was cast out of heaven for disobeying God's instruction to bow before Adam. The seducer of Adam and Eve who plotted humanity's expulsion from paradise. The unsuccessful tempter of Ibrahim, who remained ready to carry out God's order to sacrifice his son, Isma'il.

**Ibrahim. Abraham.** The founder of monotheism, who destroyed the idols of polytheism and rebuilt the *Ka'ba.* The master of Hagar and, by her, the father of Isma'il.

**'Id al-Adha.** The most important holiday in the Islamic calendar. On this day, Muslims all over the world imitate the hajjis in Mina by sacrificing an animal and distributing a portion of the meat to neighbors and poor people in their own countries. The Arabic name means the "Greater Feast"—in distinction to the "Lesser Feast" marking the end of Ramadan, the month of fasting. In Turkish, 'Id al-Adha is called Kurban Bayramı ("the Holiday of Sacrifice"); in Malay and Indonesian, it is Hari Raya ("Feast Day"); and throughout West Africa, it is known as Tabaski.

*Ihram.* The state of ritual purity that pilgrims must enter and maintain in order to perform the hajj. It also refers to the clothing that pilgrims don to symbolize their state of purity—for men, two seamless white garments worn around the waist and torso; for women, any loose-fitting garment that is modest and comfortable.

*Ijtihad.* The use of independent reason in religious questions.

**International regime.** An agreed set of rules and procedures nations adopt to achieve common goals that none can accomplish alone. Some international regimes are explicitly described in formal treaties and managed by multinational organizations. Some regimes grow out of the accretion of state practice, relying on custom and informal consensus rather than written contracts. Many international regimes, such as the law of the sea and the rules governing the hajj, originate as informal customary arrangements and evolve into more institutionalized systems.

**Isma'il.** The son of Ibrahim and Hagar. God ordered Ibrahim to kill Isma'il as a sacrificial offering but then agreed to accept an animal instead.

*Jamara* (singular form of *jamarat*). One of three stone pillars in Mina signifying Satan's repeated efforts to tempt Ibrahim into disobeying God's command to kill Ism'ail.

*Ka'ba*. "God's house" on earth. The cubelike building in the center of the Grand Mosque; the spiritual center of Islam that Muslims everywhere face during daily prayers. Ibrahim and Isma'il built it following Gabriel's instructions. According to some Meccan traditions, they built it on the foundation of an ancient *Ka'ba* that had been erected by Adam or by angels. Muhammad cleansed the *Ka'ba* of pagan idols and made it a center of the Islamic pilgrimage.

**Khan.** A tribal leader, especially in Pakistan and Afghanistan.

*Kiswa.* The ornate cover of the *Ka'ba* decorated with verses from the Qur'an embroidered in gold thread. Every year, the *Ka'ba* is "dressed" in a new *kiswa*, and pilgrims take home parts of the old one as souvenirs. Islamic dynasties competed with each other for the honor of providing the *kiswa*, viewing the gesture as a sign of their political protection over the hajj and the Holy Cities. Today, the *kiswa* is manufactured exclusively in Saudi Arabia.

*Madrasa. Medrese*, in Turkish. An Islamic school of higher learning.

*Manasik.* Rules specifying the detailed requirements of a legally valid hajj. The guidebooks containing these rules, as well as suggested prayers for each stage of the hajj, usually prepared by state-sponsored religious scholars and distributed by official pilgrimage agencies.

*Mash'ar.* The area immediately surrounding the valley of Muzdalifa, where pilgrims spend the night after completing the Day of Standing at 'Arafat and before moving on toward Mina.

*Maulvi.* A religious leader, particularly in eastern Pakistan and Afghanistan.

**Muzdalifa.** The valley between 'Arafat and Mina, where pilgrims spend the night after the Day of Standing and where they gather pebbles to throw at the devil when they arrive at Mina the next morning.

*Mesnevi.* Mathnawi, in Arabic. The title of Celaleddin Rumi's most celebrated poetic masterpiece.

**Mina.** The sprawling tent city between Mecca and 'Arafat, where pilgrims camp before and after the Day of Standing on the ninth day of Dhu al-Hijjah. Mina is where pilgrims perform the animal sacrifice on the tenth day of Dhu al-Hijjah and where they throw stones at the three pillars (*jamarat*) symbolizing Satan between the tenth and thirteenth days of the month.

*Muhajir.* A citizen of Pakistan whose family emigrated from India after partition.

*Mullah.* A religious leader. In the cities, a scholar and teacher but, in the countryside, more likely a Sufi *shaykh* or a respected prayer leader.

*Multazim.* A small portion of the *Ka'ba's* northeastern wall between the Black Stone and the *Ka'ba* door; particularly popular among women who believe that fertility is enhanced by pressing their bodies against this part of the building.

*Peci* **cap.** A narrow brimless cap typically worn by men in Indonesia.

**"Persistent objector."** See *customary international law*.

*Pir.* A leader of a Sufi organization, particularly in Pakistan.

*Rauda.* A particularly sacred spot in the Prophet's Mosque in Medina, located between Muhammad's pulpit and his tomb; known as a garden of paradise.

**Rule of recognition.** H. L. A. Hart's term for the master rule that governs how a legal

system creates all of its other rules. In reality, this is not a single rule but a bun-
dle of constitutional provisions about identifying acceptable sources of law, interpreting them, and translating those interpretations into binding obligations. Following Hart, many legal theorists argue that international law lacks a firm rule
of recognition defining its sources, particularly customary international law.
Nonetheless, they also argue that international law is gradually developing a rule
of recognition and, in any event, that the rule is already clear enough to make
international law a system of "real" law that everyone must respect.

*Sa'y.* The second half of the *'umra,* performed after the *tawaf.* Running seven times
between two hills (al-Safa and al-Marwa) on the eastern perimeter of the Grand
Mosque to commemorate Hagar's search for water and her discovery of the sacred well of Zamzam.

*Shari'ah.* Islamic law derived by legal scholars with various viewpoints relying on four
major sources: the Qur'an, the exemplary actions and sayings of Muhammad,
reasoning by analogy on a case-by-case basis, and the consensus of the community.

*Shaykh.* A leader of a mystical order.

*Sufi.* An Islamic mystic.

*Tabung Haji.* Malaysia's state-sponsored pilgrimage board and a pioneer in Islamic
banking and investment.

*Talbiya.* A greeting to God that pilgrims chant in unison as they draw closer to Mecca,
beginning in a quiet conversational tone and slowly building to a deafening roar.
The greeting signifies that pilgrims are answering God's call to visit his house
and placing themselves at his service.

*Tarikat.* An organization of Sufis, particularly in Turkey.

*Tawaf.* Circling the *Ka'ba* seven times; usually performed three times during the hajj:
upon entering Mecca (the "*tawaf* of arrival"), after returning from 'Arafat (the
"emptying *tawaf*"), and just before departing Mecca for the last time ("the farewell *tawaf*").

*'Ulama.* (plural form of *'alim*).

*Umma.* The worldwide community of Muslims.

*'Umra.* The "lesser pilgrimage," comprising the *tawaf* and the *sa'y;* it can be performed as part of the hajj or separately at any other time of the year. No number
of *'umras* can substitute for a proper hajj.

*Zakat.* The annual charitable contribution that Muslims give to religious or governmental agencies. One of the five basic obligations of Islam.

*Zamzam.* The well inside the Grand Mosque in Mecca just east of the *Ka'ba.* God
revealed the well to Hagar and Isma'il when they were abandoned in the desert
and desperately searching for water. Some of the most popular souvenirs of the
hajj are bottles of Zamzam water because of the spiritual strength it supposedly
gives to all who drink it.

*Ziyara.* "Visit." A visitation to any sacred spot but usually to the tomb of a saint anywhere in the Islamic world. Also a visit to any of the historic sites and cemeteries
in Mecca and Medina, including the Prophet's Mosque. No number of *ziyaras* of
any sort can substitute for a proper hajj.

# Selected Bibliography

Abdullah, Taufik. "Islam and the Formation of Tradition in Indonesia: A Comparative Perspective." *Itinerario* 13 (1989): 17–36.

Abdurrahman, Moeslim. "On Hajj Tourism: In Search of Piety and Identity in the New Order Indonesia." PhD diss., University of Illinois, 2000.

Abu Sulayman, Abdul Hamid A. *Towards an Islamic Theory of International Relations: New Directions for Methodology and Thought*. Herndon, VA: International Institute of Islamic Thought, 1993.

Adamu, Mahdi. *The Hausa Factor in West African History*. Zaria, Nigeria: Oxford University Press, 1978.

Ahmad, Zakaria Haji. *Government and Politics of Malaysia*. New York: Oxford University Press, 1987.

Ahmed, Akbar S. *Religion and Politics in Muslim Society: Resistance and Control in Pakistan*. New York: Routledge, 1991.

Ahmed, Akbar S., and Hastings Donnan, eds. *Islam, Globalization, and Postmodernity*. London and New York: Routledge, 1994.

Akhund, Iqbal. *Trial and Error: The Advent and Eclipse of Benazir Bhutto*. Karachi: Oxford University Press, 2000.

Al-Ahsan, Abdullah. *The Organization of the Islamic Conference: An Introduction to an Islamic Political Institution*. Herndon, VA: International Institute of Islamic Thought, 1988.

Al-Azmeh, Aziz. *Islams and Modernities*. London: Verso, 1996.

Albert, Mathias, Lothar Brock, and Klaus Dieter Wolf, eds. *Civilizing World Politics: Society and Community beyond the State*. Lanham, MD: Rowman and Littlefield, 2001.

Al-Naqar, 'Umar. *The Pilgrimage Tradition in West Africa*. Khartoum: Khartoum University Press, 1972.

Amal, Ichlasul. *Regional and Central Government in Indonesian Politics: West Sumatra and South Sulawesi, 1949–1979*. Yogyakarta: Gadjah Mada University Press, 1992.

Andrews, Peter Alford, ed. *Ethnic Groups in the Republic of Turkey*. Wiesbaden: Dr. Ludwig Reichert Verlag, 1989.

An-Na'im, Abdullahi Ahmad. *Toward an Islamic Reformation: Civil Liberties, Human Rights, and International Law*. Syracuse, NY: Syracuse University Press, 1990.

Arkoun, Mohammed. *Lectures du Coran*. Paris: Maisonneuve et Larose, 1982.

Baba, Noor Ahmad. *Organisation of Islamic Conference: Theory and Practice of Pan-Islamic Cooperation*. Karachi: Oxford University Press, 1994.

Baker, Pauline H. *Urbanization and Political Change: The Politics of Lagos, 1917–1967*. Berkeley: University of California Press, 1974.

Barkindo, Bawuro M., ed. *Kano and Some of Her Neighbors*. Kano, Nigeria: Bayero University Press, 1989.

Barlow, Colin, ed. *Modern Malaysia in the Global Economy: Political and Social Change into the 21st Century*. Cheltenham, UK: Edward Elgar, 2001.

Barnes, Sandra T. *Patrons and Power: Creating a Political Community in Metropolitan Lagos*. Bloomington: Indiana University Press, 1986.

Bassiouni, M. Cherif, ed. *The Islamic Criminal Justice System*. New York: Oceana, 1982.

Beck, Robert J., Anthony Clark Arend, and D. Vandr Lugt, eds. *International Rules: Approaches from International Law and International Relations*. New York: Oxford University Press, 1996.

Beelaert, Anna Livia F. A. "The Ka'ba as a Woman: A Topos in Classical Persian Literature." *Persica* 13 (1988–1999): 107–23.

Bell, Richard. "Muhammad's Pilgrimage Proclamation." *Journal of the Royal Central Asian Society* 24 (1937): 223–44.

Benda, Harry J. "Christiaan Snouck Hurgronje and the Foundations of Dutch Islamic Policy in Indonesia." *Journal of Modern History* 30 (1958): 338–47.

———. *The Crescent and the Rising Sun: Indonesian Islam under the Japanese Occupation, 1942–1945*. The Hague: W. van Hoeve, 1958.

Benson, Steven R. "Islam and Social Change in the Writings of 'Ali Shari'ati: His 'Hajj' as Mystical Handbook for Revolutionaries." *The Muslim World* 81 (1991): 9–26.

Bharati, Agehananda. "Pilgrimage Sites and Indian Civilization." In *Chapters in Indian Civilization*, edited by Joseph W. Elder, 84–126. Dubuque, Iowa: Kendall/Hunt, 1970.

Bhardwaj, Surinder Mohan. "Hindu Pilgrimage in America." In *Social Anthropology of Pilgrimage*, edited by Makhan Jha, 81–98. New Delhi: Inter-India Publications, 1991.

Bhardwaj, Surinder M., Gisbert Rinschede, and Angelika Sievers, eds. *Pilgrimage in the Old and New World*. Berlin: Dietrich Reimer Verlag, 1994.

Binder, Leonard. *Islamic Liberalism: A Critique of Development Ideologies*. Chicago: University of Chicago Press, 1988.

———. *Religion and Politics in Pakistan*. Berkeley: University of California Press, 1961.

Bistolfi, Robert, and François Zabbal, eds. *Islams d'Europe: Intégration ou insertion communautaire?* Paris: Edition de l'Aube, 1995.

Boland, B. J. *The Struggle of Islam in Modern Indonesia*. The Hague: Martinus Nijhoff, 1982.

Bowen, John R. *Muslims through Discourse: Religion and Ritual in Gayo Society.* Princeton, NJ: Princeton University Press, 1993.

Brenner, Louis, ed. *Muslim Identity and Social Change in Sub-Saharan Africa.* Bloomington: Indiana University Press, 1993.

Burki, Shahid Javed. *Pakistan under Bhutto, 1971–1977.* New York: St. Martin's Press, 1980.

Buzan, Barry. "From International System to International Society: Structural Realism and Regime Theory Meet the English School." *International Organization* 47 (Summer 1993): 327–52.

Byers, Michael. *Custom, Power, and the Power of Rules: International Relations and Customary International Law.* Cambridge: Cambridge University Press, 1999.

————, ed. *The Role of Law in International Politics: Essays in International Relations and International Law.* Oxford: Oxford University Press, 2000.

Callaway, Barbara J. *Muslim Hausa Women in Nigeria: Tradition and Change.* Syracuse, NY: Syracuse University Press, 1987.

Chand, Attar. *Pakistan: Party Politics, Pressure Groups, and Minorities.* New Delhi: Commonwealth, 1991.

Charney, Jonathan I. "The Persistent Objector Rule and the Development of Customary International Law." *British Yearbook of International Law* 56 (1985): 1–24.

————. "Universal International Law." *American Journal of International Law* 87 (1993): 529–51.

Chélini, Jean, and Henry Brauthomme, eds. *Histoire des pèlerinages non-chrétiens: Entre magique et sacre: le chemin des dieux.* Paris: Hachett, 1987.

Chiba, Masaji. *Legal Pluralism: Toward a General Theory through Japanese Legal Culture.* Tokyo: Tokai University Press, 1989.

Cohn, Bernard S., and McKim Marriott. "Networks and Centres in the Integration of Indian Civilisation." *Journal of Social Research* 1 (1958): 1–9.

Coleman, Simon, and John Elsner. *Pilgrimage: Past and Present in the World Religions.* Cambridge, MA: Harvard University Press, 1995.

Coles, Catherine, and Beverly Mack, eds. *Hausa Women in the Twentieth Century.* Madison: University of Wisconsin Press, 1991.

Cooper, Barbara. "The Strength in the Song: Muslim Personhood, Audible Capital, and Hausa Women's Performance of the Hajj." *Social Text* 60 (1999): 87–109.

Corbin, Henry. *Creative Imagination in the Sufism of Ibn 'Arabi.* Princeton, NJ: Princeton University Press, 1969.

Corwin, Edward S. "The Debt of American Constitutional Law to Natural Law Concepts." *Notre Dame Lawyer* 25 (1949): 258–84.

Coulon, Christian. *Les Musulmans et Le Pouvoir en Afrique Noire: Religion et Contreculture.* Paris: Éditions Karthala, 1983.

Coulson, Noel J. *Conflicts and Tensions in Islamic Jurisprudence.* Chicago: University of Chicago Press, 1969.

Crampton, E. P. T. *Christianity in Northern Nigeria.* London: Geoffrey Chapman, 1979.

Creevey, Lucy E. "Muslim Brotherhoods and Politics in Senegal in 1985." *Journal of Modern African Studies* 23 (1985): 715–21.

Crouch, Harold. *Government and Society in Malaysia.* Ithaca, NY: Cornell University Press, 1996.

Curtin, Philip D. *Cross-Cultural Trade in World History*. Cambridge: Cambridge University Press, 1984.

Danarto. *A Javanese Pilgrim in Mecca (Orang Jawa Naik Haji)*. Translated by Harry Aveling. Clayton, Victoria: Monash University Press, 1989.

Daniel, E. Valentine. *Fluid Signs: Being a Person the Tamil Way*. Berkeley: University of California Press, 1984.

Dehwar, Malik Muhammad Saeed. *Contemporary History of Balochistan*. Quetta, Pakistan: Third World Publications, 1994.

Diagne, Bachir Soleymane. *Islam et société ouverte: La fidélité et le mouvement dans la pensée de Muhammad Iqbal*. Paris: Maisonneuve et Larose, 2001.

Diamond, Larry, Anthony Kirk-Greene, and Oyeleye Oyediran, eds. *Transition without End: Nigerian Politics and Civil Society under Babangida*. Boulder, CO: Lynne Rienner, 1997.

Donnan, Hastings. "Symbol and Status: The Significance of the Hajj in Pakistan." *The Muslim World* 79 (July–October 1989): 205–16.

Drake, Christine. *National Integration in Indonesia: Patterns and Policies*. Honolulu: University of Hawaii Press, 1989.

Dubey, D. P. *Prayaga, The Site of Kumbha Mela: In Temporal and Traditional Space*. New Delhi: Aryan Books International, 2001.

Du Plessis, I. D. *The Cape Malays*. Cape Town, South Africa: Maskew Miller, 1944.

Eade, John, and Michael J. Kallnow, eds. *Contesting the Sacred: The Anthropology of Christian Pilgrimage*. New York: Routledge, 1991.

Eaton, Gai. "The Hajj: The Two Journeys to Mecca." *Parabola* 9 (1984): 18–25.

Eck, Diana L. *Banaras: City of Light*. New York: Knopf, 1982.

———. *Encountering God: A Spiritual Journey from Bozeman to Banaras*. Boston: Beacon, 1993.

Edge, Ian, ed. *Comparative Law in Global Perspective*. Ardsley, NY: Transnational, 2000.

———, ed. *Islamic Law and Legal Theory*. New York: New York University Press, 1996.

Eickelman, Dale F., and James Piscatori, eds. *Muslim Travellers: Pilgrimage, Migration, and the Religious Imagination*. Berkeley: University of California Press, 1990.

Eliade, Mircea. *The Myth of the Eternal Return or, Cosmos and History*. Princeton, NJ: Princeton University Press, 1974.

———. *The Sacred and the Profane: The Nature of Religion*. New York: Harcourt, Brace, Jovanovich, 1959.

*Encyclopaedia of Islam*, 1987 ed., s.v. "Hadjdj," by Bernard Lewis.

*Encyclopedia of Religion*, 1987 ed., s.v. "Mircea Eliade," by Joseph Kitagawa.

*Encyclopedia of the Social Sciences*, 1979 ed., s.v. "Myth and Symbol," by Victor W. Turner.

———, s.v. "Ritual," by Edmund Leach.

Enwerem, Iheanyi M. *A Dangerous Awakening: The Politicization of Religion in Nigeria*. Ibadan, Nigeria: Insitut français de recherche en Afrique, 1995.

Esack, Farid. *Qur'an, Liberation, and Pluralism: An Islamic Perspective of Interreligious Solidarity against Oppression*. Oxford: Oneworld, 1997.

———. "Three Islamic Strands in the South African Struggle for Justice." *Third World Quarterly* 10 (April 1988): 473–98.

Esposito, John L., and John O. Voll, *Makers of Contemporary Islam*. New York: Oxford University Press, 2001.

Esposito, John L., and Michael Watson, eds. *Religion and Global Order*. Cardiff: University of Wales Press, 2000.

Ewing, Katherine. "The Politics of Sufism: Redefining the Saints of Pakistan." *Journal of Asian Studies* 42 (February 1983): 251–68.

Falassi, Alessandro. *Palio*. Milan: Electa, 1983.

Falola, Toyin. *Violence in Nigeria: The Crisis of Religious Politics and Secular Ideologies*. Rochester, NY: University of Rochester Press, 1998.

Falola, Toyin, and Akanmu Adebayo. *Culture, Politics, and Money among the Yoruba*. New Brunswick, NJ: Transaction, 2000.

Farâhânî, Mirzâ Mohammad Hosayn. *A Shi'ite Pilgrimage to Mecca, 1885–1886: The Safarnâmeh of Mirzâ Mohammad Hosayn Farâhânî*. Edited, translated, and annotated by Hafez F. Farmayan and Elton L. Daniel. Austin: University of Texas Press, 1990.

Faroqhi, Suraiya. *Pilgrims and Sultans: the Hajj under the Ottomans, 1517–1683*. New York: St. Martin's Press, 1994.

Fealy, Greg, and Greg Barton, eds. *Nahdlatul Ulama, Traditional Islam and Modernity in Indonesia*. Clayton, Victoria: Monash University Asia Institute, 1996.

Feillard, Andrée. *Islam et armée dans l'Indonésie contemporaine: les pionniers de la traditions*. Paris: L'Harmattan, 1995.

Feith, Herbert. *The Decline of Constitutional Democracy in Indonesia*. Ithaca, NY: Cornell University Press, 1962.

Firestone, Reuven. *Journeys in Holy Lands: The Evolution of the Abraham-Ishmael Legends in Islamic Exegesis*. Albany: State University of New York Press, 1990.

Forrest, Tom. *The Advance of African Capital: The Growth of Nigerian Private Enterprise*. Charlottesville: University Press of Virginia, 1994.

Fuller, Graham E. *From Eastern Europe to Western China: The Growing Role of Turkey in the World and Its Implications for Western Interests*. Santa Monica, CA: RAND, 1993.

George, William. "Envisioning Global Community: The Theological Character of the Common Heritage Concept in the Law of the Sea." PhD diss., University of Chicago Divinity School, 1990.

Gluckman, Max, ed. *Essays on the Ritual of Social Relations*. Manchester, UK: Manchester University Press, 1961.

Gold, Ann Grodzins. *Fruitful Journeys: The Ways of Rajasthani Pilgrims*. Berkeley: University of California Press, 1988.

Goldstein, Judith L., Miles Kahler, Robert O. Keohane, and Anne-Marie Slaughter, eds. *Legalization and World Politics*. Cambridge, MA: MIT Press, 2001.

Gomez, Edmund Terence, and K. S. Jomo. *Malaysia's Political Economy: Politics, Patronage and Profits*. Cambridge: Cambridge University Press, 1997.

Gunter, Michael H. *The Kurds and the Future of Turkey*. New York: St. Martin's Press, 1997.

Hallaq, Wael B. "Legal Reasoning in Islamic Law and the Common Law: Logic and Method." *Cleveland State Law Review* 34 (1985–86): 79–96.

Harpur, James. *The Atlas of Sacred Places: Meeting Points of Heaven and Earth*. New York: Henry Holt, 1994.

Harrison, Christopher. *France and Islam in West Africa, 1860–1960*. Cambridge: Cambridge University Press, 1988.

Hart, H. L. A. *The Concept of Law*. London: Oxford University Press, 1961.

Harvey, Barbara S. *Permesta: Half a Rebellion*. Ithaca, NY: Cornell Modern Indonesia Project, 1977.

Hasenclever, Andreas, Peter Mayer, and Volker Rittberger. *Theories of International Regimes*. Cambridge: Cambridge University Press, 1997.

Hefner, Robert W. *Civil Islam: Muslims and Democratization in Indonesia*. Princeton, NJ: Princeton University Press, 2000.

Heim, Barbara Ellen. "Exploring the Last Frontiers for Mineral Resources: A Comparison of International Law Regarding the Deep Seabed, Outer Space, and Antarctica." *Vanderbilt Journal of Transnational Law* 23 (1990): 819–49.

Hill, Hal. *The Indonesian Economy*. New York: Cambridge University Press, 2000.

———, ed. *Unity and Diversity: Regional Economic Development in Indonesia since 1970*. New York: Oxford University Press, 1989.

Hilley, John. *Malaysia: Mahathirism, Hegemony, and the New Opposition*. London: Zed, 2001.

Hodgson, Marshall G. S. *The Venture of Islam: Conscience and History in a World Civilization*. Chicago: University of Chicago Press, 1974.

Hooker, M. B., ed. *Islam in South-East Asia*. Leiden: E. J. Brill, 1983.

Horowitz, Donald L. "The Qur'an and the Common Law: Islamic Law Reform and the Theory of Legal Change." *American Journal of Comparative Law* 42 (1994): 543–80.

Ibrahim, Jibrin. "The Politics of Religion in Nigeria: The Parameters of the 1987 Crisis in Kaduna State." *Review of African Political Economy* 45 (1989): 65–82.

Iqbal, Muhammad. *The Reconstruction of Religious Thought in Islam*. Lahore: Ashraf, 1962.

———. *The Secrets of the Self*. Translated by Reynold A. Nicholson. London: Macmillan, 1920.

Iriye, Akira. *Cultural Internationalism and World Order*. Baltimore: Johns Hopkins University Press, 1997.

Jalazai, Musa Khan, ed. *Sectarianism and Politico-Religious Terrorism in Pakistan*. Lahore, Pakistan: Tarteeb, 1993.

James, Ibrahim. *Studies in the History, Politics, and Cultures of Southern Kaduna Peoples Groups*. Jos, Nigeria: Ladsomas, 1997.

James, Wilmot G., and Mary Simons, eds. *The Angry Divide: Social and Economic History of the Western Cape*. Cape Town, South Africa: David Philip, 1989.

Janis, Mark W. *An Introduction to International Law*. Boston: Little, Brown, 1993.

Janis, Mark W., and Carolyn Evans, eds. *Religion and International Law*. The Hague: Martinus Nijhoff, 1999.

Janmahmad. *Essays on Baloch National Struggle in Pakistan*. Quetta, Pakistan: Gosh-e-Adab, 1989.

Jesudason, James V. *Ethnicity and the Economy: The State, Chinese Business, and Multinationals in Malaysia*. Singapore: Oxford University Press, 1989.

Johnston, Douglas, and Cynthia Sampson, eds. *Religion, the Missing Dimension of Statecraft*. New York: Oxford University Press, 1994.

Jomier, Jacques. *Le Mahmal et la caravane égyptienne des pèlerins de la Mekke (XIIIe–XXe siècles)*. Cairo: L'Insitut Français d'Archéologie Orientale, 1953.

Kahn, Joel S. "Class, Culture, and Malaysian Modernity." In *Social Change in Southeast Asia*, edited by Johannes Dragsbaek Schmidt, Jacques Hers, and Niels Forld, 81–97. London: Longman, 1998.

Kalu, Ogbu U. *Divided People of God: Church Union Movement in Nigeria, 1875–1966*. Lagos, Nigeria: NOK, 1978.

Kamal, Ahmad. *The Sacred Journey*. New York: Duell, Sloan and Pearce, 1961.

Keck, Margaret E., and Kathryn Sikkink. *Activists beyond Borders: Advocacy Networks in International Politics*. Ithaca, NY: Cornell University Press, 1998.

Kertzer, David. *Ritual, Politics, and Power*. New Haven: Yale University Press, 1988.

Kessler, Clive S. *Islam and Politics in a Malay State: Kelantan 1838–1969*. Ithaca, NY: Cornell University Press, 1978.

Klotz, Audie. *Norms in International Relations: The Struggle against Apartheid*. Ithaca, NY: Cornell University Press, 1995.

Koh, Harold Hongju. "Transnational Legal Process." *Nebraska Law Review* 75 (1996): 181–207.

Koon, Heng Pek. *Chinese Politics in Malaysia: A History of the Malaysian Chinese Association*. Singapore: Oxford University Press, 1988.

Koskenniemi, Martii. *From Apology to Utopia: The Structure of International Legal Argument*. Helsinki: Finnish Lawyer's Publication Co., 1989.

Kramer, Martin. "Khomeini's Messengers: The Disputed Pilgrimage of Islam." In *Religious Radicalism and Politics in the Middle East*, edited by Emmanuel Sivan and Menachem Friedman, 177–94. Albany: State University of New York Press, 1990.

Kukah, Matthew Hassan, and Toyin Falola. *Religious Militancy and Self-Assertion: Islam and Politics in Nigeria*. Aldershot, UK: Avebury, 1996.

Landau, Jacob M. *The Hejaz Railway and the Muslim Pilgrimage: A Case of Ottoman Political Propaganda*. Detroit: Wayne State University Press, 1971.

———. *The Politics of Pan-Islam: Ideology and Organization*. Oxford: Clarendon Press, 1990.

Lawyers Committee for Human Rights, ed. *Islam and Justice: Debating the Future of Human Rights in the Middle East and North Africa*. New York: Lawyers Committee for Human Rights, 1997.

Legrand, Pierre. "How to Compare Now." *Legal Studies* 16 (1996): 232–42.

———. "The Impossibility of 'Legal Transplants.'" *Maastricht Journal of European and Comparative Law* 4 (1997): 111–24.

Lev, Daniel S. *Islamic Courts in Indonesia: A Study in the Political Bases of Legal Institutions*. Berkeley: University of California Press, 1972.

Liddle, William R. "The Islamic Turn in Indonesia: A Political Explanation." *Journal of Asian Studies* 55 (August 1996): 613–34.

Lindholm, Tore, and Kari Vogt, eds. *Islamic Law Reform and Human Rights: Challenges and Rejoinders*. Oslo: Nordic Human Rights Publications, 1993.

Lodhi, Maleeha. *Pakistan's Encounter with Democracy*. Lahore, Pakistan: Vanguard, 1994.

Loimeier, Roman. *Islamic Reform and Political Change in Northern Nigeria*. Evanston, IL: Northwestern University Press, 1997.

———. "Das 'Nigerian Pilgrimage Scheme': Zum Versuch, den Hagg in Nigeria zu organisieren." *African Spectrum* 23 (1988): 201–14.

Long, David Edwin. *The Hajj Today: A Survey of the Contemporary Makkah Pilgrimage.* Albany: State University of New York Press, 1979.

Lubeck, Paul M. *Islam and Urban Labor in Northern Nigeria: The Making of a Muslim Working Class.* Cambridge: Cambridge University Press, 1986.

MacAloon, John J. *"This Great Symbol": Pierre de Coubertin and the Origins of the Modern Olympic Games.* Chicago: University of Chicago Press, 1981.

MacIntyre, Andrew, ed. *Business and Government in Industrializing Asia.* Ithaca, NY: Cornell University Press, 1994.

Madjid, Nurcholish. "Islamic Roots of Modern Pluralism: Indonesian Experiences." *Studia Islamika* 1 (April–June 1994): 55–77.

Magenda, Burhan. *East Kalimantan: The Decline of a Commercial Aristocracy.* Ithaca, NY: Cornell Modern Indonesia Project, 1991.

Mahadi, Abdullahi, George Amale Kwanashie, and Alhaji Mahmood Yakubu, eds. *Nigeria: The State of the Nation and the Way Forward.* Kaduna, Nigeria: Arewa House, 1994.

Makky, Ghazy Abdul Wahed. *Mecca, the Pilgrimage City: A Study of Pilgrim Accommodation.* London: Croom Helm, 1978.

Malik, Iftikhar H. (Gaffney, Patrick). *State and Civil Society in Pakistan: Politics of Authority, Ideology, and Ethnicity.* New York: St. Martin's Press, 1997.

Malik, Jamal. *Colonization of Islam: Dissolution of Traditional Institutions in Pakistan.* New Delhi: Manohar, 1996.

Mama, Amina. *Changes of State: Gender Politics and Transition in Nigeria.* Cape Town, South Africa: University of Cape Town Press, 2000.

Mandaville, Peter G. *Transnational Muslim Politics: Reimagining the Umma.* London: Routledge, 2001.

Mardin, Sherif. *Religion and Social Change in Modern Turkey: The Case of Bediuzzaman Said Nursi.* Albany: State University of New York Press, 1989.

Markesinis, Basil S., ed. *The Millennium Lectures: The Coming Together of the Common Law and the Civil Law.* Oxford: Hart, 2000.

Masud, Muhammad Khalid, Brinkley Messick, and David S. Powers, eds. *Islamic Legal Interpretation: Muftis and Their Fatwas.* Cambridge, MA: Harvard University Press, 1996.

Matheson, V., and A. C. Milner. *Perceptions of the Haj: Five Malay Texts.* Singapore: Institute of Southeast Asian Studies, 1984.

Mauzy, Diane K. "Malaysia in 1987: Decline of 'The Malay Way.'" *Asian Survey* 28 (February 1988): 213–22.

Mayer, Ann Elizabeth. *Islam and Human Rights: Tradition and Politics.* Boulder, CO: Westview, 1995.

Mba, Nina. "Kaba and Khaki: Women and the Militarised State in Nigeria." In *Women and the State in Africa,* edited by Jane L. Parpart and Kathleen A. Staudt, 69–90. Boulder, CO: Lynne Rienner, 1989.

Mbacké, Khadim. "Le pèlerinage à La Mecque: le cas du Sénégal de 1886 à 1986." PhD diss., Université Cheikh Anta Diop de Dakar, 1991.

———. *Soufisme et confréries religieuses au Sénégal.* Dakar, Senegal: Presses de l'Imprimerie Saint-Paul, 1995.

McDonnell, Mary Byrne. "The Conduct of Hajj from Malaysia and Its Socioeconomic Impact on Malay Society: A Descriptive and Analytical Study, 1860–1981." PhD diss., Columbia University, 1986.

Means, Gordon P. *Malaysian Politics: The Second Generation.* New York: Oxford University Press, 1991.

Meier, Fritz. "The Mystery of the Ka'ba: Symbol and Reality in Islamic Mysticism." *Eranos Yearbooks* 24 (1955): 149–168.

Melczer, William. *The Pilgrim's Guide to Santiago de Compostela.* New York: Italica, 1993.

Metcalf, Barbara Daly, ed. *Making Muslim Space in North America and Europe.* Berkeley: University of California Press, 1996.

Miles, William F. S. *Hausaland Divided: Colonialism and Independence in Nigeria and Niger.* Ithaca, NY: Cornell University Press, 1994.

Milner, A. C. "Rethinking Islamic Fundamentalism in Malaysia." *Review of Indonesian and Malayan Affairs* 20 (Summer 1988): 48–75.

Moghadam, Valentine M., ed. *Identity Politics and Women: Cultural Reassertions and Feminisms in International Perspective.* Boulder, CO: Westview, 1994.

Moinuddin, Hasan. *The Charter of the Islamic Conference and Legal Framework of Economic Co-Operation among Its Member States.* New York: Oxford University Press, 1987.

Morinins, E. Alan. *Pilgrimage in the Hindu Tradition: A Case Study of West Bengal.* Delhi: Oxford University Press, 1984.

———, ed. *Sacred Journeys: the Anthropology of Pilgrimage.* Westport, CT: Greenwood, 1992.

Munro-Kua, Anne. *Authoritarian Populism in Malaysia.* New York: St. Martin's Press, 1996.

Murphy, Cornelius F., Jr. *Theories of World Governance: A Study in the History of Ideas.* Washington, DC: Catholic University of America Press, 1999.

Muzaffer, Chandra. *Islamic Resurgence in Malaysia.* Petaling Jaya, Selangor, Malaysia: Penerbit Fajar Bakti Sdr. Bhd., 1987.

Nagata, Judith. *The Reflowering of Malaysian Islam: Modern Religious Radicals and Their Roots.* Vancouver, Canada: University of British Columbia Press, 1984.

Nakamura, Mitsuo. *The Crescent Arises over the Banyan Tree: A Study of the Muhammadiyah Movement in a Central Javanese Town.* Yogyakarta, Indonesia: Gadjah Mada University Press, 1983.

Netton, Ian Richard, ed. *Golden Roads: Migration, Pilgrimage, and Travel in Mediaeval and Modern Islam.* Richmond, UK: Curzon, 1993.

Neumann, Iver B., and Ole Waever, eds. *The Future of International Relations: Masters in the Making.* New York: Routledge, 1997.

Newberg, Paula R. *Judging the State: Courts and Constitutional Politics in Pakistan.* New York: Cambridge University Press, 1995.

Noer, Deliar. *Administration of Islam in Indonesia.* Ithaca, NY: Cornell University Southeast Asia Program, 1978.

———. *The Modernist Muslim Movement in Indonesia, 1900–1942.* London: Oxford University Press, 1973.

Nolan, Mary Lee, and Sidney Nolan. *Christian Pilgrimage in Modern Western Europe.* Chapel Hill: University of North Carolina Press, 1989.

O'Brien, Robert, Anne Marie Goetz, Jan Aart Scholte, and Marc Williams. *Contesting Global Governance: Multilateral Economic Institutions and Global Social Movements.* Cambridge: Cambridge University Press, 2000.

O'Brien, Susan. "Pilgrimage, Power, and Identity: The Role of the Hajj in the Lives of Nigerian Hausa Bori Adepts." *Africa Today* 46 (Summer 1999): 11–40.

Ochsenwald, William. *Religion, Society, and the State in Arabia: the Hijaz under Ottoman Control, 1840–1908.* Columbus: Ohio State University Press, 1984.

Örücü, Esin Elspeth Attwool, and Sean Coyle. *Studies in Legal Systems: Mixed and Mixing.* The Hague: Kluwer, 1996.

Paden, John N. *Ahmadu Bello: Sardauna of Sokoto.* London: Hodder and Stoughton, 1986.

———. *Religion and Political Culture in Kano.* Berkeley: University of California Press, 1973.

Parker, Ann, and Avon Neal. *Hajj Paintings: Folk Art of the Great Pilgrimage.* Washington, DC: Smithsonian Institution, 1995.

Pearson, Michael N. *Pilgrimage to Mecca: The Indian Experience, 1600–1800.* Princeton, NJ: Markus Wiener, 1996.

———. *Pious Passengers: The Hajj in Earlier Times.* New Delhi: Sterling, 1994.

Peters, F. E. *The Hajj: The Muslim Pilgrimage to Mecca and the Holy Places.* Princeton, NJ: Princeton University Press, 1994.

Peterson, Jeanette Favrot. "The Virgin of Guadalupe: Symbol of Conquest or Liberation?" *Art Journal* 51 (Winter 1992): 39–47.

Pitsuwan, Surin. *Islam and Malay Nationalism: A Case Study of the Malay-Muslims of Southern Thailand.* Bangkok: Thai Khadi Research Institute, Thammasat University, 1985.

Popovic, Alexandre. "Sur les recites de pèlerinage a la Mecque des musulmans Yougoslaves, 1949–1972." *Studia Islamica* 39 (1974): 129–44.

Pranowo, M. Bambang. "Islam and Party Politics in Rural Java." *Studia Islamika* 1 (1994): 1–19.

Rahman, Fazlur. *Islam and Modernity: Transformation of an Intellectual Tradition.* Chicago: University of Chicago Press, 1982.

Raillon, François. "How to Become a National Entrepreneur: The Rise of Indonesian Capitalists." *Archipel* 41 (1991): 89–116.

Rais, Mohammad Amien. "The Muslim Brotherhood in Egypt: Its Rise, Demise, and Resurgence." PhD diss., University of Chicago, 1981.

Ramage, Douglas E. *Politics in Indonesia: Democracy, Islam, and the Ideology of Tolerance.* London: Routledge, 1995.

Raphael, Freddy, ed. *Les pèlerinages de l'antiquité biblique et classique à l'occident medieval.* Paris: Librairie Orientalist Paul Geuthner, 1973.

Rasch, Bodo. *The Tent Cities of the Hajj.* Stuttgart: Institut für leichte Flächentragwerke, 1980.

Reader, Ian, and Tony Walter, eds. *Pilgrimage in Popular Culture.* Houndmills, Basingstoke, Hampshire, UK: Macmillan, 1993.

Reisman, W. Michael. "The Cult of Custom in the Late Twentieth Century." *California Western International Law Journal* 17 (1987): 133–45.

Ricklefs, M. C., ed. *Islam in the Indonesian Social Context.* Clayton, Victoria: Monash University Press, 1991.

Rittberger, Volker, ed. *Regime Theory and International Relations*. New York: Oxford University Press, 1993.

Robinson, A. E. "The Mahmal of the Moslem Pilgrimage." *Journal of the Royal Asiatic Society* 31 (January 1931): 117–27.

Rodriguez, Jeanette. *Our Lady of Guadalupe: Faith and Empowerment among Mexican-American Women*. Austin: University of Texas Press, 1994.

Roff, William. "The Meccan Pilgrimage: Its Meaning for Southeast Asian Islam." In *Islam in Asia*, edited by Raphael Israeli and Anthony H. Johns, 2:238–45. Boulder, CO: Westview, 1984.

———. "Sanitation and Security: The Imperial Powers and the Nineteenth Century Hajj." *Arabian Studies* 6 (1982): 143–60.

Rosen, Lawrence. *The Anthropology of Justice: Law as Culture in Islamic Society*. New York: Cambridge University Press, 1989.

Rosenau, James N., and Ernst-Otto Czempiel, eds. *Governance without Government: Order and Change in World Politics*. New York: Cambridge University Press, 1992.

Roussel, Romain. *Les pèlerinages à travers les siècles: chrétiens, musulmans, bouddhistes, indous, taoïstes, shintoïstes*. Paris: Payot, 1954.

Rudolph, Susanne Hoeber, and James Piscatori, eds. *Transnational Religion and Fading States*. Boulder, CO: Westview, 1997.

Ruggie, John Gerard. *Constructing the World Polity: Essays on International Institutionalization*. New York: Routledge, 1998.

———, ed. *Multilateralism Matters: The Theory and Praxis of an Institutional Form*. New York: Columbia University Press, 1993.

Rush, Alan, ed. *Records of the Hajj: A Documentary History of the Pilgrimage to Mecca*. Slough, UK: Archive Editions, 1993.

Sachedina, Abdulaziz. *The Islamic Roots of Democratic Pluralism*. New York: Oxford University Press, 2000.

Sanneh, Lamin O. *The Crown and the Turban: Muslims and West African Pluralism*. Boulder, CO: Westview Press, 1997.

Sardar, Ziauddin, and M. A. Zaki Badawi, eds. *Hajj Studies*. London: Croom Helm, 1978.

Schimmel, Annemarie. *Deciphering the Signs of God: A Phenomenological Approach to Islam*. Albany: State University of New York Press, 1994.

———. *Gabriel's Wing: A Study into the Religious Ideas of Sir Muhammad Iqbal*. Lahore: Iqbal Academy Pakistan, 1989.

———. "Iqbal in the Context of Indo-Muslim Mystical Reform Movements." In *Islam in Asia*, edited by Yohanan Friedmann, 1: 208–26. Jerusalem: Magnes, 1984.

———. *The Triumphal Sun: A Study of the Works of Jalaloddin Rumi*. London: East-West, 1988.

Schwarz, Adam. *A Nation in Waiting: Indonesia in the 1990s*. Boulder, CO: Westview, 1994.

Scott, Jamie, and Paul Simpson-Housley, eds. *Sacred Places and Profane Spaces: Essays in the Geographies of Judaism, Christianity, and Islam*. New York: Greenwood, 1991.

Scupin, Raymond. "The Social Significance of the Hajj for Thai Muslims." *The Muslim World* 72 (1982): 25–33.

Searle, Peter. *The Riddle of Malaysian Capitalism: Rent-Seekers or Real Capitalists?* Honolulu: Allen and Unwin and University of Hawaii Press, 1999.

Selim, Mohammad El Sayed, ed. *The Organization of the Islamic Conference in a Changing World.* Cairo: Cairo University Press, 1994.

Shackle, C. "Siraiki: A Language Movement in Pakistan." *Modern Asian Studies* 11 (1977): 379–403.

Shankland, David. *Islam and Society in Turkey.* Huntingdon, UK: Eothen, 1999.

Shari 'ati, 'Ali. *Hajj.* Bedford, OH: Free Islamic Literatures, 1977.

Smith, M. G. *Government in Zazzau, 1800–1950.* London: Oxford University Press, 1960.

Snouck Hurgronje, C. "Le gouvernement colonial néerlandais et le système islamique." *Revue du Monde Musulman* 14 (1911): 450–509.

———. *Mekka in the Latter Part of the 19th Century: Daily Life, Customs and Learning of the Moslims of the East Indian Archipelago.* Translated by J. H. Monahan. Leiden: E. J. Brill, 1970.

———. "Notes sur le mouvement du pèlerinage de la Mecque aux indes néerlandaises." *Revue du Monde Musulman* 10 (October 1911): 397–413.

———. "Le Pèlerinage À La Mekke." In *Selected Works of C. Snouck Hurgronje.* Edited by G. H. Bousquet and J. Schacht. Leiden: E. J. Brill, 1957.

Stein, Ted. "The Approach of the Different Drummer: The Principle of the Persistent Objector in International Law." *Harvard International Law Journal* 26 (Spring 1985): 457–82.

Stoddard, Robert H., and Alan Morinis, eds. *Sacred Places, Sacred Spaces: The Geography of Pilgrimages.* Baton Rouge: Geoscience Publications, Louisiana State University, 1997.

Strauss, Leo. *Natural Right and History.* Chicago: University of Chicago Press, 1953.

Takaya, Bala J., and Sonni Swanle Tyoden, eds. *The Kaduna Mafia: A Study of the Rise, Development, and Consolidation of a Nigerian Power Elite.* Jos, Nigeria: Jos University Press, 1987.

Tangban, O. E. "The Hajj and the Nigerian Economy, 1960–1981." *Journal of Religion in Africa* 21 (1991): 241–55.

Tanter, Richard, and Kenneth Young, eds. *The Politics of Middle Class Indonesia.* Clayton, Victoria: Monash University Press, 1990.

Taylor, William B. "The Virgin of Guadalupe in New Spain: An Inquiry into the Social History of Marian Devotion." *American Ethnologist* 14 (1987): 9–33.

Tayob, Abdulkader. *Islam in South Africa: Mosques, Imams, and Sermons.* Gainesville: University Press of Florida, 1999.

Teik, Khoo Boo. *Paradoxes of Mahathirism: An Intellectual Biography of Mahathir Mohamad.* Kuala Lumpur: Oxford University Press, 1995.

Tol, Roger, Kees van Dijk, and Greg Acciaioli, eds. *Authority and Enterprise Among the Peoples of South Sulawesi.* Leiden: KITLV Press, 2000.

Tolmacheva, Marina. "Female Piety and Patronage in the Medieval 'Hajj.' " In *Women in the Medieval Islamic World: Power, Patronage, and Piety,* edited by Gavin R. G. Hambly, 161–179. New York: St. Martin's Press, 1998.

Trimingham, J. Spencer. *The Influence of Islam upon Africa.* London: Longman, 1980.

Turner, Victor. *Dramas, Fields, and Metaphors: Symbolic Action in Human Society*. Ithaca, NY: Cornell University Press, 1974.

———. *The Ritual Process: Structure and Anti-Structure*. Ithaca, NY: Cornell University Press, 1969.

Turner, Victor, and Edith Turner. *Image and Pilgrimage in Christian Culture: Anthropological Perspectives*. New York: Columbia University Press, 1978.

Valiuddin, Mir. "The Secrets of Hajj (Pilgrimage to K'aba): The Sufi Approach." *Islam and the Modern Age* 2 (1971): 42–70.

Van Der Meulen, D. "The Mecca Pilgrimage and Its Importance to the Netherlands East Indies." *The Muslim World* 31 (1941): 48–60.

Van Dijk, Cees. *Rebellion under the Banner of Islam: The Darul Islam in Indonesia*. The Hague: Martinus Nijhoff, 1981.

Van Dijk, Kees. *A Country in Despair: Indonesia between 1997 and 2000*. Leiden, KITLV Press, 2001.

Varga, Csaba, ed. *Comparative Legal Cultures*. Aldershot, UK: Dartmouth, 1992.

Vatikiotis, Michael R. J. *Indonesian Politics under Suharto: The Rise and Fall of the New Order*. New York: Routledge, 1998.

Villalon, Leonardo A. *Islamic Society and State Power in Senegal*. Cambridge: Cambridge University Press, 1995.

Von Grunebaum, G. E. *Muhammadan Festivals*. New York: Henry Schuman, 1951.

Vredenbregt, Jacob. "The Haddj: Some of Its Features and Functions in Indonesia." *Bejdragen tot de taal-, land- en volkenkunde van Neêrlandsch Indië* 118 (1962): 91–154.

Waardenburg, Jean-Jacques. *L'Islam dans le miroir de l'occident*. Paris: Mouton, 1969.

Wagha, Ahsan. *The Siraiki Language: Its Growth and Development*. Islamabad: Dderawar, 1990.

Wahid, Abdurrahman. "Religion, Ideology and Development." *Archipel* 30 (1985): 263–74.

Walker, R. B. J. *Inside/Outside: International Relations as Political Theory*. Cambridge: Cambridge University Press, 1993.

Watts, Alan W. *Myth and Ritual in Christianity*. Boston: Beacon, 1968.

Weeramantry, C. G. *Islamic Jurisprudence: An International Perspective*. New York: St. Martin's Press, 1988.

Weiss, Anita M., and S. Zulfiqar Gilani, eds. *Power and Civil Society in Pakistan*. New York: Oxford University Press, 2001.

Wensinck, A. J. *The Ideas of the Western Semites concerning the Navel of the Earth*. Amsterdam: Johannes Müller, 1916.

Westbrook, David. "Islamic International Law and Public International Law: Separate Expressions of World Order." *Virginia Journal of International Law* 33 (1993): 818–97.

Western, John. *Outcast Cape Town*. Berkeley: University of California Press, 1996.

Wolf, Eric R. "The Virgin of Guadalupe: Mexican National Symbol." *Journal of American Folklore* 71 (1958): 34–39.

Wolfe, Michael. *One Thousand Roads to Mecca: Ten Centuries of Travelers Writing about the Muslim Pilgrimage*. New York: Grove, 1997.

Wolfke, Karol. "Some Persistent Controversies Regarding Customary International Law." *Netherlands Yearbook of International Law* 24 (1993): 2–16.

Woodward, Kenneth L. *Making Saints: How the Catholic Church Determines Who Becomes a Saint, Who Doesn't and Why*. New York: Simon and Schuster, 1990.

Woodward, Mark. *Islam in Java: Normative Piety and Mysticism in the Sultanate of Yogyakarta*. Tucson: University of Arizona Press, 1989.

Works, John A., Jr. *Pilgrims in a Strange Land: Hausa Communities in Chad*. New York: Columbia University Press, 1976.

Wright, Theodore P., Jr. "Center-Periphery Relations and Ethnic Conflict in Pakistan: Sindhis, Muhajirs, and Punjabis." *Comparative Politics* 23 (April 1991): 299–312.

X, Malcolm. *The Autobiography of Malcolm X*. With the assistance of Alex Haley. New York: Ballantine, 1992.

Yamba, C. Bawa. *Permanent Pilgrims: The Role of Pilgrimage in the Lives of West African Muslims in Sudan*. London: Edinburgh University Press, 1995.

Young, Oran R. *Governance in World Affairs*. Ithaca, NY: Cornell University Press, 1999.

Young, William C. "The Ka'ba, Gender, and the Rites of Pilgrimage." *International Journal of Middle East Studies* 25 (1993): 285–300.

Zaidi, S. Akbar, ed. *Regional Imbalances and the National Question in Pakistan*. Lahore, Pakistan: Vanguard, 1992.

# Index